African Lives

WITHDRAWN

African Lives

An Anthology of Memoirs and Autobiographies

edited by
Geoff Wisner

LYNNE
RIENNER
PUBLISHERS

BOULDER
LONDON

All acknowledgments of permission to reprint previously published material can be found on pages 395–397, which are an extension of this copyright page.

Published in the United States of America in 2013 by
Lynne Rienner Publishers, Inc.
1800 30th Street, Boulder, Colorado 80301
www.rienner.com

and in the United Kingdom by
Lynne Rienner Publishers, Inc.
3 Henrietta Street, Covent Garden, London WC2E 8LU

Library of Congress Cataloging-in-Publication Data
African lives : an anthology of memoirs and autobiographies /
edited by Geoff Wisner.
    pages   cm.
  Includes index.
  ISBN 978-1-58826-862-4 (hc : alk. paper)
  ISBN 978-1-58826-887-7 (pb : alk. paper)
  1. Africa—Biography. 2. Autobiography—Africa.
  3. Africans—Biography. I. Wisner, Geoff, editor.
  DT18.A644 2013
  920.06—dc23
                                    2012044240

British Cataloguing in Publication Data
A Cataloguing in Publication record for this book
is available from the British Library.

Printed and bound in the United States of America

The paper used in this publication meets the requirements
of the American National Standard for Permanence of
Paper for Printed Library Materials Z39.48-1992.

5 4 3 2 1

To Jenn

Contents

Acknowledgments   xi

Introduction • Geoff Wisner   1

NORTH AFRICA

Algeria
"Encounters" • Mohammed Dib   5
The Writer (excerpt) • Yasmina Khadra   11

Egypt
A Border Passage (excerpt) • Leila Ahmed   21
A Daughter of Isis (excerpt) • Nawal El Saadawi   31

Libya
"The Rabbit Club" • Hisham Matar   37

Morocco
The Travels of Ibn Battuta (excerpt) • Ibn Battuta   43
Look & Move On (excerpt) • Mohammed Mrabet   51
The Fraternal Bond (excerpt) • Tahar Ben Jelloun   59
Return to Childhood (excerpt) • Leila Abouzeid   65
"So to Speak" • Laila Lalami   71

Sudan
"Salamanca" • Jamal Mahjoub   77
"A Cold but Fertile Ground" • Leila Aboulela   85

WEST AFRICA

Burkina Faso
Thomas Sankara Speaks (excerpt) • Thomas Sankara   91

Cameroon
Three Kilos of Coffee (excerpt) • Manu Dibango   99

Ghana
Ghana: The Autobiography of Kwame Nkrumah (excerpt)
    • Kwame Nkrumah   107
A Far Cry from Plymouth Rock (excerpt) • Kwame Dawes   115

Nigeria
"My Father's English Friend" (excerpt) • Okey Ndibe   125
"Ethics and Narrative: The Human and Other" • Chris Abani   133
"African 'Authenticity' and the Biafran Experience"
    • Chimamanda Ngozi Adichie   141
"Reform, in the Name of the Father" • Adaobi Tricia Nwaubani   151

Senegal
Ousmane Sembène: Interviews (excerpt)
    • edited by Annett Busch and Max Annas   155

Sierra Leone
The Devil That Danced on the Water (excerpt) • Aminatta Forna   163

CENTRAL AFRICA

Democratic Republic of Congo
Lumumba Speaks (excerpt) • Patrice Lumumba   169

Republic of Congo
My Country, Africa (excerpt) • Andrée Blouin   175
"Hollywood, Pirated Videos, and Child Soldiers"
    • Emmanuel Dongala   185

Rwanda
Machete Season (excerpt)
    • Jean-Baptiste Murangira, as told to Jean Hatzfeld   193

EAST AFRICA

Ethiopia
"New World Alphabet" • Dagmawi Woubshet   201

Kenya
Detained: A Writer's Prison Diary (excerpt) • Ngũgĩ wa Thiong'o   205
One Day I Will Write About This Place (excerpt)
    • Binyavanga Wainaina   215

Madagascar
Childhood in Madagascar (excerpt) • Christian Dumoux   221

Seychelles
Paradise Raped (excerpt) • James R. Mancham   229

Somalia
"The Family House" • Nuruddin Farah   239

Tanzania
Memoirs of an Arabian Princess from Zanzibar (excerpt)
    • Emily Ruete   247
The Worlds of a Maasai Warrior (excerpt) • Tepilit Ole Saitoti   255

Uganda
Elizabeth of Toro (excerpt) • Elizabeth Nyabongo   265

SOUTHERN AFRICA

Botswana
Nisa: The Life and Words of a !Kung Woman (excerpt)
    • Nisa, as told to Marjorie Shostak   277
A Woman Alone (excerpt) • Bessie Head   287

Lesotho
Singing Away the Hunger (excerpt) • Mpho 'M'atsepo Nthunya   293

Namibia
Never Follow the Wolf (excerpt) • Helao Shityuwete   301

South Africa

Mafeking Diary (excerpt) • Sol T. Plaatje 307
Let My People Go (excerpt) • Albert Luthuli 315
117 Days (excerpt) • Ruth First 325
And Night Fell (excerpt) • Molefe Pheto 333
I Write What I Like (excerpt) • Steve Biko 343

Zambia

Zambia Shall Be Free (excerpt) • Kenneth Kaunda 351

Zimbabwe

With the People (excerpt) • Maurice Nyagumbo 359
Nkomo (excerpt) • Joshua Nkomo 373
"A Letter to My Mother" • Chenjerai Hove 387

Permissions 395
Index of Authors and Titles 399
About the Book 401

Acknowledgments

Thanks first to Peter VonDoepp, who shared adventures with me in Zimbabwe and Malawi, who suggested that Lynne Rienner Publishers might be a good home for this book, and who tapped his contacts in the world of African studies for suggestions and endorsements. Many thanks to Lynne Rienner herself and to Laura Logan and the rest of the staff in Boulder.

Special thanks to my colleagues at *Words Without Borders*, where I have blogged about African literature in translation since 2009. Through Susan Harris I had the opportunity to work with the translating team of Alexis Pernsteiner and Antoine Bargel, who made it possible to include excerpts from untranslated memoirs by Tahar Ben Jelloun and Yasmina Khadra, as well as a chapter from Christian Dumoux's account of growing up in Madagascar. Alexis and Antoine worked patiently with me to find graceful and accurate renderings of knotty passages.

Thanks also to the editors of other publications where I have reviewed African memoirs and other books: Marjorie Kehe of the *Christian Science Monitor*, Scott Esposito of *The Quarterly Conversation*, and Bhakti Shringarpure of *Warscapes*.

Social media gave this book a powerful boost. I am grateful to all those who helped spread the word on Twitter and Facebook, and who contributed through Peerbackers to help cover the cost of permissions and translations: Faith and Holly Adiele, Mia Adjali, Lisa Beach, Janet Bloom, Adrienne Booth, Marie Brown, Chris Carduff, Ilana DeBare, Michael DeLaney, Jill Erickson, Wes Furgiuele, Charles and Charlotte Gibbs, Robert Gibralter, Susan Harris, Gail Hovey, Brad Hurley, Rohan Kamicheril, Ron Kavanaugh, Sara Luchian, Joshua Mandelbaum, Tom McCall, Karen Odom, John and Beckie O'Neill, Bud Parr, Lee Ann Parsons, Sarah Robinson, Karl Sakas, Katharine Smithwick, Erin Underwood, David Varno, Nancy Walker, Dagmawi Woubshet, and Ilya Zarembsky.

Many of the books excerpted here were hard to locate. For help in finding them, I am grateful to the Brooklyn Public Library and New York Public Library, especially the speedy and gracious staff at the Schomburg Center for Research in Black Culture.

Finally, I am always grateful for the support and advice of my old friends Bill Schwartz and Chris Carduff, and for the love and good counsel of my wife, Jenn Brissett.

— G. W.

Introduction

In 1962, London publisher Heinemann launched its African Writers Series with the one African book that everyone seems to know, Chinua Achebe's *Things Fall Apart*. In the years that followed, orange-emblazoned Heinemann paperbacks brought attention to many African writers throughout the English-speaking world.

More recently, writers from Africa have broken free of what Wole Soyinka once called the "orange ghetto." (In 2009 the mantle of the series passed from Heinemann to Penguin, another publisher known for the color orange.) African novelists win major awards, and each year seems to bring a new collection of short stories from Africa—yet there has never been a collection of the continent's extraordinary true-life narratives. Why?

One reason may be that fiction enjoys greater prestige than nonfiction. In 2009, a panel at the PEN World Voices Festival asked the question, "Is nonfiction literature?" Panelist Philip Gourevitch noted that although Nobel Prize winners such as V. S. Naipaul have sometimes written extraordinary nonfiction, no one has yet won the prize for literature on the strength of his or her nonfiction. (He was forgetting Winston Churchill, a special case.) Nonfiction, said Gourevitch, seems to be wedged into the cracks of the literary scene. Like photography before the mid-twentieth century, it is not yet taken seriously as an art form.

So tempting is the prestige of fiction that some African memoirs have appeared in the guise of novels, including Camara Laye's *The Dark Child* and Yasmina Khadra's *The Writer*. (A chapter from *The Writer* has been translated from the French for this anthology.) *A Life Full of Holes*, a Moroccan memoir told to Paul Bowles by Driss ben Hamed Charhadi, a pseudonym for Larbi Layachi, continues to appear as a novel, though

1

Bowles in his own autobiography admits that its publisher labeled it a novel so that it would be eligible for a prize.

Despite all that the African Writers Series has done to advance the awareness of African writing, it has also furthered the impression that the memoirs of Africans are something other than literature. The series contains only a few works of nonfiction, and these were apparently chosen for their political and sociological interest. They include the memoirs of ex-slave Olaudah Equiano and of the first generation of African heads of state: Kenneth Kaunda, Kwame Nkrumah, and Nelson Mandela.

Though politicians are seldom known for their prose style, the men and women who ended white rule in Africa have extraordinary stories to tell, and they often tell them with surprising sensitivity. One of these is Maurice Nyagumbo, a guerrilla leader and friend of Robert Mugabe, who became a Zimbabwean government minister. In 1989 he committed suicide, swallowing rat poison after he was implicated in a scandal over the misallocation of cars. The following year, I saw his grave at Heroes Acres, outside Harare, where prominent veterans of the liberation struggle are buried. Unlike other cronies of Mugabe, Nyagumbo apparently had a conscience. Back home, I found Nyagumbo's memoir, *With the People*, on a shelf deep in the stacks of Harvard's Widener Library and was struck by its freshness and honesty. His memories of himself as a frightened young boy, left out in a field to scare away baboons, lingered in my memory—perhaps because one sunny afternoon in rural Zimbabwe I was asked to wait at the edge of a hot field and throw stones at any baboons that might come to raid the sunflowers. The baboons never arrived.

Many of Africa's leading writers have published extraordinary memoirs in recent years—and some have published series of memoirs. *You Must Set Forth at Dawn* is the latest in several installments of the life story of Wole Soyinka. Others include *The Man Died, Aké: The Years of Childhood, Ìsarà: A Voyage Around "Essay,"* and *Ibadan: The Penkelemes Years.* J. M. Coetzee has won acclaim for the semiautobiographical books that began with *Boyhood: Scenes from Provincial Life* and continued with *Youth* and *Summertime.* Years after the publication of his prison diary, *Detained*, Ngũgĩ wa Thiong'o explored his childhood memories in *Dreams in a Time of War.*

These books are the latest examples of a tradition that began centuries ago. In *African Lives*, I reach back as far as Ibn Battuta, the fourteenth-century Moroccan traveler. Arriving in India, Ibn Battuta is given two thousand dinars by the emperor's vizier, who tells him, "This is to enable you to get your clothes washed." His embarrassment can still be felt. I could have gone back even farther, to the *Confessions* of St. Augustine, where the future saint describes his guilt about stealing pears as a boy in what is today Algeria.

As these examples show, a memoir does not always appear under that designation. A first-person travel book may be more revealing of the author than of the place, and more worthy of the name memoir, than a book identified as "memoir" on the cover. Most of the selections in *African Lives* come from full-length memoirs and autobiographies, but in an effort to include more distinctive or significant voices, I have stretched the definition of memoir to encompass an interview with Ousmane Sembène, a speech by Patrice Lumumba, and court testimony by Steve Biko. I have also included some autobiographical essays by exceptional writers who are too young to be recalling their lives in full: Chris Abani, Chimamanda Ngozi Adichie, Laila Lalami, Jamal Mahjoub, Adaobi Tricia Nwaubani, and others.

I have made room for hard-to-find gems by leaving out works that are more readily available, with some regret. Their omission from this book should not prevent anyone from reading the memoirs of Chinua Achebe and Wole Soyinka, or *The Dark Child* by Camara Laye, a classic account of childhood suffused with piercing nostalgia for a traditional world that is slipping away. Nor should readers overlook Olaudah Equiano's classic memoir *The Interesting Narrative*, Assia Djebar's haunting *Algerian White*, Nega Mezlekia's harrowing *Notes from the Hyena's Belly*, or Zakes Mda's funny and rambunctious *Sometimes There Is a Void*. Wangari Maathai's *Unbowed* and Ellen Johnson-Sirleaf's *This Child Will Be Great* are essential volumes in the story of African women's empowerment. The journey described by Tété-Michel Kpomassie in *An African in Greenland* is one that few novelists could have imagined.

So many dramatic life stories have emerged from the struggle against apartheid that they would make an absorbing anthology of their own. The compelling story, clean prose, and calm intelligence of Nelson Mandela's *No Easy Walk to Freedom* make it one of the best political memoirs I know. Others worth seeking out include *Island in Chains* by Indres Naidoo, *My Traitor's Heart* by Rian Malan, and *Country of My Skull* by Antjie Krog.

The best African memoirs, like the best memoirs from anywhere in the world, are literature, but they are a kind of literature that is complicated by social and political dimensions. If the costs of speaking plainly were not so severe in many parts of Africa, more memoirs might have been written and published, and there might be fewer novels in which real tyrants and real countries are veiled with invented names.

More than African fiction, African memoirs demand that we come to terms with what individual Africans really think. These memoirs question our assumptions. They demand that we consider the truth of what we are being told. And in some cases, they pose questions of authenticity that do not arise so sharply in the world of fiction.

For obvious reasons, many African memoirs are stories of struggle and suffering, and many of these are "as told to" books. Because it is impossible to know how much these books owe to their coauthors, I have omitted them from this collection, with a few exceptions.

Nearly every writer included in *African Lives* was born and raised on the continent. The selections are arranged to follow the map of Africa as you would read a page in a book: top to bottom and left to right, beginning with North Africa and continuing through West Africa, Central Africa, East Africa, and Southern Africa. Within each region, the selections are in alphabetical order by country. Within each country, they are arranged chronologically, according to the date of the events described.

By a happy accident, *African Lives* begins in childhood, with Mohammed Dib's memories of growing up in Algeria. It ends in maturity and exile, on a note of leave-taking, as Chenjerai Hove writes to his mother in Zimbabwe from his new home in Norway. Between these two voices, I hope you will find many more to challenge, inspire, and enlighten you.

ALGERIA

"Encounters"
Mohammed Dib

*Mohammed Dib (1920–2003) was born in the town of Tlemcen near the
border of Morocco. He began writing poetry at the age of fifteen and as a
young man worked as a teacher, weaver, accountant, interpreter, and journalist. In 1952 he published* La Grande Maison, *his first novel and the first
volume in a trilogy completed in 1957. Two years later he was expelled
from Algeria by the French colonial authorities because of his support for
Algerian independence. He moved to France, taught at the Sorbonne, and
traveled to Finland. Dib was the author of more than thirty novels and
many other works.*

[Translated from the French by Marjolijn de Jager.]

First encounter.

A whole other world used to live next to mine but, throughout my
early childhood, I had hardly noticed it. It would happen, of course, that
I'd go into town with this or that member of my family. Consequently, we
must have run into the people of this other world. I can summon up my
memories all I want, but I swear that not one of them shows me that we
had any such encounters. My memory of that period remains a blank
where any recollections of foreigners are concerned. Either they had the
power to make themselves invisible, thus leaving no imprint on my retina,
or else my eyes were in no way made to see them. They didn't exist.

Until the day when one of them appeared in our house, landing right
in our very own home. He had crossed light-years of not being recognized.
I had just suffered a leg injury that was to keep me nailed to my bed for a
year. The extraterrestrial used to arrive cloaked in a smell of ether and
with long, dreadful needles attached to the end of his fingers. He was
solidly built and, to top it off, he had a face that was too white and pasty
and beginning to sag. He would move as one mass, putting one foot down
flat on the floor before lifting the other. Imagine the trouble such a crea-

5

ture had to go through, to lower himself all the way down to where I lay on a mattress right on the floor. I was not to know what a bed was until much later.

For some period of time he would present himself at my bedside every day and always at the same hour. Two imperious thumps on the front door with the knocker. He'd come in and there he'd be. His knocks were not only dealt to the door of the house but also to that of my heart, which would instantly crumble with sadness, just that—sadness—because I already knew how to take my pain in stride. Besides, I'd feel the moment of these knocks approach, knew when they would reverberate: as if to announce them, my mother used to boil two needles for the syringes of Dr. Photiadis in water beforehand.

He was not a descendant of the Gauls who, as I later learned at school, were my ancestors. Before me stood a Greek, who had come from another world. I would not know that until later on, of course. Like so many other things.

For now, all I saw on that huge face bent over me were black-framed glasses and, imprisoned in those lenses, the diamond-tipped gaze, radiant and all smiles. Secretly childlike. While the features of the face retained an ageless immobility, what a smile he had! I have no recollection of his ever having hurt me with his needles, not even once.

Up until that point, he was my first foreigner: before him I had never been in the presence of any other. He saved my leg, which by all logic should have been amputated. It was before the time of penicillin.

Many years passed and I'd grown into a tall young man of eighteen. I went back to see him. Early in the last war, a typhus epidemic was raging in Tlemcen that made no distinction between its all too many victims, whether they came from one shore or the other. All day long, funeral processions would follow each other in the direction of the two cemeteries in town, the Muslim and the Christian one.

As was to be expected, I had changed, but Dr. Photiadis recognized me. He was the same. The same massive build, the same broad face, on that face the same large glasses and, behind his lenses, the same gaze, as secretive as it was amused. He gave me a piece of camphor to keep on me.

Second encounter.

His name was Monsieur Souquet. I was nine years old; he about fifty, insofar as I was then able to estimate it. An ogre with an enormous, dangling, gray mustache and a big belly. He was not tall. He was French. As children we were very afraid of the French and never went near them.

Yet, just like that I found myself immured in his company, in the same room, for several hours a day and five days a week. I could do nothing other than stay there and get used to the situation; fortunately, there were another thirty in the same position as I.

He, too, wore glasses, they all wore glasses, but his were framed in thin steel.

Monsieur Souquet was a *French* teacher who had come to teach in the local public school. It was a rather large school, where we were among ourselves with our Algerian teachers with the exception of two or three teachers who came from *over there*. These remained as strange to us as foreigners. An important figure stated a profound truth these days when saying that the foreigner can be recognized by his smell. That was precisely what Monsieur Souquet, whom I could henceforth study close-up and at my leisure, gave off. A bit dry, a bit white, although not at all unpleasant. How should I say it? A smell of straw or something very much like it.

But that was not really the most important thing. It didn't take me long to discover that he embodied a kind of debonair ogre with his huge mustache, his huge voice, his huge belly, his huge eyes, and that was important in another way, too. He always caused me to tremble, but then less and less violently, then not at all anymore. It must be said that we had begun to learn a great many interesting things with him.

A good man, yes indeed, but strict where work and behavior were concerned. At a given moment, he would not shy away from raising a voice that made the windows of the classroom rattle. He used to punish bad pupils and his favorite way consisted of letting a fist drop down on your skull, a fist that may have been cushioned with flesh but was still very hard. It was a method he didn't overuse; he would apply it rather sparingly, reserving it for serious and extreme cases.

On one occasion, I also had a turn to encounter this fist. Monsieur Souquet was teaching us that as a general rule the plural of common nouns was formed by adding an *s* to the end of the word. One day we were unfortunate enough to come upon the word *corps* in a dictation. Monsieur Souquet was looking at my notebook. He immediately decreed that I'd made a mistake by writing *corp*. I answered that this word, in our dictation, was in the singular. He then responded that it nevertheless had to be spelled with an *s*. I refused to accept both the idea and the application. The question was resolved in front of the whole class with a blow of his fist on my head. A blow that I do remember caused no pain other than to my self-esteem by reducing me to silence.

Even today, I still write the word *corps* with its unwarranted appendage in the singular, though it goes against my personal conviction, solely in memory of my good teacher.

During recess, I was in my element, for in the courtyard of that local school there were only budding Algerians. I should note in passing, however, that we didn't know those words: *Algerians, Algeria, Al Djazair*.

Nobody had told us those, explained their meaning or what they were supposed to indicate. Not our parents at home, nor anyone outside. It was school that was going to teach us this. And we were then to discover that we were a specific country; we belonged to a separate land.

One day in the school playground, suddenly I forgot, we were forgetting the existence of the delegate from another planet, Monsieur Souquet. It didn't even enter my mind that he might have a home, a family life. It would have been better if I'd thought of that a little sooner, for it happened that one fine morning he brought a boy our age into the classroom, a boy with such tender, milky white skin that we were wondering how it was possible it didn't melt right off.

A child Frenchman was, in our eyes, even more astonishing than an adult Frenchman. We would not take our wide-open eyes—and rightly so—off him anymore, we weren't doing any more work, incapable as we were of doing anything else but staring. For several days, the first several days, a special atmosphere reigned over the class, an atmosphere of attention, caution, and enchantment. The effect of his mere presence, a whole new feeling, had irrefutably changed something around us, indeed, within us.

He was Monsieur Souquet's son, and his name was Georges, or maybe it wasn't, I don't really know now. He was going to be studying in his father's class, which was ours! This was an event for which nothing had prepared us. And there was quite a stir as soon as the disorderly legions of the other classes noticed him during recess. A silent revolution, in fact. Those who weren't in our class did not know who it was appearing there, and thus, as if by magic, the usual agitation suddenly stopped and all of them stood there, in shock, and we along with them. It lasted only a short moment, but it was an eternal moment.

Then we gradually approached him, still keeping a safe distance. We limited ourselves to looking at him. How he was dressed—much better than any one of us. What kind of shoes he wore—clearly better still. How his hair was cut, how he held himself. He wouldn't speak. Not once did he ever exchange a single word with us, nor we with him; we couldn't yet speak French, even if we already knew how to read it. And we didn't think we'd hear him say anything in our language.

Our customs being turned upside down like this was only an interlude of short duration. Georges, if that really was his name, soon disappeared from our class, our school, and our life. We didn't have any time to get used to him or he to us.

Souquet, the father, obviously stayed. That man, as we were discovering day after day, was the best of men for one very simple reason. He never ended his class without telling us a story, generally short and funny, but so funny that it made us shriek with joy, which he would then allow since he himself was laughing along with us. I still see him clearly, guffawing into his hairy mustache until he had tears in his eyes. This way we were never sad when we left school, where at the door the Spanish vendor of barley sugar and grilled chickpeas, the *torraïcos,* was waiting for us, anyway.

Of that man we couldn't be afraid. Not because he had a scrawny build and gummy eyes, but because he was one of us, someone close. The same thing was true for David, the Jew, who had a Tunisian pastry stand on the big square, where all the kids from our school who had a few pennies would gather. He was even more like us and so close that he never refused us any little extras, after he had given us, for our money, honeyed almond paste that was quickly gobbled up.

There is another encounter, but I was not yet aware that I had already experienced it and which, subsequently, was to reveal itself as a determining factor while changing my life with the force of a necessity or a destiny, in a sense. That was the encounter with a language, from the very start as difficult as it was seductive, the *French* language. But that is another story, one of those stories that has no end.

So, to come back to those old times: a child of the city, I obviously knew only what I saw around me in the city and nothing of what happened outside of it. For example, in the country, which always constituted a separate world as well, a world next to mine that continued to be foreign to it. But a few years later we would be taught about it, during the world conflict, when with our disbelieving eyes we would see those lines of peasants who had come to die in our very clean, very well maintained streets. For them the only enemy was hunger.

The Writer

(excerpt)

Yasmina Khadra

Yasmina Khadra is the pen name of Mohammed Moulessehoul, who was born in 1955 in the desert town of Kenadsa. As an officer in the Algerian army, he published fiction under the female name Yasmina Khadra ("green jasmine") to avoid military censorship. In 2000, he left the army and relocated in France, where in 2001 he revealed his identity. The Writer (L'Écrivain) was published that year, but has not yet been translated in full. Khadra's novels The Swallows of Kabul (2006) and The Attack (2008) were each shortlisted for the International IMPAC Dublin Literary Award.

[Translated from the French by Alexis Pernsteiner and Antoine Bargel.]

The Walls of El Mechouar

My father did not accompany us to El Mechouar school. No sooner had we crossed Tlemcen's first back streets than his stiff demeanor wavered and his driving became nervous. He started railing at pedestrians, tailgating other motorists, the corners of his mouth suddenly frothing a pallid secretion. Something had just broken in him, eroding the composure behind which he did his utmost to hide his faults. My father was careful about his appearance because of an unhappy childhood. He was the one who taught me not to be content with accepting cheerfulness at face value, and that often, if it sounded hollow, an eruption of laughter was being used as a diversion.

On the backseat, my cousin was rubbing his eyes. He asked where we were, which earned him a grunt in reply. The car negotiated many vennels teeming with onlookers before stopping in front of a squat and dirty building. Sergeant Kerzaz met us on the landing, firmly shook hands with my father, and invited us into his apartment. My cousin and I were seated around a miniature table where a meal was waiting for us: salad, a small carafe of water, and a tureen filled with a thick casserole whose smell instantly dissuaded my appetite. My father chose to speak with the sergeant in the hall. On the wall, his shadow traced embarrassed movements. His voice remained low. The sergeant had his back to us. He kept nodding his head and repeating: "Very good, lieutenant." After a brief, hushed exchange, the door creaked before softly closing again. The sergeant returned, his face expressionless. "Eat fast," he said, "We can't be late." I swerved to the side to see if my father was still there. No one was in the hall. He had left on tiptoes. Without even hugging us goodbye. I would have liked it if he had just taken a moment to talk to me, to put his hands firmly on my shoulders, or to ruffle my hair and gaze into my eyes. It wouldn't have been enough to comfort me, but maybe it would have consoled me, in the space of a smile, for a separation that resembled both breaking up and being torn apart.

Sergeant Kerzaz was a man in a hurry. He slipped on his fatigues in a flash, polished his boots, and asked us to follow him. Neither Kader nor I had the time, much less the heart, to touch a single crumb. We silently fell in step behind him, and had to hurry in order to keep up. Originally from the Great South, our guide walked very fast, as desert men tend to do. After several streets, we found ourselves running after him. He didn't turn around once. He just quickened his step, keeping his shoulders hunched, his expression impenetrable. The people around us went about their business in a chaotic merry-go-round. Veiled women and turbaned peasants assailed the stalls of traveling merchants. Punctuated with the chatter of children, the shopkeepers' cries gave the market an air of carnivalesque cheer. A fragrant warmth permeated the world, embracing it with almost human affection. It felt like springtime. It was a perfect day for skipping. Sergeant Kerzaz seemed intentionally unaware of the jubilation that surrounded us. Unfazed and almost blasé, he forged through the gaps in the crowd. In one square, a gang of kids was knocking around a cloth ball in the middle of a crystalline clamor. They played hard in an effort to catch up to their opponents, bruising their shins in hysterical confusion, exploding in joy whenever a dribble sent the other team flying or they made a shot. Without realizing it, I stopped to watch the game. "We're going to be late," the sergeant reminded me as he continued on. My cousin must have yanked my arm to shake me out of it. It was as though he were tearing me from a wonderful dream. I pushed him off fiercely, annoyed by his unfortunate gesture. The desire to turn back, to disappear into the crowd weighed heavy on my chest. I wanted my mom, my everyday rituals, my neighbors and my friends. The sergeant grudgingly retraced his steps. His hand closed coldly around my wrist. Jerking my arm, he shook me from head to toe and dragged me to the gate of a gigantic fortress with ivy-covered walls. Two on-duty soldiers opened a smaller version of the gate, exchanged salaams with the sergeant, and ignored us. Looking back, I saw the gate close inexorably on the buildings, cars, people, and noises; something told me that the outside world being erased before my very eyes was also erasing me; a page had just been arbitrarily turned once and for all. I was so distraught that I started when the soldier closed the latch.

We climbed a path lined on either side by old, stunted buildings. I was first struck by the faded tiles, the roofs sagging in places, the haggard windows, and the shocking whiteness of the façades. The individuals hanging around here and there, some in washed-out overalls, others in combat suits, looked nothing like the people that lived in my neighborhood in Oran. They appeared preoccupied and sullen, and moved without ever relaxing their crushing grimaces, or even greeting each other. A pot-bellied corporal holding a belt in his hand railed at a group of prisoners with disheveled uniforms and shaved heads. These latter were on fatigue duty; they collected trash with their bare hands and deposited it in a creaking wheelbarrow, which another frail and feverish prisoner struggled to push over the gravelly ground. Farther along, we arrived at an immense courtyard framed by colossal plane trees. There, kids cinched in squalid tunics paraded around. They all wore berets, but not the same shoes. Some had on regular shoes, others combat boots. Divided into three squads, they marched in step, arms slashing in time, backs stiff and chins high. Facing this arrangement, perched on a concrete slab, an old chief warrant officer was counting time at the top of his lungs, his eye on the lookout for the slightest false move, a shattering curse at the ready. Seeing us, he asked a subordinate to supervise the march, jumped to the ground, and came to meet us. I was astounded when, reaching our level, he withdrew a dental prosthetic from his pocket and put it in his mouth. He wiped his lips on the back of his hand, stared at us (my cousin and me), and then asked the sergeant if we were indeed Lieutenant Hadj's sons. The sergeant nodded.

"I was expecting them this morning, but whatever. You will show them their beds so they can rest. The barber won't be free at this time. They'll stay with the new recruits. Tomorrow they'll get a buzz and a shower. We don't have new uniforms yet. They'll keep their personal effects until further notice."

"Very good, sir."

The old chief warrant officer smiled at us while refraining from giving any hint of affability. He was short and spirited, with a swarthy, emaciated face that had shriveled in the scrubland. Though his jacket hung off him, one sensed his implacability, his energy in the face of all obstacles. Before going back to harass his squads, he removed his denture and put it back in his pocket. His mouth sagged with such desolation it gave me the shivers.

The sergeant led us to a building overlooking the schoolyard, a scaly and hideous edifice measuring a width of about a hundred meters. We entered through a skinny door that gave way to a long, narrow corridor that was dark and stunk of urine. There were classrooms on the ground floor lined with tables and benches. On the disquietingly gray walls drooped engravings of scenes inspired by La Fontaine's fables. Above the podium, tacked smack in the center of the blackboard, hung a cardboard headdress topped with two ass's ears to crown the dunce of the day for an entire class period. . . . The sergeant climbed to the second floor, noting the depth of the cracks on the ramp and drawing our attention to the staircase's dubious steps. He led us to a large room illuminated by a makeshift window, where he showed us two vacant box springs and how, in double-time, to fold the sheets and covers into "forty-five degree corners," according to common barracks regulations. With extreme delicacy, he spread the first blanket over the mattress, then smoothed the pair of sheets with exaggerated care, before laying out the second blanket and tucking it under the mattress from the sides; then he adjusted the pillow, straightened the bed's perimeter, and stepped back to admire his work. "Your bed should look like a munitions box," he said, "with crisp corners and a surface as flat as a board; the top sheet should be turned out exactly like this. Let me warn you that the instructor won't hesitate to throw it all on the ground if he sees a single crease, and he'll kick you up the backside until you can show him a perfectly planed bed." My cousin nodded his head, far underestimating the seriousness of these instructions. As for me, I wanted to go home at once.

The sergeant gave us a tour of *our* territory; showed us the common room, though he didn't tell us what it was for, as it was closed; and delineated our area, since if we crossed certain borders we might end up in the soldiers' quarters, which were strictly off limits. He instructed us on how to take care of ourselves, on whom to talk to when something was wrong, on how to spot an instructor in order not to trust just anyone. In the late afternoon, he took us to a small courtyard where boys in plain clothes were moping about. These new recruits had arrived a few days before us. For the most part, they were war orphans. Some had no family or surname, and had been found wandering the streets or in the charge of neighbors too destitute to take care of them. Some wore rags and had sores on their feet. Others had unkempt hair, rheumy eyes, and slugs creeping from their noses. All wore a confused and pained look, as though they were expecting the sky to fall on their heads. Visibly intrigued by our clothes, one of them approached us to get a better look. His blistered and chapped hand stroked my jacket, lingering on its cut; he stepped back, and in a dumbfounded tone said that he had thought suits were just for adults and that, with the exception of the French administrator who had managed his village during the war, he had never seen a single Arab dressed in such a fashion, much less a child. A teenager told him that we were probably bourgeois. The other kid went back to where he'd been standing but kept his eyes on us, unable to reconcile himself to the idea that the children of a rich family could fall so low. Sergeant Kerzaz took his leave, promising to be back the next day. Caught off guard, we watched him go. The second he disappeared behind a wall, my cousin fell to the ground, put his head between his knees, and started crying and calling for his mom. I could neither sit by nor talk to him. I was too overcome with grief to take care of him. . . .

A whistle blew from far off. A boy in a uniform told us it was time for dinner. The new recruits left to eat.

"Go with them," I suggested to Kader.

"What about you?"

"I'm not hungry."

"Do you want me to bring you a piece of bread?"

"That's okay."

Kader didn't insist. He ran after the others.

I was now alone. The sun was already setting, on the sly, as though it, too, were trying to give me the slip. I sat down on a slab and turned my back to the esplanade, to the clatter of forks that soon emanated from the dining hall. My shoulders sagged, weighing on my whole being. I felt as though my soul were becoming numb. Slowly, to quell the growing hunger and dizziness, I dug my hands into the hollow of my stomach and faced the night. . . .

A year before, my father had taken us to a spa in Bouhanifia, a few kilometers from Mascara. In the mornings, I would go down to the river and watch the swimming vacationers. Like young gods, they would stand erect on a rock, unleash battle cries, and jump. I was fascinated by the incredible dives they would improvise, each according to the diver's own boldness. One night while I was daydreaming on the deserted riverbank, a man came up to me. He must have been thirty or so, and seemed nice and full of goodwill. He pointed to a tree hanging over the wadi and invited me to show him what I was made of. I told him that I didn't know how to swim. He promised to watch over me and said nothing would happen to me. He was so insistent that I ended up climbing the tree. The miry, lapping water was three meters below and terrified me, but the stranger's kind smile won out. I closed my eyes and jumped. After a few desperate flails, and seeing nothing on the horizon, I started to panic. The man was still squatting on the bank, his arms wrapped around his knees; he smiled as he watched me drown. I'll never forget the calm of his face, the amusement in his eyes at my despair. As my cries grew in distress so did his smile. I now realized that he would not come to my aid. The water started to close in on me, to suck me into a dizzying whirlpool. Right as I was about to go under, the man got up and walked back up the hill, as though nothing were happening. My cousin Homaïna happened to be passing by and heard my cries for help. He had just enough time to grab my hand.

That day at cadet school, as the night spread out its black blanket above me, I was reminded of the wadi sucking me down and of the vastness of my solitude. Once more I was gripped with panic; I felt as though I were sinking, as though I were dying. . . .

A soldier sounded a bugle call for lights-out. Each bellowing note struck through me like a deathblow.

"Don't stay there, kid," he advised as he tucked his instrument under his arm. "Go find your mates in the dorm and make sure to cover up. It's going to be cold tonight."

I shared the room with twenty other kids, all restless sleepers. They had survived massacres, and their nightmares never failed to catch up to them the second they dozed off. Some cried, their fists in their mouths. Others awoke screaming, and quickly fell back into a deep sleep. But that's not what kept me awake. I was thinking of my mother, of my brothers and sisters, of my neighborhood, of the corner grocer, of my dog Rex, of the familiar sounds and my games of Hunt the Thimble. I spent hours staring at the window. Outside, the sky was teeming with stars, and the moon, a pearl hanging off a branch, tried to convince me that the tree had a cold. . . .

"I do not like to repeat myself. When I say get up, everybody had better be standing at attention at the foot of their beds before I'm done yelling."

All of a sudden, the earth was shaking. I was vaguely aware that a violent blast was catapulting me somewhere. The ceiling turned and I found myself knocked half senseless under my mattress, with my face in the tiled floor. A pair of grotesque boots was poised before my nose. A soldier crouched down to show me his angry mug:

"You think you're still at home with your dear mommy, you little snot? You better get outta here fast if you don't want my foot in your ass."

He got up, yelling after the other cadets, then left the room like a gust of wind. My cousin came to my rescue. He pushed the metal bed that was crushing me to the side, removed the mattress, and helped me get out from under the "rubble." The other kids were finishing up with making their beds, indifferent to me.

"What just happened?" I asked Kader.

"The soldier knocked over your bed."

"That guy is bad," a chubby kid explained. "When he claps his hands, nobody had better still be in bed. If you take extra time fluffing your pillow or something he'll knock you over."

"I didn't know."

"Well, now you do. If I were you, I would be getting dressed right now instead of asking questions. We have roll call in five minutes."

It was still dark when the bugle signaled roll call. The cadets rushed to the stairs, poured down the steps, and ran to the courtyard where they lined up in tight rows for the gravely waiting instructors. Unsure of where to go, I made a place for myself in a unit. Almost immediately, arms started shoving me from all sides, before ejecting me out of the line. I realized that everyone had a specific place and that no one was willing to give it up. A corporal noticed me and pointed to a corner where my cousin and a dozen new recruits joined me. All of a sudden, orders were boomed: "At ease, attention! Line up. . . . Don't move. You, number 53, stop wiggling or I'll skin your ass with my boot buckle. . . . Roll call. . . ." The instructors counted their rows, tilting a head up here, chastising a rebel there, and yelling, one after the other: "First grade, all present! . . . Second grade, all present! . . . Fourth grade, all present! . . . Fifth grade, all present!" There were no absences, so the chief warrant officer clapped his hands. The units started to jump in place, their knees pedaling up to their chests; then, row by row, the students hurried in single file to the dining hall, where they swallowed bowls of steaming coffee and slices of buttered bread before I was even able to orient myself.

After breakfast, Sergeant Kerzaz took my cousin and me to a rat hole set up as a barbershop. A man tied tightly in a puckered apron sat me down in a chair facing a dusty mirror, and cut my hair from neck to forehead while humming an Andalusian tune. His sibilant accent and marbled skin betrayed his Tlemcen roots; he was as devoid of emotion as a shepherd shearing a sheep. His graying hair was pulled into a hepcat do, his profile sharp, and his mouth deformed by giant yellow teeth that filtered his rotten breath. He seemed to have as much passion for his clippers as a sculptor for his chisel; as for the rest—his clumsiness, my resultant whimpering—he couldn't care less. He was only annoyed by my jerking around. Whenever a cut forced me to swerve to the side, he gave me a painful and authoritative clout. He clearly couldn't stand kids. After a quick back and forth of the clippers, my head looked like a smooth pebble. I didn't recognize myself. I looked completely different. The barber undid the gown, but didn't bother to brush the balls of hair from my shoulders before pulling me out of the chair and pointing Kader into it. My cousin remained rooted to the bench, terrified by my bald head. At first he gestured *no* with his hands. Then he gripped his chair in an attempt to resist the sergeant and his arms. The barber grabbed him by the collar, as though my cousin were a bundle, firmly jammed him into the chair with one hand, and with the other, quickly cropped his hair. As we left the barbershop, Kader and I gave each other a sad look, and then we both broke out—he in tears and me in laughter. We looked like two little convicts on our way to prison. Sergeant Kerzaz didn't bother consoling us. Somewhere deep down he felt sorry for us, but didn't admit it to us. He didn't have children and probably didn't know how to act. My cousin started to dry his eyes. He timidly ran a trembling hand over his scalp, feeling the tiny, prickly hairs on his head. I made a face, hoping to cheer him up. He pouted. And then, to my great relief, he burst out laughing, throwing his head back and pointing to the pumice-stone attached to my neck. "You look like a genie," he said. "You too," was my reply. Then, holding hands, we followed the sergeant to the showers, where we were probably to shed everything that, up until two days ago, made us regular children.

In the afternoon, they gathered the new recruits into a small courtyard. They had our surnames and first names on a roster; they lined us up according to height, with the littlest ones in front; they *numbered* us.

"Starting today, you will go by your number instead of your name," instructed the warrant officer, a giant beanpole with teeth crowned in gold, who kept fiddling with the cord on his whistle as he peered at us. "No more patronyms and nicknames. No more hijinks or fussing. You are now soldiers and you will conduct yourselves as such. Many of you have no family, no home, no nothing. You now have no worries. In your instructors, you will find what war took from you. We will make sure that you want for nothing. This is true for you others, as well. Rich and poor, Bedouin or urbanite, orphan or the child of a soldier, you are all equal. We will favor no student over another. In return, we expect discipline, model obedience, and unbending rectitude. Here, we make men, real and brave men, men worthy of the Algerian nation, a nation of one and a half million martyrs who cannot rest in peace until we have proved that their sacrifice was a worthy investment." My cousin was baptized *number 122,* me, *129.*

Two days later, we were each issued a bottle-green tunic, a beret, undershirts. Those with big feet got boots. Those who wore smaller sizes got rubber sandals. When we went to inspect ourselves in the mirror, we saw adorable little toy soldiers. We practiced yelling our identification numbers and putting our hands to our temples in perfect salutes. We were now *number 19, number 43, number 72, number 120,* and nothing else. We no longer existed for ourselves. . . . We had become cadets, which is to say, the adopted children of the Army and of the Revolution.

A Border Passage

(excerpt)

Leila Ahmed

Leila Ahmed was born in Cairo in 1940 to an Egyptian father and a Turkish mother. Her father, a civil engineer, ran afoul of Nasser's government because he opposed the construction of the Aswan Dam for environmental reasons. Ahmed became an important scholar of women and gender in the Islamic world and the first professor of women's studies at Harvard Divinity School. Her memoir, A Border Passage, *describes her realization that for Egyptians to identify themselves as Arabs is a relatively new phenomenon, part of a scheme supported by the British to expand and solidify Arab-identified territory as a counterweight to the Ottoman Empire. Prior to that, she writes, Egyptians thought of themselves as having a unique blend of identities: African, Mediterranean, and pharaonic. Ahmed also speaks out on behalf of the many local varieties of Arabic that have been suppressed in favor of "standard" written Arabic.*

An Expectation of Angels

I remember it as a time, that era of my childhood, when existence itself seemed to have its own music—a lilt and music that made up the ordinary fabric of living. There was the breath of the wind always, and the perpetual murmur of trees; the call of the *karawan* that came in the dusk, dying with the dying light; the reed-piper playing his pipe in the dawn and, throughout the day, the music of living: street-vendors' calls; people passing in the street, talking; the clip-clop of a donkey; the sound of a motor car; dogs barking; the cooing of pigeons in the siesta hour.

Night too had its varieties of music. The clack of the wooden clogs of village women returning home, sometimes singly, sometimes in pairs, from work or from errands among the shops in the suburb of Matariyya. And the sound, as much a part of summer nights as the croaking of frogs, of the neighbors' waterwheel creaking gently, turned by an ox whose eyes were blinkered so he would not know he was going round and round rather than forward. The neighbors had a mango grove within the dried mud walls of their land. Along one of those walls, directly opposite my bedroom window, was a stream bordered on its other side by the mud wall and fruit garden of the next neighbors. The stream, dark and still and edged with reeds, disappeared beyond the walls into open fields. It was all that remained, I was told, of the canal that had run parallel to our house until just before I was born. The canal was filled in and a road built at about the time that a railway line was laid down on the other side of our house, linking the suburbs and the distant country centers beyond our house with Cairo and with Maadi on the other side of Cairo.

In the depths of the night, one also sometimes heard hyenas somewhere out on the distant edge of the villages, in the heart of the countryside, and very occasionally but so faintly that they were like a beat on the membrane of night, one could hear drums: a village wedding. There would be pipe music, too, but only a note here and there carried to us; what one heard, or sensed rather, were the drums. The drums, I do not know why, awoke in me a kind of obscure terror. I did not think, I am frightened of the drums. Instead they seemed to bring alive in me the hidden and muffled terrors that inhered in and threaded our ordinary living. Terrors above all about death, whose presence was there in our lives in myriad ways, but also of other things, the vagaries, for instance, of why things were the way they were—the beggars, the blind, the cripples, or even just the poor and the villagers themselves, and what it was that kept us on one side of the line and them on the other.

Privilege, in a setting where the deprivation of others is glaringly obvious, no doubt produces its own mesh of anxieties and perhaps also of guilt. What does a child make of seeing another child, just like herself, on the other side of the hedge, looking in at her, hollow-eyed, in rags, as she stops in her play to stare back? I imagine that the sense of terror and precariousness that seemed to have pervaded my childhood was not unconnected with whatever conclusions I drew about the mysterious arbitrary line that divided our lives and that could quite possibly at any moment shift—people are struck blind, die, in an instant.

Sometimes the sheer pain and terror of existence would be right out in the open, in the screams, for instance, that tore through the night once, in the darkest time before dawn, when our neighbor's ox somehow fell into the well by the waterwheel. He was dragged out dead and the women's wails were shrill and endless, like the wails of villagers and poor people over the death of a person. Another time it was in the day that the screams went up from another house, farther away but still piercing. A son of the house, a young man in his twenties, had committed suicide by drinking a bottle of Lysol.

And once someone was run over by a train just outside the large, disused iron gate to our garden, a gate that had been the main entrance before the canal was filled in and the railway built. That day, unusually, the gate was open, and I saw bloodstains on the road and here and there bloodied newspapers covering something, or some things, the mangled scattered bits of a person. (No one could figure out why he was run over. It might, someone speculated, have been a suicide. Or maybe his foot got stuck.) I was five or six. I literally shivered for days after that, though it must have been early summer. I remember that I would squeeze myself in beside my mother in the stuffed easy chair near the radio where she habitually sat. She comforted me, I remember, but I must have taxed her patience because I remember her saying, "It's just too hot, dear, I can't have you sticking to me like that!"

Other one-time events also happened on that side of the house, at that gate, which seemingly opened only for those occasions. I remember standing there once watching a train full of smiling, red-faced English soldiers chug slowly by. They called out and waved to us and threw chocolates; given their cheeriness and their dispensing of chocolates, this must have been close to the end of the Second World War. I was five in 1945.

Besides the drums, there was a whole variety of other beats and rhythms that marked and threaded our days and nights, and most were not frightening. Even the trains, despite that dreadful accident, were not frightening. They mostly passed at a comfortable chug, occasionally blowing their haunting whistles. It did happen sometimes (for no better reason, I think, than that the engine driver took it into his head to put on a sudden burst of speed) that the chug would turn into a loud, gathering, hurtling sound, as if some unearthly monster would shortly be upon us. The sound would cause us children to drop whatever we were doing and race to the top or bottom of the garden or of the stairs. Safety lay in getting to wherever it was before the hurtling monster was fully upon us.

And there was the regular beat of *al-makana,* "the machine," which pumped well water to the house and to the pond and garden and the various canals and waterways of earth and concrete that ran through it. Turned on every morning, it would come on again in the afternoons when the weather grew hot, so that summer afternoons were filled with the sound of hoses, running water, the regular fall of a spade, and, in the background, the phut-phut-phut of the machine. All these, the *makana* and the running water, were good sounds, reassuring sounds, sounds about everything going forward in the way it should. Sometimes, though, the *makana* would pick up and interweave with the sound of one's heart. And for some reason, perhaps because I imagined the absence of that sound, the possibility of its ceasing, the sound of my own heartbeat reminded me of death.

The regularity of my own breath did not frighten me the way the sound of my heart sometimes did, but I remember listening for Nanny's breath, in the bed beside me, to make sure she was still alive. Nanny was sixty when I was born. She sat at the foot of the bed every night, reading her Latin Bible, turning its silky leaves, moving her lips sometimes in prayer. Her Bible had a picture of Jesus coming on clouds of glory, the light streaming out in bands from the clouds in a way that I'd never seen it do. I didn't believe that light could ever look like that, but when I got to England I discovered that that was exactly how it looked sometimes. Nanny would pause in her reading sometimes and say meditatively, "*Tu sais, Lili, moi je mourirai bientôt*" ("You know, Lili, I will die soon"). At times I would cry when she said this, and always I would beg her not to. I don't know if she said it to me in part because the depth of my distress reassured her or simply because the thought was on her mind. Perhaps a little of both.

I think that quite often when Nanny appeared to be talking to me she was, in fact, talking to herself and I was overhearing her inner monologues as I attended to my own thoughts and games. "I earn my living by the sweat of my brow," she often said, perhaps as she hung some washing (delicate items that no one else might wash) there in the sunny backyard, a cat or two rubbing back and forth across her legs, "and that is nothing to be ashamed of." She said this as if defending herself, as if some invisible interlocutor were suggesting otherwise. In truth, she rarely had anyone of her own age or background to talk to.

Still, I don't think she knew the depth of the misery she caused me by her ruminations. Her dying was my one great and secret dread in childhood. My one prayer, which I added secretly to the prayers that my sister would make me go over with her at the bottom of the stairs before I went up to bed (prayers that consisted of a litany of the names of the people we were asking God to protect: Mummy, Daddy, all of us children, Nanny, Enayat the maid, etc.), was that Nanny would not die before I was old enough to bear it. I told God that I had to be fifteen at a minimum. I think I believed that adults—which in my assessment meant anyone about fifteen or older—had less feeling than children.

It was on one such occasion, waking up in the middle of the night and lying still, listening for Nanny's breathing, that I saw my guardian angel, the angel that, Nanny had told me, was always there to protect me. It looked something like a moonbeam, standing still, touching the mosquito net by the foot of the bed. I did not dare put my head outside the mosquito net to get a better view, lest I drive it away. Yet even with all my longing to believe in my guardian angel, as well as a host of other unseen things—fairies, for example, which the books said you would see if you believed, if you looked in foxgloves, which we didn't have—and even as I made my eyes as wide as I possibly could, trying to see what exactly this angel looked like, there was deep within me a center of disbelief. It was an angel, I really had seen it, I would say to myself later, but some part of me still always thought that it was a moonbeam.

It was Nanny in particular who in some sense entered with me into the realm I inhabited where the demarcations between the realities in one's head and those that were solidly outside were matters as yet to be circumspectly investigated. The world we shared, or that she at least pretended to share with me, included ghouls as well as angels. When I dawdled about getting into bed she would threaten to call the ghoul, and if I persisted she would stick her head out the window on the street side and call "Gho-o-oul! Gho-o-oul!" getting me immediately into bed. I never, fortunately, saw a ghoul, but I did know where it would come from—from somewhere near where the drums and the hyenas were. It was Nanny, too, who told me stories in the days before I could read and maybe also after. The usual fairy tales, or versions of them. One of our favorites—she would cry when she came to the moving bits at the end—was a version of the story I encountered years later as King Lear. It was about a king who had three daughters. The first two, when he asked them how much they loved him, said more than rubies and diamonds and so on. Only the youngest refused to flatter him. She really loved him but would only say she loved him as much as salt; rubies and diamonds were nothing to her, she said, compared with salt. He became angry and exiled her. Eventually he understood that salt and not rubies and diamonds gave taste to life and that it was she alone who really loved him, and of course they found each other again and lived happily ever after. I liked the story in part, I am sure, because it was about the triumph of the youngest, my own position among the siblings. But it also encapsulated something essential about Nanny and her values. It was a story about honesty and integrity, about valuing these qualities above everything else, and it implied a distrust of people who cared too much about money. It also implied that simplicity and hard work, salt, simple things were, in the end, the real prizes.

Nanny's sense of what mattered, what was good and what was bad, manifested itself in numerous ways—for example, in her solid support and admiration for my father as against another engineer, a man called Fahmy Pasha, whose grand, sumptuous mansion on the Corniche (the broad, sweeping avenue running the length of the Alexandria coastline) we would pass every day in the summers on our way to the beach. He had built his palatial villa with ill-gotten gains, Nanny would regularly say, and consequently he would not prosper, even if he seemed to now; there would be disasters, some way or other he would suffer, and if not him, then his children and his children's children, unto the seventh generation. Nanny was responding to that episode in Father's life when, long before his troubles with Nasser, King Farouk fired him from his job; obviously he was destined to find himself compelled to stand up to one corrupt Egyptian ruler after another. All this occurred in my earliest childhood and I have no memory of these happenings, except for my father's periodic returns from abroad with suitcases full of gifts. Among these, quite unforgettably for me, was a clock, out of which, to my constant fascination, flew a bird that announced the time by saying "cuckoo."

By and large there was a congruence between Nanny's actions and her values, both professed and implicit. But there were also moments of incongruence. Her enormous and somewhat simpering admiration for Grandfather, for instance. Grandfather, Mother's father, was a man of very substantial wealth who lived his life in commensurate style. He had three Mercedes of different sizes, and he used to order his valet to have the chauffeur bring one or the other car to the door according to where he was going: the larger one for ceremonial occasions, the small one for city errands, and so on. He dressed with impeccable style and elegance. Very tall, with an elegant, athletic frame, he was an imposingly handsome figure, with strong features, piercing blue eyes, and an air and habit of command. He was also, it is true, a fine farmer, passionate about the land he farmed and the quality of fruit he produced. But I think it was all the other things that had their effect on Nanny. She was openly partial to blue eyes—her husband had had blue eyes, she told us, and the younger of my two brothers was undisguisedly her favorite in part because he had blue eyes. She doted on this brother, Karim, and accepted from him things she would not have put up with from the three others of us. I was her next favorite. Nanny herself had brown eyes and dark, straight hair that she wore in a bun and that remained mainly dark and only lightly threaded with gray well into her seventies.

In retrospect, I do not doubt that besides blue eyes the other thing Nanny favored was men—or maleness, in infant, boy, or man. I knew this then, too, or more precisely sensed it, sensed that it was something about boyness as opposed to girlness that brought about this abandonment of who she was, of her otherwise forthright and undeviating commitment to fairness and to judging things solidly for what they were. Surprisingly, perhaps, she was the only person in my childhood environment in whom I sensed this preference. Neither of my parents betrayed at any level a preference for boys; if anything, my father possibly took slightly more delight in his daughters. My mother would commonly say that she found people's prejudice toward boys unintelligible. She would recount as illustration the story of a visitor who came to our house when I was born and who exclaimed, when Mother said she had not quite decided on a name for me, "What does it matter what you call her? It's only a girl. Call her anything, call her Figla [radish]!" The woman who said this was herself, in my memory of the story, nameless. Certainly Mother never betrayed a partiality for her sons over her daughters. She kept us all, I am tempted to say, at an equal distance. But that comment is perhaps unjust. Mother did have difficulty connecting with us, and with children in general, but she did not, either in relation to her children or in talking about or relating to men as distinct from women, communicate, as Nanny did, that there was something innately preferable about the one sex over the other. Nor did my grandmother or any of my aunts convey this.

Nanny did not like Mother. This was one instance in which blue eyes did not win her over. She was plain, at least with me, about not liking Mother. *"Moi je ne peux pas mentir, je n'aime pas ta mère"* ("I cannot tell a lie, I do not like your mother"). But, she would add, Mother was the mistress, "and as the mistress I respect her." That much I remember her saying. She did not directly discuss why she disliked Mother. Still, she evidently let slip sufficient remarks to have left me with the distinct impression that she regarded Mother as an idle woman of the spoiled upper classes, someone who applied herself to no useful work but wasted her days, after a few moments in the morning instructing the servants and discussing the menu with the cook, exchanging visits and chatting with her relatives. I wonder now what it was that Nanny thought Mother should have occupied herself with—embroidering perhaps, or baking, or charity work. Nanny was herself a strict respecter of, someone who even deferred to, the conventions of life, including the hierarchies of class, so I cannot imagine that she thought Mother ought, for instance, to be cleaning the house herself or doing all the cooking.

She once hinted at something more somber, which to my child's understanding was somewhere between sinister and incomprehensible. This was that I had had another sister, born shortly before I was, who had been premature and had died within instants. I do not recall quite how she conveyed it, but something in the way she told me suggested that my sister's prematureness and consequently her death were somehow Mother's fault. Now, of course, I conclude that she was suggesting that sometime in the course of this pregnancy Mother had attempted to have an abortion; and that this somehow had later precipitated, at least in Nanny's eyes, the infant's premature birth. I have no idea if there was any truth in this. Nanny was a Catholic and to her any abortion or attempted abortion would have been abhorrent.

My own imagination supplied the detail that this sister was buried in the back garden by the Seville orange tree, close to where we had buried Mitso, our tabby cat, who had died of old age. We had held an elaborate funeral for Mitso and then had placed a cross over his grave, but Nanny, even though she had loved Mitso as she loved all cats, made us remove it. It was blasphemous, she said. Cats did not have souls like people, and in any case they were not Christians.

I think now that, apart from anything else, the fact that Mother was her employer *and* a woman would have strongly predisposed Nanny to dislike her. Nanny was someone who had her own clear, firm opinions on things and there was nothing in her makeup that would have made living as the subordinate of another woman—a man might have been a different story—a palatable situation.

Still, even though she might say to me that she did not much like my mother, it was a muttered, semi-covert dislike, not an open or a blazing defiance. And it may well be that I am exaggerating that dislike, because in daily life there was actually very little friction between them—most of the time, none. Looking after the children was Nanny's province and Mother was evidently perfectly happy to leave all the details of our lives to her. It was also always clear, however, that Mother was the supreme authority regarding us, and if there was any serious matter afoot or any major moral lesson with which Nanny thought we needed to be inculcated, Nanny would confer with Mother and then bring us before her. It was Mother who dealt with grave infractions. Not even Father superseded Mother in our house as moral authority. On the contrary, he would always say that it was she whose judgment and discernment had to be deferred to, that he himself deferred to her. And she was, when she was scrutinizing you, questioning, judging with her eyes, a very august and even a frightening presence. One would not, after being subjected to this, easily do something she had clearly interdicted.

It was evident, too, that whatever Nanny's views were of Mother, there was no disagreement between them as to the moral code to which we were to be held. Regarding how we should behave, what was permitted or not permitted, what was wrong and what was right, and the general moral framework within which we should live, there was no detectable difference in what they inculcated, in fact there was a profound and singular consonance between their views on those sorts of issues, and Father's too (although Father was less likely to defer to convention), despite the differences between their cultures, their religions. Those differences, in my experience of them, were rather nominal.

But I remember one terrible row. I remember that they shouted at each other and that I inserted myself between them, protecting Nanny. This disconcerted them only a moment and they resumed shouting over my head. Nanny said she would leave, resign, and Mother said, Yes, leave, leave, now, at once, out.

Of course Nanny did not leave, and it all blew over. But the incident left me with a fine legacy of anxieties. For one thing, Mother, in the course of their row, had said that it was disgraceful the way Nanny was using "the child," making me unnecessarily dependent on her, thinking that this would make it impossible to dismiss her. What did it mean that Nanny was using me? I didn't think she was using me. Nanny wasn't, I said, using me. But these words dropped into my life like a handful of dust, making me uncertain about yet more things, things I needed to be certain about. And what did it mean, too, that Nanny could be dismissed? Servants could be dismissed. Nanny wasn't a servant, but she wasn't a parent either. Were we, was I, more like a servant or a parent? Like Nanny? I think I felt that I occupied some marginal space, that I didn't belong quite at the center, where my parents and maybe even my siblings were. That I could be left out of things and maybe they wouldn't notice.

It may be, too, that it was in connection with this row that I was made to move into my own bed. I know that when this took place it happened at Mother's instigation and against my impassioned protestations, even though I was only being moved to another bed in the same room. I do not know what age I was—perhaps six or seven.

My confusion about categories and where exactly I belonged extended also to animals, or at least to cats. I believe I wondered, for instance, whether maybe I belonged in the category in which cats also belonged, the category of small beings. Or maybe somewhere between them and people? I vaguely remember spending a long time staring into a cat's eyes and feeling that it was like me or that I was like it. This moment and the conclusion it brought me to, which I confided to my father—that I thought that the cat and I were very alike, especially our eyes—amused and delighted him (what we said or did often delighted him) and for some while afterward he would playfully say to me, "Come here, tell me, are your eyes really like the cat's eyes?" I think it was the fact that the cat only looked—

looked rather than spoke—that made me feel we, and our eyes in particular, were alike. My father's nickname for me as a child was Wise Owl, because I spoke so little but looked always, he thought, with such an air of wisdom.

Our family, or rather Nanny, had numerous cats. She fed the cats, most of which were not strictly ours or hers but cats that simply came daily to eat the scraps on our back balcony, whose trellis was shaded with a vine and clematis flowers of the vividest blue. Usually a cat or two would be ours and would be allowed into the downstairs hallways, although nowhere else in the house. At least once or twice in my childhood a cat gave birth in the curtained-off portion under the stairs in that hallway, where empty suitcases and other odds and ends were stacked. It was here, when the kittens emerged from their lair behind the curtain, round-eyed, staggering and stumbling over themselves, absorbed in and exploring anything and everything, agog at life, that I got to know them.

Nanny, however, also sometimes drowned kittens the moment they were born. Not, as a rule, those born under the stairs, who belonged to special cats, but those she might find elsewhere, the litter of a strange cat in the garage or in the bric-a-brac room at the bottom of the garden. She said it was kinder to kill them than to let them grow up and starve or be abused by people, but I found it nearly unbearable and I would plead with her not to. She would hold them, newborn, eyes still closed, in a pail of water until they died. You could hear, I think, their squeals for a second or two. I cannot tell now whether I ever witnessed her drowning a kitten or just imagined that I did. I see her doing it in a pail by the pond in the garden where the hand pump was, a hand pump from which cascaded the sweetest, coldest water, water that had emerged only that instant out of the well, out of the depths of the earth. There were plants in the pond and goldfish that were not always easy to see in the dark waters. A vine grew over the trellis above it, putting forth small opaque grapes that for some reason never ripened.

A Daughter of Isis

(excerpt)

Nawal El Saadawi

Nawal El Saadawi, born in 1931, is best known for her Woman at Point Zero, *the scorching feminist novel she published in 1979. As a doctor and political activist, she has worked tirelessly for the rights of women, and she has fought against the practice of female genital mutilation, to which she was subjected at a young age. El Saadawi's political convictions cost her several jobs over the years, and in 1981 she was imprisoned by President Anwar El-Sadat along with others who protested the Jerusalem Peace Treaty. She was released a month after Sadat's assassination.*

[Translated from the Arabic by Sherif Hetata.]

In 1949 I entered the main building of the School of Medicine in Kasr Al-Aini Street for the first time, after completing the preparatory pre-medical year in the School of Sciences in Giza. I was now in the first year of Al-Mashraha,* and now it was the word Al-Mashraha that carried a magical ring with it, perhaps even more magical than the first chimes of the university clock that had floated to my ears in Giza. My imagination wandered wildly as I approached the entrance to the building. How could I cut up a human body? How could I cut through the muscle called my heart that never stopped beating under the ribs throughout life? How could I cut through the cells in that brain that never ceased asking questions, and bringing back memories of childhood?

In the preparatory pre-medical year I had dissected only frogs, or cockroaches, or beetles. Since the day I was born my eyes had never fallen on a dead body. A shudder went through my body at the mere mention

---

* The dissecting hall, meaning the year in which students study anatomy and physiology of the normal human body in addition to pharmacology and parasitology.

of the word "corpse." I glimpsed the door of the dissecting hall at a distance. My heart beat quickly and for a moment my breathing stopped. Would I meet with spirits and devils in that hall? A penetrating smell was carried up my nose as I drew near. Was that the smell of death?

But my curiosity overcame my fear. I walked in, followed behind by Batta and Safeya. In the hall, marble-topped tables were arranged in long rows. On each table was a body surrounded by a group of students. After a short while we realized that they were groups of eight and then somebody told us that there were seniors who were second-year students, and juniors who were first-year students like us. And so we became a group of eight students sitting around a table with a dead body, or part of one, lying on it. Then one of the senior students came up to explain things to us. That was the tradition in the dissecting hall, the older students giving a hand to the freshers and vying with one another over who would explain to the girl students the mysteries of dissection.

When we were in the dissecting hall we sat on stools. Four of us sat around the upper part of the body, that is the head and neck, and four around the lower part, what we called the lower limbs. In one of the corners of the dissecting hall, near the door were two huge wooden chests filled with formalin to prevent the bodies in them from rotting. They were like wooden tombs crouching in the corner, with the dead floating in that fluid with a penetrating smell. They were closely guarded by an orderly called Am Osman, in charge of the dissecting hall. He had narrow eyes that glinted like those of a hawk. The skin on his hands was cracked by the formalin in which he kept immersing them, to throw bodies in, or take them out, or push them around. His features were burnt by the sun to a dark pallor, like the faces of the peasants in my village.

Am Osman used to lock the huge chests with keys, as though they contained the riches of the earth, then he would stand in front of them haughtily as though he was Lord Radwan, the guardian angel of Paradise. He smiled only when a rich student went up to him to buy a corpse from him. The price of these corpses was three pounds apiece. He used to steal them in connivance with the undertaker and usually paid him fifty piastres for three dead bodies. During the night he crept into cemeteries and collected the bones of the dead which he sold to the students by the piece.

In the morning I used to see him standing in the courtyard wearing his white coat covered with formalin stains, straining his ears to catch the shrieks of the women as they followed behind the coffin of some relative. The body of the deceased was still warm but he would walk in the funeral procession, as far as the cemetery, to clinch a deal. The students said he had more money and owned more buildings than Mooro, the Dean of Medical School.

When I returned home at the end of the first day, my mother almost shrieked with fear as I came in through the door, as though I had brought back the spirits of the dead in my bag. She made me put the bag with the clothes I was wearing outside the door, then she put my white coat and my dissecting instruments, together with my clothes, in a tin full of water to boil.

In the first few days, I used to shudder whenever I cut into the body with my scalpel for I could not forget that this was human flesh I was dissecting. I stopped eating any kind of meat, and when I saw any floating in the soup tureen I had nausea. It reminded me of a dead limb floating in the formalin. Mother used to prepare a small meal for me and put it in a box, so that I could take it with me in my bag. Sandwiches of egg or meat for protein, green vegetables and fresh fruit rich in vitamins, and bread. I used to throw the box with its contents into a refuse bin, and spend the whole day without eating, except for a glass of tea with mint or lemon which Am Muhammad, the orderly, prepared for me in the female students' room.

I was seized with wonder at the sight of seniors holding a scalpel in one hand, and a sandwich into which they munched in the other, while they stood at our table explaining certain things to us. But soon the wonder evaporated and we juniors started to imitate the seniors. My female colleagues began to eat as they sat around the dissecting table with the body on it. And I started to devour the meat sandwiches that mother prepared for me. My appetite for food returned stronger than before, perhaps because the lust for life becomes greater in the proximity of death, just as light shines more brilliant in the midst of darkness.

One of the professors in the school was a relative of my colleague Batta, whether on her mother's or her father's side, I was not sure. Consequently, Am Osman never refused her any of the treasures stored in his chests, and he once gave her a complete human skeleton for half the usual price. She lived in a two-storied house on Al-Haram Road. Her mother put the skeleton together on the lower floor using wooden supports to hold it up, and Batta used to invite me to her house so that we could go over what we had to study together. This helped me because she could afford to buy whatever corpses or books were required. I, on the other hand, could not purchase from Am Osman anything more than a few pieces of bone belonging to the hand or the foot.

My father's government salary was not small but he had to pay for the education of nine boys and girls in school. He had a small piece of land in Kaft Tahla which he sold little by little to pay off money he owed. The expenses for the School of Medicine were higher than for other schools and books cost a lot. In addition, the cost of living was rising rapidly. As a result I was late paying for the fees of the pre-medical year, and again when I moved to the first year in medical school, and my father received a letter warning him that if he did not pay the fees that were long due his "honourable daughter" would be expelled.

The day came when my father gave me the envelope containing the first installment of my fees. I noticed the slight tremor in his fingers as he handed it to me. He was saving on the food of my brothers and sisters to keep me in medical school. Every day he went out early in the morning, worked hard all day and came home in the evening exhausted. At the beginning of each month he handed over his salary to my mother. With it she paid what was owed to the grocer, the butcher, the fruiterer, the vegetable shop, the bakery and the drug store. After that, little was left. We lived for almost half the month on what mother called shoukouk.* She had a small notebook in which she wrote down everything we owed, day by day.

Before I went out in the morning she used to give me the money to ride the bus or the tramcar. Often I would walk, and give it back to her at the end of the day, or save up to buy a book, or some bones, or a joint from Am Osman. I was sorry for my mother and my father, for the load they both were bearing, and did my best to make it lighter for them.

Mother worked hard all day in the house, helped by a small servant-girl like Sa'adeya. I used to stand at the sink and help her with the plates and sometimes on Fridays when I was home, I cleaned the whole house, or cooked instead of her, or prepared the table, or performed other domestic tasks.

How much I hated the repeated horrid chores I did in those days! No sooner had I finished preparing breakfast, then it was time for lunch, and no sooner had we finished lunch than it was time to prepare for supper. No sooner had I finished cleaning the floor than it was covered with dust again. The sink emptied of plates was soon full of them again. It seemed like a never-ending struggle to prevent the earth from revolving around itself, or against the movement of dust particles through the universe, or against the contraction of the muscles of the stomach and the intestines inside our bellies.

On the day when my father gave me the envelope with the first instalment of my fees, and I saw his hand tremble, saw the print of his fingers

---

* What is bought but not paid for until later, usually the beginning of the month.

on the banknote smelling of sweat, my heart was heavy with sadness as I walked down the street, carrying it in my bag, as though it was my father with his huge body that I carried in my bag, or as though I was carrying the whole world on my shoulders as I walked. Maybe it was the feeling of guilt, an uneasy conscience, for how could my small brothers and sisters go hungry, grow weak and anaemic, so that I could graduate as a doctor?

I had never carried such a big sum of money in my bag. I pushed the envelope between the pages of a notebook to hide it and put it in my bag, locked the bag and walked along holding it tightly under my arm. People seemed to be staring at me in a strange way as though they had the eyes of thieves which could penetrate through leather, and as though they had noses that could smell the odour of money at a distance.

I did not ride in a bus or a tramcar that day, for riding in them there were always pickpockets with nimble fingers capable of stealing the envelope in the wink of an eye like jinnis or hidden spirits. I walked all the way from Giza to Kasr Al-Aini Street, slipped into the building which housed the administration and stood in front of the official responsible for student affairs.

There was a long line of students waiting. The official kept leaving his desk and disappearing for a long time in some other office. In addition, he was not respecting the line. Every time one of the students gave him a card, probably with a recommendation on it from someone whom the official considered important, he would deal with him before his turn, or if one of the professors or a high official came in he would jump to his feet to finish his business for him. But none of the students protested. They just stood there looking frustrated or commenting in a low voice. I heard one of the students standing behind me saying: "It's chaos here in this school as it is everywhere else in the country. The money we pay is all wasted because of corruption. If I had an important relative or a recommendation to the dean I could be exempted from paying fees."

"The Rabbit Club"

Hisham Matar

Hisham Matar was born in New York in 1970. His parents returned to Libya when Matar was three, and he lived there until 1979, when his family was forced to flee the country due to political persecution. In 1990, while Matar was in London, his father Jaballa, a political activist, disappeared in Cairo. Letters received six years later indicated that he was kidnapped by the Egyptian secret police and turned over to the Libyan regime.

Hisham Matar's first novel, In the Country of Men, *was shortlisted for the 2006 Man Booker Prize. His second novel,* Anatomy of a Disappearance, *was published in 2011. "The Rabbit Club" was broadcast in 2011 by BBC Radio 3 as one of several authors' essays on the theme of "the team photo."*

I don't have the photograph. We must have left it behind in the rush to leave Libya. But I remember it well, leaning frameless against a row of books on one of the shelves in our old house in Tripoli. Although, sometimes, I wonder whether it ever existed, whether it was not conjured up later by my imagination or by my memory. Either way, it is vivid in my mind, I can see it: I am six, perhaps seven, standing to the far left of the frame, legs apart, my brown leather jacket zipped to the neck, and a fat rabbit under my arm. Next to me is Ziad, my older brother, looking cool and bored. Beside him stand two boys from the neighbourhood—I no longer remember their names. They are staring, curious and suspicious, at the camera or at the photographer.

This was the Rabbit Club. It took place at my grandfather's house far from our home in Tripoli. We met after lunch, when most people napped and the town was quiet. First we had to make sure all doors to the courtyard were shut; then one of us would open the pen. As if knowing our purpose, and indeed eager to start playing, the dozen or so furry rabbits would come out hopping into the hard sunlight. I loved to chase them around the courtyard and then shepherd them back into the cage. Every time I caught a rabbit, it would go still in my arms and its neck would stiffen. I still remember their small hearts knocking against the palm of my hand. I knew it was fear that they felt, but I tried to convince myself that it might be excitement. Every time I put one down gently inside the pen, I hoped that it would know next time to trust me.

We would go to my grandfather's house in Ajdabiya for an extended stay once a year. It was in the northeastern part of the country, and in those days, the 1970s, it was a small town. Jaddi Hamed, my father's father, and the rest of my paternal family lived there and it is where my father grew up. Although I didn't know it then, every time we made the ten- or twelve-hour drive from Tripoli, Father was retracing his steps, returning to the place and people he had left: first for the military academy, then on to the United States and England for further study, before returning to Libya and settling in the capital.

As a young boy, I did not like Ajdabiya and was conscious of the duty implied in these trips. I found the town's starkness unsettling: the empty dirt roads, the plain houses, the hard sea-less light. Unlike Tripoli, a city defined by the Mediterranean, Ajdabiya, according to my memory, was a village lost in the desert. This corresponds perfectly to the mythology I have somehow, from as far back as I can remember, constructed about the two different families and landscapes from which I descend. My mother's family lived in a lush and colourful world, full of exuberances and exaggerations; whereas my father's people were, like monks in the desert, wary of excessive expression or abundance.

My mother's family is from Darna. I remember the harrowing drive across the Green Mountain: the reddish rock, the grey green vegetation, the snaking black tarmac gleaming under a sky so blue it seemed drinkable, and that strange silence of the mountains, a silence deepened by what had taken place here. The Green Mountain region was where, during World War I, the Libyan resistance, under the leadership of Omar al-Mukhtar, fought some of its fiercest battles against the Italian army. And I remember also how the light changed as we approached Darna, and the sound of the sea, the way it seems to take the wind, and the smell of wild sage, mint and eucalyptus, then seeing the sea, shimmering beside the fertile plain. The people of this region are known to be lively and verbose. They sit side by side in cafés to observe the passersby. Gossip is a serious business here. And the food is good, and so are the stories. It is a place for prose, not poetry.

Ajdabiya, on the other hand, is nationally known for its poets and its high regard for poetry. Authors covet its admiration and, in return, the residents of Ajdabiya fear, maybe more than a holy man's curse, upsetting a fine poet: criticism of a person or their family immortalised in verse can be highly damaging. As for the landscape, it is bare and vacant. Two plains, the sky and the desert, dominate.

The hamlet was a cluster of buildings in the vastness. My grandfather's house was the largest in the town and occupied its centre. To my child's mind, it was the point from which not only Ajdabiya developed, but every town and city in the country, indeed the whole world. Remove Jaddi Hamed's house, and the universe might crumble. Its architecture fostered this idea. For a young boy it was as disorientating and magical as a maze. I would often lose my way through its endless rooms, corridors and courtyards. Some windows looked out on to the street, some on to one of the courtyards. Yet others, strangely, looked into other rooms. It was as if whenever the family ran out of space, they would build another room. Some of its halls and corridors were roofless, or had an opening cut into the roof through which a square or perfectly circular shaft of light leaned and slowly turned throughout the day. In fact, the light was always shifting. It was never quite clear whether you were indoors or outdoors. Some of its staircases took you outside the building, under the open sky, before winding back inside. The décor was plain. The walls were plastered and painted in two colours: a strong blue or green or purple on the lower half, and white or pale pink or yellow on the upper half. The floors were sometimes tiled but mostly covered unevenly, like cream cheese on toast, in something like concrete. In places of heavy traffic, such as the entrance, it shone smooth. Bare bulbs hung from the ceilings and there was hardly any furniture. The house was like one of my grandfather's long poems, plain yet full of surprises.

Jaddi Hamed was a poet who had fought in the resistance. I remember him once unbuttoning his shirt, pulling it over his shoulder, to show me the small rosette, between his shoulder and collarbone, where a bullet had entered.

"Where did it come out?" I asked, expecting him to point to another, identical rosette on his back.

"It's still inside," he said.

I remember how terribly upset I became, not at that moment, but a little while later, when I returned to ask again if there was no way of removing it.

At one point in the war, he was captured and sent for "trial"in Italy. In fascist Italy, the fate of such a man often ended in execution. No one expected to see him again. My grandmother did not count on Mussolini's government to return the corpse for burial either. Friends and relatives of the family began to visit, as if for a funeral. What they didn't know was that, a few days after arriving in Italy, Jaddi Hamed managed to escape. He headed for the port. A ship had just set off for Alexandria. He missed it by seconds. A fisherman agreed to take him to it, to edge close enough to the rear steps so as Jaddi Hamed could climb, unseen, aboard. He hid in the engine room for three days, eating leftovers out of rubbish bins.

From Alexandria Jaddi Hamed made his way to the Egyptian-Libyan border. He smuggled himself into his own country and eventually reached Ajdabiya. Less than two months after his capture, he was standing in front of his house. My grandmother opened the door and fainted.

Jaddi Hamed lived a long life after World War I. My father was born in 1939, when Jaddi Hamed was in his mid- to late fifties. He had two sons after my father. The youngest was born when my grandfather was in his late seventies. People, particularly in a place where life expectancy for a man hovered somewhere around 65, must have thought him mad, irresponsible, that he wouldn't live to see his newborn walk. In fact, he saw him walk, graduate from university, marry, and have children of his own.

Jaddi Hamed's house suited his history and character: its various surprising turns, its seeming endlessness, his modest manner and the depth of his presence. He would sit in the corner of the large hall, the radio and a couple of cartons of Kent cigarettes beside him. He was rarely without a cigarette between his long, slender fingers. He was tall and said very little. It embarrassed me whenever, in his presence, someone would start to speak too loudly or be too exuberant. I remember him waving to me, gathering his fingers round one of the buttons of my shirt, straightening my collar. Sitting next to him was like being beside a quiet strong stream. I was eight years old when I left Libya. That was the last time I saw him.

There are various estimates to how old Jaddi Hamed was when he died: most agree that he was somewhere between 103 and 109 years old—although I once was told, emphatically, that Jaddi Hamed was 112 when he died. This would mean he was born somewhere between 1876 and 1885. Nevertheless, when he died in 1988, it came as a shock. We were all in London. I remember the dizzy feeling, time stopping. Father had lost his mother a few years earlier, but this was the first time I saw him cry.

A little over a year after Jaddi Hamed died, my father, a leading dissident wanted by the Gaddafi regime, was kidnapped from his home in Cairo and imprisoned in Libya. Shortly before this happened, my father had confided in me a secret. In the years after we had left Libya and settled in Egypt, he would pass through the border with a fake passport, dressed as an Egyptian farmer, in order to pay Jaddi Hamed a brief, nocturnal visit.

"Was he surprised to see you?" I asked.

"Somehow he always expected it," my father said.

Father would sit in the dark beside Jaddi Hamed for an hour or two, but never more, talking in whispers, before he would kiss his father's hand and forehead and begin the dangerous long journey back.

"You didn't say hello to your sisters and brothers?" I asked.

"Too dangerous," he said.

All in all, he told me, he had done this three times.

I was cross at him for risking his life like that.

"Now that he's gone," he said to reassure me, "there's no need."

But now, after more than twenty years of not seeing my father, I think I understand his actions. But I have wondered since about the timing, about why my father had chosen that moment to tell me of his secret visits to Ajdabiya. In the beginning I had assumed it was because Jaddi Hamed had passed away not long before, but then, after my father was captured, I began to wonder if the fact that Jaddi Hamed was no longer alive had somehow emboldened my father's resistance, made him take more risks.

When we left Libya, and for several years after, I would look up my country in every atlas, encyclopaedia or dictionary I came across. I still remember the consolation I felt when I found its name: consolation and a peculiar sense of dislocation, as if seeing a photograph and not immediately recognising that the person in it is yourself. I spent afternoons in Cairo peering into maps of Libya. I could draw it from memory, knew the exact angle of its square jaw crowning Africa, and the bit that curls round and back up to the coast. Ajdabiya wasn't, as my boyish mind had always imagined, a village lost in the desert but lay only a few millimetres away from the sea, perhaps an hour's drive. And now it is no longer a village— if it ever was—but a large town.

Unexpectedly, the depth of my longing has not settled on Tripoli, where we lived and I spent a magical childhood, or Benghazi, where my brother and I spent summers with cousins, but on Ajdabiya, that earnest town I was never fond of as a boy. It is the place I long for the most and with the deepest passion. If my father is still alive, he would be seventy-two. When I imagine being reunited with him, I imagine it happening not in the family home in Cairo, the place from which he was taken, or in my flat in London, but there in my grandfather's house, not in the night hours, but in a day full of light.

The Travels of Ibn Battuta
(excerpt)

Ibn Battuta

Born in Morocco in 1304, Ibn Battuta was the greatest world traveler of his time. He began his journeys in 1325, a year after Marco Polo died in Venice, but traveled five times as far before he was done. In his journeys through Egypt, Arabia, Persia, Afghanistan, India, and China, he covered an estimated 75,000 miles.

Ibn Battuta has a plain, straightforward style and an apparent lack of interest in himself, which is sometimes frustrating. Especially in the early chapters of his narrative, he seems driven to move from one city to the next, recording their names but hardly staying long enough to look around. Along the way, though, there are wonders to be seen. In Persia he meets the members of a religious sect who wear chains around their necks. They build a fire, then "sing and walk into it." Their leader borrows Ibn Battuta's shirt, "then proceeded to roll about in the fire, and to strike it with his sleeves, until he had put it out. He then brought me the shirt, upon which the fire had not made the least impression." When Ibn Battuta reaches India, the character of the book changes entirely. Rather than repeating tales and verses he has heard, he recreates scenes in which he is an active participant. This passage begins with his arrival at the city of "Dehli," apparently a bit dusty from the road.

[Translated from the Arabic by the Reverend Samuel Lee.]

Let us now return to the description of our arrival [in] Dehli. When we arrived at this place, the Vizier having previously met us, we came to the door of the Sultan's haram, to the place in which his mother, El Makhdūma Jahān resides, the Vizier, as also the Kāzī of the place, being still with us. These paid their respects at the entrance, and we all followed their example. We also, each of us, sent his present to her, which was proportionate to his circumstances. The Queen's secretaries then registered these presents, and informed her of them. The presents were accepted, and we

43

were ordered to be seated. Her viands were then brought in; we received the greatest respect and attention in their odd way. After this, dresses of honour were put upon us, and we were ordered to withdraw to such places as had been prepared for each of us. We made our obeisance and retired accordingly. This service is presented, by one's bowing the head, placing one of the hands on the earth, and then retiring.

When I had got to the house prepared for me, I found it furnished with every carpet, vessel, couch, and fuel, one could desire. The victuals which they brought us consisted of flour, rice, and flesh, all of which was brought from the mother of the Emperor. Every morning we paid our respects to the Vizier, who on one occasion gave me two thousand dinars, and said: This is to enable you to get your clothes washed. He also gave me a large robe of honour; and to my attendants, who amounted to about forty, he gave two thousand dinars. After this, the Emperor's allowance was brought to us, which amounted to the weight of one thousand Dehli-Ritls of flour, where every Ritl is equal to five and twenty Ritls of Egypt. We also had one thousand Ritls of flesh; and of fermented liquors, oil, oil-olive, and the betel-nut, many Ritls; and also many of the betel-leaf.

During this time, and in the absence of the Emperor, a daughter of mine happened to die, which the Vizier communicated to him. The Emperor's distance from Dehli was that of ten stages; nevertheless, the Vizier had an answer from him on the morning of the day, on which the funeral was to take place. His orders were, that what was usually done on the death of any of the children of the nobility, should be done now. On the third day, therefore, the Vizier came with the judges and nobles, who spread a carpet and made the necessary preparations, consisting of incense, rose-water, readers of the koran, and panegyrists. When I proceeded with the funeral, I expected nothing of this; but upon seeing their company I was much gratified. The Vizier, on this occasion, occupied the station of the Emperor, defraying every expense, and distributing victuals to the poor, and others; and giving money to the readers, according to the order which he had received from the Emperor.

After this, the Emperor's mother sent for the mother of the child, and gave her dresses and ornaments, exceeding one thousand dinars in value. She also gave her a thousand dinars in money, and dismissed her on the second day. During the absence of the Emperor, the Vizier shewed me the greatest kindness, on the part of himself, as well as on that of his master.

Soon after, the news of the Emperor's approach was received, stating that he was within seven miles of Dehli, and ordering the Vizier to come and meet him. He went out, accordingly, accompanied by those who had arrived for the purpose of being presented; each taking his present with him. In this manner we proceeded till we arrived at the gate of the palace in which he then was. At this place the secretaries took account of the several presents, and also brought them before the Emperor. The presents were then taken away, and the travellers were presented, each according to the order in which he had been arranged. When my turn came, I went in and presented my service in the usual manner, and was very graciously received, the Emperor taking my hand, and promising me every kindness. To each of the travellers he gave a dress of honour, embroidered with gold, which had been worn by himself, and one of these he also gave to me. After this, we met without the palace, and viands were handed about for some time. On this occasion the travellers ate, the Vizier, with the great Emīrs, standing over them as servants. We then retired. After this, the Emperor sent to each of us one of the horses of his own stud, adorned and caparisoned with a saddle of silver. He then placed us in his front with the Vizier, and rode on till he arrived at his palace in Dehli. On the third day after our arrival, each of the travellers presented himself at the gate of the palace; when the Emperor sent to inquire, whether there were any among us who wished to take office, either as a writer, a judge, or a magistrate; saying, that he would give such appointments. Each, of course, gave an answer suitable to his wishes. For my own part, I answered, I have no desire either for rule or writership; but the office both of judge and of magistrate, myself and my fathers have filled. These replies were carried to the Emperor, who commanded each person to be brought before him, and he then gave him such appointment as would suit him; bestowing on him, at the same time, a dress of honour, and a horse furnished with an ornamented saddle. He also gave him money, appointing likewise the amount of his salary, which was to be drawn from the treasury. He also appointed a portion of the produce of the villages, which each was to receive annually, according to his rank.

When I was called, I went in and did homage. The Vizier said: The Lord of the world appoints you to the office of judge in Dehli. He also gives you a dress of honour with a saddled horse, as also twelve thousand dinars for your present support. He has moreover appointed you a yearly salary of twelve thousand dinars, and a portion of lands in the villages, which will produce annually an equal sum. I then did homage according to their custom, and withdrew.

We shall now proceed to give some account of the Emperor Mohammed son of Ghīā Oddīn Toglik: then of our entering and leaving Hindūstān.

This Emperor was one of the most bountiful and splendidly munificent men (where he took); but in other cases, one of the most impetuous and inexorable: and very seldom indeed did it happen, that pardon followed his anger. On one occasion he took offence at the inhabitants of Dehli, on account of the numbers of its inhabitants who had revolted, and the liberal support which these had received from the rest; and, to such a pitch did the quarrel rise, that the inhabitants wrote a letter consisting of several pages, in which they very much abused him: they then sealed it up, and directed it to the Real Head and Lord of the world, adding, "Let no other person read it." They then threw it over the gate of the palace. Those who saw it, could do no other than send it to him; and he read it accordingly. The consequence was, he ordered all the inhabitants to quit the place; and, upon some delay being evinced, he made a proclamation stating, that what person soever, being an inhabitant of that city, should be found in any of its houses or streets, should receive condign punishment. Upon this they all went out. But, his servants finding a blind man in one of the houses, and a bed-ridden one in another, the Emperor commanded the bed-ridden man to be projected from a balista, and the blind one to be dragged by his feet by Dawlatābād, which is at the distance of ten days, and he was so dragged; but, his limbs dropping off by the way, only one of his legs was brought to the place intended, and was then thrown into it: for the order had been, that they should go to this place. When I entered Dehli it was almost a desert. Its buildings were very few; in other respects it was quite empty, its houses having been forsaken by its inhabitants. The King, however, had given orders, that any one who wished to leave his own city, may come and reside there. The consequence was, the greatest city in the world had the fewest inhabitants.

Upon a certain occasion, too, the principal of the preachers, who was then keeper of the jewellery, happened to be outwitted by some of the infidel Hindoos, who came by night and stole some jewels. For this he beat the man to death with his own hand.

Upon another occasion, one of the Emīrs of Fargāna came to pay him a temporary visit. The Emperor received him very kindly, and bestowed on him some rich presents. After this the Emīr had a wish to return, but was afraid the Emperor would not allow him to do so; he began, therefore, to think of flight. Upon this a whisperer gave intimation of his design, and the Emīr was put to death: the whole of his wealth was then given to the informers. For this is their custom, that when any one gives private intimation of the designs of another, and his information turns out to be true, the person so informed of is put to death, and his property is given to the informer.

There was at this time, in the city of Kambāya, on the shores of India, a Sheikh of considerable power and note, named the Sheikh Alī Haidarī, to whom the merchants and seafaring men made many votive offerings. This Sheikh was in the habit of making many predictions for them. But when the Kāzī Jalāl Oddīn Afgāni rebelled against the Emperor, it was told him that the Sheikh Haidarī had sent for this Kāzī Jalāl Oddīn, and given him the cap off his own head. Upon this the Emperor set out for the purpose of making war upon the Kāzī Jalāl Oddīn, whom he put to flight. He then returned to his palace, leaving behind him an Emīr, who should make inquiry respecting others who had joined the Kāzī: the inquiry accordingly went on, and those who had done so were put to death. The Sheikh was then brought forward; and when it was proved that he had given his cap to the Kāzī, he was also slain. The Sheikh Hād, son of the Sheikh Bahā Oddīn Zakaryā, was also put to death, on account of some spite which he would wreak upon him. This was one of the greatest Sheikhs. His crime was, that his uncle's son had rebelled against the Emperor, when he was acting as governor in one of the provinces of India. So war was made upon him, and being overcome, his flesh was roasted with some rice, and thrown to the elephants to be devoured: but they refused to touch it.

Upon a certain day, when I myself was present, some men were brought out who had been accused of having attempted the life of the Vizier. They were ordered, accordingly, to be thrown to the elephants, which had been taught to cut their victims to pieces. Their hoofs were cased with sharp iron instruments, and the extremities of these were like knives. On such occasions the elephant-driver rode upon them: and, when a man was thrown to them, they would wrap the trunk about him and toss him up, then take him with the teeth and throw him between their fore feet upon the breast, and do just as the driver should bid them, and according to the orders of the Emperor. If the order was to cut him to pieces, the elephant would do so with his irons, and then throw the pieces among the assembled multitude: but if the order was to leave him, he would be left lying before the Emperor, until the skin should be taken off, and stuffed with hay, and the flesh given to the dogs.

On one occasion one of the Emīrs, *viz.*, the Ain El Mulk, who had the charge of the elephants and beasts of burden, revolted, and took away the greater part of these beasts and went over the Ganges, at the time the Emperor was on his march towards the Maabar districts, against the Emīr Jalāl Oddīn. Upon this occasion the people of the country proclaimed the runaway emperor: but an insurrection arising, the matter soon came to an end.

Another of his Emīrs, namely Halājūn, also revolted, and sallied out of Dehli with a large army. The Viceroy in the district of Telingāna also rebelled, and made an effort to obtain the kingdom; and very nearly succeeded, on account of the great number who were then in rebellion, and the weakness of the army of the Emperor; for a pestilence had carried off the greater part. From his extreme good fortune, however, he got the victory, collected his scattered troops, and subdued the rebellious Emīrs, killing some, torturing others, and pardoning the rest. He then returned to his residence, repaired his affairs, strengthened his empire, and took vengeance on his enemies. But let me now return to the account of my own affairs with him.

When he had appointed me to the office of Judge of Dehli, had made the necessary arrangements, and given me the presents already mentioned, the horses prepared for me, and for the other Emīrs who were about his person, were sent to each of us, who severally kissed the hoof of the horse of him who brought them, and then led our own to the gate of the palace; we then entered, and each put on a dress of honour; after which we came out, mounted, and returned to our houses.

The Emperor said to me, on this occasion, Do not suppose that our office of Judge of Dehli will cost you little trouble: on the contrary, it will require the greatest attention. I understood what he said, but did not return him a good answer. He understood the Arabic, and was not pleased with my reply. I am, said I, of the sect of Ibn Mālik, but the people of Dehli follow Hanafi; besides, I am ignorant of their language. He replied, I have appointed two learned men your deputies, who will advise with you. It will be your business to sign the legal instruments. He then added: If what I have appointed prove not an income sufficient to meet your numerous expenses, I have likewise given you a cell, the bequests appropriated to which you may expend, taking this in addition to what is already appointed. I thanked him for this, and returned to my house.

A few days after this he made me a present of twelve thousand dinars. In a short time, however, I found myself involved in great debts, amounting to about fifty-five thousand dinars, according to the computation of India, which with them amounts to five thousand five hundred tankas; but which, according to the computation of the west, will amount to thirteen thousand dinars. The reason of this debt was, the great expenses incurred in waiting on the Emperor, during his journies to repress the revolt of the Ain El Mulk. About this time, I composed a panegyric in praise of the Emperor, which I wrote in Arabic, and read to him. He translated it for himself, and was wonderfully pleased with it: for the Indians are fond of Arabic poetry, and are very desirous of [being memorialized in] it. I then informed him of the debt I had incurred; which he ordered to be discharged from his own treasury, and said: Take care, in future, not to exceed the extent of your income. May God reward him.

Some time after the Emperor's return to the Maabar districts, and his ordering my residence in Dehli, his mind happened to change respecting a Sheikh in whom he had placed great confidence, and even visited, and who then resided in a cave without the city. He took him accordingly and imprisoned him, and then interrogated his children as to who had resorted to him. They named the persons who had done so, and myself among the rest; for it happened that I had visited him in the cave. I was consequently ordered to attend at the gate of the palace, and a council to sit within. I attended in this way for four days, and few were those who did so, who escaped death. I betook myself, however, to continued fasting, and tasted nothing but water. On the first day I repeated the sentence, "God is our support, and the most excellent patron," three and thirty thousand times; and after the fourth day, by God's goodness was I delivered; but the Sheikh, and all those who had visited him, except myself, were put to death.

Upon this I gave up the office of Judge, and bidding farewell to the world, attached myself to the holy and pious Sheikh, the saint and phœnix of his age, Kamāl Oddīn Abd Ullah El Gāzī, who had wrought many open miracles. All I had I gave to the Fakeers; and, putting on the tunic of one of them, I attached myself to this Sheikh for five months, until I had kept a fast of five continued days; I then breakfasted on a little rice.

Look & Move On

(excerpt)

Mohammed Mrabet

Mohammed Mrabet, born in 1936, was one of several Moroccan story-tellers whose words were taped and translated by Paul Bowles and published as stories, novels, and memoirs. In his brief but pungent memoir, Look & Move On, *Mrabet describes his first encounters with Jane and Paul Bowles and his later meetings with their friends, including Tennessee Williams and Elia Kazan. As the passage below begins, Mrabet has just returned from an unhappy stay in the United States, where he had been invited by a young American couple he had met in Tangier.*

[Translated from the Arabic by Paul Bowles.]

Now I was able to live just as I pleased. There was no Reeves to worry about, no Maria to ask me where I was going and what time I was coming back. I could fish all day, get drunk in bars, cook the food I liked, or lie on the beach. No one cared. I had brought back dollars, so I could buy what I wanted. And meeting the right girls is a big part of having money. I found several good ones.

One of these I got to know through an accident, something I happened to see as I was getting off a bus at Souq el Bqar. A girl from my neighborhood was walking past. When she got a little further up the street, I saw a young Italian who lived in the quarter step in front of her. She tried to walk past him, but he would not let her. Then she began to yell at him, and he slapped her. That made me feel like having a fight. A Nazarene does not have the right to hit a Moslem girl.

I went over to them. What's the matter with you? The girl's just walking down the street, and you come and slap her?

He was tall and heavy, and so he thought he could swear at me. I brought my knee up to his groin, hard. When he doubled over I grabbed his ears and butted him in the face. He lay on the sidewalk and I kicked his head.

51

I had seen the girl many times in the quarter, but I did not know her name. She turned to me. Get out of here fast, she said. His father's a police inspector.

Two friends of mine who had been watching began to run toward my house with me. They helped me pack some clothes in a bag. Then the three of us set out, carrying blankets and sheepskins and pans for cooking. At the foot of the Old Mountain Mjidou and Hassan went into the baqal and bought food supplies and candles. I kept walking toward Merkala Beach, and they caught up with me. Then we went westward along the coast. We passed through Agla and kept going in the direction of the cape. Finally we came to a cave in the rocks above the sea.

First we gave the cave a thorough cleaning. We got sand and covered the floor with it. Then we set the large cartons on the sand and spread out the sheepskins. I daubed some tar around the walls of the cave, to keep out insects and snakes. And we sat down and rested.

I've got my fishing gear with me, I said. I can live on fish if I have to. Anyway, this is where I'm going to stay.

You can count on us, they said. We'll bring you whatever you need.

After a while Hassan went back to the city. Mjidou spent the night with me there in the cave. In the morning after we had eaten I gave him the keys to my house and some money.

Here's a list of everything I need today, I told him. Be sure and bring it all before night.

Mjidou said: I'll see you later, and started out. He had promised to live in my house and take care of the birds for me. I knew I could trust both him and Hassan.

It was low tide. I went down to the water and gathered shrimps for a while, putting them into a wet basket that I set in the shade of the rocks. Not far away up the coast, and above the cliffs, I could see a house. I decided to walk up and see who lived there. I found a Riffian farmer working outside the house. I said hello to him and sat down, and he sat down beside me. I took out my sebsi and filled it for him.

Where did you just come from? he asked me.

I'm living in that cave by the point, I told him.

In the cave? What for?

I explained. Then I added: So now I'm all alone here.

No, my son, he said. You're with us. If you need anything, you must come and tell me.

He got up. Just a minute. I'll be right back. He went into the house, and I heard him talking to his wife. Then he returned carrying a hen. He cut its throat, and went into the garden to dig up some potatoes and carrots for me. He even gave me a small bottle of olive oil, and put everything into a basket so I could carry it back to the cave with me.

I went back and made a fine tajine with the chicken. Later the Riffian came down to the cave with two loaves of bread. While we sat smoking, Hassan and Mjidou arrived from the city, bringing all kinds of food and equipment with them. The four of us sat down to eat.

The police have come to the house five or six times looking for you, Mjidou told me.

It doesn't matter.

The farmer got up. I've got to go home, he said.

B'slemah, sidi. And thank you for everything.

After he had gone we talked for a while. Then Hassan said they would have to leave too if they expected to get back to the town before dark.

You know the girl, don't you? I asked Mjidou. You saw the whole thing. Her name is Zineb.

I know her, all right, he said.

If you see her, tell her Mrabet would like to talk to her.

I will.

After they had gone, I sat in the cave by myself. When it got dark, I decided to go fishing. I got the basket of shrimps and used them as bait. The fish were biting. Before I stopped I had about twenty kilos of chargo. There was a pool between the rocks that was full of them.

I had brought a brazier with me, and charcoal for it, and a Primus and kerosene for that. But my idea was to use the driftwood that lay in the coves, and cook my food outside whenever I could.

And I lived on in the cave. As time went on Hassan and Mjidou did not come as often as they had in the beginning, but I had everything I needed in order to live. Whenever I caught fish, the Riffian would carry it to market and sell it for me. The summer passed, and the first rains fell. The days when it rained I stayed in the cave. It was dark and damp, and there was not much I could do but sit there and smoke kif.

One day when the Riffian farmer was sitting in the cave with me, he said he was going to take a ram and a ewe to market the next morning and sell them.

How much are you going to ask for them? I said.

Five hundred pesetas for the ewe and seven hundred for the ram.

Save yourself the trip, I told him. I'll buy them. I gave him twelve hundred pesetas for the two sheep. Now I've got a ewe and a ram. Is that right?

Yes, he said.

We smoked for a while. Twenty years ago or maybe more, he said, there were two men living here in this cave. Their clothes were nothing but rags. You should have seen them. They stayed for about seven months. But when they went away they were rich. In those days there were always all kinds of crates floating out there in the water, and they had everything you could think of inside them. Those two would swim way out and collect everything and bring it back here, and then sell it. And years later they both came back to see me, and they had cars and wives. They brought their children and stayed all day at the farm with me. They said they had made enough money here to set themselves up in good businesses. And you, you haven't found anything yet, have you?

No.

Wait, he said. If you stay on here you may make some money.

When it was nearly dark he said good-night and went back to his farm. There was a strong wind blowing, and it had brought the cold with it. I did not dare make a fire at night, or even light a candle. It would be pitch dark. I could not even smoke kif, for fear of the match. I would pull two sheepskins and two blankets outside the cave, and put them under a very low-hanging rock. Then I would creep in and sleep there. I felt safer under there than in the cave.

Early in the morning I would hear the cocks and the donkeys and the dogs up at the Riffian's farm, and the seagulls would be screaming overhead. I would climb out from under the rock and go to the cave. Everything was always in order, but I was still suspicious. Then I would walk along the shore among the boulders, to see if there was anything being washed ashore.

One morning I heard a whistle outside. It startled me, and I jumped up and ran outside. Again I heard the whistle. I began to climb up among the boulders until I came to a clump of trees. Then I saw that it was a shepherd boy signalling to his friends. He had thrown his djellaba over an animal of some sort, and was calling to the others to come and help him.

I ran over and saw that it was a young jackal he had caught. I grabbed it, and it tried to bite me. It was only about four months old, and too young to do any harm. The other shepherds came running.

Do you want to sell him? I asked them.

They said they did. I gave each one ten pesetas, and they went away happy. Then I carried the jackal down to the cave and tied him at the entrance. A little later I noticed that he was gnawing at the rope, and I saw that if I let him go on, he would soon break through it. So I put him into a crate and got a length of nylon fishing line. I made him a collar by twisting a rag, and attached the line to the collar. He did not like this any better when I tied him up again, and he tried for a long time to chew through the nylon, but it hurt his mouth. Finally he sat still. I gave him a plate of bread soaked in tajine sauce, and some fried fish. He ate whatever I gave him.

That afternoon I was sitting with him, when I looked out and saw Mjidou and Hassan coming along among the rocks toward the cave.

We began to smoke, and passed the pipe back and forth among the three of us. They tried to talk to the jackal, but he was afraid of them.

What about the Italian? I asked them.

I haven't seen him around, Hassan said. He must still be at the hospital.

They stayed all day with me. We ate lunch late and lay around smoking kif until the end of the afternoon.

Well, take good care of your jackal, they told me, and they started back to the city.

In spite of all the food I had given him, the next morning when I got up I found the jackal lying dead where he was tied outside the cave. I was sorry, but I knew that was what he wanted. I tied the nylon cord around him, weighted him with a rock, and threw him into the water.

I got into the habit of going to the old Riffian's and helping him with his farm work. Chores that he would have taken nearly all day to finish, I could do for him in an hour or so. I would take his hoe and tell him to sit down. Then I would hand him my pipe and my kif, and start to work. When I had finished I would sit down beside him and smoke with him, and he would always say: May Allah give you strength!

It was about three weeks before Mjidou and Hassan came back to see me.

We've got good news, Mrabet!

What's that?

The Italian inspector and his whole family have gone back to Europe.

Are you sure? I said.

Absolutely certain. You can come home now. Today.

But I can't! Look at all this stuff. I can't just go away. What am I going to do with all of it?

They looked at me.

We'll help you sell it, or at least get it all back to your house, they told me.

Wait, I said. I went up to the Riffian's house and asked him if he would lend me his two donkeys.

Take them, he said.

We led the donkeys down to the cave and loaded them, and Mjidou and Hassan drove them to town. The next day they came back to pack more things, and again they took the donkeys into town. In the end they made four trips back and forth between the cave and my house. The last day I went to the Riffian and said: You've got a ram and a ewe of mine.

That's right, he said.

Here's some money to feed them with. I'll come back in a month or two to see you. If the police catch me I won't be more than a year in jail.

We said good-bye, and he called after me: Be careful.

Mjidou and Hassan had gone on ahead an hour or so earlier. I climbed up the cliff to the road, and began to walk. My hair was long and matted. I looked like a wild man. As I walked along the road, I felt as though I no longer knew how to go on a flat surface. I had been living too long jumping from rock to rock. When I got to the curve at the Hotel Farhar, I found that I could not even breathe the way I should.

I came to the foot of the mountain, and cars began to pass me. In Dradeb the sight of so many people in the street made me very nervous. Then I saw that everyone was looking at me, men and women, Moslems and Nazarenes. They all stared at me and made remarks to one another. I was the first hippie they had ever seen. In those days there were no hippies in Morocco. I kept going until I got to Souq el Bqar, and there in a quarter where I knew everybody, no one at all recognized me. When I got to my house I knocked on the door. Mjidou and Hassan were there.

The first thing I did was to look into the mirror. I never would have known who it was. I thought I looked wonderful, like a man I could respect. The beard gave my eyes a nasty expression that I liked.

I turned around and looked at Mjidou and Hassan, to see if they would say something about it.

What is it?

Nothing, I said.

That night after they had gone, I shaved off the beard. Then I took a shower and had a fine long sleep. In the morning I went to the hammam and then to a barber to have my hair cut.

When I got home, I had just shut the door and set down the basket of towels and soap I had taken to the hammam with me, when there was a rap on the door.

It's the police, I said to myself, and I looked through a slit beside the door. It was a woman wearing a djellaba. I opened the door and saw that it was Zineb, the girl I had had the fight about. She came inside.

You look marvellous, Mrabet! she cried.

I burst out laughing.

I mean it. You look fantastic.

I know, I said. But thanks anyway.

I opened two bottles of Coca Cola and we sat down.

Why don't you take off your djellaba? I asked her. I was wondering why she had come to see me.

She stood up and took it off. I lighted my pipe and began to smoke. After several pipes I lay back on the cushions. She was wearing a shirt and a skirt.

Zineb, I said. How many times have we met? Four times, I think. And I've never asked you for a favor, have I?

No, you've never asked me for anything.

Why don't you take off your skirt?

What! she cried.

Your skirt.

She got up slowly and took off her skirt. She had beautiful legs. I smoked some more.

Finally I said: Why don't you take off your shirt?

She stood up again and did as I had asked. Then she looked down at me. Now what do you want? she said.

What I really want is for you to take off your bra and your slip.

And what then?

Just sit down beside me.

She undid her bra, stepped out of her slip, and sat down.

Wait a minute, I said. Go into the other room and get a pillow from the bed.

I did not want a pillow. I wanted to watch her get up and walk into the other room and come back.

She looked surprised, but she went and got the pillow. She was beautiful from head to foot, so beautiful that I put out my arms and seized her, and did not let go until I fell asleep.

The Fraternal Bond

(excerpt)

Tahar Ben Jelloun

Tahar Ben Jelloun was born in the city of Fès in 1944. He attended an Arabic-French elementary school, studied French in Tangier until the age of eighteen, then studied philosophy and wrote his first poems at Mohammed V University in Rabat. He is best known for his novels The Sand Child *and* The Sacred Night, *each of which has been translated into forty-three languages, and* Racism Explained to My Daughter, *which was translated into thirty-three languages. The winner of the Prix Goncourt, the International IMPAC Dublin Literary Award, and the Prix Ulysse, he was awarded the Grand Cross of the French Legion of Honor in 2008.*

[Translated from the French by Alexis Pernsteiner and Antoine Bargel.]

Friendship is a religion with no God or final judgment. With no devil either. A religion that is no stranger to love. But a love from which war and hate are banished, in which silence is possible. It might be the ideal state of existence. A state of calm. A necessary and rare bond. It suffers no impurity. The other before you, this loved one, is not simply a reflective mirror, but also another ideal self.

Perfect friendship ought to be a kind of happy solitude, from which sentiments of anguish, rejection, and isolation are purged. It is not simply about having a double through which to filter and examine one's self-image, exaggerating the faults and shortcomings, while diminishing the good qualities. A friend's gaze should be exacting in its reflection of ourselves. Such a friendship would belong to a space of faultless reciprocity and be guided by the same loving principle: the respect we owe ourselves, so that others might return it to us in kind, naturally.

Intentional misunderstandings, fallacious interpretations, misappropriations of feelings, errors of judgment, divergent opinions, friendship suffers from all these things: it is the least understood thing in the world.

The word has become banal. For example, people say: "They are friends." Upon closer inspection, one discovers that they are simply colleagues who get along. Efforts have been made to use different words to describe different forms of friendship: camaraderie, acquaintance, fellowship . . . but let us acknowledge that often we speak of friendship in cases of mere superficial, light, and inconsequential relationships.

To speak of friendship, I shall not consult books in great libraries. There are authorities—I am thinking notably of Cicero's book and chapter XXVIII in Montaigne's *Essays*. I shall simply look into myself, take a journey through my memory. I will tell you my own stories of friendship, fantastic and everyday stories, surprising and ordinary.

In my life, I have followed Cicero's advice to place friendship above all other human affairs. "For there is nothing which so fits with our nature, or is so exactly what we want in prosperity or adversity."

At Koranic school, we didn't have time to make friends. Every morning, we were dropped off at the little neighborhood mosque. We would take off our shoes, sit down on hard mats, and endlessly recite the day's verses. We had to learn the Koran by heart. The teacher—*faqih*—would call out the first phrase and all together we would repeat after him. It was boring and tedious. What can a five-year-old child possibly find pleasurable in memorizing verses which he cannot understand? What's more, we didn't have recess. Mornings were endless. At lunch, we would leave school, hoping never to return. We would come back in the afternoon, and take advantage of the faqih's drowsiness to say whatever we felt like.

My neighbor in class could have become a friend. He would save a place for me next to him, and, like me, he was always chomping at the bit in anticipation of the lunch hour. We both felt the same about this forced learning, but didn't dare say anything to our parents.

The faqih had this rather long stick to rouse the students who would fall asleep in the back of the class. We didn't like him. He was a mean old man. His beard was sparse and dirty. He had an evil look in his eye. We wondered why. Anyway, he didn't like my neighbor, Hafid, who had an abnormally large head. He held the fact that Hafid wasn't like the other kids against him. I never understood this bias.

Hafid and I could have become good friends, if death hadn't taken him away halfway through the year.

One morning, the faqih didn't show up. We all went home. I hadn't seen Hafid either. Soon a rumor started spreading: "Hafid died! From fluids that mixed with the blood in his brain; the faqih has gone to make the preparations to send him to heaven, for when children die, they become angels. They are not submitted to the Final Judgment."

Ever since that day, I have been afraid of faqihs, washers of the dead.

I didn't want his hand to touch mine. I also avoided kissing his hands, as was customary. I managed to get out of it by running away, until one day, he caught me and forced me to kiss both of his hands, palms and backs. I rubbed my lips to wipe off the smell of death. I was convinced that the faqih had put his hand on Hafid's head, and my classmate had caught death like you catch a cold.

I counted the days between me and school, the other one, the one where you don't learn things by heart, where you can have fun in the playground, where there's time to make friends.

My first friend was a year older than me. We didn't go to the same middle school. We met over the summer, in Ifrane, where my aunt had a vacation home (summers in Fès were unbearable). He had blond hair and was slim and handsome. I don't remember exactly how we met. We would always see each other in the afternoons near the waterfall. We were serious and spoke of our studies, our families, and even the future of our newly independent country. We were too serious, and behaved like grownups.

At the time, I was in love with one of my cousins who had blue eyes. We would talk about it with detachment. He would tell me: love only exists in marriage, otherwise it's just decadence, something you'd see in the movies. And yet my love for pictures and movies dates back exactly to that time.

Today when I recall that friendship, it is with the understanding that it was based on a lie. Even though he was a year older than me, he seemed younger. I had just started sixth grade. When I asked him what grade he was in, he answered, "seventh," in a way that seemed to say, "obviously." And, without thinking about it, I said, "me too." I kept up this lie for a whole year. We would write each other letters. He would tell me about the books they were reading in class, and, in an effort to keep up with the discussion, I'd rush to the French library to borrow them. Two years later, I wrote him a long letter in which I told him the truth. I could no longer bear the consequences of my lie. I preferred to be rid of them. That was the end of our friendship. I didn't receive any more letters from him. I learned that friendship will not tolerate disrespect, even a little lie out of pride. The lesson was simple: I lost a friend because I lied to him.

That little lie of a thirteen-year-old boy haunted me for a long time, to the point that, for me, the truth became an actual religion with serious consequences. However, it is not always advisable to tell the truth: not all truths are good to tell.

My second friend was my opposite: he was playful, adventurous, charming, and could make girls dance beautifully. Nourredine was what they call hot stuff, handsome and easygoing. He was last in our class at high school. He liked hanging out with me because he wanted to "break" my serious and sober attitude and introduce me to a world of frivolity and fun. We both liked the movies. He would always talk about the actors (he liked to identify with James Dean and Errol Flynn), while I was interested in the directors and producers. He would say: "I saw a John Wayne," and me: "I saw a John Ford or a Howard Hawks."

At our house, there was no smoking, and definitely no alcohol. No going out, either, after a certain hour. And at school, I always took my classes very seriously. Nourredine liked to talk about his nights out, and would brag about his female conquests. He claimed to have once been with Irene Papas and Dalida when they were passing through Tangier. I listened to him with envy. I was too shy to go out with him. While I was dreaming of girls, he was discovering their bodies and collecting love letters. The day I fell in love, he made fun of me. Hurt, I understood that Nourredine never listened to anybody; he just needed an audience so he could exercise his vanity. Without picking a fight, I took my distance, convinced that friendship could not exist unless both parties listened. For a long time, I had been listening to Nourredine tell his stories. Meanwhile, he was incapable of giving a little bit of his time to someone he considered a friend.

Today, Nourredine is another man. A tired seducer, old before his time. We see each other, by accident, once every three or four years. We exchange pleasantries. Every time, he tells me how much he used to envy me, because I had long hair and read two novels a week.

During this same period, I used to go to the movies with Boubker, a short boy, who was meticulous and possessive. I thought his behavior seemed strange. He scared me a little. He would tell me about his mother, how his father would lock her in the house. I remember he never invited me to his place, and would often come over to my parents' house.

One day, I learned that his mother had gone crazy, and that he had never really recovered from it. He was cruel. Sometimes he'd do mean things to cats. I felt uneasy around him. He terrified me. Ours wasn't a relationship of friendship.

It was then that I learned that friendship cannot be based on fear or tyranny. I took my distance from him without completely breaking things off.

I wasn't wrong.

Thirty years later, the same man has become a pillar of the mosque, a hard-line fundamentalist. He has grown a beard. Every time he sees a pretty girl in European dress, he invokes the wrath of God.

If I am remembering him today, it is because he was not without intelligence or a sense of humor. His mania, his angst, his malaise made me more understanding. I have to admit that I did nothing to help him get out of the long tunnel in which his family troubles had thrown him.

I never could have predicted my friendship with Lotfi. We didn't go to the same high school; we didn't live in the same neighborhood, and our families didn't know each other. He came from an old family in Tangier. I was from Fès, and my father didn't nourish much sympathy for people from Tangier. He thought they were lazy and unsociable.

Lotfi liked jazz, and me, cinema. He was always going on about his passion for freethinkers like Voltaire and Anatole France. Meanwhile, I would ask God's forgiveness for mixing with such an individual. He liked to set up hoaxes and gags; I thought that was in poor taste. He would loudly say what he thought; I cloaked my ideas in pretty sentences. He was often broke; I was a little less than him. He didn't take American cinema seriously; I would give speeches on Orson Welles, and I ran Tangier's film society at the Roxy Theater. He was a Marxist (a tradition passed down by his brothers) and I took refuge in Romanticism. He had—and still has—a sense of humor. I did not. He was bold; I was cautious. He made girls laugh; I bored them with my ridiculous little poems.

In spite of all these differences, I did not consider Lotfi my opposite. We were different but "compatible." We were attentive to one another. Our friendship began lightly. Nothing was serious. We could laugh at everything. There were no limits to his derision. Everything was submitted to his irony. I appreciated this freedom.

He taught me to listen to others, and also to appreciate jazz.

We would meet at the house of this Spanish pianist who worked at the American Cultural Center. We would religiously listen to Duke Ellington, Count Basie, Miles Davis, Dizzy Gillespie, etc. Our jazz club was over at Mr. Abrinès' place. He had exchanged his love for music for one of alcohol.

Whenever music came up, Lotfi got serious. When Mr. Abrinès got too drunk, we'd go to Lotfi's house to listen to classical music. He knew about the lives of the major composers, and would compare the different versions of this or that symphony. He was a real music lover: he intimidated us, but without pointing out our ignorance. We wondered where he'd learned all these things that we didn't know anything about. His brothers had given him his love for music, just as they had infected him with the virus of militancy.

Return to Childhood

(excerpt)

Leila Abouzeid

Leila Abouzeid, born in 1950, is best known for the story collection Year of
the Elephant. *Her memoir* Return to Childhood *is interesting not only for
its childhood memories but for its glimpses of political struggle in Morocco
around the time of independence in 1960. Abouzeid's father, an outspoken
activist, had the misfortune to be imprisoned by authorities both before and
after independence. Abouzeid was hindered in telling her story by Arabic traditions that considered memoir to be nonliterary, an expression of selfishness
and arrogance, and particularly inappropriate for a woman. "I had to wait
twenty-eight years before I dared write my autobiography," Abouzeid writes,
"and I did it in response to a request from my friend Elizabeth Fernea. The
work was meant for a non-Moroccan audience, and I felt it would give me
the opportunity to correct some American stereotypes about Muslim women."*

[Translated from the Arabic by Leila Abouzeid and Heather Logan Taylor.]

In Sefrou, we had settled in the upstairs room that became my mother's after
the distribution of her father's estate. When she went visiting my father in
prison, she would leave us with her cousins. They lived outside the old walls
of the city in a small house surrounded by fruit trees. In the early morning,
the cousin's wife used to cook harira on a wood fire outside the kitchen. Her
boys would climb a fig tree before the sun reached it, pick the figs while they
were still cool, and bring them down in a basket. Then the family would all
sit on the porch in front of the house and eat harira and figs for breakfast.

The summer was over. We were getting ready to enter school and my
mother's old aunt Zineb came to her and said, "Is it true that you intend
to enroll the girls at school?"

"Yes."

"Are you crazy? Who's going to buy them notebooks and pens?"

"The nationalists, aunt. They are taking care of us. They send us
money every month."

"Send them to learn a craft and forget about school."

"I would do that if it were only up to me, but their father says every time I visit him, 'Take them to school,' and I've never gotten a letter from him in which he does not emphasize it."

"He spent his time having affairs with other women and spending money, then he went off to prison and now he decides to say school! What will a girl study, for heaven's sake and what for? A girl's destiny is marriage, pregnancy and breast-feeding, isn't it? One would think that they are going to learn that language you need to deal with *djinns*!"

"But my dear aunt, the Sultan Sidi Mohammed Ben Youssef himself has ordered the nationalists to send their girls to school. And every time I visit Si Hmed in prison he insists that I take them to school. I can't disobey him."

"Your husband's crazy and you're crazier than he is. You should be the one to decide. The proverb says, 'Show your friend the way, but if he refuses to see it, go your own way and leave him.'"

We did go to school, as my father had insisted. But before we began, there was always laundry day and bath day. The laundry and the bath came every week, but in those days before we started school, my mother made special occasions out of these weekly rituals.

On Tuesday evening, my mother gathered the laundry: our clothes, the cushion cases, the upholstery, the curtain from the door of our room, all the kitchen and floor rugs. She did not leave a single piece of cloth in the room. On Wednesday morning, she woke up before we did and made a wood fire in a large metal brazier outside in the courtyard. She filled the water boiler and put it on the brazier. She poured out the rest of the water she had kept overnight in two wood basins to close up their cracks, set them on two wood boxes, brought out the huge bundle of laundry and started sorting it: the head scarves, the whites, the colors, the black clothing, the rugs. She poured hot water and lye into one of the basins and washed the scarves and rinsed them; she hung them up on the roof because they dried more quickly than the heavy clothes, which she would hang there later.

In the courtyard she soaked the whites in the same basin in which she had washed the scarves and rubbed them with heavy-duty laundry soap on the scrubbing board, making a regular rhythmic sound. Then she took the washboard out of the basin and scrubbed everything again with both hands, taking each item separately and dipping it every now and then in the soapy water. She wrung them out and put them aside on a low table. Then she put the pile of colors to soak in the first basin, filled the second with hot water and shook the wrung-out whites into it. She lathered and rubbed each item with soap, and, bending far over, she worked the laundry through the soapy water, her hands going back and forth in a gentle motion. Then she wrung out all the items and threw them in the boiler. She poked the partly burned wood in the brazier to revive the fire, and every now and then she would stir the white laundry in the boiler with a long stick. When she got to the heavy upholstery, she gathered the fabric together, folded it lengthwise on a stick, and, with Grandma holding the other end tight, turned the stick clockwise, until not a drop of water was left in the fabric.

After the laundry had been washed, it still had to be taken to the roof, shaken, stretched on wires, turned over, collected and folded. The folding was the last stage. It was done at night on a sheet on the floor after my mother had stretched and pressed each item with her hands.

Laundry day was a gloomy day for me. The rooms were stripped bare, cooking in the house ceased, and the women and children stayed in traditional trousers and shirts which were basically underwear. Even though my mother allowed me to wash my dolls' clothes, I did not like laundry day, just as I did not like bath day. It gave me a feeling of strenuous effort and harsh life, which stayed with me all day until the evening call to prayer.

The day after laundry day was bath day. It began in the early hours of the morning. My mother put our clean clothes and towels into two bundles, one for her and one for my two sisters and me, and put the bath things into a metal bucket. We ate an early, improvised lunch and started out for the bathhouse before the men had left it. The bathhouse was around the corner on the next street, in the Adlouni neighborhood, and on the way Fatiha lagged behind and said that she didn't want to go to the bathhouse. My mother would first cajole her, and then she'd lose her patience.

"We'll sit in the brides' compartment, ma'am," she'd say, "and you'll get cold water with the little bucket, ma'am, and I'll wash you and treat you like a little bride, and give you oranges and sweet bread and, ma'am . . . For heaven's sake! Come here! May God never make me hear of your father's family and of the day I met them. Look at this fine lady!" indicating me with her eyes. "Look how *she* likes the bathhouse!"

But the truth is that I hated it just as much as Fatiha did. The very sight of the door of that bathhouse chilled my heart, but I went along anyway. Thursday after Thursday I carried the metal bucket and walked courageously at the head of our little procession. We were not the only children of our age who hated the bathhouse. I think that every Moroccan child in the traditional urban centers felt the same way, for we were scrubbed very hard, the water was too hot, and we had to sit there in the heat for hours while the grown-ups chatted and gossiped.

Even when we actually got to the bath, Fatiha would still resist. And we would wait until the last man walked out coughing and clearing his throat, his head covered with a towel under the hood of his djellabah, clutching the collar tightly to keep his neck warm. Then we rushed inside.

In the outer room of the bathhouse, we would all take off our clothes and put them in bundles, and leave them, our clean towels, and our clean clothes with the woman who was in charge of the bathhouse. Our mother would lead, as we pushed open the heavy wooden door and stepped into the darkness and steam of the first room, finding our way with difficulty. Our mother would stop there to fill with cold water the two wooden buckets she had been given in the outer room. We girls would go on through the middle room to an alcove that was called the brides' compartment. I would set down our metal bucket containing the bath things, and as our eyes became used to the dark we could see our mother coming with the heavy buckets. She would drag them to the innermost room, and I would leave my sisters in the brides' compartment and follow her. The buckets of cold water went to Yamna, the woman who ran the inside of the bathhouse. She would pour them into a large tub where hot water ran from a faucet. My mother would then place her empty buckets on a wooden platform and squat nearby to make sure that no one moved them from their place in line. I would stay beside her. Other women would come in, dragging their own wooden buckets of cold water to go through the same procedure, until about a dozen women were grouped around the platform. After a while the heat of the room would begin to affect them and one would urge the attendant on, saying, "Well? Well? Where's the hot water?"

"Be patient," the attendant would answer. "The tub isn't full yet. Has everybody brought her cold water?"

"Yes we have."

When the tub was full, the attendant ordered us to stay where we were. "I want no mess," she'd say. "No mess! I'll fill for everyone."

But no sooner did she stand up than all the women sprang up too, pushing and shouting: "Fill my bucket, Yamna!" "My bucket before hers." Then they would rush back into the middle room with steaming buckets and start washing themselves.

My mother would take her two buckets into the brides' compartment, complaining as she came. "God! How aggressive the women of this neighborhood are! The way they talk and behave! Adlounis really have no manners!" She would set down her buckets of hot water and take our metal bucket into the first room to fill it with cold water. When she came back, she would drop two unpeeled oranges into the cold water and scrub herself. Someone would often comment on my mother's complaint: "Well, ma'am, those Adlouni women say it's their bathhouse."

"When the new one opens they can have this one all to themselves," my mother would retort. Then she would call to Yamna, "For the love of God's face, give me another empty bucket to fill with cold water so I can bathe the baby in it. The heat's going to kill her if I don't put her in some cold water."

"Okay, come and get it. But if we need that bucket you'll have to bring it right back. Tomorrow's Friday, you know, and everybody comes to the bathhouse today."

"I'll return it when I'm done with the baby," Mother would say.

My mother would bring the extra bucket full of cold water, put Naima in it to cool her down, and say to me, "Come Leila, let me wash you first so that you can look after your sisters while I wash."

She'd scrub my skin vigorously, wash my hair with *ghassoul* (a shampoo made of earth), and then start combing it. My hair was long, the bone comb was fine toothed, the water was hot, and she dug the comb into my scalp so hard that when she finally stopped and brought a towel I was seeing stars. She'd take me to the outer room, sit me on the mat of the platform, and order me to put on my clothes.

A little later she'd come out with Naima, put her next to me, dress her, and rush back to the middle room. Every time the door opened, Fatiha's screams came out with all the other noises and the steam, and made me realize how much my little sister was suffering. When my mother finally brought Fatiha out the attendant would say, "Why don't you take this child to a faqih and get her straightened out? Her behavior is too much."

"I've tried everything," my mother would answer in a discouraged tone. "I've even passed her under a camel. At El Ksiba I gave a camel owner twenty *rials* and said to him, 'Please pass this girl under your camel. They say it cures children's nervous problems.' And he did, but it didn't work."

Mother would leave us an orange and some sweet bread and say to me, "Watch your sisters, Leila! Don't let them go out in the street or uncover their heads, because they might catch a cold. Okay?" She'd turn back to the attendant: "For the love of God keep your eyes on them. I'll wash myself and come out. I won't be a minute." And she'd slip behind the heavy wet door that was standing ajar.

We would eat the bread and the orange and fall asleep on the mat. By the time our mother woke us up and we left the bathhouse, night had fallen and lights shone in the streets and shops. As soon as we got home, we'd drop the bucket and the bundle of towels and dirty clothes in the hall, go into our room and fall in our beds, too tired and sleepy to think of dinner.

The next morning at breakfast, Grandma would ask, "How was your bath?"

"A big mess," my mother would answer. "A crowd, not enough hot water, and those pushy Adlouni women. We came back and fell into bed, dead from exhaustion."

"How did Yamna behave?"

"She was okay. She gave me hot water, plus an extra empty bucket."

"She's learned her lesson, then. Not too long ago she was shouting at me about an extra bucket I had, and I said, 'Who do you think you are putting on such airs? Your job is to wait on people who need baths, and to pick up their shoes.'"

And Fatiha would say to my mother, "I peeked out at you when you were in that crowd by the hot-water tub, Mama, and I hoped that a djinn would appear and say to me, 'Make a wish.' And I would have said to him, 'I want an iron hook to take away all these women so my mother can have the hot-water tub all to herself.'"

Whenever Fatiha told that story, I would say, "You should have thought of telling the djinn to wait on us so Mother didn't have to work so hard."

Once Mother amused my grandmother with an extra piece of information: "That woman you know was there too," she said, "showing off as usual, wearing a caftan made of Khrib fabric, a silk belt, silk slippers and a scarf with Rabat embroidery."

"I hear," said Grandma, "that when she gets home she strips off the fine clothes and hangs them up. Who would wear a Khrib caftan in the public bath, for heaven's sake? It's crazy."

"Is that story about the woman who followed her home true?" asked my mother.

"Yes. That woman said to Yamna, 'I won't let her get away with showing off at the bath. I swear to God I'll follow her home and see if she still wears the fine clothes there, and then I'll come back and tell you.' The woman did go after her, then came back and told Yamna, 'I came upon her all of a sudden. The front door was open. I went in, knocked on another open door, lifted the curtain, went inside the room and there she was in rags that even a beggar wouldn't deign put on. And there was the Khrib caftan hanging on a nail.'"

"How did that woman explain her visit?" asked my mother.

"She said, 'We found this cup in the bathhouse and thought that it might be yours.'"

"'Women's stratagems caused me to flee; they use serpents as belts and scorpions as pins,' as Sidi Abdel-Rahman Al Majdoub, the old poet, says."

"So to Speak"

Laila Lalami

Born in Rabat in 1968, Laila Lalami earned a degree in English literature from Mohammed V University, studied in England, and returned to Morocco as a journalist and commentator. Her short-story collection Hope and Other Dangerous Pursuits *was published in 2005, and the following year she was shortlisted for the Caine Prize for African Writing. Her first novel,* Secret Son, *was published in 2009. She teaches creative writing at the University of California, Riverside.*

Not long ago, while cleaning out my bedroom closet, I came across a box of old family photographs. I had tied the black-and-white snapshots, dog-eared color photos, and scratched Polaroids in small bundles before moving from Morocco to the United States. There I was at age five, standing with my friend Nabil outside Sainte Marguerite-Marie primary school in Rabat; at age nine, holding on to my father's hand and squinting at the sun while on vacation in the hill station of Imouzzer; at age eleven, leaning with my mother against the limestone lion sculpture in Ifrane, in the Middle Atlas. But the picture I pulled out from the bundles and displayed in a frame on my desk was the one in which I was six years old and sat in our living room with my head buried in *Tintin and the Temple of the Sun.*

A great many of my childhood memories, like this photograph, feature books. Every night, my father would sit on one end of the living-room divan and my mother on the other, both of them with books in their hands. Neither of them had gone to college, but they read constantly—spy thrillers, mystery novels, science fiction, comic books, the newspaper, magazines, biographies, memoirs. I don't know how or why my parents came to love books so much; perhaps books provided them an education about the wider world, a sense of adventure that was missing from their lives, or an escape from the dreary official speeches that were regularly broadcast on state radio and television during the reign of King Hassan.

It was perhaps only natural that my siblings and I learned to do the same from an early age. I remember how we passed copies of *Astérix* to each other, how we lent to or borrowed from friends the latest issues of *Pif* magazine, how we fought about whose turn it was to read *Boule et Bill.* When I began to read children's novels, I found in Rabat's many bookstores regular new offerings from the Bibliothèque Rose or the Bibliothèque Verte, which included series by the Comtesse de Ségur, Jules Verne, Alexandre Dumas, Georges Bayard, and many others.

Once, when my best friend Nawal and I finished reading *Les petites filles modèles* by the Comtesse de Ségur, we wondered why the title page said "née Rostopchine." After much discussion, Nawal surmised that this must have been a disease with which the author had been afflicted since birth. It hadn't occurred to either of us that women in France might take on the names of their husbands, since our own mothers, following Moroccan tradition, kept their maiden names. After reading *The Three Musketeers* and *The Count of Monte-Cristo,* we used our bedsheets to make capes, pretended our plastic rulers were swords, and faced off while screaming, "En garde!"

Of course, none of the characters in these books looked or spoke like anyone I knew. In those days, in the late 1970s, nearly all of the children's literature that was available in Moroccan bookstores was still in French. The characters' names, their homes, their cities, their lives were wholly different from my own, and yet, because of my constant exposure to them, they had grown utterly familiar. These images invaded my imaginary world to such an extent that I never thought they came from an alien place. Over time, the fantasy in the books came to define normalcy, while my own reality somehow seemed foreign. Like my country, my imagination had been colonized.

I began to write when I was nine years old. Unsurprisingly, the stories and poems I wrote were in French and featured characters who said things like "En garde!" I had just started the fifth grade when Mère Elisabeth, the school's director, pulled my father aside one morning and asked him which junior high school he had in mind for me. She suggested the Lycée Descartes, where much of Morocco's elite—business leaders, doctors, lawyers, intellectuals of every persuasion, government ministers as well as their political opponents—sent its offspring. My father said no; he could not afford the school fees at Descartes. In fact, he had only agreed to send me to Sainte Marguerite because it was relatively inexpensive and because my mother had insisted. When my father saw that I was upset about not going to the same school as my friends, he tried to explain his decision.

"Your father is not a minister," he said in a soft, apologetic tone. Oum el-Banin, the public junior high near our house, would be fine.

At the new school, I excelled in all the subjects that were taught in French (mathematics, physics, biology) but struggled with the ones taught in Arabic (history, geography, civics). Still, the change meant that I finally started to receive proper Arabic-language instruction. The curriculum focused on excerpts from the classics of Arabic literature—the *Mu'allaqat*, al-Mutanabbi, al-Khansaa—and slowly moved on to modern authors like the Egyptians Naguib Mahfouz and Taha Husayn; the Lebanese Khalil Gibran and Elia Abu Madi; and the Palestinian Mahmoud Darwish. Because our school did not have a library, some of our teachers set up their own "lending clubs." This involved each student donating one book—any book—in order to form a classroom collection from which we could borrow Arabic novels. I don't remember ever being assigned fiction by Moroccan authors; perhaps Moroccan authors were being taught to Egyptian, Lebanese, or Palestinian schoolchildren.

It was not until the age of fourteen, when I started to read adult literature on my own, and independently from school, that I came across novels and stories featuring Moroccan characters in a Moroccan setting. The first of these was Driss Chraïbi's *La Civilisation, Ma Mère!,* which featured a heroine that was so much like the women in my family—feisty, funny, and with a sharp sense of repartee. I have a very vivid memory of my cousin Hamid giving me a copy of Tahar Ben Jelloun's *Harrouda,* a book that felt deliciously transgressive because of its frank treatment of sex. The work of Leila Abouzeid was also a revelation. To read *'Am al-Fil* was to discover that the ordinary stuff of our lives was as fertile ground for fiction as any other.

And yet, because of my early exposure to French in literature, nearly everything I wrote in my teens and early twenties was in French. This did not seem to me especially odd at the time; after all, many of Morocco's writers used the colonial tongue: Abdellatif Laâbi, Mohammed Khaïr-Eddine, Tahar Ben Jelloun, Driss Chraïbi, Fouad Laroui. My parents thought that my writing was "adorable," and praised it the way one might praise a child for a particularly good magic trick or a well-told joke, but they made it clear that writing was not a serious option for the future. I was expected to do something sensible with my life, and train in a profession that could guarantee a decent living in Morocco: medicine, engineering, or business.

Of course, their warnings did not stop me. I continued writing poems and stories and reading anything I could get my hands on at the Kalila wa

Dimna bookstore in downtown Rabat or from the used booksellers in Agdal. Still, my parents' pragmatic talk had all but convinced me that writing could merely be a hobby and not a vocation, and so I went to college to study linguistics. Since I could not make a living from using words in a creative way, at least I would be able to do it by using them in an analytical way.

After a bachelor's degree at Mohammed-V University in Rabat, I applied for, and received, a British Council Fellowship to do a master's degree at University College London. I arrived in Britain shortly after Saddam Hussein's army invaded Kuwait. I had been fairly apolitical until then, but the dislocation and racism I experienced in London, the classes I took at the School of Oriental and African Studies, and my exposure to the work of people like Edward Said changed all that. Every time I went back to Morocco, I couldn't help but notice how much and how often we moved between French and Arabic. All of us, whether we wanted to or not, went through life switching between codes: Moroccan Arabic or Amazigh in our homes, with our friends, in our places of worship; but in job interviews, in fancy stores, in formal soirées, French was *de rigueur*.

Two years later, I arrived in Los Angeles, to do a PhD in linguistics. I spent most of my days working on research articles and conference papers that had to be written and delivered in English, which made me think even more about the relationship between Arabic and French in Morocco. French was not just a prominent language in Morocco. It was the language of power; an indicator of social class; a means to include or exclude people. The education I had received had emphasized the importance of French to the detriment of Arabic. French was used in our media, our government, and our businesses. Nearly half of the shows on Moroccan television were bought from and dubbed in France. There were no neighborhood public libraries, so we often had to depend on cultural centers, like the one sponsored by the French government, for free access to books. The role of French in my life became clearer. Writing in French came at a cost; it inevitably brought with it a colonial baggage that I no longer wanted to carry. I started to suffer from a peculiar case of writer's block: If I could not write in Arabic, perhaps I should not be writing at all.

I went about the business of living. I had a degree to finish, after all, and I needed to find a job after graduate school. I tried to steer clear from writing, but writing wouldn't steer clear of me. I think that in some way we do not choose stories, but that stories choose us. A braver writer—a Ngũgĩ, say—might have immediately cast aside the colonial tongue and returned to the native one, but my literary Arabic was not good enough to allow me to produce a novel. The Arabic language is often referred to as "al-lugha al-'arabiyya al-fusha" or "the eloquent Arabic language." I sorely lacked that eloquence. One day I thought, Why not try my hand in English? I was already spending my days writing my dissertation in English, so perhaps I could use English for my fiction too. After a few tries, I noticed that the linguistic shift enabled me to approach my stories with a fresh perspective. Because English had not been forced upon me as a child, it seemed to give me a kind of salutary distance. The baggage that, to me, seemed inherent in the use of French to tell a Moroccan story seemed to lessen when I used English to tell the same story.

I have always written, because I have always had the urge to tell stories, but I cannot pinpoint the exact time when I decided that I should try to be published. I know now that it had something to do with reading work after work in which men of my race, culture, or religious persuasion were portrayed as singularly deviant, violent, backward, and prone to terrorism, while the women were depicted as silent, oppressed, helpless, and waiting to be liberated by the kind foreigner. I think I had had enough of "surrogate storytellers," to use Sherman Alexie's phrase in his introduction to Percival Everett's *Watershed*.

The surrogate storytellers told a version of Morocco—mysterious, exotic, at once overly sexual and sexually repressed—that seemed entirely removed from my reality or indeed the reality of others around me. Until I came of age and started rereading the works I had approached with great innocence as a child—books such as *Tintin in the Land of Black Gold*, for instance, or *Tintin in the Congo*—I had not had the desire to go through the trouble and sacrifice it takes to be a published writer. Still, as I was finishing graduate school, my writing path became quite clear to me. I had always told stories, but now I wanted to be heard.

"Salamanca"
Jamal Mahjoub

Born in London in 1960 to a Sudanese father and an English mother, Jamal Mahjoub was raised in Sudan. He is the author of novels including Wings of Dust, The Drift Latitudes, *and* Travelling with Djinns, *and the crime novel* The Golden Scales, *published under the pseudonym Parker Bilal. His autobiographical essay "Salamanca," which appeared in* Transition, *was included in* Best American Essays 2008, *edited by Adam Gopnik.*

The couple walked in through the door hand-in-hand, her leading him, like a pair of children who had stepped straight out of one of those tales my mother used to read to us when we were small. These two, however, had developed quite at odds with one another. She was now a tiny, wizened figure in her seventies, while he had shot up in height rather than age, sprouting from the ground like a magical beanstalk. A tower rising into the sky, a tall, brown, half-naked giant—his only concession to the ways of the city being a skimpy pair of red shorts with the number eight on one leg. The woman led him along like an overgrown child—her prize. Behind them trailed a string of curious followers picked up along the way, like human breadcrumbs dotting their route. They thronged the doorway, shoving one another aside excitedly. A couple of lithe boys managed to extricate themselves from the crush and tumbled to a halt just inside the entrance, their boxes of chewing gum and strings of lollipops all but forgotten, hanging limply from senseless fingers. The rest contented themselves with pressing their faces to the window, hands cupped to their foreheads to cut out the glare, making it look as if they were praying.

In the few years since it had opened, my mother's shop had become something of a refuge for strangers. It exercised a mysterious attraction. People walked in and buried themselves in the jumbled chaos of the interior as if they had lived there all their lives. They would turn up to pass a few hours drinking hot tea or gulping down frothy glasses of cold *limoon* summoned from Bimbo's Café around the corner while chattering about their lives. They were, for the most part, expatriate wives looking for ways to bridge the long, interminable hours that stretched across midmorning toward lunchtime, when the children were due home from school and they could all go to the swimming pool or the club to cool off and wait for sunset and cocktail hour. The shop had become a reference point, one of those stopping-off places for when you needed to get out of the sun or had an hour or so to kill downtown.

They came in all shapes, sizes, and colors, and my mother, a sociable person by nature, had the ability to make all of these wanderers feel at home. In the evenings, Sudanese couples would drop by while on their evening promenade around town—respectable people did not wander around during the day without good reason. It might have been the heat, or the fact that they were so far away from home, or maybe it had something to do with finding an Englishwoman in the midst of this foreign landscape that made it attractive to this odd collection of exiles. Some occupied humble posts in the diplomatic service or ran discrete charities— they included cultural attachés, engineers, visiting professors, technocrats, volunteer teachers, sharp-tongued novelists, deposed monarchs from mountain kingdoms you couldn't find in an atlas, would-be Lawrences who had just wandered into town on a camel, amateur artists, journalists, and photographers, all looking for someone to help make sense of what they had found here. They came and went with the seasons, and she listened to them all. Even Wasool, the Chicago-born African American whom everyone suspected of being a CIA agent even though he didn't look the part. Rabbit-toothed and lanky, with large ears that popped out from beneath the crown of his yellow skullcap, he resembled a distant relative of Goofy's. He had settled in Omdurman and married a Baggara woman who spoke not a word of English. All they had in common was love and the power of faith, which Wasool wielded like a baseball bat to thwack any "whiteys" in sight. "Islam was his saving grace," he would sigh. His past was a closely shrouded mystery from which names such as *Angela* or *Bobby* would leap cryptically. His commitment to the struggle did not explain why he spent so much time nowadays in the company of middle-aged white women. "He's a scream," my mother would declare whenever Wasool delivered one of his sermons. Everything about him was mixed-up, including his name. The story was that when he converted—at an obscure mosque in a distant icy ghetto—he was told that the name means "prophet," so now he is forever known as "The Arrival"—rather like an airport terminal. The fact was that Wasool's African side was far outweighed by his American. In my mother he had discovered a source to unveil the complex ethnographic intricacies of his adopted homeland in a language he could at least comprehend, which is what he was doing on the day when the minuscule German lady and her Nuba wrestler walked in on us. I had just come back from school and was waiting for the order to start locking up. Nebiat, our Eritrean helper, was wandering around wearing his beret, which meant that he had places to go. Nebiat's student days were cut short by the war. He had recounted the story of his personal tragedy, of his epic trek to get here, countless times. Any gap in the conversation or a slack moment would prompt him to begin again, stressing the importance of walking strictly in single file, say, or diving towards the point of impact when a shell exploded—apparently the one place where shrapnel does not penetrate. We took him on good faith, despite his shaky grasp of guerilla tactics. He liked us because we accepted him as an intellectual, not just another refugee, which is what he was to most people— hence the beret. It set him apart. Between political meetings and romantic liaisons, Nebiat always had more important places to be.

"Is that who I think it is?" Wasool whispered, wide-eyed, across the table as my mother got to her feet, eyes fixed on the stooping figure who was talking to herself, apparently in German, as she moved about. Piqued that his question had gone unanswered, Wasool turned to me. I was pressed into the gap between the painted cream and orange shelves that led through to the back. I shrugged and Wasool nodded, as if this were all the confirmation he needed.

How my parents had come up with the idea of opening a shop I will never know. For as long as I could remember, it had been a source of domestic strife. Right from the start it seemed fated to fail. In the beginning, they had envisaged a sort of health food center to provide for diabetics (my father was one) and people concerned about their weight. Khartoum was full of affluent ladies worried that their husbands might lose interest in them long enough to find themselves a younger, slimmer wife. The solution we offered was a machine that came all the way from shiny England. It had little round pads and Velcro straps to fix them on to the offending fleshy parts, which—presto!—by the miracle of modern science would disappear. That, at least, was the idea. On most days, I would walk over from school and sit in the back doing my homework. The bulky women would squeeze through the narrow gap and disappear into the shaded booth. I would listen to their snores competing with the unperturbed hum of the machine. They never looked any less plump when they emerged, and so it was perhaps not surprising that their husbands tended to grow tired of paying for treatment that had no discernible diminishing effect on anything but their wallets. The machine was our star attraction, but we had other products, such as biscuits, that helped you to diet. People would pick these up and turn them over slowly in their hands. It doesn't look like much of a meal, they grumbled. They were right. We kids were fed the broken packets, the ones with little teeth marks on the cellophane where a desperate mouse had tried to get in. And they had no effect on our appetites other than to make us feel rather sick when we overdid it. The despairing ladies of Khartoum would waddle in and slump into the big wicker chair reserved for customers, wipe the sweat from their brow, and implore my mother to find a cure for them. She offered them Greek spaghetti that contained no starch and tasted like gritty string. As my father declared whenever a damaged packet found its way onto our table, you would be better off boiling the cardboard they came in. There were preserves and marmalade which contained no refined sugar. These proved popular, not least with the customs officials in Port Sudan, who always delayed every shipment long enough for a few cases to go missing.

The sign over the doorway displayed the name painted on white glass in red and blue along with the silhouette of a rather svelte female form—the image of perfection, the goddess whom the good wives of our sleepy river town came to worship. It read *Slimming* in English. It wasn't much of a name, but it was, as my mother remarked, to the point. There is no letter corresponding to *G* in the Arabic alphabet. *Qaf* was deemed the closest substitute. That made the spelling "*Sin-lam-nun-qaf.*" "Salamanca," declared my father, half in jest, as he tried to explain to the weary sign painter how to render this unyielding word. "*Salamanca* . . . It has a ring to it." It was a dreamy sound that evoked far-off mysterious places like Samarkand or Camelot. It had nothing to do with anything, but it did have a ring to it.

But legends are sometimes not enough, and with time it became clear that people were not overly concerned about their weight, or at least not enough of them were to keep the store profitable. Heart disease and diabetes were plentiful, but being plump was a sign of well-being—only poor people were thin. Business dwindled, my parents argued, and gradually the expensive imported products gave way to local handicrafts aimed at the discerning traveler, rather than the wealthy local women.

It was these crafts that had drawn our latest visitor. The fierce little septuagenarian was digging her way furiously through every item while my mother trailed along. My mother did not take lightly to having her goods handled in such a cavalier fashion and was clearly having a hard time restraining her tongue as a cascade of leather boxes, clay pots, amber necklaces, glass beads, and hefty bedouin silver bracelets all came flying her way. The energetic little woman made her way through the shop like a furious demon, disturbing everything, ricocheting from one side to the other, knocking over lamps, copper bowls, stacks of colored baskets.

Nebiat, meanwhile, had decided it would be unfair of him to abandon his post at this time and so busied himself with clearing the onlookers from the doorway. There was some resistance, as though they were being ejected from a cinema before the film was over, and Nebiat's faith in the brotherhood of man and world revolution was sorely tested. He shooed ineffectively at them while they stared back nonchalantly in their grubby *jellabas* and ragged trousers, as if there were nowhere in the world they belonged more than here.

"Hitler," murmured Wasool, mouthing the word rather than speaking it.

"Here?" I frowned, completely at sea.

"She worked for him!" he hissed.

Whatever Wasool said had to be mulled over. He was American, and nothing he said ever made complete sense. I was coming to the conclusion that the only Americans I understood were the ones in the movies. The rest of them were completely at odds with the world. It was as if the only form in which Americans could really exist was up there on the big screen.

I looked back at the woman who was still digging things up like a manic archaeologist, examining them briefly before tossing them aside. She looked a little frantic, but *Hitler*?

"Not this. *Nein*! None of it. It is not authentic!"

Hitler or no Hitler, my mother had dealt with difficult customers before. "It's all made by people in the villages where these things come from," she explained patiently, as though her decades of living in this country were being called into question.

"No, no, no!" the woman was having none of it. "Ah. Maybe something here," she exclaimed, burrowing into the clothes rack like a ravenous predator. Shoving hangers aside, she scrabbled through the collection of *jellabas* and dresses. All "unique," all made locally for tourists looking for something colorful and, well, authentic. Then, to everyone's astonishment, she began pulling her dress off her head.

"Oh, no! Oh my god!" cried my mother in horror. "What are you doing?"

Something had become snagged and our intrepid traveler now went staggering about the floor frantically. From inside the dress the woman yelped; the inverted garment took the form of a bell-shaped flower; as she continued to struggle, the flower swayed and bent. The gathered audience howled in response, their patience finally rewarded. They clutched one another and fell about. Others went shrieking wildly down the street. Wide-eyed kids turned to stone, wads of gum tumbling from gaping jaws, not quite sure what they were witnessing as my mother tried to guide the headless white body, naked but for an enormous pair of sad gray underpants, out of sight. I stepped neatly out of the way as she crashed blindly into the shelves before making it through the gap into the back room.

"You really can't do that kind of thing here," we heard my mother chastising her loudly and in no uncertain terms. "People don't like it. You can't just start taking your clothes off." Subdued murmurs of what might have been an apology could be heard.

I glanced over at the German lady's companion. The tall Nuba wrestler stood aloof in one corner of the shop, like a piece of furniture that no one could quite place. He looked around him as though seeing nothing of what was there. Nebiat, the revolutionary in the Che Guevara beret, who had seen war and god knows what else, was looking perplexed, shaking his head as he spied the building's porter, an old soldier named Jubayr, whose bushy moustache and gnarled face was usually the portent of some form of complaint. He waved his staff at the boys and demanded to know what was going on.

"Madame," Old Jubayr called from the door. "We can't have these kind of goings-on here. This is a respectable building. What are people going to say?"

My mother went out to calm him down. Of course it wouldn't happen again. In the meantime, the German woman had made her choice and now, to everyone's relief, appeared wearing a long and very dignified kaftan. She gave a little pirouette in front of her boyfriend, who remained impassive. Impatient to conduct her business and be on her way, the woman produced a purse and shook it under my fourteen-year-old nose.

"How much? How much? *Bikum*?" she added for good measure, obviously used to dealing with the natives. I muttered something and she frowned the way you might frown at an idiot. There was some debate over the price, but all that mattered was ending this transaction as quickly as possible, and my mother, who normally drove a hard bargain, gave way without a fight. And then it was all over, and the odd couple vanished through the doorway forever, their entourage yapping at their heels, waving cigarettes and caramels under their noses.

"She was a film star in the thirties," Wasool explained as we got ready to leave. It was lunchtime and the metal shutters were clattering down into place all around us from the surrounding shops. "Hitler took a shine to her. She made films for him. *Triumph of the Will*? The Nuremberg rally?"

He was right, of course, but at the time none of us had ever heard of Leni Riefenstahl, nor could we have made the connection between that distant place in history and our little corner of the world. It was one of those strange jump cuts when time seems to fold in on itself like a closing fan. History lay dormant in black-and-white photographs in our school books. There he was, riding along with the top down, hand held high in stiff-armed salute. And here she was in living color, a little old lady. It was like staring at an electric spark, frightening and fascinating all at once.

Wasool ambled out, chuckling to himself and shaking his head. Hyuck hyuck.

"So," my mother said, arching her eyebrows mischievously, "the real question is: how did he know who she was?"

"A Cold but Fertile Ground"
Leila Aboulela

Leila Aboulela was born in Cairo in 1964 and grew up in Khartoum. She lived for much of her adult life in Scotland and now lives in Doha, the capital of Qatar. Her novels include Minaret, The Translator, *and* Lyrics Alley. *Aboulela is the winner of the first Caine Prize for African Writing, and her work has been translated into thirteen languages.*

I didn't become a writer until I had left home. That was what gave me the material and subject matter I needed. When my husband and I first settled in Aberdeen, we were not sure when we would return to Sudan, or if indeed we would never go back, remaining as immigrants in the U.K. or moving on to a second foreign country. This uncertainty gave me a sense of dislocation. There was homesickness to deal with, as well as cultural confusion and the awkwardness of being an Arab and a Muslim in the Europe of the 1990s. Exile, by definition, is a life one has not been prepared for; it is a removal from the familiar. It is "the saddest of fates," as Edward Said described it. It is an ancient form of punishment. Looking back, this trauma seems to have been the catalyst that awoke in me a dormant ability to write. Had I continued to live in Khartoum, this creativity might have slept forever.

When I left Sudan in 1987, I was twenty-three and the idea of writing was the furthest thing from my mind. Back home I had read a lot of novels. I read whatever came my way, according to an ebb and flow of books that varied in both quantity and quality. I read freely, without guidance or recommendation. I was an economics student at the University of Khartoum, specializing in statistics. Literature was not one of my subjects, and so reading was only ever a leisurely activity, a hobby. I was able to discover, alone, which books I liked, and which were superior. In English I read Charlotte Brontë, Charles Dickens, Antonia White, and Somerset Maugham. I read Dostoevsky and Tolstoy in translation and Tayeb Salih, Zeinab Bilal, Nawal Al-Sadawai and Ihsan Abdel-Qudoos in Arabic.

There were not many opportunities to discuss these books with others—reading was an entirely private affair, a secret world that was completely fulfilling. I had no urge to write.

My move from Sudan to Scotland changed all this. The ending of one kind of life and the beginning of another was dramatic enough to make me pause and reflect. The gulf of difference between Khartoum and Scotland compelled me to comment, to compare, to notice absences and observe additions. The end of my life in Khartoum demanded an elegy. And it was in fiction that I found a language to express my anxieties, my misgivings and my reactions to all that was new and surprising.

Travelling away from home is considered positive for a writer. Looking at one's home from a distance means greater detachment and that is characteristic of the writer. He is the one standing back, observing and warning. In exile there is time and space away from the throb and grind of the everyday life left behind. Describing his own development as a writer exiled from Zanzibar to London, Abdulrazak Gurnah said that, ". . . displacement is necessary— . . . the writer produces work of value in isolation because he or she is then free from responsibilities and intimacies which mute and dilute the truth of what needs to be said."

And what was it that I wanted to say, in Scotland in 1992? I wasn't sure. At first I was simply gripped by a compulsive need to express myself. Words were whizzing through my head all the time. The mechanics of constructing a coherent story or plotting a novel were far from my mind—they came later. In the beginning, there was just the need to speak out. I tried to put my thoughts into discursive articles or essays but I faltered. Disagreeing with something I had read in the newspaper one day, I tried to write a letter to the editor. Fiction came out instead.

I was obsessed with the need to express my homesickness and document the daily incidences of cultural difference that I was experiencing. I was anxious about the future of second-generation Sudanese and Muslim immigrants in the West—both from a personal and from a general perspective. Issues such as the dilution of identity and language, integration, the rights and wrongs, the gains and losses of leaving home—occupied my thoughts. Around me I could see other immigrants like myself. Many insisted that their stay in the U.K. was temporary, and yet their children were spending their entire childhoods, formative years, away from home. I watched the parents struggle to adapt to a new life, strive to benefit from it while in the background their children silently became less and less Sudanese, less and less Muslim, more and more a part of Britain.

There is something unreal and brave about a gathering of Sudanese in Britain. We get together to eat our familiar food, laugh in our familiar way.

We are replicating the past, taking comfort in each other, needing for an afternoon or an evening to forget the reality that we are not in Sudan. And of course in these warm, pleasant gatherings the difficult, sensitive topics are never discussed. When should we go back? Has it been worth it to leave? What about our children—what is their relationship to Sudan? How far away from us are they going? None of this is mentioned. We eat, we drink tea and we leave having entertained and comforted each other but those questions remain unanswered. Such questioning is a luxury, anyway, in the immigrant's struggle to survive. It felt awkward and pointed to pose these dilemmas in most social situations. As I kept my speculations and anxieties to myself, they floated down to my subconscious mind, fuelled fictions of culture clashes, loss of identity, wishful dreams.

The Croatian writer Dubravka Ugrešić describes this situation with insight and clarity in her essay "The Writer in Exile." She says, "The writer tries to rationalize his personal nightmare in writing, to calm his exile's fears in writing, to put his broken life into some sort of shape through writing, to order the chaos he has landed in through exile, to fix the insights he has come to in writing, to dilute his own bitterness in writing. . . . An exile's writings are often 'nervous' . . . subversive and nostalgic. This is because exile is itself a neurosis, a restless process of testing values and comparing worlds: the one we left and the one where we ended up."

In my case the comparisons between the world of Khartoum and the one of Aberdeen seemed endless and fascinating. I went from light into darkness, from warmth into cold; from the former colony to the land of the old colonizer, from poverty to wealth, and from a Muslim society to a secular Christian democracy. I was in awe of these differences, full of conflict and tension. It was a fertile ground for fiction.

While I can see my writing in Ugrešić's description, her words are also applicable to writers who had been writers before they left home. In my case, it was the exile itself that triggered the writing. Why? The answer, I believe, lies in the power of words, of narrative and stories, to compensate for something that is missing. In her classic book, *Becoming a Writer*, the American author Dorothea Brande instructs writers on how to increase their output without effort, how to write freely and abundantly and how to cure periods of creative drought or "writer's block." Her main advice is that while working on a story or novel, one should stop reading, watching television or going to the theatre. The writer's recreation should be wordless. In this condition, she says, "words would rush in to fill the wordless vacuum. . . . If we are left alone long enough and forbidden to read, we will very soon be talking to ourselves. . . . Prisoners who never wrote a word in the days of their freedom will write on any paper they can lay their hands on." Exile shares that characteristic with prison; the language, speech patterns and gossip of home are gone, a torrent of words rushes in to fill a vacuum.

There were other deprivations too, of colour, of scents, of know-how and the ability to penetrate depth. In my early years in Scotland, before I started to integrate, life around me seemed predictable and over-organized. All the people around me were polite and efficient; I could not distinguish them from one another. The present was sterile and alienating, so I had to live out dramas in my mind.

Starker still was the silence of the muezzin, the absence of the words *insha'Allah* and *alhamdullilah;* the absence of faith. I had left a life connected to the source; a world in which angels moved among humans and it was common to say, "If Allah gives me life tomorrow. . . ." Now I found myself praying in a place where people had stopped praying. I was as foreign and as new as the words Ramadan, hijab, haj, Eid and jihad listed in the updated editions of the English dictionary. Perhaps, I told myself, I had a calling after all; perhaps I had a role to play, a gift to give, a seed to plant. I could put Islam in British fiction, I could write novels that reflected Muslim logic with flawed and complex characters trying to practice their faith or make sense of Allah's will in difficult circumstances.

Another spur to writing was defensiveness. Suddenly I needed to express that life in Khartoum was tolerable, that the people were good, that it was circumstances and not choice that had made us all leave. Here I was, in a culture and place that asserted every minute that West was best, Africa a mess, only Islam oppresses women and that I should be grateful I had escaped. Youth and pride made me resist this description. True, I was not an expert on the Sudan, I could not challenge these judgements objectively or scientifically. But I had an intimate knowledge of both Sudan and Islam—they were in my blood. I wanted to bear witness to what I knew, to put down on paper the Khartoum I knew—a place where the impossible and the romantic pulsed within reach, a place that was easy and deep, harsh and vast, wayward and rich. I wanted to pinpoint exactly what I was missing. I wanted to show the people around me that an African city could be as atmospheric as London, livelier than Brighton, more beautiful than Edinburgh. Stories couldn't prove that but it was enough for me to express that Sudan was a real place, its culture a valid way of life. There was more to it than the stereotypical images of famine and war.

Writing is an extension of reading. It is an imitation and a development of an existing body of literature. As readers, we hold memories of prose and storylines in our consciousness. It is not just a story that stays with us, but its rhythm, its atmosphere, its voice. The writer puts his own life—his particular pain, his vision of the world, his idea of joy and beauty—into that construct called a story. But he needs to have read first in order to know what a story is. He needs to know what others are saying in order to say something new.

One of the things I enjoyed most about living in the U.K., and the thing I miss most when I am away, is the institution of the public library. Yes, it is possible to buy books anywhere in the world or order them through Amazon but it is, I think, only the free borrowing from a library that can satisfy the hunger to read. The abundance of books, the freedom of choice, the knowledge that even if you didn't enjoy a book you could return it at no loss encourages the reader to take risks, to experiment and truly fulfil himself with what he loves best. From the beginning, being in the U.K. meant more access to books and a wider scope in my reading. Despite my best efforts, access to books in Khartoum was never easy as, sadly, it is usually only the best-selling, mass-marketed books that make their way to developing countries. It is ironic to think that I had to wait until I got to the local library in Aberdeen to read Chinua Achebe or Ismail Kadare—neither of whom I had heard of in Khartoum. From Aberdeen library, I borrowed books by Scottish writers, books on poetry and biographies of authors. I borrowed books and only read half of them, or a quarter, and sometimes I borrowed the same book again and again. And it was a joy too to live in a culture where reading was valued. There were radio programmes about books, women's groups met to discuss books, the newspapers devoted pages to book reviews and there were television programmes about the lives of writers. All these I reached for and they became the activities of my new life, what I gained by moving to Britain.

Encouraged by my husband, I started to attend weekly Creative Writing classes. These were informal, held in the evening and open to the general public. One course was held at the University of Aberdeen, another in a high school, another in the central library. It was always fascinating to watch a piece of writing transform from the intimately personal into something for public consumption. I learned that a writer could easily fail in communicating his own ideas to others. Skill was necessary, practice was necessary. In my situation—writing for another culture, a place my classmates didn't know—the potential for misunderstanding was great. I learnt how to be clear and precise, how to hold the attention of a reader with a subject they could not relate to, how to present my point of view of the West without causing offence, how to entertain without degrading or belittling my own heritage.

I began to read critically instead of just for enjoyment, to discuss fiction in terms of process and craft. Gradually I developed the understated style characteristic of Scottish and American realism. This meant natural-sounding dialogue and characters grounded in their socio-economic surrounding. On a more practical level, I picked up tips on how to approach agents with my first novel synopsis and how to submit my stories to competitions.

Published writers started to visit our classes. The local library also hosted readings by established poets and novelists. I attended as many of these events as I could—they were well advertised and open to the public. This was in the early/mid-nineties, when a new Scottish realist movement emerged as an exciting feature of British writing. Those young Scottish writers who were winning prizes and gaining recognition were living close to me. I had the privilege of listening to Kathleen Jamie, Janice Galloway, Duncan McLean, Alan Spence, Robin Jenkins, and A.L. Kennedy. I was inspired by these writers. Most of them did not come from literary backgrounds and they were championing their own Scottish culture and traditions, which they saw as being marginalized and dominated by the metropolitan literary tastes of London. Instead of writing about the circles of power in London, they wrote about ordinary characters who listened to pop music and loved football. They wrote about the unemployed, the working classes, the young drug addicts. To me, this meant there was space for other marginalized characters—those who were marginalized because of religion, those who were immigrants or asylum seekers. The Muslim woman in her hijab, the reluctant Sudanese immigrant could now claim a place in literature written in English.

Thomas Sankara Speaks

(excerpt)

Thomas Sankara

Thomas Sankara (1949–1987) was a young army officer in 1983 when a coup made him prime minister under Major-Doctor Jean-Baptiste Ouédraogo. He was soon dismissed and placed under house arrest, only to be installed as president and leader of the country a few months later, after a coup led by Blaise Compaoré and supported by Libya. Sankara became famous for advancing a number of progressive causes, including reforestation, literacy campaigns, basic health care, increased government payments to peasant farmers, and an end to female circumcision. He also renamed his country from Upper Volta to Burkina Faso, "the land of upright men." In 1987 he was assassinated in yet another coup by Blaise Compaoré. Though Sankara did not live long enough to write his memoirs, this excerpt from a series of 1985 interviews by the Swiss journalist Jean-Philippe Rapp gives some insight into his origins and personality.

Jean-Philippe Rapp: Isn't the decision to become head of state a decision taken under a very definite set of circumstances?

Thomas Sankara: There are events, moments in life, that are like an encounter, a rendezvous, with the people. To understand them you have to go back a long way into the past, the background, of each individual. You don't decide to become a head of state. You decide to put an end to this or that form of bullying or humiliation, this or that type of exploitation or domination. That's all.

It's a bit like someone who has suffered from a serious illness, malaria say, and then decides to devote all his energies to vaccine research—even if it means along the way that he becomes an eminent scientist in charge of a laboratory or the head of a cutting-edge medical team.

In any event, I started out with a very clear conviction. You can fight effectively only against things you understand well, and you can't win unless you're convinced your fight is just. You can't wage a struggle as a pretext, a lever, to acquire power, because generally the mask cracks very

91

fast. You don't get involved in a struggle alongside the popular masses in order to become head of state. You fight. Then the need to organize means that someone is required for a given post.

Rapp: But why you?

Sankara: You have to convince yourself that you're capable of fighting, that you're courageous enough to fight for yourself, but above all that you have sufficient will to fight for others. You'll find men who are determined to wage a fight, and who know how to go about it. But they're doing it only for themselves and don't get very far.

Rapp: You think this is because of their origins?

Sankara: Yes. There are leaders who have natural roots, and there are those who have artificially created roots. By artificial I mean those leaders who were created by erecting a wall around themselves. Such people are definitely cut off from the popular masses. They can be generous up to a point, but that doesn't make them revolutionaries. You'll run into officials at various levels who are unhappy because no one understands them, even though they've proven their commitment. Though they're making honest sacrifices, no one understands what they're doing.

It's a little like some of the international aid volunteers who come here from Europe. They too are very sincere, but their ignorance about Africa leads them to make mistakes, blunders, that are sometimes insignificant, but that become decisive as time goes on. So after a stay of several years they go home completely disgusted with Africa. Yet it's not for lack of noble purpose. It's just that they came here with a patronizing attitude. They were lesson-givers.

Rapp: As far as you're concerned, one has to have lived the reality?

Sankara: Other leaders have had the chance to immerse themselves in the daily lives of the people. That's where they find the necessary reserves of energy. They know that by making such-and-such a decision they'll be able to solve such-and-such a problem, and that the solution they've found is going to help thousands, even millions of people. They have a perfect grasp of the question without having studied it in a sociology department. This changes your perception of things.

Rapp: But what concrete personal experiences led you to discover these realities yourself?

Sankara: There were several. For example, I remember a man I knew well. We were right in the middle of a period of drought. To avoid starvation, several families from his village collected the little money they had left and gave him the job of going to Ouagadougou to buy food. He traveled to the capital by bicycle. On arrival, he had a brutal and painful encounter with the town. He stood in line to get what he needed, without success. He watched a good many people jump ahead of him to buy their millet because they knew how to speak French. Then, to make a bad situation worse, the man's bike was stolen along with all the money the villagers had entrusted to him.

In despair, he committed suicide. The people of Ouagadougou didn't lose any sleep over him. He was just another dead body. They dug a hole and threw in the body like a useless weight they had to get rid of. The city went merrily about its business—indifferent to, and even ignorant of, this drama. In the meantime, far away, dozens of people, whole families, awaited the happy return of this man who was to give them another lease on life, but who never came back. We have to ask ourselves: Do we have the right to turn our backs on people like this?

Rapp: This shocked you?

Sankara: Yes. I think about it often, even today.

Rapp: But have you experienced inequality firsthand yourself or have you just observed its impact on other people?

Sankara: No, I've experienced it personally. When I was little I went to primary school in Gaoua. The principal there was a European and his children had a bicycle. The other children dreamed about this bicycle for months and months. We woke up thinking about it; we drew pictures of it; we tried to suppress the longing that kept welling up inside of us. We did just about everything to try to convince them to lend it to us. If the principal's children wanted sand to build sand castles, we brought them sand. If it was some other favor they wanted, we rushed to do it. And all that just in the hope of having a ride—going for a spin, as we say here. We were all the same age, but there was nothing to be done.

One day, I realized all our efforts were in vain. I grabbed the bike and said to myself: "Too bad, I'm going to treat myself to this pleasure no matter what the consequences."

Rapp: And what were the consequences?

Sankara: They arrested my father and threw him in prison. I was expelled from school. My brothers and sisters did not dare go back. It was terrifying. How could this possibly fail to create profound feelings of injustice among children of the same age?

They put my father in prison another time too, because one of my sisters had gathered some wild fruit by throwing stones up at it. Some of the stones fell on the roof of the principal's house. This disturbed his wife's nap. I understood that after a wonderful, refreshing meal, she wanted to rest, and it was irritating to be disturbed like this. But we wanted to eat. And they didn't stop at putting my father in prison. They issued a notice forbidding anyone to pick this fruit.

Rapp: Today, when you're with your father and he can see what's become of you and what you've embarked upon, what does he have to say to you?

Sankara: My father is a former soldier. He fought in the Second World War and was taken prisoner by the Germans. As a former soldier, it's his view that we haven't seen anything yet, that it was much worse for them. Let's say our discussions are more like confrontations. *[Laughter]*

Rapp: This brings us to the question of the elders, who play an important role in traditional society and who must have enormous difficulty understanding, and above all accepting, what is happening today.

Sankara: There are a lot of them, and we always need to acknowledge them with a word or two. They're surprised we mention them in different speeches. These older people have the feeling they're being excluded. This is all the more frustrating given that, when they were our age, they displayed admirable courage. Today, they're resting on their laurels. But we should still be fair by recognizing their past achievements, in order to draw from the dynamic energy they can inspire with just a simple word.

Rapp: But how are you thinking of integrating them?

Sankara: We've decided to set up an organization for this. It does not have a name yet, but we know who will be in charge. Provisional committees are being formed in all the provinces, and a national convention will be held soon where the elders will establish a national office. Different committees and leadership bodies will lay out ways of participating.*

Rapp: There is a real willingness to be open-minded?

Sankara: We are in Africa, a society where feudalism, in the broadest sense of the word, is very powerful. When the elder, the patriarch, has spoken, everyone follows. So we say, "Just as young revolutionaries must combat young reactionaries, old reactionaries will be fought by old revolutionaries." I'm sure there are ideological limits to this. But we can accept those limits as long as the elders combat those who must be combated in their sector.

Rapp: Let's come back to your childhood. Do you have other memories that could help shed light on your character and explain certain aspects of your conduct?

Sankara: I went to high school in Bobo-Dioulasso. My family lived in Gaoua and I knew no one when I arrived. As it happened the day classes were supposed to begin, we were told that, for management reasons, the school would not open until the following day. The boarding facilities were closed too, so we had to fend for ourselves for a place to sleep.

With my suitcase on my head—I was too small to carry it any other way—I wandered through the town, which was far too big for me. I got more and more tired, until finally I found myself in front of a bourgeois

---

* The National Union of Elders of Burkina (UNAB) was established in February 1986.

house. There were cars and a big dog in the yard. I rang the bell. A gentleman came to the door and eyed me disdainfully. "What's a little boy like you doing at my door?" he asked. "I saw this house and said to myself: this is where I'm going to spend the night," I told him. He let out a big sigh—he couldn't believe his ears—and then took me in. He settled me in, gave me something to eat, and then explained he had to go out because his wife was waiting in the maternity hospital. The next day I took my things, said good-bye, and left.

One day, when I had become a government minister, I named someone to the post of general secretary in the Ministry of Information. I asked him, "Don't you remember me?" He said no. A month later, same question, same answer. The day he was leaving his post I called him. "You used to work at the radio station in Bobo. You lived in such-and-such a neighborhood and you had an Ami 6 car. You opened your door to me and fed me when I was just a little boy in high school."

"So that was you?" he asked.

"Yes, it was me."

His name was Pierre Barry. When I left his house, I swore to myself that one day I would do something for this man so that he'd know his kindness had not been in vain. I searched for him. Fate was kind. We met each other. Today he's retired.

Rapp: Burkina Faso was a member of the United Nations Security Council. You yourself have addressed the General Assembly. What are your thoughts on this?

Sankara: If I hadn't gone there, I would never have had that experience, so as they say, every cloud has a silver lining. But to tell you the truth, you have to avoid becoming one of the rats in the UN corridors. Because you can very quickly fall into international complicity, a kind of acquiescence that reduces the problems people face to sterile sparring matches between theoreticians.

When you see the people there, you get the impression they're serious, but I don't enjoy being with them much. It was only at the beginning that I felt it necessary to go there.

But as you say, we were members of the Security Council. Our view was that if our role in the United Nations was not to be limited simply to filling our slot, we should have the courage to speak out on behalf of the peoples who had put their confidence in us. Burkina Faso was elected with the votes of more than 104 countries. We had to represent their interests, in particular those of the Nonaligned countries. Their interests, as well as those of other peoples in revolt, should be defended every day, constantly and courageously. Otherwise the UN would become an echo chamber manipulated by a few powerful drummers.

Rapp: Under these circumstances, have you been pressured? Have there been threats to cut off certain aid?

Sankara: At the time, the U.S. ambassador, for example, tried to pressure us in this way. It was in relation to Puerto Rico, Nicaragua, Grenada, and several other questions. We explained to him the sincere friendship we feel for the American people, but we told him it was not in their interests to cause suffering in other countries. We were so sincere in our friendship, we added, that we could not solidarize with anyone who made empty, unfounded attacks on the United States.

I should add, for the sake of intellectual honesty, that the American ambassador backpedaled after our conversation and explained our position to his government.

Rapp: Were these pressures because you were a member of the Security Council?

Sankara: In reality there were all kinds of different pressures, in different forms, by different groups of people. But could we keep quiet when a big power assaults a small country, or when one nation invades another? Our view was that we had a battle to wage there on behalf of all those who had put their trust in us and, equally important, all those who hadn't because they didn't know us well enough.

Rapp: Are you satisfied with the results?

Sankara: We took the positions we had to take. We got ourselves known by a good many people this way. We also made ourselves a good many enemies. We attacked to the left and to the right, to the East and to the West. Everyone took a bit of a beating. Was it worth making so many enemies? Should we have opened so many fronts at once? I don't know.

Rapp: Given your situation, if a big power withdraws its aid, this could cause you serious problems. This would be true, for example, in the case of France, the United States, the Soviet Union, and other Western countries.

Sankara: It's precisely for this reason that we must fight imperialism and everything connected with it. From imperialism's point of view, it's more important to dominate us culturally than militarily. Cultural domination is more flexible, more effective, less costly. This is why we say that to overturn the Burkinabè regime you don't need to bring in heavily armed mercenaries. You just need to forbid the import of champagne, lipstick, and nail polish.

Rapp: Yet these are not products often used by Burkinabè.

Sankara: Only the bourgeoisie is convinced they cannot live without them. We have to work at decolonizing our mentality and achieving happiness within the limits of sacrifices we should be willing to accept. We have to recondition our people to accept themselves as they are, to not be ashamed of their real situation, to be satisfied with it, to glory in it, even.

We must be consistent. We did not hesitate to turn down aid from the Soviet Union that, in our opinion, did not meet our expectations.* We had a frank discussion with the Soviets, and I think we understand each other. We have our dignity to protect.

Rapp: When you have a budget of 58 billion CFA francs and 12 billion are earmarked for the debt, can you really have a financial plan or strategy?

Sankara: Yes, by simply and very starkly posing the choice between champagne and water. We make every effort to reject unequal allocations. So what do we find? Out of a budget of 58 billion, 30,000 government employees monopolize 30 billion, and that leaves nothing for everyone else. This is not normal. If we want greater justice, each of us must recognize the real situation of the people and accept the sacrifices that each individual must make for justice to be done. Who are these 30,000 government employees? People like me.

Take my case. Out of 1,000 children born the same year I was, half died in the first three months. I had the great fortune to escape death, just as I had the great fortune to not die later from one of the diseases here in Africa that killed more of those born that same year.

I am one of the 16 children out of 100 who were able to go to school. That's another extraordinary piece of luck. I'm one of 18 out of 100 who managed to obtain a high school degree, and one of the 300 from the entire country who were able to go abroad and continue their education and who, on coming home, were assured of a job. I'm one of those 2 soldiers out of 100 who, on the social level, have a stable, well-paid position, because I'm an officer in an army where this rank represents something.

The number of people whose lives have been touched by even part of this luck amount to only 30,000 in a country of 7 million inhabitants. And we alone soak up more than 30 billion! This can't go on.

Rapp: Not to mention other advantages!

Sankara: In fact, it's those of us in town who set the tone, who explain to world public opinion what's running smoothly and what's not and how to interpret the situation here. We're the ones who talk about human rights, the drop in buying power, a climate of terror. We forget that we

---

* In 1984, when the country faced a major drought and a 150,000-ton food shortage, the government of Burkina Faso refused, "for reasons of dignity," an offer of 5,000 tons of food from the Soviet Union.

condemned thousands of children to death because we wouldn't agree to cutting our salaries just a tiny bit so that a little clinic could be built. And we didn't stir up international public opinion against the scandal such deaths represent. We're part of the international complicity of men of good conscience: "I'll forgive you your mistakes if you forgive me mine. I'll keep quiet about your dirty deeds if you keep quiet about mine, and we'll all be clean together." It's a veritable "gentlemen's agreement" among men of good conscience.

Rapp: Being indignant about this is one thing. But what can be done about it?

Sankara: You have to dare to look reality in the face and dare to strike hammerblows at some of the long-standing privileges—so long-standing in fact that they seem to have become normal, unquestionable. Of course, you run the risk of being violently attacked in the media. But then no one will ever ask seven million voiceless peasants if they're happy or not with a road, a little school, a clinic, or a well.

Rapp: But what would you do without international aid and structural adjustment loans?*

Sankara: In 1983, when we came to power, the state coffers were empty. The regime we overturned had negotiated and obtained a structural adjustment loan from France of 3 billion CFA francs. After a certain amount of pushing and pulling, this loan was reassigned to our government. That wasn't an easy task and I can assure you that since then no one has lent us anything at all, not France nor any other country. We receive no financial aid.

Rapp: Under these circumstances, how do you avoid a budget deficit?

Sankara: We fill the hole by preventing it from appearing—that is, we don't allow a deficit. We've lowered salaries. State officials have lost up to one month's income. Government employees have had to give up some of their benefits, which, as you can imagine, is never welcomed by anyone. These are the kinds of sacrifices we impose on members of the government, of whom we demand an extremely modest lifestyle. A minister who is a schoolteacher receives a schoolteacher's salary. The president who is a captain receives a captain's salary, nothing more.

---

* Short-term loans by the World Bank and International Monetary Fund to colonial and semicolonial countries, granted under extremely disadvantageous conditions.

Three Kilos of Coffee
(excerpt)

Manu Dibango

Manu Dibango is a jazz saxophonist with an international reputation. His song "Soul Makossa" is sometimes credited with being the first disco tune. Dibango was born in Cameroon in 1933. At the age of fifteen, he left the country for boarding school in France. His father gave him a small amount of money and three kilos of coffee to pay for his first school term. Dibango grew up, established himself as a professional musician in Brussels and Paris, then spent many years trying to return to Africa. His memoir Three Kilos of Coffee, *written in collaboration with Danielle Ruard, is largely the story of how hard going home can be. The excerpt below begins with a trip to Jamaica to record an album, following four difficult years leading a government-sponsored band in Côte d'Ivoire. Coco is Dibango's French wife and Georgia is their daughter.*

[Translated from the French by Beth G. Raps.]

On the isle of the Rastas, my blues evaporated under reggae's caresses. This was the first encounter between Africa and Jamaica. The warm, electric, sensual atmosphere reinvigorated the man who had abandoned Abidjan, his heart heavy with disappointment. The vitality of Jamaican rhythms fed my inspiration. I had prepared only three songs for this requested album, but I felt so good that compositions flowed naturally from me. Though I had come for a week, my stay extended to a month. We recorded a double album with the evocative title *Gone Clear*. Now the skies were clear; the sorrows of past days had dissipated in musical happiness. *Gone Clear* breathed. It called me to find my place again, my place as a musician. The Jamaicans surprised me, lighting little lamps of creativity. We recorded every afternoon. In the morning, I would go to Bob Marley's. He showed me his studio, his talent, and his ways of working.

99

When the month had elapsed, I went to the United States to incorporate brass, strings, and voices into our recordings—four weeks in the studio. *Gone Clear* turned out to be an expensive product, but it was worth it. Georgia and Coco came with me on this trip. "Luck" returned to me. These three months softly distanced me from my African tensions.

"Doctor Bird"

We returned to Paris in October 1979. My cousin-brother put us up until we found the right apartment. Then my little family moved into the area around the Père Lachaise Cemetery, where you'd almost think you were in the country. That part of the twentieth district in Paris gives off its own brand of village bonhomie. Georgia liked her school; Coco recovered her health. Paris gave us back our peace. It was our final harbor, we hoped. Since the age of fifteen, I had moved around Paris every time I returned from one continent or another. I've never felt like a foreigner there. Returned from my trials, strong with my successive triumphs and failures, I was becoming a Parisian African, a mutant species. The African traveler passing through Paris had given way to the Afro-European.

Now I began with nothing. Once again, I started up a band. But the thing I had for my homeland caught up with me again. Côte d'Ivoire had rejected me because I was a foreigner, but in Cameroon, it would be different; I would be at home. Little by little, self-persuasion made its inroads. I went more and more frequently to Yaoundé for "one-shot" deals; once there, I would set up bands. I had one foot in Paris and my fantasies in Cameroon. Back home, one of my close friends, a doctor in philosophy, had just been named minister of culture. His ambition was as great as it was sincere. Cameroonian music was beginning to be felt across the continent; all of Africa was dancing to makossa. My friend and I preferred not to weigh ourselves down with the individualist's yoke; we wanted to forge a unified image of Cameroon, representing all the musical currents in the country. We brought together about twenty artists, from traditional to religious to bar music. This notion resulted in a three-record set, *Fleurs Musicales du Cameroun* [Musical Flowers of Cameroon].

I believed that this was the project that would finally let me make a success of my relationship with Africa. But the project caused me mountains of agony from its conception. Out came those old jealousies again. Out of two thousand artists we considered, we chose only twenty—which gave us a hell of a lot of enemies. The elect themselves balked at being selected and lamented that only one of their pieces had been chosen. My friend was unbending under these attacks, solid as a rock. At the same time, he started a cultural magazine, *Afouacom*.

A few years before in Yaoundé I had met Hervé Bourges, founder and then-director of the École Camerounaise de Journalisme, who later became the CEO of the French TV station TF1 and then of Radio Monte Carlo. We now became friends forever. He opened my mind to politics and great causes. Another Yaoundé luminary in this period (the beginning of the eighties) was a childhood friend whose father was one of the wealthiest men in Cameroon. He had wanted to be a musician: he had the fiber of a businessman and adored music. He, too, had his own ideas, and he took me along on his dream. His father had a hotel in Douala, and my friend wanted to open an international nightclub there. He begged me ardently: "The club will shake up this city; all it's ever known is those little port bars. Once a month, we'll bring in famous foreign artists. You'll take care of that part."

"This job," he told me, "won't take up all your time, and you can continue shuttling back and forth between Paris and Cameroon." This time, Coco refused to follow me to Douala. She knew the film by heart, and she didn't plan to stay around to watch it again. Since my parents' deaths in 1976, she had remained firm in her position. She told me over and over again that my returning to Africa was just a fantasy. Once more, I didn't believe her, at least not yet. In Yaoundé, my son Michel had just turned six.

Douala was my home away from home. I had a house there—my parents' home—and a mission of national importance to fulfill. My pockets were full, thank goodness, because my life-style called for lots of money. The Japanese firm Toyota had pressed me into service for its car campaign in Africa, where the Corolla model was coming out. I signed a contract, and they financed a tour with a troupe of twenty-five people in return for one record, "Makossa-Toyota-Corolla." The kids got the records for free, and you could hear them singing the song—loudly enough to break your eardrums—in all the streets of the continent. The thing was so big that cab drivers in Yaoundé and Douala called me a two-timer if I allowed myself to be driven in anything other than a Toyota. These cabbies drove Toyotas. "Too bad for Peugeot or Renault," I told a French manager I met at a cocktail party shortly after my arrival in Yaoundé. "The Japanese wanted to corner the market. They shelled it out, and even rented a plane for my tour. French companies are resting on their monopolies."

Seen as the Toyota man, I was utterly confident. I threw myself body and soul into my new battle. This trial of truth would be my last African adventure. Of course, as always, I didn't see it coming.

"Mboa"

Douala, fall 1981: "Mboa"—"at home" on the wings of a song. The instruments I had carefully, personally chosen in the best Parisian shops finally arrived at the right port. I had even bought a Hammond organ, planning for the trios and quartets I wanted to invite to the future club. A little band wouldn't be too expensive. Soon our cabaret opened its doors with great pomp. The concept was excellent, but its operation quickly became burdensome. We had no discounted plane tickets, no money to install the soundproofing we needed, and little resistance to the "neighborhood business" that inevitably grafted onto our work. Figures in hand, we had to admit that our operation was obviously not profitable. Yet we drew such a high-class audience. I managed to bring in a pianist I really believed in, Jean-Claude Naimro, who later became Kassav's pianist. I even gave him the chance to bring out a record on Afrovision, one of the three labels I had created back home in the past few years.

Our Douala club, with its international aspirations, was a bottomless pit that devoured us. It finally closed its doors after running for six months. Perhaps Jean-Claude Naimro had made money in Douala, but I had lost a lot, and it was not over yet.

My friends in Yaoundé tried to tell me that the capital had a wider audience. "The students and expatriates are bored. Maybe you could amuse them." They bragged about the merits of a luxurious restaurant that had been set up in a fancy apartment building. "You have to open a club there. The need is there. You could get subsidized." To my mind, the time had come to open a place where people could go to listen to this famous Cameroonian music heard everywhere but in Cameroon. Here local artists could express themselves in dance, music, and skits to delight my compatriots. A national television station was going to start up in accordance with the government's wishes. I hoped to keep its shows supplied with the artists I would invite to the club. Finally, the place would acquaint local musicians with the big names on the world music scene.

My friends in Yaoundé decided to invest in my name and my responsibility. But in reality, they didn't keep their financial promises. Faced with their pulling out, I could only place my hopes in those famous subsidies, which turned out to be hypothetical. On the day I had planned to open the head of the construction crew warned me that the air-conditioning couldn't be run at night. No one had thought to tell me, and since the building was only four years old, there was no way for me to guess that we might have this problem. So off I went, looking for fans.

The club's inauguration unfolded with ministers but without air-conditioning. Me—spend ten million CFA francs to equip the club? No way. Despite my troubles, success didn't wait to come. To the hall decorated like the Don Camilo (a famous Paris cabaret) all Yaoundé came to dine and watch the show. Rhoda Scott, now a rising star, came to play the organ for a week. A woman at the organ—they had never seen that here! It was a real event.

But my clientele aroused bad feeling and envy. Those "local things," the traditional ones, made their way into my club. It was very strange: my enemies brought African "medicine" into the club to dissuade my clientele from coming in.

Black Magic

One evening when I was just returning from Paris I ran over to the club. My foot hit something sticking out. An air pocket? Had the costly rug come unstuck already because of the humidity in the air? Or had it simply been badly laid? I continued walking to the bar, and again my foot hit something. I looked, lifted up the corner of the rug, and discovered balls wrapped in cloth. What could they contain? I asked the servant boy to open them. As soon as I did, my words gave him wings. He fled; he didn't want to touch them. He knew what they were. All the rest of the staff knew what they meant, all except me. I remained aghast. Tension overtook the musicians. The city learned from sidewalk radio that "they've given Manu medicine."

From this point on, the local people didn't come to the club. Some expatriates braved the danger, but I lost an incredible amount of money. I had requested credit, and I had to honor my debts. I hung on and decided to start living here, going to see Georgia and Coco from time to time. My heart was torn between France, where my wife and Georgia lived, and Cameroon, where my son Michel and my daughter Marva lived. Telephone connections were a problem. To get my own line, I rented a luxurious villa, a real cement house. I lived alone in this too-big space.

Scarcely a month after the incident with the balls came a second and disastrous incident. One dark night after coming home from the club, I went to the toilet to read my newspaper. A moment of lovely quiet passed. The surrounding calm relaxed me. I was getting up off the seat when I saw a green snake, the kind whose bite means death. Unfortunately the telephone still wasn't connected. The villa was far from the center of town. Was I going to die here, so absurdly? How could I get out of this with just my shoes and pants? But it was decidedly not my time to go. I didn't delay reacting. I took my first slipper and held it out to the snake so he would bite it and release his venom. Then I could leave. I took off my second slipper. The reptile still had his head up. Slowly I took off my pants and threw them on him. I stepped over him, opened the door carefully, and closed it again. Early in the morning, the houseboy killed the snake. Its venom had already burned the cloth of my pants.

The next day was a memorable Monday. I went down to Douala to see my mother's sister. She had asked a friend from a village in the bush who didn't speak French to lunch with us. This woman had ability as a seer, and she started telling me about my recent misadventures. There was no way she could have known in advance. Her somber prophecies frightened me. "People are creating a lot of vibrations on you. You will have to deal with a snake again. You need to be brave, because it will be very hard." What kind of curse was I under that I couldn't create something here in Cameroon? If there were any logic in all this my mind could deal with it. Confronted with those "local things," I had no effective weapon to defend myself. I completely lost my head.

I called Coco. "I told you not to go back to Africa," she said. She wrote to me, "You'd do more for Africa far away from her." Then again, on the phone: "I'm coming to see you." Crazed, I dashed to Douala to welcome her. I asked a nephew to bring my Toyota from Yaoundé to Douala at the appointed time. The car never got there; as it arrived in the city, it had a serious accident. A car ran into it for no reason. Its driver was an influential civil servant, a surveyor with whom I was negotiating for some land. How could I fight him, or even get an honest evaluation of what had happened from the police? I had no proof. And Coco concluded, "You see, every time you achieve something, an obstacle crosses your path. On balance, you're always the loser. Why not give up Africa to return to France? You've given enough." Since 1957, the year we met, Coco had been my guardian angel. She had confronted mistrust and dislike, the pitfalls Africa can hold for foreigners.

Around me the real world, the spirit world, and the sorcerer's world mingled. The air was unbreathable. I was reeling from my debts, millions of francs to be reimbursed. These debts I took on and paid off over many years. I left Cameroon with my body and my soul raw, with my deepest wound: it was my home I was fleeing.

I had a hard time healing from this nightmare. I was sick for a long time because of Cameroon. Thank God my children Michel and Marva have helped me keep my emotional ties to my country. In this dark night, one certainty came through loud and clear: I didn't have it in me to be a businessman. Everything I had tried at home had failed. I made lots of money playing and wasted it on fantasies. Was I on the wrong path? Not completely—since my departure from Cameroon, supper clubs have flourished there. Later on, some young artists would become famous at these kind of places, groups such as Les Têtes Brûlées and Essindi Mindja. In fact, my plans had made sense.

This time, I returned to Paris for good. The page was turned forever. At least, so I thought. The misunderstanding between me and my country was a basic one. I'm beloved in Cameroon as long as I'm not there: "I love you even more when you're not here."

"Pour une Poignée de CFA"

I was back in Paris's twentieth district, under the peaceful shadow of Père Lachaise. This time, unfortunately, I didn't feel as though I had returned to the fold. Too much confusion and bitterness haunted me. I tried to see clearly. The future of my country worried me. I continued in my failure to understand any of it. Years of independence have gone by. What seed have the successive governments planted in people's heads? The kids don't believe school is useful because their fathers can buy them their diplomas. The god Money is master everywhere. People will do anything for a fistful of CFA francs, as I have said in my song. The idea of the commonweal is nonexistent. People take great care of their villas and forget the edifice they were building for the nation. They build post and telephone offices without planning for the phone booths. A budget is voted on to widen a road; someone stints on twenty centimeters the whole of its length to put more money in his pocket. No one *earns* money; everyone just knows how to use it. The dice are loaded. "Black Africa has gotten off to a bad start," the French Green Réné Dumont wrote; in fact, she may not take off during this century. While this analyst poses the problem at an economic level, I feel it in terms of more serious obstacles: Africa is having trouble finding herself.

After the colonialists left, Africa gained a margin in which to maneuver. But the whites still have some of their power, which they now exercise differently. How can Africa take over the empty margin? Everything is done to impress the onlookers. Do you have a nice house? It's empty, soulless, because it was built with no heart. There's the rub. Is my thirst for love Western or African—or simply ethical? I don't know anymore.

To succeed, I was condemned to be an expatriate. Members of the next musical generation will have to leave the continent en masse to get their place in the sun. Back home, freedom is costly; in fact, the price hasn't even been set yet. When will this flight come to an end? We can't accuse whites forever . . .

When Africa talks of ethics, it advocates a return to roots. This is a facile solution that goes nowhere. I would accept it if it opened up a new path. We have never left our roots. Like all continents, Africa has its past; like others, it has been colonized. That time is over. Creativity is our only path to health—making way for the imagination.

"Négropolitain"

Stuck in my contradictions, I suffered deeply. This story without end looked like a record turning—until a frail light went off in my head. Back home, I could talk openly: the cat never had my tongue; I had never kept from talking. I had a unique ability to put my foot in my mouth, regardless of the rank of the person listening to me. Why admire this or that dignitary who could do nothing to enrich my artistic sensibility? During my life as a musician, I had always been nourished by my encounters. But it was pointless to drive myself crazy as if, like Tintin, I had a special mission to accomplish back home. In Cameroon, no one cared; they were all too involved in their wheeling and dealing. So Tintin went into exile, to general indifference.

Once I accepted this obvious piece of information, I began to feel better. I would continue to pay off my debts and return to being a musician—my real profession. My own world is Charlie Parker, John Coltrane, Louis Armstrong, Hugh Masekela, and the Africa I keep in my head.

Ghana: The Autobiography of Kwame Nkrumah

(excerpt)

Kwame Nkrumah

Kwame Nkrumah (1909–1972) was born in the British colony of Gold Coast and became the first prime minister of the renamed country of Ghana, one of the first African nations to win its independence. A proponent of socialism and Pan-African solidarity, he was a popular figure for a time among many progressives and African Americans, some of whom were inspired to relocate to Ghana. However, policies such as appropriating the windfall profits of cocoa farmers for use in development caused him to lose political support and contributed to Ghana's economic decline. Like many political memoirs, Nkrumah's is most interesting in its early pages, before personal matters give way to accounts of meetings, speeches, and policies.

The only certain facts about my birth appear to be that I was born in the village of Nkroful in Nzima around mid-day on a Saturday in mid-September.

Nzima lies in the extreme south-west of the Gold Coast and covers an area of about a thousand square miles stretching from the river Ankobra on the east to the river Tano and its lagoons on the west. It has a population of about 100,000 people, and was known to Europeans for many years as Apollonia because it was on the feast day of St. Apollo that the white man first set foot in Nzima Land.

In the outlying areas of the Gold Coast nobody bothered to record the dates of births, marriages and deaths, as is the custom of the western world. Such happenings were remarkable only because they provided a cause for celebration. By tribal custom it was enough for a mother to assess the age of her child by calculating the number of national festivals that had been celebrated since its birth. In most cases, however, even this was unknown as nobody was concerned very much with age: time did not count in those peaceful communities.

The national festival of Nzima is called Kuntum. According to my mother's calculations, forty-five Kuntums have taken place since I was born, which makes the year of my birth 1912.

On the other hand, the priest who later baptised me into the Roman Catholic Church recorded my birth date as 21st September, 1909. Although this was a mere guess on his part, I have always used this date on official documents, not so much because I believed in its accuracy, but in so far as officialdom was concerned, it was the line of least resistance. It was not until recently that I came to realise how near the mark this guess must have been.

For recently, I spent a short holiday in Nzima and had the opportunity to revisit some of my childhood haunts and to recapture the past. As I sat with some friends on the sea shore at Half Assini our eyes were drawn to the rusty bulk of the *Bakana,* a cargo boat owned by the British and African Steam Navigation Company, which had been wrecked in 1913 and had come to rest on the sea shore.

The *Bakana* had been a landmark to me for so long that I had never realised how significant a part it could play in throwing light on my age. One of my friends asked what had happened and whether I could remember it. Although I was certainly no older than three or four years at the time, I can well remember being told the story of this disaster.

On the night of 27th August, 1913, the *Bakana,* on her way back from Nigeria to the United Kingdom with a cargo of oil, got into difficulties in a particularly heavy surf between Dixcove and Half Assini. In spite of the efforts of the captain to turn the ship seawards, the *Bakana* was dragged by a strong current nearer and nearer the shallow water until she got her propeller embedded in about five feet of sand. Two ships, the *Ebani* and the *Warri* arrived the following day and endeavoured to pull her out to sea, but the *Bakana* refused to be moved. The master, Captain Richard Williams, than gave orders to abandon ship and the crew and a few passengers were safely lowered into surf boats and taken ashore. The surf boat which was carrying the captain to one of the other ships capsized and he was drowned. His body was recovered from the sea and he was buried in the centre of Half Assini where, although the gravestone has suffered by erosion, it is still possible to read most of the inscription: "Captain Richard Williams, who perished in the surf, August 28th 1913, aged 40 years. . . . Day dawns and the shadows flee away."

I remember more vividly, however, the stories that circulated about the cause of the shipwreck, how the god of the river Ama Azule, wishing to visit his goddess of the neighbouring river Awianialuanu, had planned this disaster in order that he should have a boat at his command. The superstition surrounding this was strengthened by the fact that the *Bakana* was actually dragged nearer and nearer to the mouth of the river until eventually she reached its mouth, where she lies to-day, firmly embedded in the sand, a huge rusty shell, deserted by all but the surf that destroyed her, but majestic still in spite of her torn and broken masts and her gaping hull.

In fact the people of Half Assini still say that they see the lights of a ship—believed to be the *Bakana*—as she sets out to sea at night and ploughs her way to Awianialuanu.

My mother confirms the fact that I was a small boy at the time and that the event occurred some little time after she had brought me from Nkroful to live with my father in Half Assini. Assuming, therefore, that the year of my birth was 1909, the Saturday nearest to the middle of September in that year was the 18th. It seems likely, therefore, that I was born on Saturday, 18th September, 1909.

On the day I was born there was much celebration and beating of drums in the village of Nkroful, not, I may say, in honour of my birth, but in connection with the funeral rites of my father's mother who had died a short while before. As far as the Akan tribe (of which the Nzimas form a part) is concerned, funerals receive far greater honours than do births and marriages. The ceremonial rites performed for the dead presuppose the existence of a supernatural world and, in order that they should not be deprived of comfort there, they are buried with gold, clothes and other necessities of life. Continuous wailing is carried out by relatives and friends of the deceased person, and this goes on throughout the first few days. During the third week following the death a ceremony of remembrance of all the deceased members of the clan is held, commencing with the offering of libations to the spirits and ending in the small hours of the morning with games, dancing and feasting.

And so, on that particular day in Nkroful, my birth was of very little interest to the villagers. I am told, however, that there was a good deal of commotion going on where I was, for I apparently took so long to show any signs of life that my mother had given up all interest in me as she believed me to be dead. This is not as heartless as it may sound for it is a strong belief among the Akan that if a mother mourns the death of her child she will become sterile, and this, to an African woman, is the worst thing that can befall her.

But my female relatives, having dragged themselves away from the funeral celebrations, would not give in so easily. They were determined to put life into me and proceeded to make as much noise as they could with cymbals and other instruments, at the same time jolting me about—and even stuffing a banana into my mouth in an effort to make me cough and so draw breath. They finally succeeded in arousing my interest and, their job completed, handed me back to my anxious mother, a yelling and kicking Saturday's child.

Great importance is attached by the Akans to the day of the week on which a child is born for this determines his platonic soul. They believe that a man is possessed of three souls; the blood soul (or *moyga*) transmitted by the female and considered synonymous with the clan, the *ntoro* which is transmitted by the male and the *okra*, or platonic soul. In order that there should be no mistake about the *okra*, a specific name is given to the child according to the day of the week on which he was born. A male child born on Sunday is called Kwesi; if born on Monday he receives the name Kodjo. And so on. For a boy born on Saturday the name is Kwame. There are other superstitions surrounding a child's birth. For instance, the first child is supposed to be less bright, the third child to be precocious and incorrigible, the ninth child to bring good luck and the tenth child to bring misfortune. Sometimes the fear of bad luck at the birth of a tenth child is so strong that the infant may be smothered at birth or during early infancy.

Whilst I can claim to fall into the pattern of things by being born on a Saturday and bearing the name of Kwame, it is surely disheartening that I was the first and only child of my mother and am therefore, according to tradition, less bright than average!

Nkroful is a typical West African village composed of mud and wattle houses and bamboo compounds. The ground is high and stony leading down via a steep escarpment to a stream on one side and to a swampy lake on the other. I lived there with my mother until I was nearly three years old when we left to join my father who was a goldsmith in Half Assini.

Half Assini is about fifty miles from Nkroful and is on the borders of the French Ivory Coast and the Gold Coast. It is unfortunate for Nzimas that the Tano river and the Ayi Lagoon into which it drains were taken to form the boundary between the two countries, for the people had set up fishing villages all round the lake and are now divided. This has caused much discontent because of customs authorities, language and other barriers which they encounter when crossing from one side to the other.

Many of them still travel on foot the longer way round by the sea shore. Every day, even to-day, it is a common sight to see women with the heaviest of loads on their heads set off at a trotting pace on their seven-hour journey. And when they arrive at their destination they are still trotting! In these days it is also quite a common thing to see lorries travelling by this route, but this can only be done when the tide is low.

There were no lorries in the days of my childhood, indeed there were not even proper roads, and when I left Nkroful with my mother it was necessary to make the journey to Half Assini on foot travelling through Esiama and along the sea shore. This took nearly three days and we had to spend two nights in the villages en route. At other times when we used to journey into the bush together and we could not complete our journey in one day, we would sleep out in the open forest. I remember helping my mother to collect pieces of wood and dead leaves in order to make a fire to keep wild animals away. I had no fears of such things myself; like all small children I had complete confidence in my mother.

And she was a most worthy and vigilant protector. Although she allowed me a lot of freedom and I never felt myself tied to her apron strings, she was always at hand when I needed her and she had a knack of knowing my wants without either of us speaking a word. She never seemed to use her voice to command; there was something about her presence, her quiet, decisive movements, that placed her above most people and gave her a natural leadership.

My father was a man of strong character, extremely kind and very proud of his children. Although I was probably one of the most wilful and naughtiest of children, I can never remember his lifting a finger against me. As a matter of fact I can only remember my mother beating me really hard on one occasion. That was when, because I couldn't get my own way about something, I spat into a pan of stew that was being prepared for the family meal.

We were a large family, for, although I was the only child of my mother and father, my father had quite a number of children by other wives whom he married by native custom. Polygamy was quite legal and even to-day it is quite in order for a man to have as many wives as he can afford. In fact the more wives a man can keep the greater is his social position. However unconventional and unsatisfactory this way of life may appear to those who are confirmed monogamists, and without in any way trying to defend my own sex, it is a frequently accepted fact that man is naturally polygamous. All the African has done is to recognise this fact and to legalise, or to make socially acceptable, a thing which has been done and will doubtless continue to be done by man as long as he exists. It is interesting to note that divorce in this polygamous community is negligible compared with countries practising monogamy, especially when divorce can be obtained so much more easily than in a monogamous society. For a marriage can be brought to an end for any of the following reasons: adultery, barrenness or impotency, drunkenness, sexual incompatibility, the quarrelsome nature of the woman, inharmonious relationship with a mother-in-law, and discovery of marriage within one's own clan.

All members of a clan are considered to be blood relations, and if a marriage takes place between two of the members, it is believed that the whole clan will be visited by the wrath of the gods. In my parents' case, for instance, both were of the same tribe, but my father was of the Asona clan and my mother was from the Anonas. As heredity is governed by the matrilineal line, I belong not to my father's clan, as would be the case in western marriages, but to my mother's. My father's line descends through the eldest son of his sister, a member of the Asona clan.

Apart from our immediate family, which consisted of about fourteen people in all, there always seemed to be relatives staying with us and our little compound was usually full of people. It is a custom among Africans that any relative, however distant the relationship may be, can at any time arrive at your home and remain under your roof for as long as he wants. Nobody questions his arrival, how long he intends staying or his eventual departure. This hospitality is sometimes very much abused, for if one member of the family does well for himself he usually finds his compound filled to capacity with men and women, all claiming some distant kinship, and all prepared to live at his expense until the money runs out.

My family lived together very peaceably and I can remember very few quarrels. The women of the house used to take turns each week to cook the meals and look after my father and at the same time they either worked in the fields or did some petty trading in order to supplement the family income. It was a wonderful life for us children with nothing to do but play around all day. Our playground was vast and varied, for we had the sea, the lagoon and the thrill of unexplored bush all within easy reach.

But we had no toys. I remember one of our playmates, whose father had made some money, one day produced a child's bicycle and was to be found pedalling it up and down the beach. We were extremely envious of him and longed to be allowed to ride it, but he was very possessive and rarely let the thing out of his sight. To-day, however, it is he who may be envious of other people, for his father died and left the family not only penniless, but also quite unequipped to make their own living.

It was probably this bicycle that inspired my half-brothers to build one of a sort out of two iron hoops that they found. What I remember most about that incident is the way they treated me almost as a mascot and something rather sacred. Although they all wanted to sit on the contraption and be the first to try it out, I was placed on the seat and held firmly in case I should come to harm.

Looking back on the kindness and consideration with which they always treated me, I sometimes wonder whether they did not in their heart of hearts regard me as a spoilt little brat. Probably they were so afraid that I would run home screaming to my mother, whom they held in high regard, that they were careful to give me no cause for complaint. Certainly my mother rarely denied me anything and doubtless I took advantage of this, but I believe that she tried not to make her affection too obvious because whenever she was serving our meals, she always gave me mine last. I insisted on sleeping in her bed until, of my own free will, I decided to join my half-brothers, and I remember how I used to be angry when my father came to sleep in our bed and I insisted on sleeping between them. Several times he tried to explain to me that he was married to my mother, but I told him that I also was married to her and that it was my job to protect her.

Unlike most growing children, I was very rarely ready for my food. In fact my mother used to get worried because of the trouble she had in forcing me to eat. She discovered that I would sometimes wake up hungry in the night and so she formed the habit of putting some baked plantain under my pillow so that if I woke at any time through hunger, I could eat this and go back to sleep. I very rarely ate a meal during the day and only returned from my games in the evening to eat the food that had been prepared. My parents never complained about this and once they realised that I was flourishing in spite of my small and irregular meals, they ceased to worry.

Although there were plenty of children with whom I could play, my happiest hours were spent alone. I used to wander off on my own and spend hours on end quietly observing the birds and the lesser animals of the forest and listening to their numerous and varied calls. Sometimes, however, I was not content merely to sit and watch them; I wanted to touch and caress them. It was not long, therefore, before I devised a means of trapping them—not to kill but to bring home as pets. Many times I returned with a squirrel, a bird, a rat or a land crab. On one occasion I remember refusing to go with my mother on a journey unless she allowed me to take a pet bird along with me. Clutching the small cage against my body I suppose I either smothered the poor thing or else killed it with fright. Anyhow, we had not gone more than five miles when I suddenly discovered that my precious bird was dead. This caused me so much distress that my mother was unable to console me and there was no alternative but to return home.

I had heard many stories about ghosts, for such things are a very real part of tribal society. Instead of being afraid of these tales, however, I remember sitting for long enough on my own wishing that I could die simply because I should then rank among those privileged souls who could pass through walls and closed doors, sit among groups of people unobserved and make a general nuisance of themselves!

I do not know whether this longing for things supernatural indicated psychic power, but my mother has many times related the following incident which occurred one day, when, strapped to her back in the normal manner of a young African child, I was travelling with her on one of our frequent journeys together. It happened that she had to wade through a stream on the way and, as we neared the centre, I suddenly cried out in excitement that I was standing on a fish. Although startled by my sudden and noisy outburst, my mother was even more surprised when she discovered to her utter amazement that she had actually trapped a fish with one of her feet. It ended happily, for she managed to catch it and we had it for dinner that evening.

A Far Cry from Plymouth Rock

(excerpt)

Kwame Dawes

Kwame Dawes is a Ghanaian-Jamaican poet, novelist, playwright, biographer, and short-story writer. Born in Ghana in 1962, he moved to London and then Jamaica as a child. A professor of English at the University of Nebraska in Lincoln, he is also the Glenna Luschei Editor of Prairie Schooner *and teaches in the Pacific MFA Writing program.*

In Transit: Secret Selves

All the time we lived in Jamaica, I had the sense that I would be leaving to go somewhere else. The year and a half spent "in transit" in London in 1971 fixed that feeling in all of us. It was a year and a half of being unsettled, rootless. During that time we learned to be always ready to move. I never understood how defining that period was until recently. It was a year or so of dreams. Our days were spent in speculation about our future. It was a rough and yet an important time for the family.

Mostly, I remember that we lived like campers, nomads. We were poor. We had become, quite suddenly and unexpectedly, poor. The problem was that my father was caught between jobs. The decision to leave Ghana had not been sudden, but the execution of the move was clearly not brilliantly planned. The idea, as far as I can determine, was for my mother to travel to England with us, the children, and wait a few weeks for my father to tie up ends in Ghana. He would join us briefly in London and then go ahead to Jamaica to prepare a place for us. We would follow shortly after. The job in Jamaica was a government appointment at the Institute of Jamaica. At that time the Jamaican Labour Party was in power under Hugh Shearer, a brown-skinned Jamaican, a longtime trade unionist. Edward Seaga, who would take over the party not long after this, was actually the one who appointed my father to the post. It all seemed quite progressive: the first black man in such a position and all that.

My father was giving up his intense love of teaching to assume an administrative position. He accepted the offer because of his patriotism, his desire to give something back to Jamaica, and to give some time to his ageing mother. In letters to his friends in Jamaica, it is clear that my father had wanted to return to Jamaica even before he was offered the job. In fact, most of the letters of that period were concerned with his efforts to get an appointment at the University of the West Indies, at Mona. These efforts fell through—the result, he felt, of someone's pettiness. At one stage an appointment in Barbados was talked of, but he either rejected it, or it too fell through. I am not sure how the Institute appointment came about, but it was evidently not completely settled before he resigned his lectureship in Ghana. Had it been settled, our "in transit" stop in London would not have become the extended limbo that it was.

My father may have decided to leave Ghana because he had become disillusioned with Nkrumah's great socialist project, which had collapsed to a coup d'etat. On the evidence of letters to friends, my father's optimism about Ghana's political future had faltered. He seemed more cynical, less idealistic and fired-up than he had been in the early sixties. We did not know any of this, and if we had, we probably would not have understood it. What we did know was that we were embarked on a great migration. It would change things for ever.

The three or four weeks in London became almost two years. My father got caught in a dispute with the University of Ghana about the home in which we had lived in Legon. Without my mother there to argue, to challenge and to question, my father ended up giving up a great deal of money to satisfy the whims of the University's clerks. Now more broke than expected and still smarting at the amount of money on his booze tabs at the various clubs at the University, my father finally moved to London after we had been there for several months.

They had been hard months of moving from room to room—from Earls Court to other places in the city. Five children and a mother. We were a big family and feeding us, dressing us, being with us was difficult. My mother stretched the savings, but soon her letters to Neville asking him to send money went unheeded. It was clear that she would have to find some work or some source of income. She went for both. She worked in the kitchen at the Cumberland Hotel in the West End and did some off-track betting to augment her savings. She was doing grunge work: this artist, this university-educated woman of dignity and pragmatic humility. She worked. She worked. She would come home tired, feet in pain. We could tell that she was working hard.

Nothing was permanent. We lived out of suitcases. All our books, toys, household items, furniture—all the objects that had made our house in

Ghana a home—had been crated and shipped to Jamaica. We would lose most of that stuff to Customs in Jamaica who made it almost impossible for us to pay the duty on those things by quoting ludicrous prices. Even the suitcases and boxes of shoes and clothing we had bought in London they seized. Duty was demanded. The money was not there, and the goods stayed for a few months in Customs and then disappeared. I lost my first pair of Clarks with that important patent leather look and the carefully crafted designs, all pimples and dots. The tough leather soles were preserved by a few rows of these metal strips called Blakeys—I had been desperate for shoes like this, which were all the rage in London. We lost them. For years, I would remember my Clarks with deep sadness and resentment at the Customs people. I imagined some son of a Customs officer profiling in my good shoes. There were no good Clarks in Jamaica. Nor were there the olive-green flannel suits, one of which I had lost as well. It was in the suitcase along with most of the good clothes my mother had managed to purchase during a grand shopping expedition before we finally left London for Jamaica.

In that year and a half in London, clothes became important to me. It was during that time that I began to have an inward sense of my personality. In Ghana, the only hints at a personality amounted to anecdotes about me doing things that I am not certain I recall myself. For the most part, these "defining" recollections were part of our family lore. My self-awareness was as yet undefined. Childhood in Ghana was stable, though not void of trauma. There was the death of Arabna, a playmate who lived a few houses away in the sprawling housing complex of modern white-brick two-storey homes.

When Arabna died, a wail carried into our home: "Arabna weh woo!" It was a woman's lamentation: long, wrenching, and haunting. It would not stop. Arabna was six years old and she had choked on fufu. It was impossible to believe that our friend was gone. The mourning went on for days and the house she lived in became, for us, a gloomy hole, a place of lost childhood. It was a trauma, but hardly a defining one, except in one important sense: it presented me with the fickleness of life and the almost comic simplicity of accidental death. I knew then that a lump of fufu should not kill anyone. We all ate fufu. For quite some while afterwards our parents kept telling us to not talk while we ate. This is all it would have taken and Arabna would have lived. We stopped talking with food in our mouths. But for me it was painfully comic. The same sensation would come over me when my mother and I waited, sixteen years later, for the phone call announcing the passing of my father. Comic. Absurd. Painful.

Even the fact that, as a child in Ghana, accidental death seemed fated to be my undoing appears to have marked me only physically. The collecting and repetition of these tales of close calls had the effect of ritualizing and thus almost fictionalizing the moment. It helped us to manage the pain, if there was pain. I have come to see this family practice, which affirmed the individual quirks and narratives of each member, as perhaps the most stabilizing force in our lives. My parents understood the power of storytelling and myth-making and they passed it on to us. What I remember of my car accident is largely a blur. But the details were added in each retelling.

I hold on to the accident because it forces me to think of Ghana most days of my life. I was seven and had somehow been left by my siblings to find my way home from school. There were two significant obstacles in the journey. The first was to cross the main road, which was not a busy thoroughfare but was busy enough for a seven year old. The second was the stretch of bushes that separated each housing complex from the next. The bushes had footpaths, but the dense stretches of vegetation were infested with snakes—serious snakes. The only way to make it through the bushes alone, as far as I knew, was to sprint the entire way until you came to the opening on the far side of our backyard.

Sprinting blindly was not, however, the solution for the main road. I ran. I did not see the car coming but I saw it going—a sky-blue sedan—and that puzzled me while I lay quite shocked on the asphalt. I was waiting for it to stop. I had not experienced the business of car accidents, but I knew that the fact that the car was still moving was an absurdity. I stared at the tail smoke, then the brilliant sky. I could not move. I did not feel able to move. Time collapsed after that. I can't tell how long I lay there or when the white shirt of a teacher came into view. They knew me, the hands that lifted me from the road. I saw the white Volkswagen bug they were taking me to, remember the red upholstery and the way the front seat folded forward to fit me into the back. I remember, then, being embarrassed at the bloody mess I was making. My shirt was completely red and the people holding me seemed to be bleeding as well. They say I was quite lucid. I talked a lot. At the hospital I remember the gravel of the driveway and then I blacked out. I was in an examination room with people around when I came to. What I heard the doctor (one Dr. Frinpong) say was reassuring. He said there was no real brain damage from the vicious blow I took on the head, from where blood sprouted and crimsoned everything. Afterwards he said I had held tightly to a clutch of movie-star chewing-gum cards and that, as long as I was conscious, I was explaining each cowboy to those who were around. I would not let them go. Frinpong said this meant I was not going to suffer brain trauma.

I blame him, though, for the mangling of my right ankle. It had been crushed by the wheels of the car. The foot was placed in a cast that I wore for weeks. It became a nuisance when, as was his custom, my father punished me by sending me into a corner to kneel down. I could not kneel because the cast ended above my knee. I have always assumed that I had broken only my ankle, but some other fracture must have occurred. When the cast was removed, my foot was deformed. I had no jutting anklebone on the inside of my right foot but the outside bones jutted out obscenely. My foot was turned slightly inwards. Frinpong assured my mother that I would "grow out of it."

I have not. I suffer pains because of this ankle. I live with this pain. According to recent x-rays, the bones are loose in the ankle. They slip in and out of the wrong grooves. I have to find the best position, the best pressure spot to work things into place. Sometimes I simply limp gingerly on it, stiffly, afraid of the sudden consuming pinch on a nerve.

I remember Ghana. I remember that I was surrounded by black leaders, black teachers, black doctors, black writers—I had taken it all for granted. Nationalism was easy because race was hardly an issue.

Ironically, I grew up with a strange complex that made me associate whiteness with a negative sense of self. In Ghana I was teased for being white. I was called "obroni." This was more defining. It was not about life and death, but it was about the way I would begin to shape my own understanding of race. I have not, in any other society, been called white or anything close to it. My complexion is hard to describe, but photographs would assure anyone that whatever whiteness was in our family genes (as I mentioned earlier, my Jamaican great-grandparents were the products of a mixture of slaves and white Irish immigrants to Jamaica), little appeared in me. But *I* was "obroni." Not my siblings, who were all darker than I was. It may have had to do with the fact that my father was a lighter-hued black man from abroad. For obroni did not simply mean white man, it also meant foreigner, alien.

My nose was the other culprit. Obviously African in its spread and substance, it tended to announce itself too loudly for comfort's sake because I was always blowing it, pulling at it, sneezing from it, and picking at it because of my chronic sinus problem (another diagnosed as "he will grow out of it"—this by Frinpong and a British doctor in London—both were wrong) and the allergy I had to cigarette smoke. My parents smoked chronically. My nose was constantly inflamed and I was nicknamed "cherry-blossom nose." Not an original idea, but one that bothered me. Combined with "obroni," I was taking the worst disenfranchisement. There was no language available to me to articulate pride in being in any measure close to whiteness. I would have to learn that reactionary and self-hating language in England, Jamaica and, most eloquently, in America. In Ghana, I made up for the absence of such a language with absurdity. The conversation I had with my amused mother on these issues is one that she repeats as evidence of my ability as a freethinking artist.

"I am not obroni! I am not white!"

"Who said you are obroni?"

"Everybody. I am not obroni. I am not white!"

"No? Oh, so what are you then?"

"I am . . . I am . . . I am green!"

We did not have a television set at the time and Kermit's song had not yet been written, so this was a wholly original thought that made my mother fall about laughing and retelling the tale to anyone she saw. I was pleased with my ability to finally settle the issue of my colour.

For the poet looking around for childhood germs of the future, my answer is clear genius. The truth is more prosaic; I had few options when my mother asked what I was. I could have said black, but I knew it was not entirely true, but I also knew something deeper: that my greatest objection to the name "obroni" was that it made me alien with a particular and negative identity. It made me a known antagonist, a known stranger. It placed me squarely in the limited Ghanaian dialect of race and left me with little that was useful. It was not that I minded being different. In fact, I liked being different, but *I* wanted to define that difference.

Perhaps I had no real understanding of colour at the time; perhaps green was a colour I blurted out because of the pressure to say something, anything. But I don't think so. I think I turned to green because I had understood something about race and racism, something about self-awareness and identity. It would characterize the rest of my life. Being green was not about denying my blackness, or whiteness, for that matter. Sitting here more than thirty years later, and retrieving this as myth, offers a wonderful opportunity for fanciful interpretation. I now treat that moment, which I recall only as a memory granted me by my mother and siblings, as sweetly symbolic. The details of the language clearly belong to my mother and her telling, but not the emotions, which I recall quite well and associate very specifically with Cape Coast where we spent summers with my Pentecostal grandmother and our wild and engaging cousins (the ones who first called me *obroni*), with the smell of yeast and baking bread that my grandmother made in an outdoor mud kiln and sold for a living, with the rugged Atlantic coast, with missing my parents. I regard these memories as important groundings for much that I write. The way I retrieve them and grant them a certain symbolic quality is symptomatic of my inclinations as a poet so that, in many ways, these memories are the seeds of my poetry writing, and the earliest signs of the shaping of a personality, the original DNA traces of the clown, mimic and artist that I would become.

These anecdotal hints of a personality would join other stories to form a received sense of self. But before I developed a secret life, my sense of being an individual, of having a private self, was undefined. For example, my sense of being a good child who would do anything to reduce tension and conflict in the house, was, like many things that come to define who we think we are, a product of another series of stories handed to me. The closeness I felt for my older sister Aba was rooted in the family myth of the famous shared meal. What I remember most about that incident was that, after a while, I continued to eat more and more, not so much because I was relishing the food, but because I could sense a love and solidarity emerging between my sister and I.

There were other stories for the archives. There was the day we all cut school to go and play with a white boy who had a house full of toys. All four of us went roaming through Legon looking for mischief. We settled on visiting this white boy whose parents must have been some kind of American diplomats in Ghana. Maybe they were British, but the story works better if they were American. This visit confirmed what we had always suspected: that white people had a lot more fun in life than we did. He did not seem to go to school and he had all kinds of toys. We did not care too much for him—he was a spoilt brat—but we scavenged his toys, playing with them and enjoying them. For us, America was toy heaven.

This was not the only evidence of American superabundance. There was, apparently, a good trade in second-hand furniture, kitchen utensils, and other household items owned usually by American and sometimes European (rarely English) diplomats or expatriates who would leave the country suddenly for a variety of reasons: coups, diplomatic fracas, anxiety about encroaching Marxism, and so on. My mother, always the entrepreneur, was constantly in search of good deals. We would accompany her to these places and burden the car with games: Monopoly, Stratego, Scrabble—and with toys, utensils, anything that did not seem completely overused. The revelation, of course, was the material plenty of these people. White people, we could tell, defined their lives by material things. The objects were well-preserved. We, on the other hand, found these toys to be quite disposable—as disposable as the cardboard dolls we would make ourselves, dressing them in the silver and gold wrappers from cigarette cartons—designer fashions of some genius. For these dolls, we built houses, cars, submarines, aeroplanes—all from boxes and scraps. Manufactured toys would come in waves, but these, our homemade toys, were our mainstay. We were good at entertaining ourselves.

But the day we cut school to indulge in Americana, we also faced a serious and unprecedented round of whippings. My mother actually had to borrow a cane from a neighbour to exact our punishment. She had discovered we were missing by chance. One of us had forgotten his or her lunch. When my mother arrived at the school, she learnt that we were not there. She panicked. We had been kidnapped—all of us. She called the police, called relatives, called friends. The prospect of losing us in one fell swoop was unbearable.

In the meantime, I had grown tired of America. I wanted to return to the comforts of the Third World. I was whining and complaining, arguing that what we were doing was wrong. Our leader, my eldest brother, Kojo, tried to cow me into silence. It did not work. Eventually, they made the mistake of sending me away. "Crybaby!" he teased. My sisters did not come to my defence. So I ran through the bushes, frightened to death and terribly uncertain. When I came to the edge of our backyard, I saw my mother. She grabbed me, held me close. I started to cry.

"Where are the others?"

I pointed.

"Where, where?"

I explained. She sent me inside. My brother hated me. He got the worst of the punishment, at least if one went by the howling he made. I got the least: the value of copping a plea bargain as a snitch, I suppose. My eldest sister, actually, may have been the most severely tested because she chose to be defiant and not cry. My brother, skilled and experienced in being punished with beatings, knew that early, melodramatic caterwauling reduced the punishment. Stoic, tearless silence simply annoyed the punisher. Aba cried eventually, but by then she had received more than any of us weaker souls.

Excursions to America were clearly not a good thing. This idea, too, would last. For me, the label of a good boy was taking shape. I was the good one. It would take London and the development of a secret life to complicate my personality, to provide me with a layered sense of myself.

Retrieving such instances of personality-shaping, particularly those connected with Ghana, is, in fact, a process of recovering the path of a writer and artist, just as being the son of my father helps to define much of what I have become and may give clues as to what I will become as my years of fatherhood continue. Ghana, my life there, and the manner of my encounter with America in that country, still affects what I feel about America today. Dreamer that my father was, he provided an ideological framework for me that was constantly crashing against stark reality. It has always been the shock of the clash between dream and reality that has sustained me or moved me as a writer, as a person fascinated by people. The London my father painted for us—the London we had seen briefly on visits to Oxford where we lived out his dream of British rural quiet—came heavily up against the poverty and struggle of the London we had to survive for two years in the early seventies. Jamaica, too, was a shadow offered by my father, and by the time I hit America, I was prepared for revelations. They came, too.

NIGERIA

"My Father's English Friend"

(excerpt)

Okey Ndibe

Okey Ndibe, born in 1960, is a professor at Bard College at Simon's Rock and the author of the novel Arrows of Rain *and the forthcoming* foreign gods, inc. *Following a career as a magazine editor in Nigeria, Ndibe moved to the United States to become the founding editor of* African Commentary. *He writes a weekly column for* The Guardian *in Nigeria and has contributed poems to* An Anthology of New West African Poets, *edited by the Gambian poet Tijan Sallah. "My Father's English Friend" is an essay that appeared in the magazine* Guernica.

During a visit to my native Nigeria in January 1993, I saw signs that some dreadful illness had crept into my father. His spare body had filled out in a way that did not seem to spell well-being. His face had become rounder, paler, a little sadder. When he hugged me, I missed the sinewy strength that, in the past, his arms easily commanded. His gait, once brisk, had slowed to the cautious pace of somebody plagued by aches. His clear ringing voice was gone; there was, instead, a slightly enfeebled pattern to his speech, as if his body was no longer able to support the generousness of his spirits.

In June, I received news that he had been diagnosed with renal disease. Thus began my version of a son's worst nightmare. The most graceful man I knew was beginning his final somber dance. In my adolescent days, I had often looked upon my father, first as stronger than everybody else's father; then as simply immortal.

Christopher Chidebe Ndibe was a genial man of noble bearing, and quietly brave. His own father's fame lay in two simple facts. In his day, he had been an invincible traditional wrestler, one of the best in his village, Amawbia. The story is still told there of his wrestling exploits, especially a comical incident during one communal festival. Cowed by my grandfather's wrestling prowess, his opponent had lost his nerve and pleaded,

125

"May we wrestle tomorrow instead?" To which my grandfather responded, "What then shall we do about today?" Till my father's death, villagers saluted him with the statement, "May it be tomorrow," a paraphrase of those plaintive words spoken by his father's opponent.

My grandfather's other claim to fame had to do with white men. When the first white men appeared in Amawbia, my grandfather had been one of the few men to go away with them, drawn by the economic possibilities promised by the nascent world, complete with a new cash nexus. He had hired himself out to the Europeans as a hewer of timber around the delta of Warri, in Nigeria's midwest region, some 200 miles from his village. In those days, modern highways were nonexistent and travelers trekked long distances. When, several years later, my grandfather had not returned, his relatives, presuming him dead, performed his funeral.

Soon after, my grandfather reappeared in the village. His relatives, though much relieved, were bound by tradition not to touch him or welcome him back into the community of the living until the funeral rites were reversed. Until that was done, he remained for the villagers a dead man, a spirit.

My father married my mother in 1958, when she was 33 and he was 36. At the time, any woman past 20 was considered an unviable spouse, dangerously close to a museum piece. In fact, many of his relatives had opposed the marriage, certain that age must have weakened my mother's womb, rendering her incapable of bearing children. He had countered their plaint with the simple point that this was the woman he loved. To his scandalized relatives, this was not a simple matter; theirs was, after all, a world in which the romantic notion of love was hardly a ranking consideration in taking a wife. Having children was by far more important.

Poor for most of his life, my father nevertheless carried himself with an assured nobility. He labored at his postmaster's job with the cheery spirit of one determined that dignity would never be foreign to him. He never raised his voice against his fellows, never became surly, never bore his circumstance, however hard and trying, on his face.

The news of his ailment stabbed me with sharp anxiety attacks. A large part of it owed to the fact that I resided in the United States, separated from my father by 7,000 miles. Besides, I was aware that his illness amounted to a death sentence, slowly, painfully, executed; Nigerian hospitals, like much else in that oil-producing country that has been misruled by a succession of military dictators, are little more than ghastly caricatures of medical care. Dialysis machines are unavailable in most hospitals. The few that have the equipment are flooded by rows upon rows of patients lying in shattering anguish, hoping their turn might come faster than death.

The greater source of my anxiety lay in realizing how much I didn't know about my father. I knew little about his life before he became my father, before he and my mother married and had five children, four sons and one daughter, myself as the second child. My parents, of course, had told us, their children, many stories: about their own childhood, about their parents, and about that distant time of their own youth, full of excitement and peril. I had simply not paid much attention.

The reason was simple: the stories were often told in the context of rebuking shameful conduct. I was the rebellious child in the family, drawn early to smoking, hankering after all-night parties, committed to truancy, and, worst of all (in the opinion of my parents), driven to sex.

Callow and self-absorbed, I felt affronted, diminished by my parents' stories. I quickly learned a way to distract myself during those storytelling sessions. I would focus on some cheeky fantasy, daydreaming about some girl with whom I was infatuated, or thinking about the day when I would be grown and wealthy, able to live my dream life of prurient liberty. The particular fantasy changed, but never the objective—to block out the lessons contained in the personal histories my parents shared.

I did an effective job of it. As I tried to grapple with the news of my father's illness, I was struck by the paltriness of the memories I had of him. It suddenly dawned on me how sorely I missed the treasure of stories I had once spurned.

Visiting Nigeria in 1994—a more or less annual ritual for me—I made sure I spent long hours with my father, asking him questions. There was so much ground we could never hope to cover, but that hardly blunted my joy that, in the race against time, I had reduced my margin of loss, however fractionally.

The first blurry persona I asked about was the Reverend John Tucker, an Englishman who had been my father's regular correspondent for as long as I could remember. For many years, Tucker had been an alluringly misty figure. All I knew was that he wrote to my father once or twice each year, but unfailingly at Christmas. As a child, when my parents were away, I would pilfer his letter and run off to a quiet spot to read it. Many of Tucker's letters were mundane affairs: a quick statement about his pastoral work, a report of the progress in school of his three children, something about his wife's job, an expression of delight at the news from my father that his own wife and children were also doing quite nicely. There was nothing in the letters that could lift the cloak of mystery that surrounded the Englishman in my mind. Nothing explained who he was and why he and my father had become friends. There was little in the letters to reward the punishment I surely would have received had my parents found out I was peeking in their mail.

In a way, the absence of clues suited me quite well in those youthful days. It enabled me to invent a place for Tucker in what I saw as my impoverished life. My parents were lower middle class, and I wanted for symbols to bolster my social standing among my high school friends, some of whom spent summer vacations with their parents in England. I made my father's English friend serve as my own claim to status; he became my peculiar fashion of visiting England, a country linked in my juvenile mind with idyllic beauty. If my father had an English friend, I reasoned, then what edge could my friends from wealthier homes possibly have over me?

In time I outgrew this quaint fantasy, but not my curiosity about where or how my father's story with Reverend Tucker had begun. They had met in Burma, my father told me, a few months after World War II ended. Tucker, a lieutenant in the British Army, had been detailed as the officer in charge of the Signals platoon where my father had served for a good part of the war. My father was a non-commissioned officer with the rank of lance corporal.

My father was not one to rhapsodize war, but he took unmistakable pride in the four medals he had earned. Among the few items of memorabilia that survived Nigeria's political crisis—a crisis that culminated in the Biafran civil war of 1967–70—is one of those medals, as well as his discharge certificate, dated Dec. 31, 1946, from the Royal West African Frontier Force. The document notes "one small scar on the belly" as my father's only wartime injury. Its final testimonial captured the essence of the man who would become, years later, my father. "Honest, sober and trustworthy. Used to handling men. Works efficiently without supervision. Gives great support to his superiors," wrote his officers in the discharge certificate.

Educated only up to elementary school level, my father was able to acquire from the war the necessary skills for his postwar employment with Nigeria's Posts and Telegraphs Department.

I remember the day when, visited by two Nigerian veterans of the war, my father brought out his lone surviving medal from the box where it was kept, like a rare totem. Though too young to make much sense of what was said, I was impressed by the passion with which they shared their experiences, how they recounted their gallantry in such and such a campaign, recalling the number of enemy forces they had, in their own words, "wiped out."

I was always proud that my father took part in World War II, the most meaningful conflict of the modern era. I found myself awed by the war's moral dimensions, the strange configurations of alliances it engendered, its geopolitical consequences, the sheer scale of its prosecution, and its gargantuan cost in lives. It was not until I became a serious student of African history—especially the history of Africans' struggle to reclaim their autonomy from several centuries of European derogation and control—that I began to see the war in an entirely broader light. I was shocked—almost incredulous—when I learned that some 100,000 Nigerians had fought in the war. Other African countries, most of them under the colonial tutelage of Britain or France, also sent several hundreds of thousands of combatants.

Why was this fact glossed over in the major books on the war that I read? Why were Africans consigned to the margins, sometimes altogether erased, when the drama of this war was narrated?

Discussing the war with my father, I came close to grasping a sense of how the African combatants felt as they fought a war that was, in an important respect, the logical culmination of a species of racism with which Europe had yoked Africa. In Burma, my father was a budding nationalist. "I was constantly disgusted at the way European officers treated African soldiers," he said. Tucker was not as haughty as some, but could not help carrying himself, much to my father's detestation, with that very British of airs, a mixture of detachment and purse-lipped confidence, the carriage of a man secure in his place in the world, affecting an easy swagger.

Silently, my father seethed. He considered himself far more adept than his superior officer at using the signalling equipment. Tucker and the other British officers, by their presence and attitude, reminded my father of his wretched place, as an African, in the world. They reminded him that, though fighting side by side with Europeans (and for the same cause), he was a conquered man, subject to the whim of his British conquerors, his life less prized. He was a man whose world had been turned upside down by the English.

Deep down, however, my father saw himself differently; he saw himself as better than some of his British subjugators where it counted. The thinker of such thoughts is a dangerous man. My father was constantly on the verge of explosion. "One day, I angrily told Tucker that he had his rank because he was British, not because he knew signalling as well as some of the African soldiers," said my father.

My father's brusque manner alarmed his African compatriots. "Many of them dropped their jaws in shock," recalled my father. "They were sure I would be court-martialed for insubordination. Some of them even feared I would be shot." But my father remained indifferent to whatever fate awaited him. As it turned out, Tucker chose not to pursue the incident. Instead, recognizing that his less-than-respectful subordinate burned with nationalist ideas, Tucker went out of his way to befriend him. The two began to hold long discussions, often touching on the likely developments in British colonial possessions.

Tucker assured my father that Nigeria, like other British colonies in Africa, would regain political autonomy soon after the war. It was a view other officers mocked, convinced as they were that Africans were little more than bumbling children who would profit by submitting to many more years of stern guidance by their European masters. Tucker's generosity began to make a good impression on my father. He began to reassess the Englishman. As he did, his mistrust of all people British soon thawed where Tucker was concerned.

The two men, defying the gulf of history that separated them, began to build a new relationship that—even in the uncertain time and turf of war-worn Burma—could be called friendship. The British officer and the African soldier, in deciding to meet on an even ground, were saying, in effect, that the arrangements of history were subordinate to the call of friendship. Their friendship was, therefore, at once beautiful and, yes, subversive.

As my father spoke, I could see that his fiery outburst against Tucker had drawn on an uncommon depth of courage from within him, to say nothing of his disregard for the imperative of personal safety. The world of 1946 was one in which my father's kind were meant to be seen, not heard. Not heard, at any rate, speaking in irreverent terms to any British citizen, much less an officer. For in 1946, Britain owned Nigeria, and Tucker was—military ranks aside—literally my father's master. Improbable as my father's conduct was—in a sense, because of it—the two men would go ahead to become lifelong friends.

Back from Nigeria in the spring of 1994, I kept thinking about the meaning of my father's friendship with the Englishman. Still excited from listening to my father recreate his Burmese encounter with Tucker, I decided to arrange a telephone conversation between the two friends. I called my father in Nigeria and linked him up, in a conference call, with Tucker in England. It was the first time they would have heard each other's voice in nearly fifty years. I had pictured them exploding in uproarious excitement, perhaps too choked with joy to find words. How wrong I was. The two friends spoke with an unbelievable emotional restraint, their voices controlled. Their calmness at first struck me as odd, as if somehow they had betrayed their own sense of friendship.

Yet, as I thought about it later, their reserve began to serve as illustration of the character of both men, perhaps even a definition of the spirit of their times. I decided that there was a lot to admire in these men who, despite the seduction of the telephone, simply preferred to stay in touch through the rigorous habit of writing letters. I felt mildly rebuked by their equanimity, as though I had rudely disrupted the familiar rhythm of their routine. A few days after the telephone link-up, Tucker wrote my father a letter that made it clear that my trouble was not wasted. "May I say," he wrote, "how delighted I was to receive the telephone call from Anthony [my English name; I now use Okey] some weeks ago and was amazed to be able to speak to you, as well. I would never have imagined it was possible. Will you please thank Anthony for his forethought and kindness. For days after the phone call, I was filled with pleasure to be able to speak to you after an interval of 48 years." He underlined "delighted," as if, now safe within the letter, he could finally express his excitement.

"Ethics and Narrative: The Human and Other"

Chris Abani

Chris Abani was born in 1966 to an Igbo father and an English-born mother. A professor at the University of California, Riverside, he is the author of novels and novellas including GraceLand, The Virgin of Flames, *and* Becoming Abigail, *and of poetry collections including* Hands Washing Water *and* Sanctificum. *His awards include the PEN USA Freedom-to-Write Award, the Lannan Literary Fellowship, the California Book Award, and the Hurston/Wright Legacy Award.*

> Love for the weak always includes a certain murderous intent.
> —*Kobo Abe*

> Liberty is not the power of doing what we like,
> but the right to do what we ought. —*Lord Dalberg-Acton*

Let us not begin with definitions. With academic references. With proof that many books have been studied on the subject. With the notion that for an idea to be singular, purposeful, or even useful it must be backed up by the research of others. Let us begin with a smaller gesture. If small things can defeat us, and they can if we are to believe the old Igbo proverbs, then they are enough, perhaps, to hang so much upon. A cup of tea and a cold winter morning. Or a story, perhaps. Imagine this: a young boy of ten sets off down a village path to a stream, the part where animals are killed and dressed so that their offal washes away from everything holy. This boy has to become a man. He has to kill a goat. I was that boy. There is nothing harder to do in this world than kill something. I tell a lie; roaches are the exception. But everything else dies hard, struggles to live. Imagine if you will the cry of a goat. So human that the Greeks named catharsis after it. And goats' eyes? So human. In Igbo culture, children are told when lost in the forest to seek a goat and follow it, as it will always lead back to habitation.

Anyway, the story. I have to kill this goat, not much bigger than a kid. A kid to kill a kid. This is the reality—it wasn't cruelty that demanded this of me. It was simply the reality of a culture that killed its own meat, coupled with the process of masculine initiation that demanded the sacrifice of innocence as its entrance. Of course, arguably, I wasn't that innocent, having already killed chickens and turkeys, but birds are dinosaurs and retain their reptilian evil. It is easy to kill reptiles; they're just asking for it. But I didn't want to kill that goat. I wanted to read my new Silver Surfer comic in the shade of a mango tree. I wanted to hide behind the woodshed and drink cokes and smoke cigarettes. I wanted to do anything but kill that goat. It was a lonely walk down to the killing spot, dragging the reluctant, crying kid behind me. The rules were simple: kill and dress the kid alone. But then, halfway to the river, out of sight of the elders, a familiar figure emerged from the underbrush: my school friend and former boy soldier Emmanuel. Emmanuel was hard; he had seen many terrible things. Taken the lives of men. Yet here he was to help me with something as ordinary as killing a goat. As I struggled to hold the animal down, my knees pinning its legs to the ground, my hands on its horns, pulling its throat back to ready it for the bite of the knife, I froze as our eyes met and the goat cried. Tears welled and Emmanuel, sensing I was about to fail this test, came over and with one hand covered the goat's eyes, and with the other, closed its mouth against its own cries. "Steady," he said. Such simple gestures, pedestrian even, but coming from someone like him who should have cared less whether I could kill a goat or not, they meant more. I was crying louder than the goat as I pulled my knife across its throat and held its head, draining the blood into the ritual pot. When Emmanuel let go, the goat's eyes were cloudy and the last blood gurgled through its lips. I jumped back. Emmanuel cleaned and dressed the goat as I sat sobbing. When he was done, he came over to me and sat down. He lit a cigarette, sucked on it and passed it to me, then said: Listen. It will always be hard to kill. But if you cry like this every time, you'll die of heartbreak. Sometimes it is enough to know it will be hard.

Until I began to write this essay, I had forgotten that though I killed maybe two goats in my life, my elder brother Charles had to undertake the responsibility of killing and dressing the goats we cooked for Easter and Christmas and birthdays and when we had special guests—quite a number. Until now, it never occurred to me to question whether this was hard for him. It might have been harder for him. Charles has always loved animals. As a kid, he took in stray cats and dogs, and once even built my sister and me a toy zoo complete with a lizard as a crocodile. Charles had a cat that got bitten by a snake and died in the backyard, crying horribly and foaming at the mouth. We all gathered to watch it with differing degrees of fascination and repulsion, but Charles held the dying animal. The look on his face comes easily to me as I write this, even though it has been over thirty years. Every writer thinks he feels things the most, that he is somehow special because he gets to narrate the world to everyone else as though they aren't living it. Pride is one of the deadly sins, one writers commit every time we put pen to paper.

A lot has happened between then and now. A lot of blood. Not all animal. The thing is, my knowledge of blood, of the terrible intimacy of killing, has taught me that though I have never killed a man, I know how, I know I could. The only thing that terrifies me is that I may not feel sorry. And even as I make this terrible confession, what can it mean? What does the moment offer? Affirmation of something already suspected? Or something else, the recognition perhaps that we all stand at the edge of the same abyss?

This is what the art I make requires of me: that in order to have an honest conversation with a reader, I must reveal myself in all my vulnerability. Reveal myself, not in the sense of my autobiography, but in the sense of the deeper self, the one we keep too often hidden even from ourselves. This revelation is not designed to engender sympathy, or compassion, or even pity. These sentiments, while generous on the part of the reader, obscure the deeper intent, the deeper possibility. The point is to dissolve oneself into the journey of the protagonist, to face the most terrifying thing in narrative, the thing that has been at its heart since the earliest campfire and story. To dare ourselves to imagine, to conjure and then face all of our darkness and all of our light simultaneously. To stand in that liminal moment when we have no solid ground beneath us, no clear firmament above, when the ambiguity of our nature reveals what we are capable of, on both sides. The intensity of that confrontation is the only gift the writer has to offer, the only redemption that is possible.

This is perhaps the awe of us, this attempt we undertake to juggle the dialectic. To accept that all acts, every intervention in the world, requires judgment and that judgment by its very nature conjures up the specter of shame. Between these two things, so far, the only language we have of defining self does violence to another.

> Like a piece of ice on a hot stove,
> the poem must ride on its own melting. —*Robert Frost*

We have wrestled with the question of our humanity since man pointed to a star and saw that his finger was not connected to the night sky. Our humanity, this humanness, is something we still cannot fully define. It is in fact more like a black hole. We know that it is there simply by observing and charting the phenomenology of our reactions. Wise ones amongst us know that it is the sum of all the play and field and the phenomena and the black hole. But we are not all wise, at least I am not, and while the knowledge can be present in its academic sense, we embody it only once in a while. But to stretch the physics analogy, the measuring of a black hole entails the elimination of phenomena one at a time, so we as humans, in the measuring of our humanness, remove these phenomena (or add) depending on our worldview. What if we think of those phenomena for a moment as facades, or the masks of identity, and there are so many that we layer upon whatever is human about us to be seen in the world? I think, then, that we can all agree that even though we don't know exactly what this humanness is, we know that being human, the process itself, forces us to release the masks that we hide behind. Masks we believe we cannot live without, even though we know deep inside that we all hate being measured by them, even as we realize it is impossible to go on living behind them. These masks have many names—fear, hate, pain, love, jealousy, self-loathing, and on—but share very similar archetypal origins regardless of where in the world we are from.

This is what I know about being human—that we all desire to live without fear, or disease, or affliction, but that we all refuse to give up our crutches. James Baldwin said it better: "I imagine one of the reasons people cling to their hates so stubbornly is because they sense, once hate is gone, they will be forced to deal with pain."

In making my art, and sometimes when I teach, I am like a crazed, spirit-filled, snake-handling, speaking-in-tongues, spell-casting, Babylon-chanting-down, new-age, evangelical preacher wildly kicking the crutches away from my characters, forcing them into their pain and potential transformation. Alas, or maybe not, I also kick the crutches away from my readers. And many have fled from the revival tents of my art, screaming in terror.

What of compassion, you might ask? Is that the measure of it? Aristotle liked conditions and listed three that must exist before compassion can take place:

1. That a serious and bad thing has happened to somebody other than us.
2. That this bad event was not (at least not entirely) the person's own fault.

3. That we know ourselves to be vulnerable in the same ways to the same bad thing.

Baldwin said, and I paraphrase, that suffering means something only in so much as someone else can attach his or her suffering to yours. He offered this as a point for young writers to find ways to make their work compelling, but it speaks often to our general tendencies towards the relational. We feel things for others only in so much as those things can fall within the realm of our understanding. This relational model, while laudable, is also, sadly, delusional.

French writer Marguerite Yourcenar says this: "Compassion emphasizes the experience of suffering with those who suffer and it is far from according a sentimental conception of life. It inflicts its knife-like pain only on those who, strong or not, brave or not, intelligent or not, have been granted the humble gift of looking the world in the face and seeing it as it is." But what if we change the idea of gift to choice? What if compassion, true compassion, requires not the gift to see the world as it is, but the choice to be open to seeing the world as it really is, or as it can be?

This is my hope—to create an art that can catalog the phenomenon of our nature, all of it, without sentimentality, but rather by leaning into transformation, so as to offer up what Diane Arbus would call the veritable, inevitable, or the possible, so that we can all have that terrible but necessary confrontation with all of ourselves. Whatever we feel about specific situations, we must at all costs avoid the sentimental.

When I was a younger man, I was engaged in an ideological war with the Nigerian dictatorships under which we lived. I use the plural because there were many coups and counter-coups, and many governments were replaced, but they all had one common denominator: they were dictatorships. Upper-middle-class, educated, privileged (although not bulletproof), I campaigned tirelessly to organize protests to rid us of that oppression. I marched with the people I helped to organize—mostly poor, working-class or yet-to-be working-class citizens. Together, we faced down riot police and tear gas and beatings and bullets with nothing more than songs and the uncrushable belief that nothing good could die. But many did, and I paid little attention. I speak only for myself here and not the many good and wonderful thousands of other Nigerians engaged in that struggle with me. But I hardly questioned myself about my privilege and my right to organize these people. Any questions that did come up I rationalized. Had I not myself been imprisoned? Was I not also facing beatings and bullets? I was engaged in a righteous war. Now I have to ask myself if I had the right to place others in harm's way in the battle for our country's soul. And it is not because I have regrets, or because I suffer from survivor's guilt. It is simply that I have to accept this discomfort—that being human, being courageous, requires the ambiguity of doubt. Would I do it again? Probably. Would I feel this conflicted again? Probably. I have no answers. I have no crutches. I told you the terms at the beginning.

Let us return to the small things. The stories that hold all this transformation that I am trying to articulate, because they are far more reliable than anything I can say. As a child growing up in post–civil war Nigeria, I had the unique opportunity to spend time working on the rice fields that my father owned. I say it was a unique opportunity because farm work, particularly the growing of rice, was considered women's work. My father wanted us to learn everything about our culture, though, so as boys we were free to take part. I remember that as the women planted rice, they would sing mournful songs, dirges that were made up of the names of everyone in the town that had died during the civil war, as though the women could somehow seed the souls of the dead into the tender shoots of green they threaded through the mud of the rice fields. I learned the songs and sang along, threading with them, back bent. Months later, as we harvested the rice, the women would sing happy songs, and woven through them would be the names of all the babies born that year. The following planting season, we went back to the dirges. I had always assumed the songs were fixed seasonal ditties, designed to make the work easier. Later, I learned that this tradition was new and began just after the civil war, and that far from being seasonal, the songs were magical. I began to notice that the number of dead who appeared in the dirges dropped in proportion to the number of births that year. This wasn't a simple belief in reincarnation, but the palpable and powerful transformation of sorrow and pain, and even an underlying anger and hate, into absolute redemption. These women, quietly, textually and bodily, in their way, were changing the narrative of the world.

Writing *Song for Night,* my novella, was a strange journey. It is a quest story and part of the quest is a spiritual one, as the protagonist looks for a way to accept death. The month before the book's U.S. debut, my publisher sent finished copies. I was in Thailand teaching when they arrived. I went out with some students to celebrate when I got the call that my mother had just had a heart attack. I rushed to England to see her. The first thing she did was grab the book and start to devour it greedily. When she got tired, she asked my brother, Greg, to read it to her. I spent ten days with her before heading back to the U.S. A couple of days later, before my plane left Los Angeles for a gig in New York, my mother called. She was too tired to finish the book, she said, but wanted to know if the protagonist, My Luck, ever made peace with death. Yes, I said, he did. I'm glad, she said. She died the next day.

This sometimes happens to us, that we write the song that sings our mother across to the other side. That the narrative is beyond even the ethical work we wanted it to be. That it is sometimes a good yarn, that it sometimes brings comfort to others, that it sometimes makes our people proud of us. It doesn't matter in the end; integrity will find its own way.

> . . . terror is a state of complete understanding . . .
> —*Larry Levis*

As terrifying as things we see are, perhaps more terrifying are the things that, once seen, cannot be unseen. This is a difficulty I think we all recognize in the most instinctual way, and perhaps this is why we all look away as often as we can from the things that have the power to unmake us. We do this in every way, every day.

But what if you cannot? What if you had to arrive at a tree? A lynching tree bearing the burned-out husk of a person. Not male, perhaps because his genitals have been cut away, or because it was a woman to begin with; no matter. This body, before the torture, before the fire, before the dying, this person you have come to meet, this being, this no-longer human, this body, is no stranger to you. This is someone you loved. Someone whose smile you can still imagine under the crinkle of the crackled skin, even though, sans lips, there is only a snarl. What do you do with all that anger, all that rage that burns through you? How do you not pass it on to your kin, if not in words, then in blood, in the silence of the heart where unknowable things become illuminated even without thought? The point of the purposeful narrative, of the ethical story, is to draw all the courage, kindness, goodness, and hope from the world into the open, where everyone can share it.

To be human requires no action. What is required, though, is harder: the non-judgmental (and I don't mean non-discerning) daily accounting of our lives and narratives to ourselves. It is owning all the power and privilege we have wielded that day, as well as its true cost. Perhaps this is what makes my work hard, and human—a difficulty I disguise in beautiful language like any good lover knows to do. One of my earliest spiritual advisers told me that to be human is to accept that there will never be world peace, but to live life as though it is possible. This is the core of my aesthetic: belief in a deeper humanness that is beyond race, class, gender, and power, even as I know that it is not possible. And yet I strive for it in every way, even when I fail. In the end, we may never know. Perhaps it is enough, as Emmanuel said, to know that it will always be hard. May we cry, but may we never die of heartbreak.

"African 'Authenticity' and the Biafran Experience"

Chimamanda Ngozi Adichie

Born in 1977, Chimamanda Ngozi Adichie is one of the most accomplished and celebrated of the younger generation of African writers. She grew up in Nsukka, where her father was a professor of statistics and her mother the first female registrar, and her family lived in a house that was once the home of Chinua Achebe. She is the author of the novels Purple Hibiscus *and* Half of a Yellow Sun, *and the short-story collection* The Thing Around Your Neck. *She was awarded a MacArthur Foundation grant in 2008. This essay, published in* Transition *the same year, was adapted from a presentation at the Christopher Okigbo International Conference at Harvard University in 2007.*

I grew up in Nsukka, a small university town in southeastern Nigeria, and started reading when I was perhaps four years old. I read a lot of British children's literature, and I was particularly enamored of Enid Blyton. I thought that all books had to have white people in them, by their very nature, and so when I started to write, as soon as I was old enough to spell, I wrote the kinds of stories that I was reading. All my characters were white and had blue eyes and played in the snow and ate apples and had dogs called Socks. This, by the way, at a time when I had not been to England and had never seen snow and was more familiar with mangoes than apples. My characters drank ginger beer, a staple of Enid Blyton's characters. Never mind that I had no idea what ginger beer was. For many years afterward, I would have a desperate fascination for ginger beer, but that is another story.

Then, when I was perhaps eight or nine, I read Chinua Achebe's *Things Fall Apart* (1958). It was a glorious shock of discovery. Here were characters who had Igbo names and ate yams and inhabited a world similar to mine. Okonkwo and Ezinma and Ikemefuna taught me that *my* world was worthy of literature, that books could also have people like me

141

in them. It was about the same time that I read Camara Laye's novel *The Dark Child* (1953), a beautiful, elegiac, and in some ways a wonderfully defensive book that also played a role in making me see my African world as a worthy subject of literature.

I like to think of Achebe as the writer whose work gave me permission to write my own stories. But, although Achebe's characters were familiar to me in many ways, their world was also incredibly exotic because they lived without the things that I saw as the norm in my life: they did not have cars and electricity and telephones. They did not eat fried rice. They lived a life that my great-grandfather might have lived, which brings me to a second *Things Fall Apart* story.

I came to the United States about ten years ago to go to college because I was fleeing the study of medicine in Nigeria. As is the case in many places, when you do well in school in Nigeria, you are expected to become a doctor or to pursue some other exalted science. I had been in the science track in secondary school and matriculated at the University of Nigeria to study medicine, but after a year I realized I would be a very unhappy doctor. To prevent the future inadvertent deaths of patients, I fled. Before I arrived in Philadelphia, my friend Ada, who had been in the United States for some years, found a four-bedroom apartment which I would share with three American students. Because Ada had made all the arrangements, my future roommates did not see me until I arrived at the door. I remember them opening the door and looking at me in shock. There was also some disappointment on their faces: I was not what they had expected. "You are wearing American clothes," they said (about the jeans I had bought in the Nsukka market). "Where did you learn to speak English so well?" They were surprised that I knew who Mariah Carey was; they had assumed that I listened to what they called "tribal music." I remember looking at them and being surprised that twenty-year-olds knew so little about the world. And then I realized that perhaps *Things Fall Apart* had played a role in this. These students, like many Americans, had read Achebe's novel in high school, but I suspect that their teacher forgot to explain to them that it was a book set in the Nigeria of a hundred years ago. Later, one of my new roommates told me that I just didn't seem *African*. Clearly, they had expected that I would step out of the pages of *Things Fall Apart*.

My *Things Fall Apart* experience was a point of departure for reflections on authenticity, for the idea that there is a single definition of African and, related to that, for thinking about stereotypes. There is a lot of talk about stereotypes as being automatically bad, and I am not sure that I agree. I think that some stereotypes can be interesting and useful. The problem with stereotypes, however, particularly in literature, is that one story can become the only story: stereotypes straitjacket our ability to think in complex ways. I have a friend from Korea who complains about being thought of as intelligent by Americans just because she is Asian, and I often tell her that I wish I had that problem. While I'd rather not have any stereotypes attached to me at all, if I had to choose, I would prefer a more benign one. Unfortunately, however, the stereotypes in the West about Black Africa are anything but benign. Africa has a long history of being maligned. Racism, the idea of the black race as inferior to the white race, and even the construction of race itself as a biological and social reality, was of course used by Western Europeans to justify slavery and later to justify colonialism. The brilliant Zimbabwean writer Dambudzo Marechera describes colonialism as "that great principle which put anyone who was not white in the wrong." It was an economic enterprise, sustained by superior arms, but it was one that depended on racism for its survival. The ideology of racism was derived from ancient and medieval ideas, biblical references, linguistic connections to the idea of blackness, all of which said, in the end: *Black is not as good as white*. And it therefore became morally acceptable to engage in unfair trade with Black Africans, to take their agricultural resources, to take their land, to "civilize" them. These dangerous stereotypes that originated from the need to justify the economic enterprises of slavery and colonialism meant that the inhabitants of Black Africa were no longer looked at with the mere curiosity that one may have for somebody who is different: instead, they were regarded with contempt. And these stereotypes found their way into the popular imagination and literature.

Some of the books I read as a child—such as those by Rider Haggard—dehumanized Africans. All the Africans in those books were spectacularly simple, if not stupid. The adults were like children who needed a Westerner to teach them everything; they were uncivilized; or they were dark and inscrutable and dangerous in the way that wild animals are. I loved many of those books. I simply didn't get that they were supposed to be about *me*. I did not, of course, identify with any of these African characters. Even the more serious books which I read later, those with well-meaning intentions, such as Joseph Conrad's *Heart of Darkness* (1902)—essentially about the evils of colonialism—did not have a single African character portrayed as fully human. A more recent anti-imperial book which castigates European evils in Africa, Sven Lindqvist's *"Exterminate All the Brutes": One Man's Odyssey into the Heart of Darkness and the Origins of European Genocide* (1995) still manages not to depict a single human African. There are many other examples. Africans become dispensable; Africans don't matter, not even in narratives ostensibly about Africa. The old stereotypes are repeated, feeding on one another and self-perpetuating in the many other books that have been written about Africa since.

A different manifestation of stereotypes is the present sexiness and hipness of Africa in the Western media. Africa has for the past two years or so been very fashionable in the United States and Europe, and this new "afro-fashion" is based in part on the stereotype of the poor starving African in need of salvation by the West. So we have celebrities not only adopting babies but recommending that baby adoption is the way to save Africa. And we have tons of people who go to Africa to show us how much they care and who take pictures with starving African babies, and that sort of thing. Now, I don't want to appear facile about this issue. I recognize that there are huge problems in my continent, and I certainly want them fixed, and I believe that aid can be useful—although I do have trouble with the idea of adoption or distributing bags of grain as the solution. I would rather think of aid not merely as bags of grain but as infrastructure and trade. However, the ways in which Africa is being portrayed today—from CNN to the *New York Times*—reduce Africa to a simple story and often neglect African actors. So we see Africans receiving, we see Africans who are limp with gratitude or limp with hunger, but we do not see Africans who act, although there are many who do. If I were not African, and if all I knew of Africa came from the U.S. media, I would think that all Africans were incomprehensible people perpetually fighting wars that make no sense, drinking muddy water from rivers, almost all dying of AIDS and incredibly poor. This kind of portrayal makes it difficult for outsiders to see an African as equally human, prompting the Westerner to ask, even if secretly, "Is something innately *wrong* with these people?"

And this is perhaps the central point of what I want to say: I believe that it is important that we recognize the equal humanity of the people with whom we inhabit this earth. There is no doubt that we are all equally human, but the course of history has made it possible for some people to question the humanity of others, which has grave consequences for all of us. And so, we need to combat and challenge and complicate stereotypes. We need to conceive of a world in which the idea of difference is just that: *difference,* rather than something necessarily better or worse. I am obviously biased, but I think that literature is one of the best ways to come closer to the idea of a common humanity, to see that we may be kind and unkind in different ways, but that we are all capable of kindness and unkindness. I remember reading Balzac's *Père Goriot* (1835) many years ago and being a bit alarmed because the behavior of these nineteenth-century women in Paris was exactly like the behavior of twentieth-century women in Lagos—for example, they both lied about how much money they had paid for domestic services so that they could fleece money from their wealthy husbands. Of course, their clothes and food and mannerisms were different, as well they should be. What they had in common was being of a certain class with its attendant expectations and hypocrisies.

While I do feel strongly about literature being the best way to combat stereotypes, I am wary of the idea of literature as anthropology. It is not without its problems, one of which is generalizing from the particular. At an Oklahoma university where I spoke not too long ago, a well-meaning student expressed sadness that most Nigerian men were like the physically abusive father in my novel *Purple Hibiscus* (2003). I replied that I had just read Bret Easton Ellis's *American Psycho* (1991) and that perhaps all American twenty-something-year-olds were serial murderers. A short story of mine published in the *New Yorker* in 2007 is about Nigerian university student gangs, which are called *cults*. I received an email from an American woman who was horrified by what happened in the story, although she guessed I was used to it, having grown up in Nigeria. I was not used to it. I wrote about it because in many ways I found it just as horrifying as she did. And of course a part of me wanted to ask her to go to any U.S. inner city if she wanted to encounter something similar to Nigerian university cults.

The films and books I had consumed about America before I first visited did not prepare me for West Philadelphia. I knew there was poverty in the United States, but my conception of it was more like that of people living off the land, in conflict with nature, brave and dignified, even if poor, in worlds like Willa Cather's. But the first time I drove through the inner city of West Philadelphia, I was shocked. It was not mere poverty. It was the sense that these were a people who had been forgotten. But, to return to the woman who wrote to me about the story, if we had an African Al-Jazeera that broadcast worldwide, if we had diverse African stories told by Africans available all over the world, she would perhaps not have assumed that I was immune to horror, and there would be no need to say any of this. Knowing that so little is known about Africa, however, does make me wary in writing truthfully about what interests me. When I write about war, I think: Will this only perpetuate stereotypes of Africa as a place of war? I have so far kept away from making artistic choices based on this concern, but I do think about it, and there is a certain discomfort that it brings. My vision of the world is largely a dark one, and I sometimes wonder whether being African means that I must always indulge in fragile negotiations in order to fully explore my artistic vision.

Literature as one way of combating stereotypes brings me back to Chinua Achebe's *Things Fall Apart*. There are many ways to read this book, but I think most people will agree that it challenges the idea of an Africa without a past, as well as the idea of an Africa with one unchanging past. And so, even if it did not ultimately prepare my roommates for the strange and disappointing vision that I presented at the door, *Things Fall Apart* certainly disabused many of those who felt that the Igbo—as only one example of Africa's diverse peoples—lived in anarchic darkness before their contact with Europeans. The allusions that Achebe's work makes to customs that have changed, to what people did but no longer do, remind us that human history is a collection of stories, of people borrowing from one another, and African cultures, too, have always been dynamic. The Igbo culture changed over and over again, even before the missionaries came. To be an African in precolonial Africa was not one single thing.

After my first novel, *Purple Hibiscus*, was published, a professor at Johns Hopkins informed me that it was not authentically African. My characters were educated and middle class. They drove cars. They were not starving. Therefore, they were not authentically African. It made me wonder why I had never heard anybody speak of "authentically American" characters. Is F. Scott Fitzgerald's Jay Gatsby, with his love of money and position, any more or less authentic than John Steinbeck's altogether dissimilar characters? Both Fitzgerald and Steinbeck are American writers, and their stories are American. I do not accept the idea of monolithic authenticity. To insist that there is one thing that is authentically African is to diminish the African experience. That kind professor wanted to see in my work what he had come to expect from Africa, having consumed the long literary tradition of the Africa of Joseph Conrad and Karen Blixen. Somewhat related to what that professor had to say (and related to the distinction between universal and parochial writers underscored by Ali Mazrui), I am often told by Western journalists that my work is "universal." Sometimes this is said with some surprise, as if by setting a book in a small Nigerian town one risks losing the ability to be universal. I feel very strongly that it is from the specific that universalism arises, that it is through anchoring one's narrative in so-called parochial details that universalism becomes possible, and that it is therefore counterintuitive to make a distinction between *universalism* and *particularity*. When William Faulkner, whose work I admire, writes about life in small, closed, and very specific communities in the U.S. South, his universalism is never in doubt. Nor did the specific Russian realities described in the novels of Dostoevsky and Gogol, which I read and loved as a teenager, make it difficult for me to see that the characters were human like me—even if I had no idea what a *samovar* was.

One can ask of Christopher Okigbo: Was he Nigerian, a poet, or an Igbo first? I find it reductive that the different identity labels we carry must somehow be arranged in some sort of ascending or descending order. I am Igbo because I grew up speaking Igbo and was raised with Igbo cultural norms—I did not quite grasp some of the subtle differences until my Yoruba sister-in-law spent time with us and kept shaking her head in bemused wonder at some of the things we did, such as saying "thank you" to every adult after we had a meal. I am Nigerian because of the passport I carry and the football team I root for in the World Cup. I am African because I find similar concerns, similar ways of looking at the world, in a lot of African people and literature and history. And I am all of these and more at the same time. Apropos of nothing, I read books about bagels as a child. I thought they sounded very elegant, very chic, this thing I pronounced as *bah-gel* that characters ate. I desperately wanted to have a bah-gel. My family visited New York for the first time when I was nine. At the airport I told my mother that we had to get a bah-gel. Finally. You can imagine my intense disappointment when I discovered that this bah-gel, this glorious bah-gel from the books, was only just a dense doughnut.

I have often been asked why I chose to write about Biafra, and I like to say that I did not choose Biafra, it chose me. I cannot honestly intellectualize my interest in the war. It is a subject I have known for very long that I would write about. I was born seven years after the Nigeria-Biafra war ended, and yet the war is not mere history for me, it is also memory, for I grew up in the shadow of Biafra. I knew vaguely about the war as a child—that my grandfathers had died, that my parents had lost everything they owned. Long before my parents began to talk, under my keen questioning, about their specific experiences, I was aware of how this war haunted my family, how it colored the paths our lives had taken. My paternal grandfather died more than a year before the war ended, and because he was in $Biafra_1$, and my father in $Biafra_2$, which were divided by an occupied road, my father could not go to bury his father, and did not see where his father was buried until a year later, when the war ended and somebody showed him an unmarked area of graves. My father, the most undramatic and stoic of men, tells me that he bent down there and took a handful of sand that he has kept ever since. My mother has never spoken very much about losing her father in a refugee camp in Uke. She has, however, often spoken of the things she lost: her wig, the china she had brought back from the United States, how she went from making toast and scrambled eggs for her two little daughters to standing in line and fighting for dried egg yolk from the relief center.

I am still known to cry stupidly about some stories, about some tiny losses that so many people endured, about this trail of physical and metaphysical losses. If anything, learning of the war left me with great respect for a generation of people who had the courage to believe so fervently in something, something I find sadly lacking in the Nigeria of today. But I wanted to write a novel. I had no interest in writing a polemic. I was aware that the book would in the end reflect my world view—it would be a book concerned with the ordinary person, a book with unapologetic Biafran sympathies, but also a book that would absolutely refuse to romanticize the war. I was very aware, as I wrote, of the problem that often comes with being a defeated people—and the Igbo are in many ways a defeated people. It is not only that you learn to bear a collective shame, but that you sometimes go to extremes of reaction. The survivors' sense of defeat and injustice can result in their making a utopia of Biafra, when it may very well have become yet another state of tyranny. I wanted to avoid making Biafra a *utopia-in-retrospect,* which would have been disingenuous—it would have sullied the memories of all those who died. What illuminated my choices as I wrote was remembering and reliving through books and oral accounts remarkable stories of the courage of ordinary people. Chinua Achebe, in his story collection *Girls at War* (1972), writes of Biafran heroism often happening "in out-of-the-way refugee camps, in the damp tatters, in the hungry and bare-handed courage of the first line of fire." I was also determined to make my novel about what I like to think of as the *grittiness* of being human—a book about relationships, about people who have sex and eat food and laugh, about people who are fierce consumers of life. The only major aesthetic I had, if one can call it that, was the idea of writing "the kind of book that I like to read."

I was concerned with certain questions about what it means to be *human.* When you are deprived of the comforts of the life you know, when you go from eating sandwiches to eating lizards, how does this change your relationship, your sense of self, your idea of self-confidence, your relationship with the people you love? How does it change the things you value? I was particularly interested in class and race and gender, which I think affect everything about life in every part of the world—in some ways, the amount of humanity and dignity the world allows depends on what race and class and gender you are. I wanted to have a number of characters so that I could come close to having a portrait of the dynamics of race and class and gender and, even more importantly, how the war complicated these dynamics. It was an emotionally exhausting book to write, and I often stopped just to cry.

One of the books that was important in my research into Biafra was Wole Soyinka's *The Man Died* (1972), a magnificent memoir about his time in prison during the war. It is a brilliant, funny, honest, and courageous book, and, apart from being useful and interesting, it also gave me the image of Christopher Okigbo, which ultimately inspired the character of Okeoma in my own *Half of a Yellow Sun* (2006). In *The Man Died*, Soyinka writes of seeing Okigbo shortly after the secession of Biafra. He tells Soyinka, "You know, I learnt to use a gun right in the field. I had never fired even an air-rifle in my life. But this thing [the Biafra War], I am going to stay with till the end." I read that line over and over, in awe, in wonder, and I imagined this immensely talented poet and thinker, this wonderfully complex man who had dared to believe, and who consumed life so fiercely. And I fear that it is on this terribly romanticized image of Okigbo that the character of Okeoma was based. I wanted to pay tribute to Okigbo, who exemplifies the monumental loss of human capital that Biafra represented, but I used only an essence of the real Okigbo. My character Okeoma, for example, does not comb his hair, though I suspect that Christopher Okigbo did comb his hair. I also wanted to find ways to celebrate the poet's work, as a part of this tribute. I am one of those prose writers for whom most poetry is mysterious and esoteric, and I struggled through Okigbo's *Labyrinths* (1971). Still, I gathered the courage to play with one of the poems by doing a very crude and very simple word substitution with an excerpt from his poem "Water Maid," which reads:

Bright
with the armpit dazzle of a lioness,
she answers,
wearing white light about her;
and the waves escort her,
my lioness,
crowned with moonlight.

My crude word substitution verse, attributed to Okeoma, reads:

Brown
With the fish-glow sheen of a mermaid,
She appears,
Bearing silver dawn;
And the sun attends her,
The mermaid
Who will never be mine.

I also wrote my own original poem, "Were You Silent When We Died?" which is attributed to the character Ugwu, and I like to think that it was Christopher Okigbo's sparkling, intrepid, and unforgettable spirit that guided me as I wrote:

Were You Silent When We Died?

Did you see photos in '68
Of children with their hair changing to rust?
Sickly patches nestled on those small heads
Then falling off, like rotten leaves on dust

Imagine children with arms like toothpicks
With footballs for bellies and skin stretched thin
It was kwashiorkor—difficult word,
A word that was not quite ugly enough, a sin

You needn't imagine. There were photos
Displayed in gloss-filled pages of your "Life"
Did you see? Did you feel sorry briefly
Then turn round to hold your lover or wife?

Their skin had turned the tawny of weak tea,
And showed cobwebs of vein and brittle bone
Naked children laughing, as if the man
Would not take his photos, then leave alone

Wole Soyinka writes in *The Man Died* that "there is something shabby about all unequal conflicts," and he is right. The war was in many ways shabby, painfully shabby. And yet, it was also a time when my brother was born, when people discovered strength and talent and courage, when people got married and found reasons to laugh, when people came together in different ways. Another Soyinka quote from *The Man Died* reads: "It will be a long long long time, possibly generations, before passions die out over the Nigerian civil war." Again, I think Soyinka is right. I think, however, that sometimes that passion comes from not knowing. Nobody taught me about the war in school. It is a part of our history that we like to pretend never existed, that we hide, as if hiding it will make it go away, which of course it doesn't. As if hiding it will make the legacies any easier. One of my hopes was that my novel about the Biafran experience would make Nigerians, particularly Nigerians of my generation, aware of their history and ask questions of that history, that talking and knowing about it would, if not make passions die out, then at least make it possible for us to collectively acknowledge what happened.

In the end, though, *Half of a Yellow Sun* is for me more a love story than a war story; it is a book about love, about the human complexity of our flawed and rich African world.

For, while the tale of how we suffer, and how we are delighted,
and how we may triumph is never new, it must always be heard.
—*James Baldwin*

"Reform,
in the Name of the Father"
Adaobi Tricia Nwaubani

Born in Enugu in 1976, Adaobi Tricia Nwaubani gained attention with her comic debut novel I Do Not Come to You by Chance, *which takes place in the world of Nigerian "419" Internet scams. The book won the 2010 Commonwealth Writer's Prize. The essay below, in a much more serious vein, appeared in the* New York Times *in 2012.*

Some of the best nights at our home in Umuahia were those when Emma Nsofor, my father's lawyer, came to dinner. Not only did he bring me and my four siblings Smarties—a novelty in a house where sweets were never bought for children—but his presence guaranteed that we could get away with almost anything, since our father would be in a state of euphoria. He was rarely as thrilled as when they sat talking late into the night, with dozens of law books strewed about the living room floor.

Over the years, I watched my father, who ran an accounting firm by day, embroil himself in one fight for justice after another, causes that were technically none of his business. The most famous of his battles was against the government of Imo State, which he sued for increasing the number of local government areas from 21 to 59—a ploy to gain more votes and to receive more money from the federal government. The Nigerian Constitution did not authorize states to create LGAs.

Back then, in the early '80s, no one had ever sued the state government before. Relatives arrived in contingents to express their alarm. But their attempts to dissuade my father only ended with his yelling: "What they've done is wrong!"

My father's legal victory over the government stole local headlines. It also attracted the ire of the powers that be. They found a perfect outlet for their fury in my mother, who worked as a top official in the local government. Each new day brought her a fresh experience of workplace victim-

151

ization until eventually she was forced to react. My father summoned a family meeting.

"Your mummy has been transferred," he said.

She was being sent to a remote post—a fate usually reserved for civil servants considered nobody because of their low status in society or lack of connections to anybody who was somebody.

My siblings and I received the news in terrified silence. The transfer meant that our mummy would no longer pick us up from school every afternoon. We would see her only at weekends. And her journey to and from this new post would involve a tortuous journey on a perilous road. Just a few weeks earlier, our family friends had lost their mother to a car crash on such a road.

"The government could even arrange for someone to cause a crash," my father said.

We listened with increasing terror. My mother remained sullen. She and my father must have already dissected the matter. This meeting was simply fulfilling his policy of keeping the children involved. He wanted our input on their decision.

"Your mummy is going to resign."

None of us disagreed.

If only my father had confined his battles to the government. With time, his enemy base expanded. He criticized community leaders who tried to wangle their indigenes into positions of authority in a manner that contravened the 1946 regulations to which my grandfather had been signatory. He alerted the board of the now defunct Golden Guinea Breweries to some decisions of its executive which were not in the company's long-term interests. He went after government commissioners who were not constitutionally eligible for their appointments.

By the time the dead cats, monkey paws and severed heads of chickens started appearing on our front porch, no one was sure exactly who was trying to get rid of him.

One day, a dibia—a seasoned native doctor who had been a friend of my grandfather—paid a visit to our home.

"There are negative forces all over the place," he said.

Using supernatural detectors, he led his apprentices around our backyard, stopping after every few paces and commanding his boys to dig. Hours later, when he declared the proceedings over, the excavations had uncovered evidence of "remote control" juju rituals—earthen pots containing animal parts and herbs, some mingled with items of clothing filched from our clothesline.

The dibia explained that the alligator pepper seed concoction was designed to make my father constantly irritable and ill-tempered; the animal dung was to fetch him miscellaneous shame; the dog's teeth were to instigate quarrels between my parents. To think that, while we slept, diabolical strangers had been planting evil devices on our manicured premises. At least, unlike in today's Nigeria, where assassination is the preferred method of getting rid of opposition nuisances, my father's enemies apparently wanted him alive, just well tormented.

The dibia advised him to forestall future attacks by subscribing to juju. My grandmother, a founding member of the local Assemblies of God church, stretched her palms over our heads and rattled off strange tongues, interjecting in Ibo to ask Jesus to protect and prosper her children, and their children, and their children's children, forever.

The excavated items were piled up and burned. My grandfather's friend died the following Tuesday. Everyone believed that the evil forces he'd dislodged had struck him down in revenge. The mangoes and pawpaws and guavas in our backyard orchard, suspected of contamination, were left to rot on the trees or on the ground.

My father also stopped eating at events.

"They might try to poison me," he said.

When any of us children reported a headache or tummy ache or whatever, my father's first response was, "Did someone give you something to eat?"

Still, my father did not relent in his outspokenness. His reputation as a troublemaker grew. With time, he also became known as a man of principle. By the '90s, after we moved from the town to our ancestral village, we began hosting dusk visits from dignitaries seeking election into some of the highest offices in the land.

"I hope the men who come to marry you won't turn back after seeing the state of our road," my father often joked to me and my sister, referring to the bumpy miles leading to our house.

Yet, those dignitaries—the sorts of potbellied men you saw speechifying on TV—braved the journey. They knew that Chukwuma Hope Nwaubani had earned the respect of his community. The troublemaker had become a kingmaker.

A few years ago, my father took his romance with the courtroom to another level. He enrolled to study law. At the age of 63, he graduated with the highest GPA in his class. Shortly after being called to the bar, he summoned a family meeting to announce that he was going back into politics. He was no longer satisfied with pulling strings behind the scenes; he wanted to run for office.

"No," my mother responded. "You'll have to find yourself another wife."

My father turned to me.

"What do you think?" he asked.

I'd always felt that he had constrained himself too much to the local scene, that the rest of Nigeria could benefit from the valour he had to offer. But one look at my mother's face made me reconsider.

My father has done his bit, and more. Today, my country faces one of the most trying periods in our 52-year history: terrorist attacks, calls for splitting the country along ethnic lines, insecurity, inhumanity and alarming decay in our medical and education systems. I realize that it is now the children's turn to follow in our parents' footsteps, to take on the challenges of our time.

Ousmane Sembène: Interviews
(excerpt)
edited by Annett Busch and Max Annas

Ousmane Sembène (1923–2007), the author of novels including The Black Docker *and* God's Bits of Wood, *was not only one of Africa's leading writers but one of its leading filmmakers. His films, some of them based on his own fiction, included* Black Girl, Xala, *and* Camp de Thiaroye. *Sembène never wrote his memoirs. Speaking to Bonnie Greer in 2005, he said, "I am really unable to talk about my life—I don't know my life. I've traveled a lot and this is the life that I have lived, but that doesn't mean that I know myself." But despite this modest disclaimer, he left behind a number of revealing interviews. The interview below was conducted by Michael Dembrow and Klaus Troller in 1975.*

[Translated from the French by Michael Dembrow.]

Dembrow/Troller: How does the process of creation occur for you?

Sembène: It is very difficult to explain the question of creation, in that I myself don't believe in what one might call a formal manner of inspiration. I think that if I must create something I pose questions somehow or other at my level—why this subject and not another, why I should do this and not something else, what is the objective, what aspect of human beings do I want to reveal, in a general setting. If it is a personal film, I concern myself further with knowing if the problem I'm raising would interest everyone, and how to go about making it of interest to others.

And there, I think that for me it is that moment that the work of investigating the very level of human beings, of the nature of this subject with individuals, with other subjects, begins. I don't know if I'm making myself understood; creation is never detached from the social context of the man himself.

155

Dembrow/Troller: You've said that you personally aren't interested in making "direct cinema." What is the difference between your films and "direct cinema"?

Sembène: I'm not sure what's meant here by cinema direct, or cinema vérité. As for Jean Rouch, he says, "I place my camera in the street, the subject enters, and that's it." I don't think that's true at the level of cinema. One is obliged to select, to point out, to edit, to collate, to make a collage from beginning to end, and one must make a segregation of images, because if you place your camera at the corner of the street, everyone is going to pass by, but if you project that in front of people, there's nothing new there. One sees the street, one sees the automobiles, one sees the people—perhaps they stop to speak, but that means nothing. Jean Rouch and Edgar Morin do that, I've seen it. Perhaps it's right, but I don't believe so, because they're taking up these ideas again from Vertov—Vertov the Russian who in 1917 after the revolution spoke of cinema direct in trains and other things. Perhaps in his context, that was one thing.

But in the context of Africa, I think that a kind of cinema can be created, but the director is obliged to select and to sort out, so that there's a head and a tail to what one is narrating. And I think that at this time direct cinema has no chance for life. The people who go to the theater or to the cinema or what not, they want, I think, to be told a story—I don't know whether that's good or bad. At any rate, they want to have a subject. It depends on how you regard them. At least if it were an underground cinema, a parallel cinema, it would have a chance to live. It touches perhaps the cinephiles, those who love cinema, who think they're satiated with narratives, and who seek another form of truth-masturbation, saying, "That, that's very good!"

You see, I think cinema vérité is like the product of a bad painter who buys an empty frame and who goes among flowers and there hangs the frame, saying, "I have a very pretty picture," ignoring all there is around, that's that. Someone who buys a frame, who goes in a very pretty garden and who frames the flowers and says, "Here's a pretty picture. Here."

Dembrow/Troller: You've said that at the moment you begin, you ask yourself questions such as, "Is this relevant or not," but where do these questions come from? What is there before that?

Sembène: Everything is there! For example, at the moment I'm working on a scenario. It will soon be six months that I've been working on it, every morning, even here [in Bloomington, Indiana]. It's difficult for me to say, it's an aspect that escapes me perhaps, why this must come first. I think that when things are collected there's a mathematical law which escapes us all. But I think it is a mathematical law. And in matters of cinema it is very technical and rigid. Because I only have a certain amount of time in which to tell a story, which can recount fifty years or twenty years of a person's life. I must tell the story of that life in an hour and a half. Therefore I've got to choose. From the moments, the actions, the looks which enfold the entire past or the period of which I can depict so little in the film. It's a different thing with literature. In a literary work you can say, "Fifty years later," one knows then that it's fifty years later. But as for the cinema, you can put in a written title, but it interrupts the story. The film has to move forward. The filmmaker has to select. But this selection process, I think a director has difficulty explaining it in a truly technical, formulaic manner.

Dembrow/Troller: But where do you find your stories?

Sembène: How do I find my ideas? Ah, that's another story! Perhaps . . . I have many ideas in my head, because I see things around me, and every event deserves to be recounted, it seems. But aside from that, it's usually a little bit of news, a speck of an event. I see something, I tell myself, "Wait, that's got to be told." I don't know whether or not you were at the showing of my film last night. [The film was *Borom Sarret,* 1963.] The story of that baby, I'd like to write a book about that.

The story hit me so hard that I was obligated to it from that moment on. I had to reenact the events myself, in my own mind, the tragedy of the bus, to know at what hour the story takes place, to imagine how many people are there, where they come from. You see, from this moment on, I dig, dig, dig, dig, until I find the end of my story. And I think that in my case, this is the hardest time. Because I also have to try to see why this, and why that. I write the same things over four or five times. I ask myself if I'm satisfied. Then I reformulate the questions, and I believe it's there that the mathematical side of creation enters. I remain convinced that there is a very emotional side, but there is also an important intellectual element. Yet this mathematical element escapes even the author.

Dembrow/Troller: When you're developing your ideas, do you begin by establishing individual images, or is it the continuity of the story which interests you?

Sembène: I think it's the continuity of the story which interests me. I don't know what's going to follow. There are times when there are people obsessing me, figures whom I didn't expect to find. You see, these people are pressing themselves on me.

For example, if I take the case of that baby, it's the individuals I see, these characters pressing, jostling one another in front of me—there's this father and son whom I don't know. I must therefore invent a father and a son. Good, I have to go to the hospital, more or less, to see what occurred previously. Perhaps a vision of one of the deaths there is going to spring to my mind. As soon as I begin to set them on an itinerary, to locate them, other ideas and characters have already begun to appear, characters who speak to me. To me. At that time I make a note of these people, I mark them as X, Y, Z, but advancing the story all the while.

Dembrow/Troller: You've said that for several films you've prepared note cards on which the shooting script is broken down to individual scenes. For which films did you do this?

Sembène: I did it for *Borom Sarret, Black Girl,* and another film, *Niaye. Niaye* is the story of incest in a village. It was easier for me to work that way because I was working in the bush and all that. I had my knapsack. And on each card was written a character or a scene of the film. Because I'm always pressed for time when I film. When I'm filming a room, I have to film the entire scene at the same time. Perhaps even later scenes, i.e., the room as it must appear ten or twenty years after the initial scene. Therefore, I have all these cards with the characters, their dress, their dialogue, the appearance of the room, set out as much as possible. Barring accidents, I cannot modify them.

But now, in my room here, in Bloomington, I'm working on an event which took place in Africa during the last century. Good. Here I can think what I like, and that's what I do. I write it down and all that. But when the time comes for me to be out there, what I thought in Bloomington is perhaps no longer true, and doesn't jibe with, say, the lay of the land where I'm filming. But as I have all my little pieces of paper, I know what improvisation is not going to work. Because I'm in a real setting, I have to scratch things out, add others. What I've altered becomes something new. It sometimes happens that by chance, I'd already been thinking along those lines, but I'd fashioned it in a way that didn't correspond to reality.

For example, I'm at a wine merchant's, one who sells wine to the natives at the beginning of the century. He had huge jugs and he had amphorae. Good. I like his shop and, imagining myself the merchant as I prepare my script, I hang as many guns or whatever as I like all over the place. But when I go to make the story, in reality, perhaps the real shop on location has no guns hanging. You see, for me, an image is charged with something, it should correspond to an action that must come from somewhere—if the merchant doesn't hang his rifles, if he places them on a table, then I have to change the whole scene that treats those rifles. To align it with these rifles that are on a table or wherever. And that's why the cards are utilized, because already they are serving as a memory pad.

Dembrow/Troller: You mean at the moment you arrive on location it becomes necessary to change certain things to accord with the physical reality that you find?

Sembène: Yes, it's I, not the actors. Their phrases are the same, their acting is the same, it's the things around them which change. For example, let's say this room is, I don't know, before television. You try to shoot in this room around the TV. Bah! You have to take out the TV or at least find something to mask it with. You see . . . it's always the little things and so on which can encourage creation or make it grind to a halt.

But still I doubt that one can actually teach the creative process. You can teach methods in a technical manner—that was true for me. In Moscow there is a school for cinema, a school for literature, and so on. Good, there were many Africans with me who went to these schools. But I took a shortcut. I didn't stay five years, and I didn't take any courses in theory. But I would be present at all the filming, even if it was snowing. For me, that's how you learn technique, and I think it's most important. When the directors had time, I'd ask them questions: "Why this?" Good, I'd write it down. "Why that?" I'd write it down. And afterwards, when he had the time, he'd say, "This fits with this or that; look in the scenario." Good, I'd write it down, tell him, "OK, I've got it." I think that often in filmmaking schools—I'm speaking of schools where films are made, not just studied, there are so many theories on the creative process that the students pay too much attention to theory and don't think about all these problems.

Dembrow/Troller: Can you give us an example of where you've had to improvise on location?

Sembène: Often. There are many, many examples. I spoke earlier of that child with the gun. [Sembène is speaking of a scene in *Emitai* where the woman and children of a village which had refused to give up its corn to the French are forced to sit in the town square. At one point during the shooting of this scene, a child surprised everyone by suddenly leaving her place, wandering over to where the "French soldiers" were standing guard, and picking up one of their rifles, which had been stacked nearby. This unexpected element works extremely well in the film.] And the same thing occurs in my last film also. I place the actor in a framework and leave possibilities open.

Because sometimes everything looks fine on paper and as long as it's on paper, it's fine. But on location, when we're shooting, we need transitional elements, and it's often the actors who give them to me. An actor might say, "Wait, what if this is done?" I look, I say OK, I see the cameraman and say to him, "Wait, we've got to do this. It's not my idea, it's his." Then he looks, says OK. We change the placement of the camera, do what the actor suggested, and we continue with our work. It doesn't cost us anything and it makes him happy. All it takes perhaps to make him feel good is this little gesture of improvisation.

For example, in my last film [*Xala*] I had once again as my leading actor the man from *Mandabi*. He had a pair of glasses which I'd never seen him with. These glasses could be taken apart, and when we weren't shooting he would take them apart piece by piece and then put them back together. Then when we were shooting he did the same thing. I said OK, we've got to film it, so we filmed it and he was happy. And I myself hadn't foreseen this action.

There are many such instances with women in my films, and it's often with women that I find myself doing the most improvisation. I usually give them more freedom than I give the guys. Because the women are usually playing themselves, their own roles, and on paper I'm very limited by the fact that I don't know them very well. They modify the scenario accordingly. And that also, I think, that brings something to the act of creation.

Particularly in Africa, where we shoot outdoors in direct sunlight. It's not the same in a studio, because in a studio there are a number of steps which must be taken. With studio lighting you're limited, since the zone of illumination extends only three meters before and three meters behind the subject, so he can't move more than six meters. Whereas I have over a hundred meters at my disposal. I place my camera in such a position that I leave the subject time and space to move around.

Dembrow/Troller: How do you choose the roles that you yourself play in your films?

Sembène: Myself? No, you see, these are tricks, there are times when actors who've promised to come—because often certain actors aren't paid, they just promise me they'll come—but they don't show up. Then I say, "OK, I can do it, I think I can do it." Though I don't plan to play a part at the beginning. Except in April a friend of mine asked me to play the leading role in his film, but that's different: it was he who asked me. But I never intend to do it in my own films. I haven't chosen to play a part in my next film, but I have to be ready in case of an absence.

Dembrow/Troller: You mean the choice of playing a soldier in *Emitai* was purely the result of an accident? [There is a satiric sequence in *Emitai* in which the picture of Marshal Pétain in the local army headquarters is replaced by one of General de Gaulle. A Senegalese native soldier, played by Sembène, finds this "changing of the guards from the 'fascist' to the 'republican'" rather incomprehensible, and he makes some humorous comments regarding it. Sembène was himself a soldier in the French colonial army in Senegal during this period.]

Sembène: It was by accident. We had an actor who was supposed to do it, but unfortunately he couldn't come. Because this man who was supposed to act in *Emitai* is the village clerk, and is therefore a member of the town council, an elected position. The day we were supposed to film him there was a meeting of the town council. OK, what were we going to do? Because I'm limited for time by the sunlight, and I can't allow myself to stop shooting every time somebody doesn't show up. You know that when they're in session these council meetings can last four or five days. So I couldn't wait—I did it. The same for *Mandabi* and so on.

When someone's missing, you've got to take their place. It often happens in our films. You don't know it, but everyone in my crew appears in the films, even the cameraman at times. It happens that we're missing a character, so everyone says, "Hold it, the cameraman's got to do it." I take over the camera, he does it, and we continue. So that in each film there are always one or two guys from our crew who appear in it; but it's never planned that way a priori.

Dembrow/Troller: In *Mandabi* you played . . .
Sembène: The scribe, yes.

Dembrow/Troller: And I've read that in reality you do sometimes serve as scribe in your village. Is this the same thing?
Sembène: Yes, but that's, no, you see, in the village they're perhaps illiterate. In French. And there are times when things have to be written. That's neighborliness. You help out, it's not an obligation. I do it a lot, but I think it's the laws of being a good neighbor that are responsible. Because I am a neighbor in the village, and they know I am lettered in French, naturally they come to see me. I can't say no to my neighbor, for in exchange I receive a good deal of recompense. It's a village of fishermen, and sometimes they give me fish, sometimes they give me lobsters, sometimes they give me vegetables, and so on. It's not payment, it's returning a service—so by this act we're more or less joined in this solidarity.

Dembrow/Troller: You see, I have the impression that for you it's all very simple when you explain your choice of roles. We've been taught to make theoretical statements. So we asked ourselves if it perhaps wasn't by accident that it should be the scribe here, or the soldier in the other case—because the day before you had told us of the changeover from Pétain to de Gaulle, when you were in the army. So for us there was a particular significance in that.

Sembène: Yes, of course. I lived that story myself, but in the film I didn't plan to play the role. I think that in the schools . . . you see, schools are a good thing. I've always wanted there to be schools. But the relationship between the theoretical teaching and the actual work with cinema, particularly, I think is very hard. Very hard, whether it be in Africa, in America, or elsewhere. The cinema is too hard because its existence rests on money. There is its industrial aspect to consider. The producers don't want to lose money, so they don't allow certain improvisations. They really want something tidy, so they can count on the returns. In the case of Africa, we have an advantage, I think, in that we can do pretty much what we want, since most African directors up to now have been their own scriptwriters. It's they themselves who write their scripts. You see, it's still very rare in many countries today for the director to both write and direct. They are real creators. In the evolution of our cinema there is nevertheless a new method: scripts created by two filmmakers—a director and a writer. That's a good thing, but still, on location it's another story—it's the director alone who is in fact the owner of the film.

Dembrow/Troller: The other day you said that, for you, there is a medley of film techniques that you could learn in Europe, but your narrative methods are perhaps the contribution of African storytellers.

Sembène: Yes, storytellers . . . yes, that's perhaps why the African cinema is slower. It's slower, admitted. Often, the people who are making films in Africa, the majority never attended the great European schools. For a long time they remained very attached to their culture, in which stories are told. We say that they are storytellers. The story is clear and simple. At first glance you say good, that's really clear, but when you dig, you find philosophy. You find that there is something within that simplicity.

Dembrow/Troller: This story you're talking about, did you find it in the "faits divers" ("human interest") section of a newspaper?

Sembène: No, no, no. Some people told us that story. Because these people went to see *Borom Sarret.* They discussed the story of this boy. Good, OK, this is after 1963, but people didn't want to believe that in Africa a person could go all by himself to bury his child. But when they saw this happen, they ran to tell me about it.

The Devil That Danced on the Water
(excerpt)

Aminatta Forna

*Aminatta Forna, born in Glasgow in 1964, is the daughter of Mohamed
Forna, a doctor who became finance minister under Prime Minister Siaka
Stevens, and a Scottish mother. The parents had a stormy relationship.
Forna's memoir* The Devil That Danced on the Water *weaves together
past and present, the personal and the political, to tell not only her father's
story but her own: that of a small girl growing up under wrenching circumstances. The book circles around a childhood memory: the day a man
appeared at her father's clinic with wounded hands, hours before two men
with the improbable names of Prince Ba and Newlove came to take him
away.*

Last night it did not rain. I lay on my bed reading a book and outside the
night was still. In the middle of the ceiling a naked sixty-watt bulb glowed.
Above me my mosquito net was draped over itself. A few insects were
beginning to gather around the light, but it was still early, only a little after
seven. Daylight had just departed. It would stay dark another twelve hours.
This close to the Equator the days and nights are measured with precision.
Long before bed time Morlai would spray the room with repellent and
leave a mosquito coil burning under my window.

My rubber flip-flops had fallen off my feet onto the bare, stone floor
at the end of the bed. I was lying on my stomach in shorts and T-shirt, lost
in the lives of Gerald Durrell's family and their anthropomorphic pets,
when my brother's head appeared at the door. His face was riven with the
excitement of one who knows and is about to tell: "Have you seen the
man?" was all he asked.

Our house has two verandas. The one at the back, away from the road,
overlooks the crevasse and is next to the kitchen. We reached it in
moments. We ran along the corridor, skidded round the corner, raced

through the living room, past the dining-room table and out of the kitchen door. There were a number of people already out there and they were crowded around in a semicircle facing the other way from me. The span of their backs blocked my view. People were talking in low voices. I edged around the outside of the group.

A man sat almost motionless on one of the hard-backed chairs. His face was damp, great globes of sweat hung on his forehead, his head and eyes rolled slightly backward. Our father, balanced on the arm of an old black plastic easy-chair, was bent towards him.

I pushed in past them all and eased myself in next to my father. I smelled stagnant sweat and alcohol rising from the man, who must have been in his twenties. His skin was dusty grey. It reminded me of something I once saw on a trip we made up-country. We were driving back to Freetown, late at night; everyone around me in the car was asleep. Our driver swung the car around a bend and we came suddenly upon a dark figure walking at the side of the road, miles from any village, petrol station or even crossroads. The walker turned abruptly and the headlights lit up his face. I gasped and so did Sullay, the driver. The man's black face was smeared with pale ashes. His robes were dark, their color obscured by the darkness. He came like an apparition out of the night. Seconds later the car had left him far behind. That, and the time a boy I knew was stung by a scorpion, were the only occasions on which I had ever seen someone turn that colour.

The light was yellow and poor. I peered down until I was able to see what my father was doing. In the man's lap there lay a bloodied object. I thought at first he was holding onto something, a wounded creature maybe, so badly hurt as to be unrecognisable. Then I realised it wasn't an animal but a hand—his own hand. Or rather, what remained of his hand. It lay in tatters. There were no fingers, no fingernails, no palm to speak of. The flesh seemed to be everywhere and nowhere at once. It looked just like raw meat. Amid the quantities of blood there was a gleam: a nub of bone, a sliver of white tendon, a glint of grey muscle. I stood mesmerised, as my father set to work removing pieces of dead flesh with a pair of tweezers.

There was no breeze; the air was close. I began to sweat. I wanted to stay and watch but my father ordered me quietly: "Am, you go and help with the bandages."

My cousins were sitting at the dining-room table just inside the door. They were tearing a sheet into strips and sewing the pieces end to end. I moved to obey, disappointed at being sent away, placated that I had a task.

My father called for antiseptic and Morlai dashed into the house at once. A moment later he reappeared with a near empty plastic bottle.

"Uncle, the Dettol is all done." He gestured with the bottle, half shrug, half question.

A beat passed and then I pitched in: "I have some." I saw my opportunity to be of real use and seized it.

I raced to my room, slid to my knees and reached under the bed. One day I wanted to be a vet. In a cardboard box that I kept hidden was my first aid kit for injured animals. Week by week I used my pocket money to add something new: gauze, tape, splints. Everything else I foraged, like the cotton wool, or else was donated: my father had given me a couple of plastic syringes from his own medical bag. So far I had effectively treated only the dogs and, with less success, a lizard that lost its tail.

At Choithrams supermarket a few days before I had bought a tiny glass quarter-bottle of Dettol. It was still new and unopened, easily the most prized piece in the entire collection. I loved the long Excalibur sword on the label and the sharp scent when I unscrewed the top. It was this I returned bearing, primed with self-importance.

"Here's some Dettol. It's mine but you can use it." I held the little bottle up high. I took up the position next to my father again, and again he sent me away. For the next hour I sat with my cousins and stitched yards of bandages—more, I imagined, than anyone could possibly need.

A long time later, after the wounded man had been taken away and the detritus of soiled dressings cleared, I fell asleep on the same plastic-covered armchair where my father had been sitting. Someone must have carried me to my bed. When I woke up this morning, less than half an hour ago, I was lying under my mosquito net, sheets tangled round my legs. Dawn was barely a memory across the sky. For a little while I stayed there half dreaming until images of the previous evening began to come back to me.

In her bed on the other side of the room my elder sister lay still sleeping: I could hear her breathing. Outside a cock crowed, a tuneless, inarticulate and abrupt cry. It was a young cockerel and it hadn't quite mastered the full-throated song of the rooster. It annoyed me because it often woke me up. One morning I went outside and threw a stone at it.

I lay there listening to the ordinary sounds. I hadn't fallen asleep and been put to bed for years. Had I somehow imagined all of it? I wriggled free of my sheets and yanked up the mosquito net. Pulling it over my head, I leaned out, balancing myself with both hands on the floor. I ducked my head under the bed and slid out my vet's box. The tiny bottle of Dettol was still inside, the top was on. Everything else was in place. I was about to close the lid and push the box back, when I paused and instead I removed the bottle to inspect it. It was my bottle, that was certain, and someone had returned it to the box. But there were no more than a few drops of liquid left inside. And the label was spoiled. It was bloodstained and covered in reddish-brown fingerprints so that you couldn't even read the words any more.

At breakfast our father tells us the man had a car accident. He is wearing a brown suit, ready for the office. I am eating Weetabix, soaking them in milk and mashing the biscuits up. At the weekends my stepmother supervises in the kitchen and we have *akara*, deep-fried balls of banana, rice flour and nutmeg; or else fried plantains with a hot peppery sauce made with fish and black-eyed beans. On weekdays we eat cereal and toast.

"How did he crash?" we ask. I layer sugar thickly over the cereal.

"I don't know," our father replies.

"What happened to him?"

"He's gone to a hospital."

We nod. I spoon the soft brown mush into my mouth while I begin to formulate another question, but my father's next statement stops me dead in my tracks.

"Am, I'm seeing someone today. A maths tutor. I want you to have some extra lessons during the holidays."

My mouth is full of Weetabix and I am left speechless. It's true that my maths is not good. I routinely come midway down my class, unacceptable by my father's standards. Every term he hands out awards for first, second and third place but I rarely manage to make the grade. At the last minute he comes up with a booby prize "for effort" which somehow always has my name on it. But the holidays have only just begun; we arrived home from our boarding schools in England ten days ago. I cannot decide whether I am affronted or pleased to be singled out for such attention, to have my own maths tutor. While I am considering all this my father finishes his breakfast and borrows my milk glass. He pours himself a glass from one of the bottles of boiled water he keep in the fridge. As the glass fills the water turns cloudy. It doesn't look very appealing.

"Ugh!" I say.

"It all goes to the same place." My father smiles, amuses us by draining the whole glass with exaggerated delectation. He kisses us and he is gone.

In the afternoon the rain begins. The ground around the house fills up with rust-coloured puddles. Little rivulets of blood join into ever larger tributaries which weave down the slopes to the slaughterhouse stream. The heat doesn't abate and the smell of steaming dirt is like a wet dog. The drops hurtle onto the corrugated roof of the garage, bouncing obliquely on the curves of tin and crashing like a thousand demented timpanists.

Through their discordant rhythm rises the regular beat of the man with a pickaxe, who keeps on splitting stones. He has stripped down to a pair of torn shorts and the water washes away the sweat and shimmers on his torso. The man doesn't pause once. On his right a second mound of small stones has begun to overtake the original pile of rocks.

On the balcony, below the curled iron railings, pools of water form and stretch out over the tiles. I take my book and sit in one of the long line of chairs. I am alone. No one comes to the house today. Ordinarily, by mid-afternoon the people have begun to arrive alone and in pairs, usually on foot from Kissy Bye-Pass Road, more rarely by taxi. Anyone known to the family goes through the house and keeps company on the back veranda. The others sit out front on the roadside. They come from Freetown and from the provinces in need of help.

The chairs are strung with green and yellow plastic cord which is no longer taut and cuts into the flesh. The people sit uncomplaining on the uncomfortable chairs, nursing their requests until my father comes home from work. If he is late or busy, they come back the next day. Some of them are his former patients wanting further treatment but without money to pay for another doctor; others bring news of a death or need help to school a child. Sometimes he is asked to intercede in a family dispute or help find someone a job. Most of them just want a little money.

When they start to arrive I usually disappear somewhere else. Once a blind man climbed up the stairs from the road and accidentally sat on top of me. In school we were taught that blind people had super sensory powers and hearing like a bat's radar; we were warned never to treat them as though they're helpless. So I watched as the blind man lowered his bottom, believing, until it was too late, that he must somehow know I was underneath him, my tongue locked with the shame of the moment. As soon as his buttocks touched me the blind man shot up in the air like a jack-in-the-box and groped his way silently into another seat. The blind man isn't here today. There are no visitors at all. Perhaps it is the rain that is keeping them away.

DEMOCRATIC REPUBLIC OF CONGO

Lumumba Speaks

(excerpt)

Patrice Lumumba

Patrice Lumumba (1925–1961) was a nationalist leader who became the first prime minister of an independent Congo. Born in the Kasai province, he was educated at Protestant and Catholic schools and worked as a postal clerk and a beer salesman before becoming politically active. In 1958 he helped found the Mouvement National Congolais (MNC) and became its leader. In October 1959 he was arrested for inciting a riot in Stanleyville (now Kisangani) and imprisoned while awaiting trial. In January 1960, as his trial was about to begin, delegates to a conference in Brussels on the future of Congo applied pressure to have him released. National elections were held in May, and in June Lumumba became prime minister. Shortly after independence, the province of Katanga declared its independence, and Lumumba turned to the Soviet Union for help in suppressing the rebellion. President Kasa-Vubu, who was more politically moderate, dismissed Lumumba from office, and in September Colonel Joseph Mobutu (later known as Mobutu Sese Seko) overthrew the government in a coup. Lumumba was placed under house arrest, escaped, was captured by soldiers loyal to Mobutu, and in January 1961 was executed by a firing squad.

Below is a selection from a speech made to a public meeting of the Amis de Présence Africaine in Brussels on February 6, 1960, four months before Congo's independence.

[Translated from the French by Helen R. Lane.]

From Prison to the Round Table

I came to Belgium last year to organize a lecture tour. The aim of my trip was to put the real aspirations of the Congolese people before the Belgian people. I told you what these aspirations were, in this very auditorium. I told you that the Congolese people were no longer willing to tolerate the colonial regime that was an open defiance of human dignity.

When I returned to the Congo following this lecture tour, I resigned from my job in order to put myself entirely at the service of the Congolese people. I encountered a great many difficulties and a great many hardships, leaving my wife and my four children behind, traveling to every corner of the country to prepare the people, educate them politically, and teach them their duties as citizens.

You are well aware that Belgium came out in favor of the independence of the Congo in its declaration of January 13. But it was a very vague sort of independence, for no definite date was set. We presented several resolutions to the minister of the Congo; we repeatedly demanded to know when the Congo would be granted its independence.

Subsequently, toward the end of the year, we held a congress in Stanleyville. This congress brought together the representatives of the various provinces of the Congo. More than forty tribal chieftains attended this congress. We decided to participate in the elections to be held in December 1959, but only on condition that the minister open negotiations with us, because the minister had stated in his message of September 16, 1959, that communal and territorial elections would be held first, in December 1959; and then later, in March 1960, the communal and territorial advisers could get together to appoint the provincial advisers; and around September 1960 there would be a central government, presided over by the governor-general; he also stated that the Congo could not hope to be independent for four years. Our congress did not approve of this government plan at all. We therefore asked the minister to open negotiations with us immediately. The minister flatly refused to do so.

Receiving this negative answer, the congress decided not to subscribe to the government's plan, because we failed to see how a Congolese government could continue to be headed by a governor-general. We were well aware that it was not genuine independence that we were being promised. And we said that we would die rather than vote for this plan, which was merely a cover-up for the perpetuation of a colonial regime in the Congo. The entire populace was standing up for its rights; the entire populace was demanding immediate independence; and we said that we were going to mobilize every man, woman, and child in the country to serve the cause of Congolese revolution, to serve the cause of peaceful revolution, because our fundamental doctrine, as I stated in this very auditorium, as I have always stated in all our public meetings, is based on nonviolence.

Seeing that the populace agreed with us (thousands and thousands of people, since no one wanted to go along with the administration any more), the authorities decided to make an all-out effort to arrest me. The local administration then carefully hatched and staged a plot to allow them to do so. A police officer came to our meetings and recorded my speeches on tape. After all my speeches had been recorded, the tapes were taken to the Office of the Public Prosecutor, and immediately afterward I was issued a summons. They told me: "You are to appear in the Office of the Royal Prosecutor." This occurred while we were still holding not only the MNC congress, which ended on the twenty-ninth of September—or rather, the twenty-eighth—but also another congress bringing together the six [*sic*] political parties, which opened on the twenty-ninth. There was a delegation from Rwanda-Burundi, and the other political parties had come from all over the Congo. All of them had taken the same stand, and the officials had said: "Lumumba is a dangerous individual because everywhere he goes the people follow him. If we let him run around loose, our plans will fail, because the populace is going to follow him. We must stop him."

Since there was no possibility of stopping me, they then planned and staged a repressive attack on the people of Stanleyville, as I explained. We were holding a private meeting behind closed doors in a private home. We heard rifle shots—the beginning of the repression. Immediately thereafter, we saw dead bodies lying all over; there was widespread panic; the people were overwrought and asking: "Why is this happening, what have we done?" Then I hid for several days in a house. "We'll see what's going to happen now," I said. They were looking everywhere for me. And after a few days, when things had calmed down somewhat, I came out of hiding. When the repression first began I went to the police and asked them to stop shooting. I said: "Officers, there is no reason for you to behave like this." They shot at me. Even though I had an immatriculation card and had the same legal rights as Europeans, I was arrested and physically assaulted and thrown into a pitch-dark little cell where I was forced to lie on the floor and was given a blanket only when I protested and demanded one.

A week later I was transferred to a military camp, where I spent a month in a combination toilet and shower room with no opening and no ventilation. I wrote to the royal prosecutor and informed him that the conditions in which I was being held were horrible. Nothing happened. It was not until my children went to the governor-general and the general prosecutor and pleaded with them on my behalf that I was finally taken out of this military camp, after several months, and transferred on December twelfth to a prison, where conditions were somewhat better than the ones I had had to endure previously. Everything possible was done to break my spirit, but I knew that freedom is the ideal for which from time immemorial, in every country in the world, men have fought and died, and I made a choice: to serve my country. I bore all my troubles courageously.

Eventually I appeared in court, but before that the governor, two days before my arrest, made speeches saying: "Lumumba has tried to dig a bloody trench between whites and blacks, and Lumumba was trained in revolutionary techniques abroad," and claiming that I was the one who had incited the populace to riot. I was vilified in every possible way; I was jeered at, insulted, and dragged in the mud simply because I demanded our country's freedom. I have never been against the white man; I have never been against individual persons; what I have always rebelled against is injustice. Against a regime whose time was long past. I went before the tribunal. An investigation was conducted: several witnesses were summoned, and each and every one of them declared that it was not Lumumba who was responsible for the incidents in Stanleyville. "He never incited us to any sort of violence," they said, and testified that I had always called upon people to remain calm.

Then when I appeared before the magistrates, they insisted that no mention whatsoever be made of the tragic events of October 30; they insisted that no mention be made of the bloody events of the thirtieth of October: [there had been violence, they claimed] simply because Lumumba had made inflammatory speeches, because in his speeches he had said, "Down with the Belgian colonial policy." Because in his speeches he had called the Belgian government a conservative and dictatorial government, because in his speeches Lumumba had attacked the prestige of the Congo administration, because Lumumba had incited the populace to refuse to vote. All these accusations were proved to be totally false, and if I was sentenced to six months in prison, it was only so that no one would publicly declare that it was the administration that was guilty; it was a pretext: I was in no way guilty. It was the local administration that planned the repression; it was the governor of Stanleyville who was responsible for what happened in Stanleyville. Thirty Congolese were literally murdered, for no plausible reason whatsoever. There was no unrest whatsoever in the African quarter of the city; there was no uprising, absolutely nothing; everything was calm. But for years now in the Congo it has been necessary to bow and scrape, to say amen continually, to say yes continually when people should be saying no, in order to enjoy the favor of the administration or of certain colonial circles. When a person wishes to defend his country, when he wishes to defend freedom, the label "revolutionary" is immediately pinned on him; he is immediately called an agitator, a petty hoodlum—all sorts of names.

After these events, the minister came to the Congo and saw the realities of the situation. Then the king came to the Congo, directly to Stanleyville. He saw with his own eyes that the populace was no longer willing to tolerate the colonial regime. The very same day that the king arrived, thousands and thousands of people went to the prison and said, "We want Lumumba released from prison today." The king realized that this was the situation throughout the country, and finally, after all the misunderstandings and the lack of comprehension, the Belgians bowed to the evidence: the Congolese people had to be free. The Round Table Conference was then called.

I appeared before the tribunal on January 18, 1960. I was sentenced on the twenty-first. The royal prosecutor asked for a prison sentence of four years; the government sentenced me to six months. That very day, despite the fact that any gathering of more than five people had been forbidden, several thousand people came to the prison after I had been sentenced. They surrounded it and said, "If Lumumba isn't let out of prison, things are going to go very badly."

On the twenty-second, one day after I had been sentenced, I was in my cell reading, barefoot, in my undershirt, without a shirt. The director of the prison came in and said, "We've got bad news for you." I thought that perhaps a member of my family had died. He was accompanied by a group of police officers. He said to me, "You are to be taken to Jadotville immediately." I said to him, "How can that possibly be?" and he replied, "It's true; you're being transferred." I said, "But how can I leave here on such short notice? . . . I should have been advised at least a day in advance so I could pack my things and see my attorneys." "No, that is out of the question." I said, "Will you please send for my attorneys?" "Seeing your attorneys is out of the question," he answered. They came for me immediately thereafter, and as you can see I was physically assaulted. [Lumumba was wearing bandages on his wrists.] They took me away. I was not even allowed to walk to the police van; they threw me in it like a stick of wood. I was taken to the airfield, made to get out of the van, and thrown onto the plane. My neck was twisted, I was manhandled, and all my things were still in the prison. When I arrived in Elisabethville I was taken off the plane as if I were a common thief, and certain Europeans took great delight in photographing me, and from there I was taken directly to Jadotville, where I was thrown in a maximum security prison, where only common criminals or prisoners who have been condemned to death or been given life sentences are kept. I was locked in a cell there.

When the populace learned that I had been physically assaulted, several hundred people immediately surrounded the Jadotville prison. The local authorities were sympathetic. I was able to receive at least a hundred visitors that same day, and on the following day I received many more visitors, from Bukama, from Elisabethville, from all over, more or less, and on the third day news came that I was to leave for Belgium.

I didn't have anything, no suit, no shoes, absolutely nothing. The authorities had to find me a suit and other things so I could get dressed. The Africans took up a collection and bought me the rest of the clothes I needed. I was escorted from Jadotville by the district commissioner and military jeeps. When I got to the airport, there were at least ten thousand Congolese there; they were delighted, and kept shouting, right there in front of the provincial commissioner: "Down with colonialism, down with the colonialists, long live immediate independence!" and the atmosphere was now entirely different. Reporters came to ask me what my impressions were. And I told them: "Gentlemen, you may tell the people of the Congo, and the Europeans in particular, that I am not at all bitter, that this is a page of history, and that I am going to Brussels to defend the interests of the country, the interests of the Congo, and that I have no intention of exploiting the personal hardships I have suffered, all the injustices of which I was a victim, so as to damage future relations between the Congo and Belgium."

My Country, Africa

(excerpt)

Andrée Blouin

The child of a forty-year-old French businessman and the fourteen-year-old daughter of an African chief, Andrée Blouin was born in 1921 in what she describes as "the French colony of Oubangui-Chari"—today's Central African Republic. At the age of three she was placed in an orphanage in Brazzaville, now the capital of the Republic of Congo, where the children of inconvenient interracial relationships were raised under the harsh rule of Catholic nuns. As a woman, she spoke passionately on behalf of African independence, and she was chosen by Patrice Lumumba as his first minister of protocol. Her autobiography, published in 1983, was praised by Jessica Mitford, Tillie Olsen, and Studs Terkel, but it has been largely forgotten. The passage below describes her departure from the orphanage at the age of seventeen, an early indication of the rebellious spirit that would rule her life.

Flight to a New Life

It was not enough that the nuns controlled every aspect of our existence, from our ignorant, frightened minds as children to our prudish, submissive ways as adolescents. The nuns aspired to manage our futures even after we left the orphanage, through the simple device of arranging our marriages.

The evil of our mixed blood, it was easy to see, should not be allowed to do further damage to the fabric of the colonialist society by mingling with that of either the blacks or the whites. The female of mixed blood was seen as a particular threat to the order of the system. It would not be good for black men to have access to lighter skinned women, it would make them uppity and harder to govern. If the white male had already proved vulnerable to the seductions of the black female, the *métisse* was even more dangerous to him. And what was to be done with the offspring of a white and a *métisse*? Why, one might not even be able to distinguish its having black blood. Clearly, such situations should not be allowed to develop.

The girls of mixed blood, then, should be married to men of mixed blood so that the confusion should go no further. The problem of their special appearance, their special psychology, and their potentially dangerous aspirations after being blessed with a youth in the care of the mission and learning a little French, must be carefully contained.

One kilometer away from us was an orphanage for boys of mixed blood that was run by the Mission of the Fathers of the Holy Ghost. It was with someone from this pool of outcasts like ourselves that we should be united. When the Fathers of the Mission had a young man whom it seemed advisable to marry off, they proposed his name to the nuns, who found a suitable candidate for him among their older girls. When the couple had been agreed upon by both orders, the day was set for the young people to meet.

This event took place in the Parlor of Saint Joseph and Saint Mary. The straight chairs were set in a row and there was a white doily lying on the table in the middle of the room. The girl was seated on one side of the Mother Superior and the young man, scrubbed clean, his pants in pleats sharp as an accordion, on the other.

The Mother Superior asked a few questions of each of them: how many times a week they went to mass or catechism, where their parents lived. Then, without further tiresome conversation, she stated the purpose of the occasion. To the girl she said, "My daughter, this is your fiancé. Now that you are 17 years old it is time for you to be married. This young man is a good Christian. It is up to you to be a good wife to him and a good mother to your family."

To the young man she offered the same genre of sound advice, then concluded "Shall we set the marriage date three months from now?"

Usually the young girl was so terrified by the event that she could hardly raise her eyes to look at this phenomenon, a young male, the man with whom the rest of her life was to be entwined. And avid though she was to stare at him—such an uncommon sight were young men in our lives—she sometimes became engaged hardly knowing what her proposed husband looked like. If the girl was lucky, she might see her young man on two more occasions before they were wed, although always in the parlor, under the vigilant eye of the Mother Superior.

During the months that followed, preparations were made for the marriage; the older girls helped the betrothed to sew what was ostentatiously referred to as "the trousseau of the bride." It was traditional that the young man should buy some cloth for his fiancée; from this she made an embroidered table cloth and napkins. He also bought the fabric for her wedding dress, which she made herself. A small suitcase with some night gowns, dish cloths, and sheets was considered a fine trousseau. The initials of the couple were elaborately embroidered on all the household linens, in imitation of the haughtiest bourgeois customs.

Uniting these two like aberrations of the species, however, did not provide all the necessary safeguards against their potential for disrupting the order of things. Their presence, as a couple, a kind of third species in this black and white society, tended to present questions without comfortable answers. Obviously, the best thing would be to keep this third species together and removed, for the most part, from the rest of the system.

This, it was decided, could be done by creating a special village for them. The French government had turned over a large piece of undeveloped land at some distance from Brazzaville to the Mission of the Fathers of the Holy Ghost. There, in the middle of a wasteland of tall coarse grass and a few trees, the fathers made a clearing and constructed, as a beginning, four small houses. The clearing was connected with the town by one lonely footpath. This place was known as the village of Saint Firmin, after Monseignor Firmin Guichard, whose diabolical plan it was to keep the couples of mixed blood under the surveillance of the Catholic missions forever.

I was about ten years old when I first saw a marriage of this kind, arranged through the machinations of the holy orders. After the ceremony we girls were taken to see "the house of happiness" where the young couple was to live. It was an ugly brick building of two rooms and a roof of corrugated iron. I found the whole place repellent and shuddered to think of those young people, sequestered in that solitude. Even when they had left the orphanage and were ready to found their own families, still they were not free.

I swore that this would not be my fate. I would choose my own husband and make a home only with love. In the years that followed I saw several more of these made-to-order marriages of the missions and each of them only served to strengthen my resolve. When we visited the village, the women looked miserable. They always had their eyes down in front of their husbands. Perhaps they looked at each other when we were not there, but it seemed to me that they were just enduring that wretched life.

One evening when I was 15 years old the Mother Superior called me to her. "A young man is asking to marry you," she announced. "You should be very pleased. He has heard about you and has decided that it is you and no other that he wishes for his wife."

"But Mother," I answered, "I'm too young. I don't want to be married."

"You are quite right," said the Mother Superior smoothly. "And that is why the arrangement is perfect. This young man is going to Chad as a veterinarian aid, but before he leaves he wants to become engaged. You have only to promise to wait for him for four years. Then you will be 19, which will be quite suitable."

I listened, appalled, as she spoke of this young man with the brilliant future for whom I had only to wait and pray for four years. "You are very fortunate because this young man is of an exemplary character. It seems that he is a good worker and extremely pious. He goes to mass faithfully not only on Sundays but on days of the week, too. His name is Luc Pacoteaux," she added, as if that should complete all I could possibly want to know about my future husband. Mother Superior's tones, her gestures, had the final air of a business well concluded. At last she paused for the meek "Yes, Mother" that was customary and would seal the affair.

"I am sorry, Mother, but my answer is no," I said firmly. "I cannot become engaged to him."

"What do you mean 'no'?" Mother Superior lifted her chin indignantly. "You have here an honorable offer of marriage. Of course you will accept it."

"I do not want to become engaged to this man. I don't want to become engaged at all."

"My child, you know nothing about life. Such an opportunity may never come again. Think how you would feel if you were never to be married, never to have children. It would be abnormal!"

"Perhaps my life will be abnormal, but I cannot agree to this engagement."

Mother Superior was extremely provoked by my attitude and made every effort to persuade me that I should accept. But I would not. I was to have a number of other offers of marriage during the succeeding years which I rejected in the same way. I had seen how unhappy these forced unions were, and I resolved not to let the nuns bully me into one of them.

After all these years with the nuns I was convinced that they were the last to know or care where my real happiness lay. I had no idea what the future of a *métisse* like myself should be, no real image of what to hope for, or aspire to. But the methods of the nuns, from what I knew of them, should be no part of it.

I was determined to forge my own future, however good or bad that might turn out to be.

By 1938 my life with the nuns had become intolerable. At 17, more than ever I was of a proud, combative temperament. I was considered the rebel of the institution, the likely source of whatever disciplinary problems arose. The only fate in sight for me was an arranged marriage. I was afraid I might not be able to resist the nuns' intrigues indefinitely. Whatever the price, I decided, I must get away from the orphanage. I made plans to escape. I discussed my plans with my two best friends, Louisa and Madeleine, who were also unhappy enough, I thought, to make the break with me. Louisa was the oldest, she knew that she could not hold out against a forced marriage much longer and often cried in dread of this. Madeleine—she was number 19 at the orphanage and had been deposited there just shortly before me—I had really hated when we were younger. It was she who taunted me, wearing my father's dress and shoes. But later we made it up, and I knew that, like me, she wanted desperately to flee. The three of us agreed to make the unheard of break together.

Mother Germaine, we learned, was to return to the mother house in Europe in two weeks. Even the prospect of relief offered by getting rid of her, the cause of so much of our misery, did not change our plans. We decided, in fact, to use her departure to help us in our escape, to profit by the confusion that this extraordinary event would create. After all those years of grief under her, at last Mother Germaine would be useful to us.

Permission was given for all the girls to go to the train station and see Mother Germaine off. This was already a great concession and a change in our routine. We knew it was that day or never. It was impossible to escape during the night when everyone was asleep as the windows of the bedroom were barred and the bedroom doors were locked by the guardian nuns who hung the keys on a board in their room. The gate of the orphanage was kept heavily locked. We would have to go over the walls that had kept us prisoners so long.

The day of the departure was one of great turmoil and emotion. The girls were crying—it was weeping for the devil, but even a change for good can provoke a sense of malaise, loss—and wailing. "She's leaving, she's leaving!" Mother Germaine was embracing everyone. A very special atmosphere existed. Madeleine, Louisa, and I acted out our roles and wailed with the rest.

Profiting by the license and disorder of the day, as soon as we got back from the train station the three of us slipped out of the building and into the garden. We had already hidden the little bundles of personal things that we wanted to take with us among the branches of the thorny lemon trees. Twilight comes early and quickly in the tropics and after seven o'clock it was already dark. In the garden I led the way, following paths that, after 14 years, I knew all too well. I squeezed my friends' hands hard; I knew by their trembling that they were frightened to death. We found our little bundles of possessions, as planned, but we could not go over the wall there because the police station, with officers on guard outside in little huts of straw, was directly on the other side. Behind the kitchen was a guava tree that leaned over the wall toward the Street of Paradise. Feeling for branches in the eerie gloom, I climbed and they followed. We lowered ourselves onto the wall. The bottle shards along its top immediately cut our hands and feet. We began to bleed.

I looked down into the street for a good place to jump. There were no street lights or cars, so we had only to be sure that no one was walking past. It was totally black below and the wall seemed fearfully high. Behind us was the detested garden, before us the unknown.

Squatting there on the top of the wall, the broken glass slashing our feet, we steeled ourselves for the jump. Madeleine and Louisa began to cry.

"It's too high," Madeleine whimpered. "I'm scared. We can't do it."

"We'll be killed," sobbed Louisa. "I'm going back."

I had no alternative. Ignoring their protests, I pushed Madeleine, then Louisa, and jumped after them. We landed on the hard dirt below without being too badly hurt. Limping and leaving bloody traces behind us, we took our first steps toward freedom at last.

Louisa had told us we could find shelter at the home of her cousin, Martha, who herself had been raised at the orphanage and married through the good offices of the Mother Superior. However, Martha and her husband had managed to escape being confined in Saint Firmin, and lived in a little house in the native village of Poto-Poto.

I did not think for a moment of turning to my father whom I had not seen since his half-hour visit when I was eight years old. As a matter of form, and to salve their consciences, the nuns required that each girl write one carefully supervised letter a year to her white father. This I faithfully did. During my 14 years in the orphanage I had received one, perhaps two letters in return. My ideas about life outside the orphanage therefore did not in any way involve my unknown father who, I could only suppose, would be furious at my running away. Since he had placed me there, mustn't he support its principles?

Martha received us with kindness and that first night I slept not under a sheet but an immense, colorful African cloth. It seemed wonderful to me. At last I was to know my Africa! The next day, we had to remain in hiding, although we were longing to go out and see the world. We knew that the police, summoned by the Mother Superior, would be looking everywhere for us. To make a clean break with our past of submission and obedience, we cut our hair. My hair was very long, down to my hips, like a skirt. We didn't have a razor blade so we did the job with a piece of broken bottle, badly. The fashion then, according to the gravure magazines we had seen, was to wear one's hair short and combed straight back, behind one's ears. We shaved the back of our necks with broken glass, too. It was frightfully done, but it was proof of our freedom, an irrevocable step of defiance. For years we had worn our hair always in the same way, parted in the middle, the sides plastered down, and a flat chignon in back; it had been a torment to us. Now our hair looked terrible, raggedly short as it was, but at least we were no longer marked by its style as belonging to the orphanage.

All day we remained indoors; in the evening we could bear the confinement no longer. We went walking in the quarter, lit only by the flickering lights of the little cooking fires, or a kerosene lantern, where a family was gathered on a mat in the yard. Each hut was set off in its own yard with a tiny, rickety, imperialistic fence. Even in this poverty there was a high sense of "This is mine, poor as it is, let no one intrude on my poverty!" As the houses did not have kitchens, the cooking was done on wood fires outside. Around us we could hear people doing their chores, laughing and talking in the warm evening air. It was so different from the orphanage where everything was foreseen, regimented, stale, and sad! Here, we were seeing real life at last.

The sight of a *métisse* always aroused comment and questions; three *métisses* could not go unnoticed. The next day a group of police encircled Martha's house, and without bothering to ascertain if we would come out peaceably, broke down the door. We three girls were arrested and led off like criminals to the city hall of Brazzaville.

It was the mayor, himself, who questioned us. "I want the truth from you, my children. Why did you run away from the orphanage?"

The most important man in Brazzaville was calling us to account. Madeleine and Louisa were tongue-tied, shaking with fear. I had to answer for the three of us.

"Sir, we couldn't bear to stay there anymore. We were too unhappy." This was my chance. Unsparingly I described the torments, the humiliations that comprised our lives. I pointed out the ragged dresses we were wearing that, in fact, were a disgrace. I bared one shoulder and showed him the lashes from a whipping I had received earlier. "Worst of all," I pled, "they're always telling us that we will go to hell because we have inherited our father's sinfulness and our mother's primitive nature. How can we live in such misery?"

The mayor listened with an intent air. I brought out the ultimate proof of our desperation. "We are determined not to return to the orphanage, sir. If you send us back—" Here I paused for the full effect, "we have taken an oath. Each of us will kill herself."

A strange expression passed over the mayor's face. Later I was to learn that he had fathered a son by a black woman and had given this boy to the Fathers of the Holy Ghost to raise.

An hour later the Father Superior of the Mission, looking stern, and the Mother Superior of the Convent, pale and furious, arrived at the city hall at the request of the mayor, to deliberate our case.

"I have decided that these girls are not to return to the orphanage," the mayor informed them. "The problem is, they are still young. Where are they to go? Who can we have take care of them?"

For Madeleine and Louisa the solution was not difficult as they had black relatives in Brazzaville to whom they could be entrusted. For me it was a problem, as I had no one. I waited for endless minutes in the anteroom while they discussed my case.

As I reentered the mayor's office I heard the Mother Superior, in silky tones of persuasion say "But Mister Mayor, Andrée cannot be removed from our boarding school. Her father, who is very interested in her, insists that we keep her." After this last outrage she was not going to let me go, like that!

It was a drawn battle between two deeply antipathetic natures. Mother Superior was more experienced than I, and had her reputation to defend, but the cause was mine. I saw that to win it I would have to be very convincing indeed. The theatrics into which I threw myself had 14 years of anguish behind them, to add to their effects.

"Oh, Mother," I wept, "Listen to me! I beg you . . . I'm young! I have a right to live! If you force me to return to the orphanage you are condemning me to death!" Tears streamed down my face, I wrung my hands. "The responsibility for my death will be yours!" To underline the effect I was achieving, I added solemnly, in spite of my sobs, "I have sworn it before, and I swear it again, now, before all of you, that if I am returned to that place, I will kill myself." I was in fact prepared to do just that.

The mayor's face twitched with consternation. Again he asked me to leave his office and again they conferred.

Finally, Madeleine, Louisa, and I were once more before our judges, awaiting the verdict.

"You will go to the homes of your relatives here in Brazzaville, as we discussed, Madeleine and Louisa. As for you, Andrée," the mayor continued while the Mother Superior looked coldly on, "for the moment you will stay with Louisa's family. I am going to write to your father and tell him what has happened. We shall wait for his reply before we make a final decision on what to do with you. I will let you know when I have received his instructions."

It was necessary to add a sweetener for the holy orders. "But now that you girls are to live on the outside, you must promise to go to mass every Sunday, and to make confession and take communion."

We agreed to this, hardly able to believe what had happened. Never before had we counted for anything. Now we had been heard by no less a personage than the mayor, the man whom other whites obeyed. We were not behind bars, we were not whipped, we were hardly reprimanded. Life outside was too extraordinary! Dazed, alternately laughing and crying with emotion, I went home with Louisa.

Life in Poto-Poto after the orphanage was a rebirth for me. At last I was to live something different from that hell. There was not enough oxygen in the air for me to cram into my lungs with my new freedom, this freedom that I had wrenched away for myself. With a passionate interest I examined everything around me. In the evening I walked the streets, looking at the little fires in the yards where the mamas were cooking the meal in their blackened pots. The odors from those pots were delicious. Each woman had her own pot; that, to me, was freedom. There was a warmth, a human presence in the smoke of those little fires, those good foods being cooked, and in the voices of the people, at the close of day. For me those sounds and smells were a concert of joy, the first real joy of my life, as a conscious being. Finally. I walked the blocks, looking into the little yards, listening to the talk, the laughter, overwhelmed by my feelings. To think that for 14 years I had been dying of hunger while everyone else ate! I did not know what was in the pots, their contents sometimes were no doubt poor. Still, they boiled; over those fires something was being prepared for dinner. What simplicity, and yet what splendor. Yes, I have seen it—splendor in the poorest huts.

I threw myself into learning about African life. After 14 years behind the walls with shards of glass my vision of life was that all was fabulous. I looked at the huts of straw, at the houses made of flattened kerosene cans, and found them all wonderful. When I saw a house with a corrugated iron roof on it (although it was idiotic in that hot sun, it was considered very chic) I thought "How well they must eat in that house!" When I saw a man riding a bicycle I thought "How marvellous life must be for him!"

A trip to the market of Poto-Poto was for me an extraordinary adventure. With my eyes I devoured all that I looked at; I wanted everything I saw. My stomach, as always, was raw with hunger. But I almost forgot it in looking at the bunches of bananas heaped up, piles of mangoes, guavas, or peanuts. Pineapples! I hadn't know such marvels existed on earth. Even though I couldn't have them, just to feast my eyes on them, just to know that those wonderful things were there: it was fabulous, fabulous, fabulous.

I watched people buying live chickens and dazzling slabs of meat. There were fish 20 times as big as a sardine! Piles of rice, millet, beans, dried red peppers, onions, garlic. Anyone could walk by and look at them, smell them, watch the mamas handle them and make their purchases. The Portuguese merchants' shops presented me with a delirium of new images: stacks of enamel cups and dishes, pots and basins. European articles: soap wrapped in green paper with the name Palmolive printed on it. Boxes of sugar, one of them opened to show the hard little cubes inside. Needles! Ten of them in a package of black paper. Pins! Razor blades! Scissors! All these things were astonishing to me in proportion to what I had known, my own hunger, my own need.

I particularly liked to watch the food vendors, and especially the mamas who prepared and sold *mikate*. This is what the French call a *beignet*, a banana fritter, and it is quite simply one of the most delicious things in the world. The patties were made the night before. Then early in the morning the women took their place on a street corner, and seated on a little three-legged stool in front of a boiling pot of oil, they fried the fritters, as they were needed, for passers-by, all day long.

For a young girl to whom hunger was a way of life, the smell was maddening. Fascinated, without any hope of such a treat for myself, I would stand nearby, just to smell that wonderful smell and to watch the woman as she made her calm, methodical gestures. She would drop the fritter into the pot of oil, then retrieve it a moment later and lay it on a clean green leaf. With a few words she would hand the *mikate* to her customer and receive her payment, which she tucked into the fold of her *pagne*. I found this marvellous to watch. Once a kind mama beckoned me to her and gave me one to eat. I nearly swooned with pleasure.

How rich these people are, I thought. They have so much food, they even have enough left over, to sell. They can even give me a sample. For me it was a sign of opulence. I thought "Now I can have the joy of living in the midst of all this! If I work, then I can become a part of such things, this too can be mine." It gave me the exhilarating hope that, with hard work I, too, could some day aspire to such a sumptuous life.

"Hollywood, Pirated Videos, and Child Soldiers"

Emmanuel Dongala

Emmanuel Dongala, born in 1941, was the dean of Marien Ngouabi University in Brazzaville when war broke out in 1997, causing him to leave the country. A chemist by profession, he holds a chair in natural sciences at Bard College at Simon's Rock. The author of novels including Little Boys Come from the Stars *and* Johnny Mad Dog, *Dongala is on the advisory board of* Warscapes *magazine, where this essay first appeared.*

It is one thing to be prepared intellectually for violence, but it is quite another to experience the real thing in the form of a gun pointed at your head or the cutting edge of a machete being wielded before your eyes. You never really know how you will behave in such circumstances. You may act courageously, or you may act cowardly. It is really a roll of the dice.

Since the 1990s, my work as a writer has led me to study violence in Africa in all its forms. Those who have read my novels can testify to this. I have always been a social activist, and I have written many articles criticizing the passivity and cowardice of many of my intellectual peers who have stood by silently in the face of political corruption and the violation of human rights in their countries. I have always seen myself on the side of the weak and the oppressed, ready to pounce on the offender and save the victim whenever I witness an injustice or whenever I see a person brutalized. There was never any doubt in my mind that had I lived in Nazi Germany, I would have been among the Righteous, those heroic men and women who protected the persecuted. And by dint of creating and manipulating characters in novels, I sincerely believed that I was better than my fellow humans, until, one morning in October 1997 in Brazzaville, Congo, before a makeshift roadblock, everything changed.

The roadblock barring the street in front of us was merely a long bamboo pole with each end sitting on an old oil barrel. A simple kick could have sent it flying and yet none of us was so brave. We were a group of about thirty, all living in the same area, who decided to leave because the fighting between the different militias, the extortions, and the looting had transformed the city into a hell of blood and fire. To avoid being spotted, we took small back streets, away from the center where the fighting was fiercest. After forty-five minutes or so of silent walking, anxious and fearful of stray bullets, we were relieved to see wooden shacks with corrugated iron roofs, typical of the shanties built by rural people who had left the countryside in the hope of making a living in the city but having no place to go ended up living on its edge. This meant that we had finally reached the periphery. Salvation was at hand. We began to relax. One more turn and we would be out of the city.

It was only after we took the turn that we saw the roadblock. A dozen kids were in charge of it. The oldest was probably no more than 18, and he was the only one who wore a helmet. He was clearly the boss. Brandishing Kalashnikovs and dressed in the most bizarre ways with sunglasses, wigs, and gris-gris around their arms or their necks, some of the child soldiers had darkened their faces with coal or ashes. Three bodies, including that of a woman, were lying next to one of the barrels. Some of our group tried to run away in panic, but gunshots (fortunately, above our heads), yelling and warnings not to move froze them on the spot. Afraid of making any movement which could be misinterpreted, I was scared stiff, nervously watching these trigger-happy kids. And yet we were more than twice their number!

Suddenly and brutally, they pulled a man from our ranks and two or three of these youngsters started hitting him. Numbed by fear, my brain did not register the incident which led to that poor man's beating. None of us dared to say a word, much less come to his aid. It was one thing for the others in our group not to say anything, but I knew that man very well! He was my next door neighbor, a high school teacher for whom I was a role model. He had always admired the professor and writer I was, often speaking of me as *the* epitome of the honest, upright and courageous intellectual compared to other Congolese intellectuals who had betrayed their principles and had sold their souls for money or had become political prostitutes. Yet there I was, indignant, imperceptibly clenching my fists, but incapable of moving or looking away, my body paralyzed by the horror of this terrible scene.

All of a sudden, unexpectedly, a shrill scream pierced the air: the man's wife broke away from us and futilely hurled herself, not against the militia men, but upon her husband in order to protect him with her body. In a spectacular role reversal, it was the woman who was trying to protect her man. One of the militia kids, taken by surprise, started kicking her. She screamed in pain but remained firmly stretched across her husband's body. Another aimed his gun, threatening to kill her. He did not shoot, though; instead, laughing coarsely and uttering obscenities, they started pulling off her clothes in order to humiliate her—and believe me, except for rape, there is nothing more humiliating for a woman than being stripped naked in front of her children and a bunch of gazing onlookers. It was unbearable. "Do something, Emmanuel," I silently repeated several times to myself and yet, the valiant defender of the weak and the down-trodden, the self-righteous writer, crippled with fear, was still looking the other way in order not to see. Was it because I was a coward or was it because I wanted to protect the group from any retaliation?

Just the previous week, at the beginning of the conflict, a friend of mine trying to get back home from work was caught up in such a road-block. The kids who manned it demanded a 100 francs ransom to let any-one through. While he stood in line waiting his turn, he watched a relatively young man, who obviously did not have enough money, as he counted and recounted the change he had in his pocket and each time came up short by 20 francs. When the kids pulled him out of the line and started roughing him up with the butts of their guns, one of my friend's colleagues could not stand it any more and said, "I have 20 francs. I would like to pay for him." "Shut up, you shit head," yelled one of the kids, abruptly turning towards him. "It is *his* money we want, not yours. Who do you think you are?" And bang, the man was dead!

Was he courageous or foolhardy? Neither, probably. He was perhaps instinctively driven into action by this quality embedded in our DNA, human compassion. If these kids cannot understand such a simple and basic concept as human compassion, what could I have done for this woman and her man which would not in turn endanger the other people in our group? Or was I only trying to rationalize my unworthy behavior?

Even today, I still do not want to confront this question; rather, I pre-fer to keep myself in a comfortable safety zone by not seeking an answer. And not knowing the answer is the only way I can still preserve a tad of my self-esteem.

Suddenly, the boss, the boy with the olive-green metal helmet, yelled: "Hey, Chuck Norris, bring me a grenade!" "Yes, chief, I am coming," came a voice from a hut on the side of the road, probably where the weapons were stocked. I was on the verge of nervous laughter when I saw a kid no taller than the Kalashnikov he was carrying come out with the grenade. It was surreal: here we were, in a back street of a miserable neighborhood of a city in strife in Equatorial Africa; and a young boy had chosen the name of an American actor of B movies as his nom de guerre. Where in the world had he ever heard of Chuck Norris?

The phenomenon of child soldiers in Africa has been so well documented by many reports of international organizations, documentary films, scholarly publications and novels that there is no new information for me to give. It is very difficult to know the exact number of child soldiers but as of 2010, it was estimated that there were about 300,000 in the world, a "child soldier" being defined as an enrolled child under age 18. Unfortunately as so often, Africa holds the record with about 120,000 of them. What I would like to point out here is that most of these studies concern child soldiers who were recruited by force or who chose to enroll because they had no alternative means of survival.

The case of the Republic of Congo, a.k.a. Congo-Brazzaville, is somewhat different. In 1997–1998, a fratricidal war erupted after disputed elections. Both sides in the conflict recruited and used child soldiers. These children were in no way kidnapped or coerced to join the combatants. Their histories were very different from the well documented ones of Uganda, Sierra Leone or Liberia where children were forced to enroll and where, after systematic brainwashing, they were brought back to their villages to commit unforgivable crimes like killing a family member or raping their grandmother, mother, or sister. The aim of these ritual killings and rapes was to break all links between the child soldiers and their villages or their clans, thus making them completely dependent on the warlords and more easily manipulated. As for the girl soldiers, they had the extra burden of being sexual objects.

In Congo, by contrast, these kids joined voluntarily, often with enthusiasm. But even though they joined the fighting groups along ethnic lines, this did not mean that they were less cruel towards their own kin than those in Liberia or Sierra Leone who were coerced into fighting.

It was only after the shock of that unforgettable 1997 October morning that I realized that I should not have been at all surprised by the fact that that kid had called himself Chuck Norris and had joined a group of child soldiers.

In cities like Brazzaville or Kinshasa where movie theaters no longer exist, enterprising young men equipped with TVs, VCRs or DVD players earn their living by projecting pirated films in simply constructed spaces. Often they create these spaces in their own bedrooms or living rooms by pushing a bed here or a table there against the wall, and then adding a couple of benches. Or when they do not have their own rooms they improvise a projection room. With some poles, they delimit a rectangular area in the yard of the lot where they live and encircle it with corrugated iron or old jute sacks called "nguiri" which are sacks used to carry cassava flour. To have the darkness necessary for projection, they top the room with a tarpaulin or black plastic sheets. Every time rain threatens, the session is suspended, the electronic equipment promptly disconnected and brought to safety. They are geniuses at fixing their equipment. For example, for continuity of business in a city where electricity is as iffy as winning the lottery, they have adapted their equipment so that it runs on car batteries.

To advertise the films, they photocopy the illustrations and blurbs written on the cover of the DVD or videocassette boxes and post the images on walls. The matinee sessions for children cost 25 CFA francs (about ten cents), and those prices are doubled or tripled for what they call "adult" movies, a code word for porn films. It goes without saying that there is no selection—everything they can put their hands on in this wild market is good. A pirated DVD costs only five thousand francs (about $9.00) while the original fetches more than double that price.

I once asked a young boy to write down for me the titles of the projected films screened over the course of a month. As expected, the most popular ones were violent action and karate films, followed by Bollywood films from India. It is only very recently that live broadcasts of European football championship matches have become most popular. Inexpensive Nigerian video films, Nollywood films as they are known, have also made their appearance on the market. Names like Schwarzenegger, Stallone, Van Damme, Jackie Chan, Chuck Norris were household names. This is quite incredible when you realize that these kids could not name a single Congolese government minister! Only some star soccer players were able to compete with these Hollywood names.

These kids do not know that films are "made." For them, this "imaginary" violence they see in movies has the same reality as the violence in the real world which they watch on the international satellite televisions one can get these days in any big African city. They watch this violence from Kosovo, Rwanda, Iraq, Afghanistan, or Sierra Leone almost in real time, without any mediation or contextual explanation. They internalize even more violence when they go to what are called "casinos" in Brazzaville, places with PlayStations where they play video games such as "Bloody Roar" or "Street Fighter" or "God of War" or "Tekken." With these games, where they interact physically with the machine, they have the feeling that they are also participating physically in the actions of their heroes.

This inability to differentiate between reality and fantasy makes these children redoubtable fighters. They have no real consciousness of what they are doing; they have no sense of danger. They can be cruel without having any idea of the suffering they are inflicting. I suspect that for them there is not much difference between real killing and killing on video.

To all the preceding factors, one has to add their African cultural background, the belief in magic, which leads them to believe that their charms, amulets, and the potions they are made to drink by their recruiters make them invisible, invincible, and invulnerable to bullets— that they can fly like birds if ever they are cornered.

Now, I am not so naïve as to believe that these films and these video games with their violence are the sole reasons that lead these kids voluntarily to become child soldiers. It is rather that, when conflicts erupt and the State fails as it did in Congo, these children, lacking guidance, are naturally drawn to where the action is and they instinctively mimic their heroes. It is their chance to live for real what they have been living vicariously through their imaginations. A very good example of this is that during the conflict in Congo, whole neighborhoods in the capital city of Brazzaville were renamed Sarajevo, Kosovo, Beyrouth or Koweit; fighters took Rambo, Ninja, Cobra, Saddam as noms de guerre. Though their parents' generation dreamed of big luxurious cars, large houses with swimming pools and bundles of greenback dollars when they thought of America, these children now dream of Hollywood or PlayStation heroes.

And that's not all. One has to add the influence of one of the characteristics of African political culture since independence in the 1960s, the cult of the "strong man." Kwame Nkrumah, Sekou Toure, Robert Mugabe, Mobutu Sese Seko, all of them were "strong men." Even today, with few exceptions, behind the smokescreen of model constitutions which guarantee democratic liberties and human rights, the "strong man" still exists. He has the absolute power to nominate and repudiate anyone he wants, to use state violence against his opponents, to dispose of the country's finances as he pleases with no accountability whatsoever, and to change the constitution as it suits him. Just look at Chad, Cameroon, Congo, Zimbabwe and Niger. This quasi-absolute power does not come from ballots but from bullets, and is caricatured by the posse that escorts the President any time he moves through the city. This "strong man" culture has so completely permeated all society that, for instance in Brazzaville, neither a minister nor a high ranking military officer stops at a red light, thus showing that they have power, since only common people obey the rules of law.

Thus, for the urban youth from whom are recruited the majority of child soldiers in Congo, the epitome of the respected and feared person is *that* kind of politician. Therefore when the state no longer exists and chaos takes its place, to possess a weapon is the shortest road to respect and power. Since all their lives they have learned that power, brutal and pitiless, is the "normal" way of getting what one wants, be it money, girls, cars, DVDs, or TV, nothing is more natural than to become a Rambo or a Chuck Norris in order to transform one's fantasies into reality.

Once fighting ceases, the big challenge in the rehabilitation of these kids is to find a way to reorient their violent fantasies into positive, non-violent visions, to make them understand, for example, that the magic of education is mightier than that of a gris-gris or of an amulet, and that the real power of a gun is when you use it to protect a human life.

All things considered, we got out of our situation rather cheaply. After threatening to blow us up with the grenade brought by Chuck Norris, the head of the soldiers was probably satisfied by what he looted from us, including a Yankee baseball cap worn by one of the children in our group. He let us go. He also let go the couple they had beaten up so badly for no apparent reason. The woman was transformed in my eyes; she radiated a tranquil dignity. She had become a lesson in courage for me. I avoided her eyes when, still clutching the arm of the man she protected, she walked past me. After glancing obliquely at the three bodies still lying next to the oil barrel, I put one foot in front of me, then the other, and started walking away.

Machete Season

(excerpt)

Jean-Baptiste Murangira, as told to Jean Hatzfeld

Jean-Baptiste Murangira was born in central Rwanda, attended secondary school, and became a census taker and local official. After losing these jobs, he returned to farming. At the time of the Rwandan genocide in 1994, Murangira was thirty-eight years old. He was among the killers who took part in the massacre of Tutsis in and around the district of Nyamata, south of Kigali. Many of the victims fled into the nearby papyrus swamps and were killed there. His own wife, a Tutsi woman, was spared.

Murangira was one of the gang of ten génocidaires *interviewed by the French reporter Jean Hatzfeld for the oral history* Machete Season, *which was published in 2003. Hatzfeld writes that Murangira was the first of his gang to be tried for murder. He pleaded guilty to several killings and was sentenced in 1997 to fifteen years in prison. In 2003, he was released and returned to his wife and land.*

[Translated from the French by Linda Coverdale.]

When you get right down to it, it is a gross exaggeration to say we organized ourselves up on the hills. The plane came down April 6. A very small number of local Hutus went straight for retaliation. But most waited four days in their houses and in the nearest *cabarets,* listening to the radio, watching Tutsis flee, chatting and joking without planning a thing.

On April 10 the burgomaster in a pressed suit and all the authorities gathered us together. They lectured us, they threatened in advance anyone who bungled the job, and the killings began without much planning. The only regulation was to keep going till the end, maintain a satisfactory pace, spare no one, and loot what we found. It was impossible to screw up.

We were on a path coming back from the marshes. Some youths searched the house of a gentleman named Ababanganyingabo. They frowned on him because this Hutu from Gisenyi was known to consort with Tutsis and might well lend them a hand. They discovered he had helped some Tutsis getaway their cows—behind his house, in a pen, I think. They surrounded the man and pinned him down helpless. Then I heard my name.

They called me out because they knew I was married to a Tutsi. The news about Ababanganyingabo's fix was spreading, people were waiting, all fired up because they had been killing. Someone said to the audience: "Jean-Baptiste, if you want to save the life of your wife Spéciose Mukandahunga, you have to cut this man right now. He is a cheater! Show us that you're not that kind." This person turned and ordered, "Bring me a blade." Me, I had chosen my wife for love of her beauty; she was tall and very considerate, she was fond of me, and I felt great pain to think of losing her.

The crowd had grown. I seized the machete, I struck a first blow. When I saw the blood bubble up, I jumped back a step. Someone blocked me from behind and shoved me forward by both elbows. I closed my eyes in the brouhaha and I delivered a second blow like the first. It was done, people approved, they were satisfied and moved away. I drew back. I went off to sit on the bench of a small *cabaret*, I picked up a drink, I never looked back in that unhappy direction. Afterward I learned that the man had kept moving for two long hours before finishing.

Later on we got used to killing without so much dodging around.

If you proved too green with the machete, you could find yourself deprived of rewards, to nudge you in the right direction. If you got laughed at one day, you did not take long to shape up. If you went home empty-handed, you might even be scolded by your wife or your children.

In any case, everybody killed in his own way. Someone who couldn't get used to polishing off his victim could just walk on or ask for help. He would find a supportive comrade behind him.

No colleague ever complained of being mistreated for his awkwardness. Mockery and taunts—they could happen, but harsh treatment, never.

The more we killed, the more greediness urged us on. Greediness—if left unpunished, it never lets you go. You could see it in our eyes bugged out by the killings. It was even dangersome. There were those who came back in bloodstained shirts, brandishing their machetes, shrieking like madmen, saying they wanted to grab everything. We had to calm them with drinks and soothing words. Because they could turn ugly for those around them.

No one was going to their fields anymore. Why dig in the dirt when we were harvesting without working, eating our fill without growing a thing? The only chore was to bury bananas in pits, out in abandoned banana groves, to allow the next batch of *urwagwa* to ferment. We became lazy. We did not bury the bodies—it was wasted effort—except, of course, if by bad luck a Tutsi was killed in his own field, which would bring a stench, dogs, and voracious animals.

At first killing was obligatory; afterward we got used to it. We became naturally cruel. We no longer needed encouragement or fines to kill, or even orders or advice. Discipline was relaxed because it wasn't necessary anymore.

I don't know anyone who was struck because he refused to kill. I know of one case of punishment by death, a special case, a woman. Some young people cut her to punish her husband, who had refused to kill. But she was in fact Tutsi. Afterward the husband took part without whining—in fact, he was one of the busiest in the marshes.

If one morning you felt worn out, you would offer to contribute with drink and then you went along the next day. You could also replace killing with other useful tasks, like preparing meals for the visiting *interahamwe,* or rounding up cows scattered in the bush, so they could be eaten. And when your bravery returned, you would take up the tool again and return to the swamps.

If the *inkotanyi* [derogatory name for Tutsis] had not taken over the country and put us to flight, we would have killed one another after the death of the last Tutsi—that's how hooked we were by the madness of dividing up their land. We could no longer stop ourselves from wielding the machete, it brought us so much profit.

It was clear that after our victory, life would be truly rearranged. The obedient ones would no longer obey the authorities as before, accepting poverty and riches the usual way. They had tasted comfort and overflowing plenty. They were sated with their own willfulness. They felt fat with new strength and insolence. They had cast off obedience and the inconveniences of poverty. Greed had corrupted us.

Evenings the gang would get together in a *cabaret,* in Nyarunazi or Kibungo, it depended. We might also go from one to the other. We ordered cans of Primus, we drank, and we fooled around to rest up from our day.

Some spent sleepless nights emptying bottles and became even wilder. Others went on home to rest after having an ordinary relaxing evening. Rowdies kept on slaughtering cows after the killings because they couldn't put down their machetes. So it wasn't possible to herd the cows for the future, and they had to be eaten on the spot.

Me, I went through those festivities with a pretend smile and a worried ear. I had posted a young watcher to make rounds about my house, but I stayed on the alert. The safety of my Tutsi wife tormented me, especially during the drinking sessions.

It is a country custom that women do not concern themselves with any bothersome task of cutting. The machete is for a man's work. This was as true for the farming as for the killing.

So during the killings, the women continued to prepare the meals in the morning, and during the rest of the day they went looting. They were storing up goods instead of crops, so they were not unhappy. They didn't complain because they knew that in any case the operation was intended to succeed completely. They dared not show any sign of disagreement with the men's brutality, not even the simple gesture of a mama's kindness.

In Ntarama I do not know of a single Hutu woman who hid away a little Tutsi child to save it from the massacre of its family. Not even a toddler wrapped in a cloth or a nursling unrecognizable to her neighbors because of its tender age. Not one woman on the whole hill cheated in the way of a rescue, not even for a short moment of trying.

During the killings, much jealousy spilled from the mouths of our women because of the constant talk about the Tutsi women's slender figures, their smooth skin thanks to drinking milk, and so on. When those envious women came upon a Tutsi searching for food in the forest, they called their neighbors to taunt her for crawling around that way all slovenly. Sometimes women shoved a neighbor to the bottom of the hill and threw her bodily into the waters of the Nyabarongo.

I know the case of a Hutu boy who fled into the marshes with the Tutsis. After two or three weeks they pointed out to him that he was Hutu and so could be saved. He left the marshes and was not attacked. He had spent so much time with Tutsis in his early childhood that he was a bit mixed up. His mind no longer knew how to draw the proper line between the ethnic groups. Afterward he did not get involved in the killings. That is the sole exception. The only able-bodied person not forced to raise the machete, even coming along behind. It was clear his mind was overwhelmed, and he was not penalized.

Extreme agonies were worked on important people, well-known businessmen. It was to punish them for past misdeeds or make them cough up their hidden savings. Also torments were done to people with whom there had been a stubborn grievance—a bargain that had not been settled or bad blood over some trampling by cows, for example. But not often. No orders were given about this. The bosses would say, "Kill, and fast, that's all. There's no point in taking your time."

In Congo, on the way back, I knew some perpetrators who were driven by madness into Lake Kivu. Fright plunged them into an engulfing grave. They thought death would welcome them more mercifully in the waters than on the hills. Horrible threats were flying in all directions as the return drew close. Terror gave them detailed promises of a wretched death, since they had themselves cut a great many in a vicious way. But they were the exceptions.

Only dogs and wild beasts ventured into the church and its slaughterhouse stench. When we walked alongside the parish wall to go to Kanzenze or down into the marshes, that stink turned us even farther away from reading the gospels.

Truly, the times no longer wanted us to worry about God, and we went along. Deep down we knew that Christ was not on our side in this situation, but since He was not saying anything through the priests' mouths, that suited us.

We could not ask time to give us a firm deadline for such a long program. Time seemed to smile on us, desiring only that we no longer worry about God. So we obeyed, and we kept on killing, aiming for the last one. Even though the work went on and on because of the looting and the fatigues of drinking, we never doubted, since no one could stop the work. But God slipped in among the killings to hurry along the *inkotanyi*. In the end God did not accept a definitive conclusion—that's the lesson.

I often dream I am walking in freedom on the road to Ntarama. I go along, among the familiar trees. I feel refreshed and at ease, and I am content. I wake up full of nostalgia on my pallet.

Other nights dreaming tips into calamity. I see again the people I killed with my own hand. When that happens, every awful detail of blood and terror comes back: the mud, the heat of the chase, the colleagues. . . . Only the cries are missing. These are silent killings, which seem slow but are as dreadful as before. My dreams in prison are of various kinds, sometimes somber, sometimes calm; perhaps they flow from the various situations of my life here, whether I am sick or in good health. Who can tell if they will change when I get out? My hope is they'll forget about me.

All the prisoners live unhappily since the genocide. Many complain about their fate, but not to the point of turning to a deadly remedy. I know of no one driven by remorse or nightmares to extreme measures. I know of no case of suicide in prison during my seven years here. There are a dozen cases of people eating filth, tearing their clothes, writhing on the ground, or screaming in waking dreams—but raving enough to take their own lives, never.

When Habyiramana's republic was forced to become a multiparty state, all the different Hutu parties recruited militias, at first to protect themselves from one another, because things were really hot among the Hutu extremists, and then to focus on the Tutsis.

The *interahamwe* were the most visible: they sang in the meetings, paraded in the streets, got together for exercise workouts at the cultural center. They received food, drinks, and little gifts of money from shopkeepers.

They were preparing for small massacres of Tutsis, the way we had been doing them since 1959—punishment massacres, caused by envy, or the *inkotanyi*, or revenge, or greed for Tutsi cows and plots of land. But the removal of all Tutsis—that they thought of only after the plane crash.

Through my job as the municipal census taker, I was well acquainted with the councilor at Ntarama, and I know he did not use the word *genocide* before it began, not even in his innermost thoughts. The higher-ups in Kigali had planned it all behind blank faces.

I feel more at peace since I began to speak. After I have endured my punishment, I see nothing to prevent me from returning to my wife, my place in society, my six children, even if they have grown up without me and no longer recognize me. I must point out something, however: there is now a crack in my life. I don't know about the others. I don't know if it's because of my Tutsi wife. But I do know that the clemency of justice or the compassion of the stricken families can never fix this crack. Even the resurrection of the victims might not fix it. Perhaps not even my death will fix it.

In prison most inmates reject forgiveness. They say, "I apologized and I am still in prison. So what use is it, besides pleasing the authorities?" Or else they keep saying, "Look at that man. He asked forgiveness of everyone at his trial, and he still got a heavy sentence. Forgiveness, for us, from now on it's a waste of time." That is why they prefer to stand fast on their old opinions.

But I am very concerned with forgiveness. And I am certain of being forgiven, because I confessed, because I am convinced of my offense and determined to live in the right way, like before. If someone who has suffered cannot forgive me at first, time will help this person manage it on a better occasion. Forgiveness will help us to forget together, even though in both camps each person may hide away memories of deepest pain and sorrow.

Hutus have always reproached Tutsis for their great height and for trying to use this to rule. Time has never dried up that bitterness. In Nyamata, as I told you, people said that Tutsi women seemed too slender to stay on our hills, that their skin was smooth from their secret drinking of milk, that their fingers were too delicate to grab a hoe, and all that foolishness.

In truth, Hutus noticed none of that hearsay in the Tutsi women of their neighborhood, who bent their backs beside the Hutu wives and lugged water home the same way they did. Yet Hutus enjoyed repeating such common talk. They would also murmur that a Hutu with a Tutsi wife, like me, was trying to show off.

They took pleasure in spreading the most unlikely rubbish so as to drive a thin wedge of discord between the two ethnic groups. The important thing was to keep a distance between them and try to aggravate the situation. For example, on the first day of school the teacher had to call out the background of every pupil, so that the Tutsis would feel timid about taking their seats in a class of Hutus.

The whole time the killings went on, I never heard the word *genocide*. It reached our ears only through the voices of international reporters and humanitarian officials, first on the road into exile—but we did not know what the word meant—and then in the camps in Congo.

This is a truth: among ourselves, we never said that word. Many did not even know the meaning of *genocide*. It was of no use. And yet if we were getting up every morning to go hunting, even when we were tired or had other work left unfinished, it was certainly because we thought we had to kill them all. People knew what job they were doing without needing to name it.

After the plane crash, we talked from group to group about wiping out the Tutsis. But to me, the words didn't ring true, I was thinking only about doing some killing soon. The evening of the massacre in the church, the seriousness of it overturned everything: I understood that words and deeds had come together. The deeds now promised to be definitive, and the words useless.

You could feel uneasy about the activity waiting for you in the marshes. But you whispered, This job is going to be completely finished, and if I don't contribute my share, I will seem a defeatist afterward, and that's too penalizing. So you followed close on your colleagues' heels, you did it without a word, and after a while you got used to it and you joked around like before. But speaking true words about that situation, that is risky no matter what.

"New World Alphabet"
Dagmawi Woubshet

Born in Addis Ababa in 1976, Dagmawi Woubshet is a professor of English at Cornell University. He has published essays in Art South Africa, Callaloo, Nka: Journal of Contemporary African Art, *and* Transition, *where "New World Alphabet" first appeared. Woubshet is the author of the forthcoming* Looking for the Dead: AIDS, Poetics and Politics, *a comparative study of AIDS writing in the United States, South Africa, and Ethiopia.*

The first word I learned in the New World was *faggot*. It was autumn 1989, and I was groping my way through a new country and an all-boys boarding school. What little English I knew came from basic grammar classes in Ethiopia and American pop songs, some of which I transcribed from cassette tapes to ease the restlessness of rainy seasons. Already, I was a quiet, inward child, but in another country I became terrified of speaking. I'd panic when a teacher asked me to read aloud, or when I raised my hand to ask, *May I go urinate?* The kids would erupt into wild laughter at my strange expressions—at how I said *za, zat, zis, zerfore,* unable to mouth their lisp. The tongue is hard to tame, language difficult to master. So, when my new roommate JR called me *faggot!* I thought he meant maggot, a reasonable slur in the country from which I'd just emigrated. I said nothing to the boy; silently, I cursed him back, *you za faget!*

I didn't know the label for it at thirteen, but by then the desire for my own sex was instinct; and I had already been intimate with my boy mates in Addis Ababa—the rituals of boy bonding being different there. Like the grown men around us, we held hands and kissed on the cheeks—free to be sensual and easy to express tenderness in public. Alone, we burrowed ourselves into some nook to masturbate and grind together, and did so with little qualm and complete boyhood abandon. I remember the intoxicating smell of spit and cum on our hands, and the bits of a jingle we used to sing—*bah Lux samuna, bah Lux samuna* [with the lather of Lux soap, the lather of Lux soap]—to signify to ourselves our private pleasures.

Bushti [faggot in Amharic] was not a compulsory term for kids my age. I knew it referred to an outlier, but one whose profile I couldn't really

201

make out. I heard men in the streets exclaiming it regularly, and exclusively at each other, and could sense that in their arsenal of invectives it was the key unmanning term. Not to mention, everyone knew that *bushti* was Colonel Mengistu's choice term for castigating foes and dissenters.

We glean meaning from repetition. It took me little time to realize that faggot did not mean maggot, since it was the singular term against which, by rote, American boys defined themselves. And they used it wildly, and pointedly, to police difference: lisps, limp wrists, dangling pinkies, arms akimbo; boys who wore tight pants, who couldn't play ball, who switched; boys who were funny, sweet, fruity, queer; a homo, a fairy, a sissy, a girl, a bitch.

Initially, bewildered by the fact that I was a fat kid from Ethiopia, the boys overlooked my sissy ways; and, it turned out, my place of origin alone was ample fodder for dining hall gags.

"What do you call a five-ounce Ethiopian? Lucky."

"What do you call an Ethiopian with a yeast infection? A quarter pounder with cheese."

"Why are Ethiopians starving? 'Cause Dag ate all the food."

Their laughter baffled me when I didn't get the punch line. Since we used a different metric system, I didn't know what an ounce was, or a quarter pounder, let alone one with cheese. When I got the joke, I laughed guardedly at its base humor and often out of humiliation. And, as if hitting an air pocket, my heart stammered each time the humiliation came unexpected; huddled before the dorm TV, when our reverie was shattered by ads like:

> Did you know in Ethiopia for twenty-one dollars a month, you could feed a child like him nourishing meals each day? Please call now. Sponsorship is just twenty-one dollars a month. That breaks down to seventy cents a day.

During these thirty-second intervals, I tried to avert their gaze full of pity and spite.

"Hey Dag? You know we sponsored you, right?"

Enveloped in shame, I sat still or walked out the room resentful of the bare life I saw on the screen.

My roommate JR, mercy on his soul, was relentless with his disses and quick to suss out my homo ways. JR was the first to call me *faggot!* Then, he coined, *bitch lashes!* for my long eyelashes, which I trimmed to be inconspicuous; then, *bitch fingers!* for my slender fingers, which were harder to alter. Persecution in the tongue of the persecuted: we spent the remainder of 1989 knocking down each other's country (he was from

Puerto Rico), our Englishes jockeying for position. He'd itemize abject Ethiopia like Sally Struthers, and I'd strike back, *At least I have a country!* In the hush of night, though, we traded our chauvinism for furtive exploits and English for native tongues. *Koño,* he'd sigh in my ear; *k'onjo,* I'd sigh back.

Like me, the boys had marked JR. He was too sensual and kitsch for boys hatched in America. And, despite how much he tried to be otherwise, he remained a kind of ballast until we graduated.

Both of us were desperate in our antics to pass. Once, in the ninth grade, a year after we stopped rooming together, JR tried to out me as a preemptive, defensive measure. He told me, poking at his cupped palm, "I gotcha right here." Somehow, he'd managed to record (and isolate from his) my surreptitious moans from one of our faux sex sessions, and was now keen to share it with others. *You're crazy,* I thought, but bluffed and told him, "I don't care." Panic-stricken, the next day I sneaked into his room, rummaging frantically through the pile of tapes by his boombox for the one bearing my voice. Luckily, I found the tape, already cued up to muted sounds in Amharic, over which I swiftly dubbed static on the radio.

When raising the name of the dead, I was taught to implore for their soul. JR, mercy on his soul, killed himself shortly after we graduated from high school. He parked his car on the side of a highway and, seized by something intractable, walked out into the flying traffic. Looking back, now, I am melancholy over all the wasted feelings, the spilled effort it took to live a lie—how we deprived ourselves of records, when we were already silenced and banished. *Mercy.* I remember how JR taught me to do the running man (like MC Hammer) and the snake (like Janet Jackson). I remember his body's weight on mine. His sharp jaw lines. His sweet, wayward breath. All the words he taught me.

Detained:
A Writer's Prison Diary
(excerpt)

Ngũgĩ wa Thiong'o

Born in Kenya in 1938, Ngũgĩ wa Thiong'o is one of Africa's leading writers. He is a playwright and the author of novels including The River Between, Petals of Blood, *and* Wizard of the Crow. *An advocate of the use by African writers of their indigenous languages, he ran afoul of the Kenyan government in 1977 when he wrote and produced a play in the Gikuyu language called* Ngaahika Ndeenda, *or* I Will Marry When I Want. *As he writes in his book* Detained, *"I have never tried to write an autobiography—even when publishers have requested it—for my life has been ordinary, average really, and it would bore me to death." Nonetheless, he says, "I will try a diary of life in prison. I'll record everything that happens: what I see, touch, smell, hear and think." In this selection, he describes the writing of his novel* Devil on the Cross *in Gikuyu, but it is striking how much of his diary he devotes to other writers and activists who have shared the experience of incarceration.*

Warĩĩnga ngatha ya wĩra . . . Warĩĩnga heroine of toil . . . there she walks haughtily carrying her freedom in her hands . . .

12 December 1978: I am in cell 16 in a detention block enclosing eighteen other political prisoners. Here I have no name. I am just a number in a file: K6, 77. A tiny iron frame against one wall serves as a bed and a tiny board against another wall serves as a desk. These fill up the minute cell.

It is past midnight. Unable to face the prickly bristles of three see-through blankets on a mattress whose sisal stuffing has folded into innumerable lumps as hard as stones, I am at the desk, under the full electric glare of a hundred-watt naked bulb, scribbling words on toilet-paper. Along the passageway which separates the two lines of Kenyatta's tiger cages, I can hear the heavy bootsteps of the night warder. He is going on his rounds.

205

At the one end, the passageway leads into a cul-de-sac of two latrines, a wash-room with only one sink and a shower-room for four. These are all open: no doors. At the other end, next to my cell, the passageway opens into a tiny exercise-yard whose major features are one aluminium rubbish-bin and a falling apart tenniquoit-cum-volleyball net hung on two iron poles. There is a door of iron bars at this opening—between the exercise-yard and the block of cells—and it is always shut and locked at night. The block of "tiger cages" and the yard are enclosed by four double stone walls so high that they have completely cut off any part of the skyline of trees and buildings which might give us a glimpse of the world of active life.

This is Kamĩtĩ Maximum Security Prison, one of the largest prisons in post-colonial Africa. It is situated near three towns—Rũirũ, Kĩambu and Nairobi—and literally next-door to Kenyatta University College but we could as easily have been on the moon or on Mars. We have been completely quarantined from everything and everybody except for a highly drilled select squad of prison guards and their commanding officers.

Maximum security: the idea used to fill me with terror whenever I met it in fiction, Dickens mostly, and I have always associated it with England and Englishmen and with Robben Island in South Africa: it conjured up images of hoards of dangerous killers always ready to escape through thick forests and marshes, to unleash yet more havoc and terror on an otherwise stable, peaceful and godfearing community of property-owners that sees itself as the whole society. A year as an inmate at Kamĩtĩ has taught me what should have been obvious: that the prison system is a repressive weapon in the hands of a ruling minority determined to ensure maximum security for its class dictatorship over the rest of the population, and it is not a monopoly exclusive to South Africa and England.

The menacing bootsteps come nearer. But I know that the prowling warder cannot enter my cell—it is always double-locked and the keys in turn locked inside a box which at five o'clock is promptly taken away by the corporal on duty to a safe somewhere outside the double walls—but of course he can look into the cell through an iron-barred rectangular slit in the upper half of the door. The slit is built so as to only contain the face.

The bootsteps stop. I take my time in turning to the door although I can feel in my bones that the warder is watching me. It is an instinct that one develops in prison, the cunning instinct of the hunted. The face of the warder fills the whole slit: I know nothing so menacingly sinister in its silent stillness as that trunkless face glaring at you through the iron bars of a prison cell.

"Professor . . . why are you not in bed?" the voice redeems the face. "What are you doing?"

Relief! I fall back on the current witticism in the detention block.

"I am writing to Jomo Kenyatta in his capacity as an ex-detainee."

"His case was different," the warder argues back.

"How?"

"His was a colonial affair."

"And this, a neo-colonial affair? What's the difference?"

"A colonial affair . . . now we are independent . . . that's the difference . . ." he says.

"A colonial affair in an independent country, eh? The British jailed an innocent Kenyatta. Thus Kenyatta learnt to jail innocent Kenyans. Is that the difference?"

He laughs. Then he repeats it. "The British jailed Kenyatta. Kenyatta jails Kenyans." He laughs again, adding:

"Take it any way you like . . . but write a good petition . . . you might get a hearing this time. . . . Your star shines bright in the sky . . . ex-detainee . . ." he chuckles to himself. "Does 'ex-' mean the same thing as 'late'—*hayati*?"

"What do you mean?"

"Can I say the late detainee instead of the ex-detainee?"

The tone tells me that he knows the difference and that he is trying to communicate something. But tonight I feel a little impatient.

"You know I no longer teach English," I say to him.

"You can never tell the language of the stars," he persists. "Once a teacher, always a teacher," he says, and goes away laughing.

In his prison notes, *The Man Died,* Wole Soyinka aptly comments that "no matter how cunning a prisoner, the humanitarian act of courage among his gaolers plays a key rôle in his survival." This warder is a good illustration of the truth of that observation. He is the one who in March told me about the formation of the London-based *Ngũgĩ Defence Committee* and the subsequent picketing of the Kenyan Embassy on 3 March 1978. He enjoys talking in riddles and communicating in roundabouts. It's a way of protecting himself, of course, but he enjoys seeing a prisoner grope for the hidden meanings.

Tonight, his laughter sounds more direct and sympathetic, or perhaps it is another kind of riddle to be taken any way I like.

Two warders guard the passageway in turns. One sleeps, the other guards. At one o'clock they change places. They too cannot get out because the door between the passageway and the exercise-yard is locked and the keys taken away. Night warders are themselves prisoners guarding other prisoners. Only they are paid for it and their captivity is self-inflicted or else imposed by lack of alternative means of life. One very young warder—a Standard Seven drop-out—tells me that his ambition is to be a fighter pilot! Another, a grandfather, tells me his ambition once was to become a musician.

To hell with the warders! Away with intruding thoughts! Tonight I don't want to think about warders and prisoners, colonial or neo-colonial affairs. I am totally engrossed in Waríínga, the fictional heroine of the novel I have been writing on toilet-paper for the last ten months or so!

Toilet-paper: when in the sixties I first read in Kwame Nkrumah's autobiography, *Ghana,* how he used to hoard toilet-paper in his cell at James Fort Prison to write on, I thought it was romantic and a little unreal despite the photographic evidence reproduced in the book. Writing on toilet-paper?

Now, I know: paper, any paper, is about the most precious article for a political prisoner, more so for one like me, who was in political detention because of his writing. For the urge to write:

> Picking the jagged bits embedded in my mind,
> Partly to wrench some ease for my own mind,
> And partly that some world sometime may know

is almost irresistible to a political prisoner. At Kamítí, virtually all the detainees are writers or composers. Wasonga Sijeyo has volumes of notes on his life, Kenyan history, botany, zoology, astronomy and Luo culture. Koigi wa Wamwere has many essays on politics and culture, several political fables, a short novel, an autobiography, and a long poem on his prison experience. Gíceru wa Njaũ has a novel in Kiswahili. Thairũ wa Mũthíga has a few poems. Simba Ongongi Were composes heart-rending songs; while Mahat Kuno Roble, though illiterate, is a highly accomplished poet. And from Shimo-la-Tewa Prison, I have received two huge manuscripts written on toilet-paper. Now the same good old toilet-paper—which had been useful to Kwame Nkrumah in James Fort Prison, to Dennis Brutus on Robben Island, to Abdilatif Abdalla in G Block, Kamítí, and to countless other persons with similar urges—has enabled me to defy daily the intended detention of my mind.

> A flicker, pulse, mere vital hint
> which speaks of the stubborn will
> the grim assertion of some sense of worth
> in the teeth of the wind
> on a stony beach, or among rocks
> where the brute hammers fall unceasingly
> on the mind.

I now know what Dennis Brutus meant. Writing this novel has been a daily, almost hourly, assertion of my will to remain human and free despite the Kenya African National Union (KANU) official government programme of animal degradation of political prisoners.

Privacy, for instance. I mean its brutal invasion. Thus, I was daily trailed by a warder for twenty-four hours, in waking and sleeping. It was unnerving, truly unnerving, to find a warder watching me shit and urinate into a children's chamberpot in my cell, or to find him standing by the entrance to the toilet to watch me do the same exercise. The electric light is on the night long. To induce sleep, I had to tie a towel over my eyes. This ended in straining them so that after a month they started smarting and watering. But even more painful was to suddenly wake up in the middle of the night, from a dreamless slumber or one softened by sweet illusion or riddled with nightmares, to find two bodiless eyes fixed on me through the iron bars.

Or monotony: the human mind revolts against endless sameness. In ordinary social life, even the closest-knit family hardly ever spends a whole day together in meaningless circles on their compound. Man, woman and child go about their different activities in different places and they only meet in the evening to recount their different experiences. Experiments done on animals show that when they are confined to a small space and subjected to the same routine they end up tearing each other. Now the KANU government was doing the same experiment on human beings.

At Kamĩtĩ, we daily saw the same faces in the same white kũũngũrũ prison uniforms; we daily fed on unga and beans in the morning, at noon and at three o'clock; we daily went through the same motions, and this, in a confined space of reliefless dust and grey stones. The two most dominant colours in the detention block were white and grey and I am convinced these are the colours of death.

The government could not have been ignorant about the possible results of these experiments in mental torment: valium was the most frequently prescribed drug in Kamĩtĩ Prison. The doctor expected a detainee to be mad or depressed unless proven otherwise.

There was a history to it. I was told a harrowing story about one detainee before my time who had a mental breakdown in that very block. The authorities watched him going down the drain until he was reduced to eating his own faeces. Yet the regime kept him in that condition for two years. This is normal practice in regimes with no popular roots in the masses, and Kenyatta's KANU government was one: but this did not make the horror easier to contemplate.

A week after my incarceration, Wasonga Sijeyo, who had been in that block for nine years but had managed to keep a razor-sharp mind and a heart of steel, eluded the vigilant eyes of the warders then guarding me and within seconds he told me words that I came to treasure:

"It may sound a strange thing to say to you, but in a sense I am glad they brought you here. The other day—in fact a week or so before you came—we were saying that it would be a good thing for Kenya if more intellectuals were imprisoned. First, it would wake most of them from their illusions. And some of them might outlive jail to tell the world. The thing is . . . just watch your mind . . . don't let them break you and you'll be all right even if they keep you for life . . . but you must try . . . you have to, for us, for the ones you left behind."

Thus in addition to it being an insurrection of a detained intellect, writing this novel has been one way of keeping my mind and heart together like Sijeyo.

Free thoughts on toilet-paper! I had deliberately given myself a difficult task. I had resolved to use a language which did not have a modern novel, a challenge to myself, and a way of affirming my faith in the possibilities of the languages of all the different Kenyan nationalities, languages whose development as vehicles for the Kenyan people's anti-imperialist struggles has been actively suppressed by the British colonial regime (1895–1963) and by the neo-colonial regime of Kenyatta and his comprador KANU cohorts. I had also resolved not to make any concessions to the language. I would not avoid any subject—science, technology, philosophy, religion, music, political economy—provided it logically arose out of the development of theme, character, plot, story, and world view. Further I would use any and everything I had ever learnt about the craft of fiction—allegory, parable, satire, narrative, description, reminiscence, flash-back, interior monologue, stream of consciousness, dialogue, drama—provided it came naturally in the development of character, theme and story. But content—not language and technique—would determine the eventual form of the novel. And the content? The Kenyan people's struggles against the neo-colonial form and stage of imperialism!

Easier said than done: where was I to get the inspiration? A writer needs people around him. He needs live struggles of active life. Contrary to popular mythology, a novel is not a product of the imaginative feats of a single individual but the work of many hands and tongues. A writer just takes down notes dictated to him by life among the people, which he then arranges in this or that form. For me, in writing a novel, I love to hear the voices of the people working on the land, forging metal in a factory, telling anecdotes in crowded matatus and buses, gyrating their hips in a crowded bar before a jukebox or a live band, people playing games of love and hate and fear and glory in their struggle to live. I need to look at different people's faces, their gestures, their gait, their clothes, and to hear the variegated modulations of their voices in different moods. I need the vibrant voices of beautiful women: their touch, their sighs, their tears, their laughter. I like the presence of children prancing about, fighting, laughing, crying. I need life to write about life.

But it is also true that nobody writes under circumstances chosen by him and on material invented by him. He can only seize the time to select from material handed to him by whomever and whatever is around him. So my case now: I had not chosen prison, I was forced into it, but now that I was there, I would try and turn the double-walled enclosure into a special school where, like Shakespeare's Richard II, I would study how I might compare:

> This prison where I live unto the world . . .
> My brain I'll prove the female to my soul,
> My soul the father; and these two beget
> A generation of still-breeding thoughts,
> And these same thoughts people this little world,
> In humours like the people of this world,
> For no thought is contented.

In this literary target I was lucky to have for teachers, detainees and a few warders, who were very co-operative and generous in sharing their different mines of information and experience. For instance, Thairũ wa Mũthĩga, Gĩcerũ wa Njaũ and Koigi wa Wamwere taught me a lot of Gĩkũyũ vocabulary, proverbs, riddles and songs; Wasonga Sijeyo was an expert on the nationalist anti-imperialist struggles before 1963 and on the beginnings of land grabbing and foreigners' bribery of former nationalists with token shares in their companies; Gĩkonyo wa Rũkũũngũ gave me books on rituals of Catholic worship; Simba Ongongi Were taught me some Zairean tunes and words; Mũhoro wa Mũthoga, Koigi wa Wamwere and Adamu Matheenge gave me topographical details of Nakuru; while Gĩcerũ wa Njaũ, Thairũ wa Mũthĩga and I often discussed women of different careers, especially barmaids, secretaries and engineers, as well as different aspects of social life and bourgeois rivalry in Nairobi. I learnt a lot about business acumen and the whole practice and culture of accumulation from stories and real-life anecdotes narrated to us by the only millionaire in detention, Mahat Kuno Roble.

Not only from conscious discussions and direct inquiries: whispered news of happenings outside the walls would often provide me with material that I would later weave into the fabric of the novel. For instance, the main theme and story line emerged when I learnt that two members of parliament were serving sentences after being convicted of coffee theft. The shocking news of Professor Barnard's visit and the generous provision by his Kenya hosts of public platforms to air his racist pro-apartheid views prompted the philosophical discussion in a matatu about "life to come" and the problems of rival claims to the same heart on the day of resurrection; it also prompted the satirical depiction of a vision of one robber character, for a world in which a rich few would ensure their immortality through the purchase of spare organs of the human body, thus leaving death as the sole prerogative of the poor.

In the daytime, I would take hasty notes on empty spaces of any book I might be reading. I would scribble notes on the bare walls of my cell, then in the evening I would try to put it all together on toilet-paper.

Sometimes I would be seized with the usual literary boredom and despair—those painful moments when a writer begins to doubt the value of what he is scribbling or the possibility of ever completing the task in hand—those moments when a writer restrains himself with difficulty from setting the whole thing on fire, or tearing it all into pieces, or abandoning the whole project to dust and cobwebs. These moments are worse in prison because there are no distractions to massage the tired imagination: a glass of beer, a sound of music, or a long walk in sun and wind or in a starry night.

But at those very moments, I would remind myself that the KANU-led comprador ruling class had sent me here so that my brain would turn into a mess of rot. The defiance of this bestial purpose always charged me with new energy and determination: I would cheat them out of that last laugh by letting my imagination loose over the kind of society this class, in nakedly treacherous alliance with imperialist foreigners, were building in Kenya in total cynical disregard of the wishes of over fourteen-million Kenyans.

Because the women are the most exploited and oppressed section of the entire working class, I would create a picture of a strong determined woman with a will to resist and to struggle against the conditions of her present being. Had I not seen glimpses of this type in real life among the women of Kamīrīīthū Community Education and Cultural Centre? Isn't Kenyan history replete with this type of woman? Me Kitilili, Muraa wa Ngiti, Mary Mūthoni Nyanjirū? Mau Mau women cadres? Warīīnga will be the fictional reflection of this resistance heroine of Kenyan history. Warīīnga heroine of toil . . . there she walks . . .

I am now on the last chapter. I have given myself 25 December as the deadline. 25 December 1978 has a special significance to me. In February or March I had told the other detainees that we would all "eat" Christmas at home. I had even invited them to a Christmas goat-meat roasting party at my home in Gītogoothi, Bibirioni, Limuru. It was said half-in-joke, like so many other prison wagers related to dreams of eventual liberty, but I secretly believed it and inwardly clung to the date though becoming less and less openly assertive about it as days and nights rolled away. Now only twelve days are left. Twelve days to eat Christmas at home. Twelve days to meet my self-imposed literary deadline!

But tonight something else, an impulse, a voice, is urging me to run this last lap faster. The voice is not all that secret. Maybe it is born of the feverish expectation of early release which has been building up in the block for the last four months, though nobody is now sure of its "ifs" and "whens." Maybe it is also born of a writer's usual excitement of seeing the light at the end of a long hazardous tunnel. Or maybe it is a combination of both. But whatever its source, the voice remains insistent.

The heart is willing. The hand which has been scribbling non-stop since about seven o'clock is weak. But the voice is relentless: Write On!

I rise to stretch my legs. I walk to the iron-barred rectangular slit and peer into the passageway. Neither of the two warders is asleep. They are playing draughts, but they are murmuring more than they are playing. I ask the same warder about the time.

"Half-past twelve," he says, and then adds: "Why do you want to know the time, Professor?"

"I wanted to know if my star is still shining in the sky," I answer back.

"You better have some sleep. You might need it."

No. I don't feel like any sleep tonight. I go back to the desk to resume the race to the literary tape only a couple of paragraphs away.

KENYA

One Day
I Will Write About This Place
(excerpt)

Binyavanga Wainaina

Binyavanga Wainaina, born in 1971, may be best known for his essay "How to Write About Africa," which mercilessly satirizes many of the cliché conventions of literature and journalism about Africa. The founder of the influential magazine Kwani?, *he published his memoir* One Day I Will Write About This Place *in 2011. The* New York Times *named it one of the 100 notable books of the year. The passage below illustrates Wainaina's impressionistic, present-tense rendering of his childhood thoughts and experiences. Jimmy is his older brother, and Ciru and Chiqy are younger sisters. The invented word "kimay" stands for gibberish, sometimes threatening, that may come in musical or linguistic form. "Kimay is the talking jazz trumpet: sneering skewing sounds, squeaks and strains. . . . Ki-may is any language that I cannot speak, but I hear every day in Nakuru."*

Ciru and I are still in Lena Moi Primary School. Jimmy is now in form three in a boarding school called St. Patrick's Iten. Chiqy is four, and looks a lot like me. I am eleven.

Last night we had a storm, the biggest one anyone can remember. Two windows broke, and this morning we found a giant eucalyptus tree lying flat on the ground, its roots muddy and shivering with dew and earth. There are flat clouds where sky meets earth. Flat and clean and gray, like old suds. The light of the sun falls in soft shafts and everything gleams with God behind it. The air is fresh, and we are all quiet in the car on our way to school: fences, trees, and garbage are piled on every elbow of road and land.

We drive into school but can't see anybody. My father is irritated with me. He makes me tie my shoelaces. He redoes my tie. For years I will hide from my inability to tie a tie, to tie my shoelaces, to tell the time, and, later on, my inability to do long multiplication. Friends will tie my tie for me, and I will keep it tied for a whole term.

But today seems special. The soft mouth of God is blowing moist air at us; we run through dots and dashes of shadow into soft peeping light. We run onto the pavements; long bungalows of classrooms stretch. We run zigzag, swing off one pole and vault to the next. We break out to the back, past the drinking-water tap, past the long line of caterpillar trees, which nobody will stand under for fear that the hairy green caterpillars will fall on their heads, to the field, where everybody is playing. The caterpillars cover the tree, like leaves.

In one week, all of Nakuru will be covered by a million white butterflies with pink nostrils. The grass is still damp, still long from the rain, and we watch for knots. When the grass is long we all like to tie clumps into knots that people can trip on. People are spread out all over the field, and we have no idea what they are doing. It is drizzling softly.

Then we see them. All over the field. Brought down from the sky, by the storm. Furry balls of gray. Other clumps of pink and gray. And just pink. Many of them are dead. Others have been eaten by dogs, others flutter about weakly. There are pink feathers everywhere; entrails and bones and soft, beautiful pink and string and jelly flesh. Feathers everywhere. There are clumps of ant sculptures, rolling and reshaping like clouds. Bubbles of blood. Crunched bone. For the whole morning, we pick up the baby flamingos that are still alive, and hand them to Kenya Wildlife Service people.

Lena Moi Primary School used to be Lugard School, a whites-only school until the 1960s. Now it is named after Lena Moi, the abandoned wife of our president, Daniel Toroitich arap Moi. When Moi was vice president, she slapped him during a Madaraka Day dance, in front of President Kenyatta, who laughed at him, and that made him angry and now we hear she cannot leave her farm. She comes from an important Kalenjin family, the Bommets, a big farming family, one of the first in the Rift Valley to become Christians and go to mission school. Some of them go to my school. Many Nakuru people like Lena Moi, because it used to be the white school in Nakuru. There are no whites left. There is one Japanese student.

President Moi doesn't come from an important family. He was only a primary school teacher before entering politics. He is always being shamed. When Moi was vice president, Kenyatta's friends treated him like a child. One policeman, a Gikuyu, would stop and search his car whenever he was going home. The policeman's name is Mr. Mungai, and two of his sons are in our school. He is very short, and he keeps horses. Once Mr. Mungai slapped Moi. Now that Moi is president, Mr. Mungai has left the country. President Moi wants to detain him. The school hedge runs along the road where this happened, the road to Kabarak, his wife's home, now Moi's home. Past the road to Eldoret and finally to Uganda. President Moi likes primary school choirs and gives choirmasters big promotions.

One Sunday afternoon we go to town, Mum, Ciru, and I, to buy chicken and chips for supper. Kukuden. The streets of Nakuru are empty. People are at home. Even from here, two miles away, I can hear the Salvation Army band at the bottom of town, near Lake Nakuru. There is a lorry parking lot across the road from Kukuden. And from one of the lorries a cassette tape is playing.

Congo music, with wayward voices as thick as hot honey. This sound is dangerous; it promises to lift you from where you are and drop you into a hot upside-down place twenty thousand leagues under the sea. *Kimay*. Guitar and trumpet, parched like before the rains, dive into the honey and out again. A group of men unloads sacks of potatoes, and they are singing to the music. The song bursts out with the odd Kiswahili phrase, then forgets itself and starts on its gibberish again.

The voices plead in a strange jangling language, Lingala, which sounds familiar—it has Kiswahili patterns and words—but I can't understand it. It stirs something green and creamy in my belly, and I am nauseous. Men are sending their voices higher than voices should travel, letting their voices flow, slow and thick. The song's structure is . . . different, not like the easy melodies of school, the tamed do-re-mi-fa Kiswahili songs we sing for choir.

I am starting to read storybooks. If words, in English, arranged on the page have the power to control my body in the world, this sound and language can close its folds, like a fan, and I will slide into its world, where things are arranged differently, where people like Jonas, the Pokot guard, live, and in that place anything can happen to you.

I like choir. The school lets choir members off class twice a week in the afternoons to meet kids from other schools and practice for a giant group called Massed Choir that has kids from all twenty-two municipal schools. We go to the stadium and practice, over a thousand of us, to sing praise songs composed by our teachers for the president on Madaraka Day on June 1. It is fun. The music teachers of several schools compose the praise songs, and the best ones get to become headmasters or even go to work at the Presidential Music Commission near State House in Nairobi.

English is Kenya's official language. All documents that are legal and official must be in English. Kiswahili is not compulsory in school; it is our national language. That is what our constitution says. So, we have news in English and Kiswahili. Most Kenyans speak some Kiswahili. Our constitution does not name other languages. I think it is because we want to eradicate tribalism. We are not allowed to speak "mother tongue" in school. In school, Mrs. Gichiri, our headmistress, reacts strongly to girls who are prrr-oud, who show vanity, who prrr-een themselves. Naughty boys get four on the buttocks; proud girls get four on their palm.

Prrr, said the whistle. A warning not to exceed yourself. The world in English has sharp edges. *Pr* words in English promise good futures to people who stick to brittle boundaries; *prrr* words promise breaking to those who dare to dance to *kimay*. Kenyan English places have stainless steel whistles, which tell you to march this way; they shrill sharply when you cross a line. There are bells and parades and posted rules and glasses and cups, which are all breakable. People who do not speak Kiswahili use enamel cups.

Prrr-oud. I like those sharp shrill controlling words that sound like they come from an officer's whistle. Prim. Prude. Proper. Price. Probe. Prance. Preen. Prrr-een. Baba says the pound is growing rich against the shilling. More white people are leaving Kenya, more Indians. The shops that supplied us with books and toys and British comics like *Beezer, Beano,* and *Topper* are becoming expensive.

If I visit you in your home and your mother starts to speak to you in your language while I am there, you will roll your eyes at me, and reply to her in English or in Kiswahili, because we have agreed that parents are ridiculous that way. More than anything, we laugh at and dislike those kids who seem unable to escape their tribe.

Sometimes we practice traditional songs for the interschool music festival. We try to make sure we do not shake our bodies too much so that we step out of the lines and lose our place. It is important that we move our limbs together and keep in tune, and follow the conductor. At practice, the conductor, our music teacher Mr. Dondo, keeps us in do-re-mi-fa key with his mouth organ before we start. Don't move like a villager, he likes to say. We often do not know the meaning of the traditional song we are singing, but we learn the words well. Mr. Dondo has been promoted. He is now the deputy headmaster.

When two boys come to school one day sunburned and smelling of the village, where they had gone for a funeral, their hair was gone, shaved clear with a razor blade, scalps shining from animal fat.

They are toxic. They do not turn up for choir practice.

As money gets tighter, middle-class parents prefer to have their kids walking to school, and don't mind the shortcuts. Soon kids are buying lunch in little illegal kiosks outside the school. Soon we cross into the other world, to buy handmade wire cars and trade homing pigeons from kids who speak strange languages, who laugh if you speak English to them—they understand it, but find it pretentious; kids who wear no shoes, kids who miss school a lot, and have babies very early and smell of smoke from charcoal cooking, who go hunting with dogs and catapults for antelopes and rabbits and pigeons, in the forest above our home, for fun.

Outside the once neat school hedge, through its holes, zigzag paths make their way through every part of town. Andazi, the school gardener, is getting old; he has been in this school since white people were here, and he says we have spoiled it.

I grew two inches this term, and my voice just broke, and I got kicked out of the choir because I squeak a lot. There are informal kiosks sprouting everywhere, selling everything from batteries to fresh vegetables, between the thorny hedges that are starting to grow wild in English-speaking Nakuru. There are a lot of things coming from Taiwan, and fewer things coming from Britain. Baba says the British make good things but never learned how to market them, because the colonials had to buy what they made. There are hawkers now, walking the streets selling Taiwan things, and more shops are closing.

Look! Look at Michael Jackson move, as if he cannot break. We try to dance like him.

Baba wakes us up this morning and tells us that there has been a coup d'etat led by junior soldiers in the air force. There is shooting all over Kenya. We stay home the whole day. The government was taken over by an air force private. There is shooting in Nairobi all day, and rumors that the streets are piled high with bodies. Indian shops are looted. Many women are raped. There are curfews, for months, and arrests. Some of the Gujarati-speaking kids from school have left for London and Toronto. Nobody really can keep the holes in the hedges sealed.

Kenya is not Uganda. Kenya has big roads and railways and tall build-ings, science and technology, research and big planes and thousands of troops and machine guns and missiles. With only a few guns and some raging soldiers, air force Private Ochuka is, for six hours, the president of Kenya. In the afternoon, the coup is put down, and thousands are killed. Nairobi has corpses everywhere.

Childhood in Madagascar
(excerpt)
Christian Dumoux

Christian Dumoux was born around 1950 and grew up as a mixed-race child in Madagascar. He went on to live in Benin, Côte d'Ivoire, Cameroon, and Chad before moving to Paris. Dumoux's memoir, published in French in 2005, is one of the few available from the island country. He tells his story in the third person, in a series of chapters named after the house he was living in at the time.

[Translated from the French by Alexis Pernsteiner and Antoine Bargel.]

Tenth House

It was in Antsaralalana, which meant beautiful road. It was left of the station, with a restaurant, "The Lyonnais," at the end of the street.

The house had the peculiarity of being partially collapsed and having three floors: they lived on the third floor and shared the apartment with a co-worker of his mom's, a single woman who had a separate room, but with whom they had a bathroom in common. With a roommate they could make rent. A Malagasy family lived on the second floor and had two boys who were his age. He spent a lot of time there; their servant boy, the unforgettable Lita, told incredible stories inspired by the coal stove's shadows: the glowing coal had a tendency to fall behind a kind of luminous screen which stimulated the servant-cook's imagination to concoct thousands of fantastic tales with dragons, witches, and legendary warriors.

The courtyard was a huge mess, a helter-skelter including the remains of the collapsed part of the house, a workshop with machines, a corner with dumbbells, scrap metal scavenged from the railway at the nearby station, and the monkey bars where all the kids would play, not to mention compete to see who could pee the farthest. It was during one of these competitions that he discovered he hadn't been circumcised, and his little Malagasy friends made fun of him. His mom told him that since he didn't have a grandfather anymore they had decided not to circumcise him: it was customary for the foreskin to be mixed with banana and eaten by the grandfather. They didn't want to impose that on Dadabé, the family elder. . . . He figured he'd gotten off easy, and the "Old Man" too.

It was rumored that the house had partially collapsed because the Greek merchant next door had built a five-storey building. The merchant had a son who was also his age, and when he wasn't with the Malagasy children, he would play with the Greek kid: they would go into the stock-room of the dad's wholesale store and eat cheese from Holland wrapped in red wax, or make toys out of "jourjour," a wood from the veins of palm leaves. For the most part, they fashioned airplanes pricked with bent needles, through which they extended a taut string in order to glide them from the balconies on the fifth floor to the open field across the way. They made spinning tops by cutting loquat pits in half and sticking half a match in one side.

The boys on the second floor had what they called "kalèches," wooden planks with three ball bearings, one of which served as the steering wheel, and they would speed over the sidewalk, either by pushing each other along, or by propelling themselves with one leg. It was a kind of horizontal scooter made out of whatever they could find: they crafted their own toys.

His mom worked late, and his dad, after closing the shop, would often play dice or Belote at the neighborhood bar/restaurant. He got along well with a French kid from the mainland who lived down the street, but when he went over to the kid's house, he got the feeling the mom didn't trust him. He wasn't allowed over there anymore, probably because they took him for a little Creole hoodlum, with too little supervision and too much time spent with the neighborhood's Malagasies. He did have his "gang," which did not include the Greek friend or the downstairs neighbors, and sometimes there would be scuffles with gangs from other neighborhoods. He would go with a group over to the Chinese grocer, and while the others ran diversion, he would steal chewing gum and licorice. The chewing-gum wrappers had pictures of American movie stars. They would throw them in the air two by two, and anybody whose picture landed face up got to keep it. Everybody knew about John Wayne and Gary Cooper. . . .

He was proud to be known as the "zlamboty," the neighborhood gangster, but that didn't keep him from quaking with fear whenever he was in the field and saw the moths with what looked like skulls on their wings. He firmly believed—a common belief—that these were the errant souls of the dead, and that they were dangerous to the touch.

He really liked the great Tananarive flood: when the whole neighborhood was submerged in water. For several days, the water stagnated at the midpoint of the stairs that went up to the second floor. He still remembers his delight at going home in a dugout.

His sister got baptized, even though she wasn't little anymore. The godfather, a certain L., came from Iosy, in the south of the Island, where he was bailiff. He was a big man whom the boy's dad had known when he was in Fianarantsoa. He had a reputation for being broke and drinking a lot.

The boy later learned that, a few years earlier, this man had married his father's eldest daughter from another marriage, but against his father's wishes. Since the daughter had been sixteen and the parents divorced, the mom had given her consent for the marriage.

He often heard his father talk about this act of disobedience, which he considered a betrayal. Apparently he had told his daughter that if she married against his wishes, he would disown her. That's what he did. And he never saw her again, as long as he lived.

However, the bailiff he did forgive after the couple got divorced. It was only many years later that the boy learned of the bailiff's impotence, of the wife's "phantom pregnancy," and that the local doctor who had diagnosed her had also "cured" her. . . . They told him that the marriage had been "broken," in both legal and religious terms.

On Saturday evenings, he often took a long walk with his parents down Libération Avenue. It was a big treat when they bought peanuts, which they would shell and eat with bread. The walk often ended up over a drink at the terrace of The Glacier, where the boy was fascinated by one work of art: thousands of bottle caps, tossed out by the restaurant's waiters, encrusted into the melting tar of the road. The bottle caps gave a festive air to the "studded street crossings," so called because, at the time, pedestrian crosswalks were made of giant aluminum nails hammered into the road.

Long after, he would angrily recall a few tortured days he had spent with his sister: it was a day of crisis when his father, probably mad at his mother for a bout of unfounded jealousy, took them from the house with some clothes packed in a suitcase and hid them in a hotel which they were not to leave. How many days did they spend alone with their father, terrorized by his anger, longing for their mother without daring to admit it, imprisoned in the hotel, where the staff and the manager gave them funny looks? Meals were tense with their father, who would eat without saying anything. And then Grandma Félicie played mediator, and they were able to go home: how happy they were when their mother came to get them at the hotel, how angry he was at his parents for never explaining themselves.

It was around this same time that he met Luc Donat, a famous musician from Réunion who played sega, *the* dance in Réunion. His father often saw him at a bar and when the boy found out, he asked if he could learn the violin. He started by learning music theory over at the musician's apartment, which was near Libération Avenue. He learned to read music very fast, but it was all abruptly cut short: the musician said that in order to continue he'd have to get his own violin; after a thousand promises, his dad admitted he didn't have the means to buy a violin. . . . For a while, the kid would dream in front of the violin shop's window. He later learned that none of his classes had been paid for. . . . What a disappointment! But, whatever, he was used to it by now. He gave up on his dream of playing music, yet another of so many. His heart was beginning to harden, it was better not to want anything, things were easier that way.

The only thing that was truly his and that he really loved was his butterfly collection: they were pinned in a glass box; he had chased after and caught them in the open field facing his house. He had a net made out of mosquito netting and some formalin he would dot on them to preserve them: there weren't very many but they were beautiful.

He often went to see his Grandma Félicie, mounting and descending the interminable staircase's thousand and one steps that went from Colbert Square to the marketplace square to where his grandmother's house was situated on Faravohitra hill. His city was really beautiful, seen from the top of all those stairs. The way to the public school took just as long. He had gone from last in the class to first, after the school's headmistress had called his father and he had gotten a severe spanking.

His father opened a shop on Libération Avenue near a Greek bakery. There, on a major public holiday, he once saw a standing General de Gaulle go by in a big black car. He had just announced the Enabling Law, which was supposed to pave the way to greater autonomy under what was being called the Great French Community. On his father's shoulders, the boy was one in the crowd. What he couldn't understand was why de Gaulle was inaugurating a statue of Joan of Arc. He wondered, though he didn't dare ask, what Joan of Arc was doing at this party.

This was in August of 1958.

To him, what seemed important was the word independence since, outside his little Greek friend and his father, he lived in a "Malagasy" world, and every time there was talk of independence, his classmates' eyes would light up, probably because their parents put their hopes in it.

He often recalls one afternoon when his mother asked him to accompany her to an "uncle's" house. He lived fairly far away, in the Besarety Quarter out in a suburb of Tananarive. He was called, and his name was pronounced with respect and a lowered tone, Edmond Ravelonahina. After a long trip in a shared taxi, during which his mother told him she had a heart disease and that she was going to get treatment through radi-esthesia, they arrived at the uncle's house. He welcomed them warmly, speaking only in Malagasy. He put them in a secluded room, and his mother spent more than an hour holding a kind of iron-gray "magne-tized" rectangle against her chest. The uncle was a kind of "healer" accord-ing to his mother, who felt much better after the session, but the man was also "in politics and had almost been killed." Had she done other sessions of radiesthesia? He isn't sure, but it probably cost less than going to the doctor. He learned many years later—for it was taboo to speak of "the events of 1947"—that Edmond Ravelonahina had been sentenced to death after the 1947 revolt, but had then been pardoned. In the twenties, he had been deported to Mayotte, a little island in the Comoros, for his activities in nationalist circles. How proud he felt the day he learned that a member of his own family had risen up against colonization, even though there were some rumors that he had worked for a time as an informant for the French secret service, rumors that he had "played for both sides."

Bear in mind that, according to the French army's archives, at least in what is accessible, in the two years following the rebellion's outbreak on March 29, 1947, approximately 100,000 Malagasies were killed or died as a result of the military action taken to suppress it. There was the massacre in the sealed cars of the Moramanga train, a grisly memory: on May 5, 1947, in Ambatondrazaka, with the last-minute arrival of reinforcements sent to quash the rebellion, three train cars typically used to transport zebus were loaded with one hundred sixty-six hostages. The train arrived in Moramanga in the early afternoon, and the hostages were left in their cars. At midnight, the soldiers on guard were given an order to open fire on the train cars. The train doors opened to seventy-one survivors, who were taken to Moramanga prison, where they were interrogated and tor-tured for two days before being put back on the train. They were taken out of the train on May 8 and executed according to the orders of a certain General Casseville, the head of the French military's high command in Madagascar. The hostages were slaughtered over a mass grave, where the bodies were piled. One hostage, who was only wounded, was able to escape at nightfall and give his testimony.

The horror of the Moramanga train is but a reflection of the fear in which the French lived during the first months of the rebellion, when almost five hundred of their own were massacred.

The boy's maternal family, which was made up of half-bloods and Malagasies, spent this entire period in a state of trauma and fear, since half-bloods usually had French citizenship and at least one among them was a senior civil servant. One of his mother's great-uncles, Marcel Riddell, was half Scottish, half Malagasy, and was mayor of Tananarive during the rebellion—at the time, mayors were appointed by the colonial authority. He had made a career out of administration after having gone to the French Overseas School. In 1946, he was tasked with neutralizing any overt demonstration of popular support organized by the three leaders of the party for independence, the MDRM.

The boy's godmother was married to a well-established French entrepreneur. . . .

Edmond Ravelonahina had been at the heart of the rebellion, and the fact that he hadn't been executed after being sentenced to death had served for some—other nationalist rebels expressing jealousy?—as proof of his role as a double agent.

For his close family members, the uncompromising character of this uncle, who, moreover, was married to a staunch nationalist, was incompatible with this "rumor." If such a rumor were true, would the colonial in him have really let the "collaborator" rot in the Nosy-Lava labor camp until 1956?

Much later, an anecdote—well or poorly interpreted?—was disclosed to him: Ravelonahina went to visit the Riddells in Tananarive a few days before the March 29, 1947, rebellion broke out: he seemed off and uncomfortable during the visit. As part of the rebellion in Tananarive, the Riddell family was to be poisoned; their morning milk, which was delivered daily to the Administrator, was to be laced with a strong poison on March 30.

However, following a series of last-minute defections, the plans of rebellion in Tananarive were aborted. Was this why the milk didn't get poisoned? Some close to the rebellion who knew about the assassination plot thought so. They also saw it as proof that Ravelonahina couldn't have possibly betrayed the cause, since, even though members of his own family had been at risk, he'd said nothing. And the sense of unease that had been felt during his visit had undoubtedly been due to the fact that he'd known of the plans.

Ravelonahina's pardon was most likely the result of "interventions" with the colonial authorities on his behalf, and family alliances also probably played a role. With the exception of the events of 1947, the history of Madagascar would never be bloody, since the culture of clan and family alliances would help to resolve tensions, even after independence.

There was also the "bizarre" death of his father's brother, whom the boy did not know because they had been angry with each other ever since he was born. He died of a poorly treated "ingrown nail" on his plantation in Ambohimasoa. In the time it took to charter a small plane, gas gangrene had reached the torso, at which point he was doomed. When his father learned that his older brother was going to die in Girard and Robic Hospital, he went to see him and make amends; no sooner had he entered the room than the man at death's door shouted at him to "get the hell out!" The damage caused from the time each brother had slept with the wife of the other was irreparable, but he wouldn't know that secret in its entirety until fifty years later; there was another bone of contention that he would only begin to understand in part at the next house, since his father did not tend to expand much on his family's past, that is, with the exception of his being proud of having a parent who had gone to the best engineering school in France, which was not exactly true, and that his first wife would sleep with anybody.

As a side note, the man who had just died a stupid death was, it seems, about to have his divorce made official by the court in Tananarive. And, as it happens, his wife, thanks to this abrupt death, made off with a fortune, which she would have otherwise been denied. Her lover, the priest at her backwoods church, was apparently later defrocked, but, even if true, this was only a little scandal typical of the white colonials.

And boom!, one day it was announced that the house where they lived was going to be torn down and rebuilt. The owner had gotten a construction permit and insurance money.

It was goodbye again to all his neighborhood friends, since the trip to school would take up a lot of his time, there was no telephone at the house, and no parent drivers to take him to see them, seeing as how they didn't have a car. With all this moving, the only friends he had left were his classmates, but they lived so far away he only saw them at school.

Paradise Raped

(excerpt)

James R. Mancham

Born in the Seychelles archipelago in 1939, James R. Mancham studied law in England, returned to found the Democratic Party, and promoted tourism as chief minister of the colony. In 1976, when Seychelles won its independence, he was elected president, but he was deposed less than a year later while he was attending a Commonwealth conference in London. These events are described in Paradise Raped, *which was published in 1983. In 2010 he was awarded the International Jurists Award for his work on behalf of world peace.*

I was born on 11 August 1939. Soon after, all the bells on every populated island of Seychelles rang out. For some time my parents mischievously led me to believe that there was a connection, before eventually deflating me with the news that the bells had not tolled for me but for the outbreak of something called the Second World War. The effects of that terrible conflict reached out as far as our islands when two British troopships arrived and took away two thousand young Seychellois to fight for King and Country in the Egyptian desert, seducing them with the offer of bully beef and a pair of Army boots. Even as the islanders sampled the new culinary delights and squeezed previously unshod feet into the boots, they had no inkling that the nights in the desert would be cold and that camels were no substitute for women. The result was that many returned with two previously unknown afflictions—tuberculosis and homosexuality. The lesson was not lost on us. Contact with the world outside could be dangerous. It was a lesson that was to be taught again and again over the years.

Another result of the war was that my father Richard Mancham became prosperous. He had a provisions business in Victoria on the main island of Mahé and a ship-chandler's licence, and with the increased naval activity he was constantly busy. Like most Seychellois, he was of mixed blood, his mother French and his father Chinese. He was eight when his

229

father died and he was sent to relatives in South China. There was a war on and by the time he returned to the islands at the age of thirteen he had matured into an adult with a clear sense of values.

My mother Evelyn is French Seychellois. Orphaned at six, she was brought up in a convent by French and Irish nuns. She met my father when she was fifteen and they married in 1935. She was sixteen, he was twenty-one. I was their first child and my early memories were of the regular arrival of brothers. First there was Thomas who, for some reason, was always known as Billy; then Francis, known as Babi; then Michael and Frank and finally a sister, Anne Marie. In addition there was Philip, our half-brother, the result of a pre-marital relationship of my father's. Philip lived with our paternal grandmother but spent most of his time with us.

No-one could have asked for a better start to life. Our house was large and comfortable, a wooden building of several bedrooms. From my room I could see below the rooftops of Victoria, the only town on the islands. The garden was surrounded by a tropical orchard of mango groves and apples, and the sun shone continually.

At that time few people had heard of Seychelles. Mahé was accessible only by the passenger ships which called every six or seven weeks on the run between Mombasa and Bombay. The islands were beautiful, tranquil and poor. In Victoria, magnificent *sang-dragon* trees (so called because when scratched they drip red sap which looks like blood) stood like a guard of honour above the road to Government House. Fish, eggs and rice were cheap but wages were correspondingly low, and there were more rickshaws than bicycles in the streets, and few cars. Nevertheless, with war raging outside, Seychelles seemed more like the world as God intended it to be. Each morning was fresh and new, and evenings brought peace and companionship.

I knew that other islands were often hit by cyclones and that in other countries the seasons could be described in terms of weather, but I did not know what they meant by cold or fog or snow. There are no seasons in Seychelles. The temperature rarely drops below 75°F or rises above 85°. When the rains come, they come down fast and furious and usually leave quickly.

Mother had her own philosophical outlook on life. I particularly remember her happy vitality; she gave much of her time to church and parish activities as well as caring for her large and growing family. She had a fine voice and would sing the children to sleep from her extensive repertoire of romantic French songs.

Naturally, knowing nothing different, I took the beauty of my surroundings for granted. The water was warm and clear. The sand was white, the vegetation lush. It was not until I had travelled that I realised that, by comparison, the Seychelles were indeed paradise islands, that I had been brought up in technicolour while much of the rest of the world was painted in greys.

I took for granted the fact that my friends came in all shapes and colours, that a Seychellois could be blond with blue eyes or as black as night, or any shade in between. It was not until I had travelled that I discovered something called racial prejudice, although I was conscious of a certain aloofness from those who called themselves the *grand blancs* and who claimed to be directly descended from the original French settlers.

In Victoria I would meet my friends under the Clock Tower, which is a replica of the clock in front of Victoria Station in London, and I thought nothing of the fact that the clock of the Roman Catholic cathedral always chimed twice: the first time on the hour, then three minutes later, in case you hadn't heard it the first time. I learnt that a man could be fined for taking a coconut out of a plantation but I knew nothing of crime. There was some petty larceny on the islands and occasionally we heard terrible stories of years ago when a murder had been committed. I knew the policemen in Victoria and the fact that they had very little to do.

And I knew why some of the coconut palms were numbered and known as toddy trees. Their sap produced a potent drink called *calou* which could make the adults sing and dance and sometimes fall down, to such an extent that the government was compelled to control their tapping by licensing the trees. It seemed that everything we needed was close at hand.

At weekends we would go to our beach house at Glacis where we would swim and fish. During the week, when I was not studying, I would play football with my brothers and the boys who came to our garden. We were fortunate in having proper footballs. There were others who had to make do with kicking breadfruits around.

It was a good life, the highlights being the arrival of a boat from overseas. We had no television or newspapers, only the radio which occasionally received the BBC World Service, and so the boat was our only physical link with the outside world. I remember the excitement caused when the harbour siren would blast after a ship had been sighted from Signal Hill. The whole town would gaze out to sea, each one trying to be the first to catch a glimpse of the approaching vessel; then we would run to the pier to wait for her to come in. There would be friends on board and strangers from distant corners of the world.

Memory can be a faulty indicator and in my case it conjures up only the good things. If there were times of pain and tears, then they have been forgotten. If there were teenage tantrums or adolescent rebellion, then they must have passed in the night, because I have no recollection of them.

Each day I cycled two miles to the Seychelles College which was run by missionaries of the Order of Christian Instruction, most of whom came from Quebec. They were dedicated and strict but I enjoyed the work. I did not need to be dragged to school. From the first day my father encouraged me to study. Like many successful self-made men, he was conscious of the fact that he had never gone to university and he was determined that his children should not lack the opportunity; and like most islanders he looked up to doctors and lawyers as men of unfathomable knowledge.

"Study well," he would tell me in a serious tone, "and when you leave school I will send you to Europe to become a lawyer. I want you to be a man of letters and culture."

There was no question about it. He wanted me to be a lawyer and so a lawyer I would be, if I could.

At school I learned about the islands, their geography and history. I learned that Mahé is situated just south of the equator, that the group comprises ninety-two islands spread over 200,000 square miles. Some were granite mountain peaks of a sunken continent; others were of coral formation with their attendant reefs, all uninhabited until French pirates discovered them two hundred years before. The buccaneers were followed by French settlers, refugees from the revolutionary fervour of France or the collapse of the French Empire in India. They were wealthy and brought slaves with them. At the time of the French Revolution, someone conducted a head-count and wrote that the population of the Seychelles— which had been named after a Controller-General of Finance, Vicomte Moreau de Séchelles—consisted of "69 persons of French blood, three soldiers of the garrison, 32 coloured persons and 487 slaves."

It might have been idyllic had not the islands already become a victim of their geographic position. The British were engaged in naval rivalry with the French for control of the sea routes to the East Indies and piracy in the area was also becoming rampant, with the British merchant fleet suffering colossal losses. Thus it was that in 1794 a British frigate sailed in and demanded the unconditional surrender of the islands. Twenty years later the French ceded sovereignty to the British who remained in charge till 1976, although the French influence is still strongly apparent, in religion, language and law.

Britain ruled, or rather neglected to rule, the islands as a dependency of Mauritius until 1903 when Seychelles became a Crown Colony, complete with a cast list of Governors which might have been invented by

Noël Coward. There was Sir Bickham Sweet-Escott, followed later by Lt. Col. the Hon. Sir E.E. Twistleton-Fiennes, grandfather of Ranulph Fiennes who recently crossed the North and South Poles. Still later came Sir De S.M.G. Honey; compared with them, the first Governor I became friends with had the almost commonplace name of Sir Selwyn Selwyn-Clarke.

My teachers took their work seriously, yet ironically it was two of them who unwittingly furthered my less formal education. The first turned up one evening with her young man in a quiet spot frequented by lovers and proceeded to enjoy themselves, unaware that a friend and I were watching from behind a tree. To us, the sound and the sight of love-making was absurd and hilarious. We could not contain our laughter and when we ran away we were recognised. Next morning our teacher had reported us to the headmaster, the Rev. Brother Norbert, saying that we had been shouting names at her. The punishment was ten cuts of the heavy wooden ruler and as I stretched out my hands, I closed my eyes and saw again in my imagination my teacher's wonderful legs thrashing around in the moonlight.

Not long afterwards, another teacher took us on a nature ramble to the Botanical Gardens. When we arrived, we were met by a young agricultural officer who lived in a timber cottage among the tropical flowers.

"Children," said our teacher, "I want you to collect butterflies this afternoon. Catch as many as you can. At the end of the day, the gentleman here . . ." (pointing to the young man) "will give each one of you a mango. Now, all of you disappear and let me see who will bring back the most butterflies."

We all ran off. Looking back I saw the teacher and the agricultural officer sneak into his cottage. Wise now to the ways of the world, I decided to forget about butterflies and crept back to the cottage where I saw my teacher in all kinds of positions. It was the most instructive hour of nature study I ever had.

Seychelles was an ideal place for budding peeping Toms. With no distractions like television (which still has not been introduced to the islands) and no commercial cinema, except for an irregular showing of outdated British newsreels by the Government Information Unit, the islanders enjoyed themselves as nature intended, and much of the activity took place out of doors. In other parts of the world a married man on the loose traditionally needs to check his collar or handkerchiefs for lipstick. In Seychelles, he was given away either by grass stains or adhesive grains of sand.

Although I knew the facts of life before I was ten, it was five years later before I took an active part in these mysteries. As a practising Roman Catholic I had been taught that to have carnal knowledge of a girl outside marriage is a mortal sin, and I always dreaded the idea of having to tell my confessor about such a terrible thing.

One evening I had been doing some extra work in the school library and was walking back home, some two miles away. The moon was half full and the atmosphere balmy and sensuous. As I approached the Botanical Gardens, with visions of my teacher's and the agricultural officer's performance flooding my mind, I saw walking alone towards me a maid from a nearby village, about twenty and very attractive. In Creole the words appropriate to such occasions are "Donne moi un petit coup," meaning "Give me a little kick," and sure enough the lady was ready and willing to do so and knew the right spot for it, a mango tree behind the enclosure where some giant tortoises were kept. But as we walked, she leading the way, I started to think about the serious sin I was about to commit and became suddenly engulfed by a strong feeling of guilt. When we got to the mango tree my friend took off her knickers, lay down on the grass, lifted her skirt and revealed to me, for the first time at close quarters, a woman's private parts. I do not think I much liked what I saw, but in no time my mating chemistry acted prematurely and soon I was fleeing the scene, feeling more guilty than ever before and leaving a confused girl wondering what had caused me to desert her.

Back home I realised it was Friday night. Had I to go to confession? Had I committed a mortal sin? When did I commit it? Was it when the thought of having sex first came to mind? Was it when I made the suggestion to the girl, or was it when nature did its work? I was, to say the least, confused in my mind and decided that for the sake of inner peace I had to face my confessor. Father Eustace was an elderly priest in charge of the parish of Plaisance.

On Saturday afternoon I went to confession.

"Forgive me, Father, because I have sinned. I accuse myself of having done bad things."

"The bad things you did, son, was it with a boy or a girl?"

"With a girl, Father."

"What about boys, have you ever done any bad things with them?"

"I do not know what you mean, Father."

"Have you ever played with your body?"

"Not deliberately, Father."

"Tell me, my son, this woman you did bad things with, was she married or single?"

"I do not know, Father."

"All right, my son, you will recite ten Our Fathers and six Hail Marys. Your sin is forgiven. You can go in peace."

Another lesson had been learned. Absolution, it seemed, can come easily.

In early 1947 father made plans to take my mother, my brother Billy and me on a three-month holiday to Kenya. It was to be the first time that I had left the islands and my excitement was tempered by doubt that we would get a passage, since there was always a long waiting list and the British India Company's official policy was "first come, first served." But father had his ship-chandler's connections and at the eleventh hour it was confirmed that we had secured passage. We were to travel in the ship's hospital, on the pretext that Billy and I were in need of "urgent specialist attention in Nairobi."

Father was a man of tremendous *joie de vivre* and every evening for the three days of the voyage the hospital of the SS Aronda saw some lively drinking. Each morning it fell to Billy and me to tidy up and remove the empty beer and whisky bottles in time for the captain's inspection. When the uniformed captain and his entourage arrived, Billy and I would try to look ill and father would put on his most lugubrious face, which after the previous night's party was not all artifice. The inspection party included the English purser and the Indian doctor, father's accomplices and drinking companions.

In Kenya we stayed with my mother's cousin, Mr. Michel Hoareau, an official of the East African Railways and Harbours, and even then it was obvious that trouble was brewing in that most beautiful of African countries. People were classified by race, European, Asian or African, each with a corresponding pay scale. The injustices and pressures which this system created were nowhere more apparent than among the multiracial Seychellois who had found jobs in East Africa. Because Uncle Hoareau was classed as a European he had a large home and a much higher salary than Mr. Dagama, a Seychellois of Asian extraction who was three times more competent. No one could blame Mr. Hoareau for taking advantage of the situation, but it caused severe social strains which divided the Seychellois community in Kenya.

I worked happily through my years of secondary education, fit and strong and without a care in the world. Jacques Yves Cousteau, the French underwater pioneer and inventor of the aqualung, came to Mahé to make his famous film, *The Silent World*. As a member of the Seychelles Sea Scouts I visited his ship-cum-laboratory, the *Calypso*, and went away, like most of the islanders, with a new enthusiasm for underwater exploration. After Cousteau's visit, I spent most of my weekends spear-fishing, unconcerned about any danger. There were plenty of sharks around the Seychelles but they had never been known to attack anyone. They did not bother us and we, in turn, did not worry about them. In a paradise island you can coexist quite happily with almost any living creature.

At school I became friendly with Robin Crawford, the son of Sir Frederick, who became Governor in 1951. Robin became my classmate and close friend for two years and I was often a guest at Government House. I had no idea, of course, that years later I would occupy the house as President, nor, looking at the dignified figure of the Governor, so apparently secure in his position, that he would be so shabbily treated by his colleagues in Whitehall. (Sir Frederick's passport was confiscated in 1967 by the British Government because he had appeared in public places with members of the Ian Smith government. He died in Cape Town in South Africa in 1978, a bitter man, sacrificed on the altar of political convenience and the shabby diplomacy which often surrounds it.)

I also became fascinated with another visitor to the islands. Archbishop Makarios of Cyprus was sent into exile by the British Government and lived for a year in Sans Souci, a magnificent house which commanded one of the most beautiful views on earth. Occasionally I saw him walking in Victoria, wearing his heavy black cassock and black hat, his beard and hair immaculately groomed. To a schoolboy he looked impressive and dignified. I think I was slightly in awe of the man with his vaguely sinister smile and I could never have imagined that only a few years later he would be coming to me in my position as Chief Minister asking to revisit the islands.

At that time I was busy working under the progressive tutelage of a kind British teacher called Brother Austin O'Donnell. I spent the last three years at college under his instruction and it was through his efforts and encouragement that I passed my exams. I became captain of the football XI, then house captain and finally head prefect. At Speech Day in my final year I addressed the annual gathering of parents and students. I was seventeen and had been accepted as a law student by the Middle Temple in London. I had my father's blessing to go abroad and a testimonial from Brother Austin that I was "full of initiative" and that I had "on several occasions displayed leadership qualities."

A few weeks later I packed my bags and made my way to the pier, waved my parents, family and friends goodbye and climbed aboard the SS *Amra* bound for Mombasa. I was on my way to London with an imagination filled with preconceptions and bolstered by the blind confidence and enthusiasm of youth. I stood motionless on deck for what seemed like hours, watching Mahé becoming smaller as the vessel steamed across a featureless ocean.

Suddenly the ship's radio blasted out a message for me from a girl-friend, followed by a song request. It was Harry Belafonte singing about leaving a little girl in Kingston Town.

'Cause I'm sad to say
I'm on my way.
Won't be back
For many a day . . .

I cried, laughed, was excited . . . a new dawn was before me.

"The Family House"

Nuruddin Farah

Nuruddin Farah, born in Baidoa, Somalia, in 1945, is a winner of the Neustadt International Prize for Literature. His works include three trilogies: Variations on the Theme of an African Dictatorship, Blood in the Sun, *and a recent trilogy that includes the novels* Links, Knots, *and* Crossbones. *"The Family House" was first published in 2008.*

Early one January morning in Mogadiscio, I was awakened by a phone call from a woman I didn't know. I was the first member of my family to have returned to Somalia since the outbreak of civil war, when Mogadiscio descended into anarchy following the collapse of the dictatorial regime of Siad Barre. After more than a decade of turmoil, an interim government had been set up, and I went to the country on a one-man peace mission, hoping that, in my role as a writer, I might be able to bring the politicians and the warlords closer to one another. But the phone call wasn't about peace. The woman, describing herself as a "looker-after" of my older brother's property, wanted me or my brother to pay her fifty dollars a month for having kept the house in as good a state as she had found it when the city went up in flames, back in 1991.

I had no idea what to say. I assumed that this woman had occupied my brother's house because it happened to be in an area controlled by a warlord belonging to her clan family, yet she somehow was not satisfied with having lived for free on the property. She wanted to be paid for her pain. Fifty dollars a month for the last eleven years was no paltry sum, and far more than my brother, who now lived in North America with his family, could ever afford. I asked her, what would she do if my brother couldn't pay? She said that a refusal to pay would prove most regrettable. Then she hung up.

I was overwhelmed by a sense of agitation. If my brother's house had been taken over by a stranger, what had happened to the first home we had owned in Mogadiscio, the family house?

239

I grew up a couple of hundred miles away from Mogadiscio, in a small town in Ogaden, the Somali-speaking territory under dispute by Ethiopia and Somalia. When I was seventeen, fierce fighting erupted between the two countries, and our family and many others fled to Mogadiscio, abandoning our home and property, including a large commercial farm where my father grew maize, millet, sesame, vegetables, and fruit.

My father's farm, which yielded two crops in a good year, was in a fertile triangle about a three-hour walk away from Kallafo, a town astraddle the River Shabelle, one of two permanent rivers that rise in Ethiopia and flow southward into Somalia to empty into the Indian Ocean. Because our town boasted the most grain production in the entire region, it attracted a variety of residents, some from the Somali-speaking peninsula, others from Ethiopia. There was a large community of Yemenis engaged in business, and a garrison of Ethiopian soldiers recruited from all the various ethnic groupings of the Empire. At one point, during the better part of a year, the town hosted a small community of Palestinian refugee families whose children attended our school.

The town had two schools, both on the other side of the river, right under the watchful eyes of the Ethiopian garrison stationed up on Government Hill. One of them was largely the consequence of my father's commitment to community-funded education, and the fact that the Ethiopian government, which administered the disputed region, was not keen on providing schooling for us. The other school offered its classes in English, having been established by the American churches. There was a bridge dividing the section of town where we lived from the barracks where the Ethiopians camped. Because their salaries were seldom paid on time, the Ethiopian soldiers were in the habit of levying their expenses by intimidating the civilian population and taking everything at gunpoint. We lived in daily fear for our lives, and suffered humiliation at the hands of the soldiers, who behaved as they pleased. We dreaded crossing the bridge on our walk to school alone, and avoided encounters with the soldiers after dark.

My family had a very large compound that was alive with activity all day long and all year round. There were lots of comings and goings, of relatives visiting from the hinterland, or herdsmen tying their beasts in our huge pen for several days, time enough for them to sell their cattle. Then they would give their customs duty to my father, to buy what they needed from his general store. Our compound was busy, too, because my father, a stalwart supporter of community education, provided free housing and gave his produce gratis to the teachers there. My mother had her own dozen or so head of cattle, received in advance from my father's holdings in the event of a divorce. We, the boys, helped her milk the cows in the mornings and evenings, and on occasion we assisted the herdsman hired to escort the cattle out of town, where they were meant to graze. One of my younger sisters was assigned to deliver the milk to a restaurant where it was sold.

There were eleven of us when we fled the fighting, and it wasn't easy to start over from scratch. My parents had lived in Mogadiscio before, and my two older brothers had been born there, but the city still felt alien to us. We weren't used to living in rented accommodations, or to sharing our space with others. My father fell into a depression that he never came out of altogether.

Mogadiscio, which had existed as a city-state from the tenth century on, had its own cosmopolitan charm. Its history had been that of a prosperous city, beautiful, peaceful, and receptive to newcomers. It had teahouses and restaurants with terraces, and cinemas and theaters. The mysterious quality of the city also had a way of drawing interest. Compared to the hick town where we had lived in constant fear for our lives, Mogadiscio was welcoming, a city synonymous with civility. Moreover, most everybody was in a celebratory mood. If you were lucky, as I was, you got invited to parties every weekend, to dance to the latest music or listen to a singer of the more popular Somali tunes from a musical that had just hit town. I would have myself fitted for a new pair of trousers— when I could afford to—and I often enjoyed my cappuccino along with a sandwich wrapped in take-away foil while sitting with a friend in a car after an evening at the movies. My friends took every opportunity that came their way to throw a party or to go out to one.

When I first arrived in Mogadiscio, I loved the labyrinthine networks of the city's alleyways; I loved the *mélange* of its cultures—an eleventh-century minaret cheek to jowl with a glass house. *Mogadiscians* spoke every language in an idiom of their own manufacture. I loved the contrasts on display at every turn, from the monument raised in memory of Mussolini to the palace in which the city's Zanzibari sovereign defined the city's cosmopolite. I adored the sea that served as the city's face. Above all, I loved the Tamarind shopping complex, the city's traditional prize market and joy, where the shoppers, dressed in their finest getups, sauntered in, in search of an after-siesta bargain. The city put on a sunny smile soon after siesta; the evenings were starry fun, and the city came alive. In those days, the city was innocent of the meanness of crime.

There was an epic dustiness to the pre-monsoon storms, as the sea raged and the minarets blared, praying for rain. We were poor, though, and our prayers were to own our own house again one day. Meanwhile, we did what we could to survive. I am the third of four brothers, and my older brothers and I landed jobs relatively quickly: one as a teacher, one as an administrator, and I as a clerk and typist. One of my sisters stayed at home to help my mother, and the younger siblings went to school. My three brothers and I, "the boys," rented a very large room, with its own outhouse, close to where "the family"—my parents and younger brothers and sisters—lived in two rooms. Our food was prepared at the family kitchen, and we all ate together.

Six years later, we were still living in temporary accommodations. I was married and had a young son by then. One day he was playing outside, opening and closing the gate, when the landlady came to collect the rent. I heard her shout, "Stop it!" My son started screaming fitfully and wouldn't be silenced. When I came to see what was afoot, the landlady was telling my mother off for letting "this small thing destroy my house!" Without thinking, I gave the landlady our notice and told my worried mother to find us a house.

My mother found a six-room house in the district of Howl-Wadaag. Three of the rooms were tolerably livable; the other three were half mud and half stone. I arranged a loan through a friend at a bank, and we moved into the tolerable part of the house. After having paid off the loan, we hired masons to rebuild the other three rooms and a spacious courtyard. There was also a bathroom with a shower and a kitchen where my mother and her friends used to sit talking as they sifted rice and cooked. We all found ourselves working harder, and even my father's depressed spirit was somewhat lifted. Now that we had our own house, we no longer felt as if we were strangers in this city.

We registered the property in the name of my youngest brother, being aware that most of us wouldn't be living there forever. In 1974, I left Somalia on a scholarship to Britain, soon after which it proved unwise to return. I had been threatened with a thirty-year detention by Siad Barre's regime for a novel I had published in London. My brothers and sisters had stayed on in Mogadiscio throughout this period, gradually acquiring their own homes but continuing to meet every Friday for lunch at the family house.

Near the end of the 1980s, the internal politics of Somalia erupted. Siad Barre had come to power through a military coup in 1969 and was determined to hold onto it until he was run out by a ragtag of armed militiamen. A cold war strategist, he played the Soviets against the United States and its allies, now befriending one who supported him, now turning to the other in search of further military and financial assistance. He was a dictator, divisive in his politics, aligning himself with this or that clan family until he ran out of friends—when everyone had become his foe. He came to rely more and more on his immediate family, in whom he invested politically, militarily, and financially. Several powerful clan families had rebelled against Siad Barre's regime, and there were insurrections throughout the country. The *clan*, let me explain, is an extended patrilineal network that owes its existence to a political construction whose aim was to provide the blood community with an imagined identity. That the concept of a clan was artificially constructed is evident from the notion of *tol*, a Somali word meaning both "kinship" and "to stitch together"! I am of the heretical view that it is worthwhile to find out *what* has made two clan-based militia groupings clash, not just *who* is fighting whom. Power (who is to become the head of state) and wealth (who has the right to collect taxes or tributes and keep them) are two of the primary reasons for all of the fighting between clans. To prove that he had more right than anyone else to remain president, Barre sent in his army to quell the militiamen fighting to overthrow him, and he also employed South African mercenary pilots to raze entire cities, killing hundreds of thousands of civilians. As a result, Mogadiscio came under attack from a confederacy of clans, and Barre took to bombing those parts of the city suspected of harboring dissidents.

At the time, I was living close by in Uganda, where I was teaching at the university. I remained aware of what was going on through contact with family and friends. My mother had died a few months before the fierce fighting broke out. As the conflict worsened, the clans that had variously collaborated with the regime until Siad Barre's overthrow began to fall out with one another. With the situation growing worse by the day, the rest of my family locked up their houses as though they were going away for the weekend. First they went to the coastal city of Kismayo, where they camped for a week while awaiting news. When rumors spread that Kismayo would soon come under attack, they left by boat for Mombasa, in Kenya, where they were put into a refugee camp.

Eventually, one of my sisters migrated to the United States. My father died two days before he was due to join her. One of my brothers made his way to Minnesota. My eldest brother died in Addis Ababa in 2007, and my youngest now lives in Britain, while I am in Cape Town. We're scattered across the world, but the memory of our family house unites us whenever we talk.

I was so disturbed by the early morning phone call in Mogadiscio that I spent the day talking about it to as many people as I could, including some whose own property was now in the hands of militiamen. The family house was located in an area that had lately come to be known as *Bermuda* because it was thought to be so dangerous. Everyone advised me not to go there without first getting in touch with either the deputy chief of the police force, who could provide a security detail for me, or the warlord whose militiamen controlled the area. I also sought the opinion of the manager of the hotel where I was staying, in the north of the city. He was a stalwart politician with many connections, and, as luck had it, he knew a distant cousin of mine. Perhaps she could enlighten me as to what had become of our family home, he said.

The following day, the young woman came to see me. Clearly worried, she explained that Bermuda was a no-go area, notorious for its years of fierce street-by-street gunfights between militiamen allied with the most ruthless of the warlords. She had lived there herself until the fighting drove her out. When I insisted on going to find the house, she suggested that I call on "Warlord G," whose militiamen were said to run Bermuda as their fiefdom these days, and request that he provide me with a clearance so that I wouldn't come to harm if I were stopped there.

I had met Warlord G once before, in 1996, and he struck me as a man with whom one could do business. I arranged to be taken to his stronghold by two men related to him: one was a former colonel in the defunct national army who was now chief of the prime minister's security detail; the other was a member of parliament.

Only one route linked the northern part of Mogadiscio, once under the control of the warlord Aideed's faction, to the south, formerly under the control of the warlord Ali Mahdi. The traffic was very heavy: taxis, trucks, private saloon cars, government-owned vehicles bearing military or police insignia, "technicals" carrying their warlord *en route* to or from their reduced power base.

Today, Mogadiscio is relatively peaceful, and Somalia's interim government, the Transitional National Government, exists alongside the warlords in an uneasy cohabitation. Some warlords, including Warlord G, hold ministerial positions in the transitional government and thus are not in opposition to it, yet they continue to strengthen their hand in any way they can. Others have allies in neighboring Ethiopia, which is interested in keeping Somalia from being divided into fiefdoms. Even though the city is awash with weapons—some going back to the Soviet era, and many more from the time when the United States was an ally of Siad Barre's regime—people are not disturbed by the presence of these weapons until there is a shooting, which is rare these days. At the time of my visit, however, a spirit of danger still reigned.

When we arrived at Warlord G's redoubt, he and I talked about peace for a good two hours. He wore jeans and trainers, and was so relaxed— even when he called over a young militiaman who had misbehaved—that he might have been a man on safari. (I had no idea what the man being admonished had done.) Just before we left, I asked Warlord G if he thought it safe for me to go to Bermuda to see what state our family house was in. He responded that, as far as he knew, the area was now very safe. He offered to send in his special commando, if need be, but he doubted that it would be necessary. Still, it took some arm-twisting to make the colonel who had driven me to Warlord G's stronghold agree to let us use his personal car, and even more to convince the member of parliament to come with us.

We were well on our way when the colonel revealed that he knew that our family home was two doors away from his uncle's property. We entered Bermuda from the south and drove as slow as a snail in an effort to avoid impact from the deep depressions in the roads. The colonel explained that the ditches had contained sewage system drainage pipes rumored to have been sold in Nairobi and the Arabian Gulf by militiamen. The telephone poles had no wires, and you could be sure that the water pipes had been removed, too.

As we drove slowly along, suddenly the earth gave way under the tires of our car, and we fell into one of the ditches. The two front tires spun round and round, covering us with fine red sand. By now the whole place was alive with curious onlookers. We clambered out of the vehicle and pushed it out of the sand, back onto firmer ground. A bare-chested man in a sarong, between forty and fifty years of age, came forward in the self-important manner that some men display in such situations.

When he asked the purpose of our visit, the colonel introduced himself in a way that made it clear that we had been sent there by Warlord G. "We're looking for my uncle's house," he said, mentioning his uncle by name. Could the man take us there? "No problem," the man in the sarong told us, instructing us to park the car under the tree in front of his house, lock it up, and follow him.

We walked eastward, away from the inhabited area of Bermuda and into a zone of total grief. I had never seen so much devastation in my life. What I saw called to mind wartime images of humans with their eye sockets emptied, their noses removed, heads bashed in until they were featureless and couldn't be recognized as humans anymore. The houses of Bermuda looked like no houses at all. Having been exposed to the elements for several years, vandalized, and not lived in, they had no roofs, no windows, no doors. We stopped walking, and the man in the sarong pointed at a house, saying to the colonel, "That's your uncle's house." Whereupon the colonel turned to me and said, "In that case, it's yours." I couldn't believe that I was looking at my family's savings so recklessly wasted. I refused to go inside, fearful that I might do or say something stupid, or perhaps even faint from the shock of the destruction before my eyes. Could someone else please go inside and tell me if it was really our family house? I stayed where I was, and described to the others what I remembered about the layout of the six rooms.

The others went inside and then came back out, confirming that it was indeed as I had described. But I dared not step inside, lest I should feel sadder than I already felt, having seen so much devastation all around. This was judgment day, and I didn't like the thoughts that were crossing my mind.

I met Warlord G once again, at an airport, when I was leaving Somalia. He asked if I had found our family house. I told him about its state of ruin, how there was no roof, the windows had been removed, and the doors, too. He called a construction engineer over and then offered—if I would put in about two thousand dollars to have it redone—to rent the house for me and send the rent money to me anywhere I liked, even Cape Town. I said I would think it over.

Memoirs of an
Arabian Princess from Zanzibar
(excerpt)

Emily Ruete

*Before Zanzibar joined Tanganyika to form the nation of Tanzania, it was
part of an Arab kingdom that also included Muscat on the Arabian peninsula. Born in 1844, Salamah bint Saïd was a princess in the royal family of
Zanzibar. Her father was the sultan, Seyyid Saïd, and her mother was a
Circassian concubine. Salamah was a young woman who combined a spirit
of independence with rather poor judgment. She was unusual in having
learned to read and write, but her decision to back an attempted palace
coup led to her exile. She married a German trader and took the name
Emily Ruete. After her husband was killed in an accident, she wrote her
memoirs in German.* Memoirs of an Arabian Princess from Zanzibar *is
said to be the first biography of an Arab woman ever written.*

[Translated from the German by Lionel Strachey.]

It was at Bet il Mtoni, our oldest palace in the island of Zanzibar, that I
first saw the light of day, and I remained there until I reached my seventh
year. Bet il Mtoni is charmingly situated on the seashore, at a distance of
about five miles from the town of Zanzibar, in a grove of magnificent
cocoanut palms, mango trees, and other tropical giants. My birthplace
takes its name from the little stream Mtoni, which, running down a short
way from the interior, forks out into several branches as it flows through
the palace grounds, in whose immediate rear it empties into the beautiful
sparkling sheet of water dividing Zanzibar from the continent of Africa.

A single, spacious courtyard is allotted to the whole body of buildings
that compose the palace, and in consequence of the variety of these structures, probably put up by degrees as necessity demanded, the general
effect was repellent rather than attractive. Most perplexing to the uniniti-
ated were the innumerable passages and corridors. Countless, too, were

247

the apartments of the palace; their exact disposition has escaped my memory, though I have a very distinct recollection of the bathing arrangements at Bet il Mtoni. A dozen basins lay all in a row at the extreme end of the courtyard, so that when it rained you could visit this favourite place of recuperation only with the help of an umbrella. The so-called "Persian" bath stood apart from the rest; it was really a Turkish bath, and there was no other in Zanzibar. Each bath-house contained two basins of about four yards by three, the water reaching to the breast of a grown-up person. This resort was highly popular with the residents of the palace, most of whom were in the habit of spending several hours a day there, saying their prayers, doing their work, reading, sleeping, or even eating and drinking. From four o'clock in the morning until twelve at night there was constant movement; the stream of people coming and leaving never ceased.

Entering one of the bath-houses—they were all built on the same plan—you beheld two raised platforms, one at the right and one at the left, laid with finely woven matting, for praying or simply resting on. Anything in the way of luxury, such as a carpet, was forbidden here. Whenever the Mahometan says his prayers he is supposed to put on a special garment, perfectly clean—white if possible—and used for no other purpose. Of course this rather exacting rule is obeyed only by the extremely pious. Narrow colonnades ran between the platforms and the basins, which were uncovered except for the blue vault of heaven. Arched stone bridges and steps led to other, entirely separate apartments. Each bath-house had its own public; for, be it known, a severe system of caste ruled at Bet il Mtoni, rigidly observed by high and low.

Orange trees, as tall as the biggest cherry trees here in Germany, bloomed in profusion all along the front of the bath-houses, and in their hospitable branches we frightened children found refuge many a time from our horribly strict schoolmistress! Human beings and animals occupied the vast courtyard together quite amicably, without disturbing each other in the very least; gazelles, peacocks, flamingoes, guinea fowl, ducks, and geese strayed about at their pleasure, and were fed and petted by old and young. A great delight for us little ones was to gather up the eggs lying on the ground, especially the enormous ostrich eggs, and to convey them to the head-cook, who would reward us for our pains with choice sweetmeats.

Twice a day, early in the morning and again in the evening, we children—those of us who were over five years old—were given riding lessons by a eunuch in this courtyard, without at all disturbing the tranquillity of our animal friends. As soon as we had attained sufficient skill in the equestrian art, our father presented us with beasts of our own. A boy would be allowed to pick out a horse from the Sultan's stables, while the girls received handsome, white Muscat mules, richly caparisoned. Riding is a favourite amusement in a country where theatres and concerts are unknown, and frequently races were held out in the open, which but too often would end with an accident. On one occasion a race nearly cost me my life. In my great eagerness not to be outstripped by my brother Hamdan, I galloped madly onward without observing a huge bent palm tree before me; I did not become aware of the obstacle until I was just about to run my head against it, and, threw myself back, greatly terrified, in time to escape a catastrophe.

A peculiar feature of Bet il Mtoni were the multitudinous stairways, quite precipitous and with steps apparently calculated for Goliath. And even at that you went straight on, up and up, with never a landing and never a turn, so that there was scarcely any hope of reaching the top unless you hoisted yourself there by the primitive balustrade. The stairways were used so much that the balustrades had to be constantly repaired, and I remember how frightened everybody was in our wing, one morning, to find how both rails had broken down during the night, and to this very day I am surprised that no accident occurred on those dreadful inclines, with so many people going up and down, the round of the clock.

Statistics being a science unfamiliar to the inhabitants of Zanzibar, no one knew exactly how many persons lived at the palace of Bet il Mtoni, but were I to hazard an estimate, I think I should not be exaggerating if I put the total population at a thousand. Nor will this large number seem excessive if one considers that whoever wants to be regarded as wealthy and important in the East must have an army of servants. No less populous, in fact, was my father's town palace, called Bet il Sahel, or Shore House. His habit was to spend three days a week there, and the other four at Bet il Mtoni, where resided his principal wife, once a distant relative.

My father, Seyyid Saïd, bore the double appellation of Sultan of Zanzibar and Imam of Muscat, that of Imam being a religious title and one originally borne by my great-grandfather Ahmed, a hereditary title, moreover, which every member of our family has a right to append to his signature.

As one of Seyyid Saïd's youngest children, I never knew him without his venerable white beard. Taller in stature than the average, his face expressed remarkable kindness and amiability though at the same time his appearance could not but command immediate respect. Despite his pleasure in war and conquest, he was a model for us all, whether as parent or ruler. His highest ideal was justice, and in a case of delinquency he would make no distinction between one of his own sons and an ordinary slave. Above all, he was humility itself before God the Almighty; unlike so many of great estate, arrogant pride was foreign to his nature, and more than once, when a common slave of long and faithful service took a wife, my father would have a horse saddled, and ride off alone to offer the newly wedded couple his good wishes in person.

My mother was a Circassian by birth. She, together with a brother and a sister, led a peaceful existence on my father's farm. Of a sudden, war broke out, the country was overrun by lawless hordes, and our little family took refuge "in a place that was under the ground"—as my mother put it, probably meaning a cellar, a thing unknown in Zanzibar. But the desperate ruffians found them out; they murdered both of my mother's parents, and carried away the three children on horseback. No tidings ever reached my mother as to the fate of either brother, or sister. She must have come into my father's possession at a tender age, as she lost her first tooth at his home, and was brought up with two of my sisters of her own years as companions. Like them she learned to read, an accomplishment which distinguished her above the other women in her position, who usually came when they were at least sixteen or eighteen, and by that time of course had no ambition to sit with little tots on a hard schoolroom mat. She was not good-looking, but was tall and well-built, and had black eyes; her hair also was black, and it reached down to her knees. Of a sweet, gentle disposition, nothing appealed to her more than to help someone who might be in trouble. She was always ready to visit, and even to nurse invalids; to this very day I remember how she would go from one sick bed to another, book in hand, to read out pious counsels of comfort.

My mother had considerable influence with Seyyid Saïd, who rarely denied her wishes, though they were for the most part put forward on behalf of others. Then, too, when she came to see him, he would rise, and step toward her—a signal distinction. Mild and quiet by nature, she was conspicuously modest, and was honest and open in all things. Her intellectual attainments were of no great account; on the other hand, she showed admirable skill at needlework. To me she was a tender, loving mother, which, however, did not prevent her from punishing me severely when I deserved it. Her friends at Bet il Mtoni were numerous, a rare circumstance for a woman belonging to an Arab household. No one's faith in God could have been stronger. I call to mind a fire, which broke out one moonlight night in the stables, while my father was in town with his retinue. Upon a false alarm that our house had caught, my mother seized me under one arm and her large Koran under the other, and ran out of doors. Nothing else concerned her, in that moment of peril.

So far as I can remember, my father—the Seyyid, or Sultan—had only one principal wife, from the time I was born; the other, secondary wives, numbering seventy-five at his death, he had bought from time to time. His principal wife, Azze bint Sef, of the royal house of Oman, held absolute sway in his home. Although small and insignificant-looking, she exercised a singular power over her husband, who fell in readily with all of her ideas. Toward the Sultan's other wives and to his children she behaved with domineering haughtiness and censoriousness; luckily she had no children of her own, else their tyranny would certainly have been unendurable. Every one of my father's children—there were thirty-six when he died—was by a secondary wife, so that we were all equals, and no questions as to the colour of our blood needed to be raised.

This principal wife, who had to be addressed as "Highness" (for which the Arabic is Seyyid, and the Suahili Bibi), was hated and feared by young and old, high and low, and liked by none. To this day I remember how stiffly she would pass everybody by, hardly ever dropping a smile or a word. How different was our kind old father! He always had a pleasant greeting to give, whether the person was one of consequence or a lowly subordinate. But my high and mighty stepmother knew how to keep herself on the top of her exalted rank, and no one ever ventured into her presence without being specially invited. I never observed her to go out unless grandly escorted, excepting when she went with the Sultan to their bathhouse, intended for their exclusive use. Indoor, whoever met her was completely awestruck, as is a private soldier here in the presence of a general. Thus the importance she gave herself was felt plainly enough, although upon the whole it did not seriously spoil the charm of life at Bet il Mtoni. Custom demanded that all of my brothers and sisters should go and wish her a "good morning" every day; but we detested her so cordially that scarcely one of us ever went before breakfast, which was served in her apartments, and in this way she lost a lot of the deference she was so fond of exacting.

Of my senior brothers and sisters some were old enough to have been my grandparents, and one of my sisters had a son with a grey beard. In our home no preference was shown to the sons above the daughters, as seems to be imagined in Germany. I do not know of a single case in which a father or mother cared more for a son than for a daughter simply because he was a son. All that is quite a mistake. If the law allows the male offspring certain privileges and advantages—for example, in the matter of inheritance—no distinction is made in the home treatment given to children. It is natural enough, and human too, that sometimes one child should be preferred to another, whether here in this country or in that far southern land, even though the fact may not be openly acknowledged. So with my father; only it happened that his favourite children were not boys, but two of my sisters, Sharife and Chole. One day my lively young brother Hamdan—we were both about nine years old at the time—accidentally shot an arrow into my side, without, however, doing me much injury. The affair coming to my father's ears, he said to me: "Salamah, send Hamdan here"; and he scolded the offender in such terms as to make his ears tingle for many a day after.

The pleasantest spot at Bet il Mtoni was the *benjile*—close to the sea, in front of the main building—a huge, circular, open structure where a ball could have been given, had such a custom been in vogue with our people. This *benjile* somewhat resembled a merry-go-round, since the roof, too, was circular; the tent-shaped roof, the flooring, the balustrades, all were of painted wood. Here my dear father was wont to pace up and down by the hour with bent brow, sunk in deep reflection. He limped slightly; during a battle a ball had struck his thigh, where it was now permanently lodged, hindering his gait, and occasionally giving him pains. A great many cane chairs—several dozen, I am sure—stood about the *benjile*, but besides these, and an enormous telescope for general use, it contained nothing else. The view from our circular look-out was splendid. The Sultan was in the habit of taking coffee here two or three times a day with Azze bint Sef and all of his adult offspring. Whoever wanted to speak to my father in private would be apt to find him alone in this place at certain hours. Opposite the *benjile* the warship *Il Ramahni* lay at anchor the year round, her purpose being to wake us up early by a discharge of cannon during the month of fasting, and to man the rowboats we so often employed. A tall mast was planted before the *benjile*, intended for the hoisting of the signal flags which ordered the desired boats and sailors ashore.

As for our culinary department, Arabian cooking, and Persian and Turkish as well, prevailed both at Bet il Mtoni and Bet il Sahel. For both establishments harboured persons of various races, with bewitching loveliness and the other extreme fully represented. But only Arabian dress was allowed to us, while the blacks wore the Suahili costume. If a Circassian arrived in her flapping garments or an Abyssinian in her fantastic draperies, either was obliged to change within three days, and to wear the Arabian clothes provided her. As in this country every woman of good standing considers a hat and a pair of gloves indispensable articles, in the East ornaments are essential. In fact ornaments are so imperative that one even sees beggar-women wearing them while plying their trade.

At his Zanzibar residences and at his palace of Muscat, in Oman, my father kept treasuries full of Spanish gold coins, English guineas, and French louis; but they contained as well all sorts of jewellery and kindred female adornments, from the simplest trifles to coronets set in diamonds, all acquired with the object of being given away. Whenever the family was increased, through the purchase of another secondary wife or the birth— a very frequent event—of a new prince or princess, the door of the treasury was opened, so that the newcomer might be suitably endowed according to his, or her rank and position. In case of a child being born, the Sultan would usually visit mother and child on the seventh day, when he would bring ornaments for the infant. A newly arrived secondary wife would likewise be presented with the proper jewellery soon after she was bought, and at the same time the head eunuch would appoint the domestics for her special service.

Although my father observed the greatest simplicity for himself, he was exacting toward the members of his household. None of us, from the oldest child to the youngest eunuch, might ever appear before him except in full dress. We small girls used to wear our hair braided in a lot of slender little plaits, as many as twenty of them, sometimes; the ends were tied together; and from the middle a massive gold ornament, often embellished with precious stones, hung down the back. Or a minute gold medal, with a pious inscription, was appended to each little plait, a much more becoming way of dressing the hair. At bed-time nothing was taken off us but these ornaments, which were restored next morning. Until we were old enough to go about veiled, we girls wore fringes, the same that are fashionable in Germany now. One morning I surreptitiously escaped without having my fringe dressed, and went to my father for the French bonbons he used to distribute among his children every morning, but instead of receiving the anticipated sweetmeats, I was packed out of the room because of my unfinished toilette, and marched off by an attendant to the place from which I had decamped. Thenceforth I took good care never to present myself incompletely beautified before the paternal eye!

Among my mother's intimates were two of the secondary wives who were Circassian, like herself, and who came from the same district as she did. Now, one of my Circassian stepmothers had two children, Chaduji and her younger brother Majid, and their mother had made an agreement with mine that whichever parent survived, should care for the children of both. However, when Chaduji and Majid lost their mother they were big enough to do without the help of mine. It was usual in our family for the boys to remain under maternal tutelage until they were about eighteen to twenty, and when a prince reached this age he was declared to have come to his majority, that is to say, the formalities took place sooner or later, according to his good or bad conduct. He was then considered an adult, a distinction as eagerly coveted in that country as anywhere else; and he was at the same time made the recipient of a house, servants, horses, and so on, beside a liberal monthly allowance.

So my brother Majid attained his majority, which he had merited rather by his disposition than his years. He was modesty itself, and won all hearts through his charming, lovable ways. Not a week passed but he rode out to Bet il Mtoni (for, like his deceased mother, he lived at Bet il Sahel), and although my senior by a dozen years played games with me as if we had both been of the same age.

One day, then, he arrived with the glad news that his majority had been announced by his father, who had granted him an independent position and a house of his own. And he besought my mother most urgently to come and live, with me, in his new quarters, Chaduji sending the same message. To his impetuous pleading my mother objected that without his father's consent she could not accept, and said she must therefore first consult him; as for her, she was willing enough to share Majid's and Chaduji's dwelling if they wished it. But Majid offered to save my mother this trouble by himself asking the Sultan's sanction, and the next day, in fact—my father happening to be at Bet il Sahel—he brought back the coveted permission. Thus our transmigration was decided upon. After a long talk between my mother and Majid, it was concluded that we should not move for a few days, when he and Chaduji would have had time to make the necessary arrangements for accommodating us.

The Worlds of a Maasai Warrior

(excerpt)

Tepilit Ole Saitoti

Tepilit Ole Saitoti was born in 1949 into the nomadic Maasai people of Kenya and Tanzania. Educated at a mission school, Saitoti later became a park ranger and guide, and he was featured in the National Geographic *film* Man of the Serengeti. *He furthered his education in Germany and the United States before returning to Tanzania. The chapter below describes his initiation into manhood, which traditionally requires the killing of a lion.*

The Door to Manhood

Mount Lengai, the flaming beacon, has guarded our land throughout time immemorial. This rumbling deity is a sentinel of geological upheavals. Its colors are governed by the sun's movement and the seasons. I have seen a contemplative Mount Lengai in the light of the full moon; I have seen it golden at dawn and turning purple just before sunset in the rainy season. It sometimes has white and black stripes, a pattern created by volcanic ash (and maybe snow) that has led people to call it Ol Doinyo Osira Lengai (Striped God Mountain). I have seen it calm and clear as if in meditation, sometimes attended by only a single cloud.

In the year 1966, God, who my people believe dwells in this holy mountain, unleashed Her fury unsparingly. The mountain thunder shook the earth and the volcanic flame, which came from deep down in the earth's crust, was like a continuous flash of lightning. During days when the eruption was most powerful, clouds of smoke and steam appeared. Many cattle died, and still more would die. Poisonous volcanic ash spewed all over the land as far as a hundred miles away, completely covering the pastures and the leaves of trees. Cattle swallowed ash each time they tried to graze, and were weakened. They could not wake up without human assistance. We had to carry long wooden staffs to put under the fallen animals to lift them up.

There must have been more than enough reason for God to have unleashed Her anger on us, and all we could do was pray for mercy. My pastoral people stubbornly braved the gusting warm winds as they approached the flaming mountain to pray. Women and men dressed in their best walked in stately lines toward God, singing.

The mountain was unappeased and cattle died in the thousands. Just before the people started dying too, my father decided to move; as he put it, "We must move while we still have children, or else we will also lose them." My father usually summoned all his youths and warriors to consult with whenever there was a major decision to be made. This time I was among them.

I had observed the angry mountain fuming and had even suffered its rage. I had inhaled ash and started feeling the effects in my leg joints. Afraid that I too would die, I eagerly concurred with my father's wish to move.

We left Olngosua le Sanjan the following day early in the morning to avoid the infernal heat. Our household belongings were packed on donkeys driven by women and young children, accompanied by one elder. All other able bodies attended the cattle. Even then my father had more than six hundred head of cattle, although he had lost many to the poisonous ash. In the herd were strong and weak animals. The weak animals had to be practically carried by hand; therefore, we needed all the help we could summon. Eight strong men followed the herd with long poles.

That sunny day Mount Lengai directed its eruption elsewhere and our path was clear and visible. We crossed gorges and horseshoe-like ridges and stretches of plain and headed to the Korongoro Highlands. The barren rocky mountains called Ildonyo Ogol (Difficult Mountains) to our right witnessed our departure. Going downhill was more difficult for the cattle than going uphill. The weak cows tried to waggle along, fell down, and had to be helped up again. My father's distinctive voice could be heard pleading for more and more help for fallen creatures. It was a very tiring and difficult undertaking.

By midday we were hungry and exhausted, and despair was overwhelming us. My father, sensing that we were about to give up, suggested that we rest for a while. He spent our rest period haranguing us about the importance of the task at hand and of persistence. His words went like this: "Fellows, I realize how tired everyone is, but this is the sacred task of caring for cattle which no Maasai man can back away from."

He went so far as to suggest that if an animal was immobile, someone should stay with it overnight, with his expectation being that the animal would be able to walk the next day. My father insisted that we either help the animals or die with them. "This is our ultimate survival," he said.

When we started again, we ascended Waitoni Plateau, where the country leveled and the herd was able to travel better.

We could see Olomorti and Makarot mountains in the distance. As if to welcome us, clouds started forming at Olomorti, and soon there was a shower. We could hear freakish thunder far away, disproportionately loud in comparison with the lightness of the shower.

The rain winds blew our way and we all breathed deeply, including the cattle, who lifted their nostrils to the wind. The cattle started walking with determination toward the rain; even the weakest of the herd quickened their pace. Our spirits and hopes were high again, and my father said, "The darkest hour came just before the dawn, so let us not give in." With those words, our caravan moved on. We passed the now-empty temporal water pools and headed to Esieki and Singau Enkutuk, lion country. So we decided to spend the night in an abandoned kraal overlooking Esieki and proceed the next day. We kept a vigilant watch all night, taking turns to keep the lions away from the herd.

At dawn we started out once again. The trip was not as long as the one the day before, but the area was known for its heat. At midday we arrived at Meshili, our destination. The grass had started to turn green and our cattle cropped it eagerly.

It rained almost every day, and our animals kept getting healthier and healthier. They had become so weakened that they had been unable to turn themselves over at night, but now they could do so without our help.

Now that the rain had come and bad times were behind us, I decided to approach my father concerning my manhood. Such a topic must be discussed with the utmost care before my father or any Maasai elder. The slightest hesitation could be misinterpreted as a lack of seriousness, as unfitness to become a reliable man.

Had my mother been alive, I could have sent her to my father first to smooth the way before me. She would have gone and told my father that I wanted to be circumcised.

One evening after my father had eaten and was lying on his bed contemplating, a common habit of his, I went to him. "Father, I have been wanting to talk to you for a while now, but you have been very busy lately."

"How can I not be busy, son, when God deliberately nearly killed all of us."

"Yes, I know, Father, but the bad days are behind us now."

After a long silence my father cleared his throat and said, "What brings you to me, son?"

"Father, I am grown up enough to become a man. Having no mother, I must tell you this myself. You are my only father and mother, Father."

Recalling my mother's death again, the words were like a knife in my heart. Tears welled in my eyes. I could not bring myself to say another word.

My father cleared his throat and said, "My Tepilit [meaning "my dawn"], keep quiet, because I will consider your words despite all the complications ahead."

He went on to explain the difficulties. "The period for circumcision of the present generation is over, and if the elders allowed you to be circumcised because you are a schoolboy, there is the problem of Moinjet. He will not be allowed and he is older than you. By tradition, the younger one must not surpass the older." After another long silence he said, "Go, son, because I have heard what you have asked."

I left feeling better than when I had arrived; at least the door had not been closed.

Two of my half-brothers who were warriors suggested we move the herd to the lower highlands, as it was greener than the lowland where we were. They asked me to accompany them with another younger half-brother named Shaangwa. We kept our decision from our father because he, always wanting the family to stay together, would have tried to discourage or even prevent our move. We brothers discussed the matter among ourselves and agreed to separate out the cows for milking, which we had to leave behind with the rest of the family. We took the rest of the herd, including a few milk cows. The herd was eager to climb the highland, and that made our work easy.

One of us, a warrior, went ahead to build a thorn fence to enclose the herd at night, and the rest followed with the herd and calves, which were driven separately. The highland was green and the cattle did not have to go a long distance to get enough feed. During watering days, because water was not available, we had to trek far away to the river.

My warrior brothers looked after the larger herd. I was entrusted with the calves, who had to travel the same distance as the cattle for water. Shaangwa was left behind with the newborn calves, who were still too young to require water and who grazed around the kraal.

One day when I was driving calves home from the watering hole, a lioness attacked the herd. I had been away searching for a cow I had lost the previous morning when I heard the commotion. I felt as if ants were crawling all over me; instinctively I spat on my palm to get a better grip on the spear I held at the ready as I walked cautiously toward the herd. Ahead of me in a small opening I saw three donkeys and one lame old cow and headed toward them. The terror on their faces made me think twice. At first I thought the predator might be a rhino, but cattle were never too afraid of that animal. The cow was practically trembling like any terrified human being.

Facing east, I heard a calf coughing and walked toward it. Through thicket branches I was able to make out something brown; I took it to be a hyena, an animal the Maasai are not afraid of. I started to relax, but wanting to kill the predator, I checked for the direction of the wind. Luckily it was blowing away from the animal toward me, and therefore it couldn't get my scent. I planned to stab the hyena repeatedly with my spear. When dealing with a dangerous animal, however, a Maasai would aim for a spot which would speed its death, throwing the spear from a good distance and getting set to run for his life if the animal charged.

After passing the thickets separating me from the beast, I soon realized that it was not a hyena but a lioness, the first I had ever seen. Her majestic muscles and mighty paws had rendered the three-year-old calf helpless. Only the tail was moving. Facing the lioness, I had to change my strategy entirely. I knew that if the wind changed direction, the lioness would catch my scent and I would be done for.

A miscalculation on my part could mean death for me and the calf. My first step was to move far away from the lioness. I had to be close enough to spear the lioness but far enough away to escape if I missed it. I listened for people nearby, in the event I needed help. All I heard were birds and a gang of baboons feeding nearby. I knew the lioness could not see me, for it was preoccupied with killing the calf, and lions usually close their eyes during a struggle to avoid being blinded. But the response of a lion to any human smell is immediate, so I had to act quickly before the wind changed direction, or before the lion finished off the calf and was free to look around. Lying on its back, the lioness held the calf in a deadly embrace. Its huge front paws were around the calf's neck. The calf's muzzle was in its mouth. The lioness was trying to kill the calf by suffocation so as not to attract attention. It was the sound of the calf still trying desperately to breathe that had attracted my attention.

The most crucial moment of my life had arrived. There was no question of turning back now; I had to spear the lioness in the heart and speed her death before she could get to me.

I realized that I could not aim for the heart of the lioness without hurting the calf. There have been embarrassing incidents in Maasailand in which would-be rescuers have accidentally killed people or cattle instead of the predators they were trying to spear. Afraid of losing their own lives, they would spear the attacker while running, and would not aim accurately.

The body of the lioness and that of the calf were inseparable. My only alternative was to aim for the lioness' kidneys, a strike that would kill her, but slowly. The lioness would still be able to fight for a while. I let my spear fly. I saw it cutting the air until it penetrated the lioness' body.

The lioness roared and jumped straight into the air, flinging the helpless calf away. The lioness swirled in midair and landed on all four feet. Her mouth was fully open, her fangs red. Her eyes searched the bushes all around, but fury blinded her. She did not see me.

I should have waited long enough to see which way she went and then gone the opposite way so as to avoid a head-on confrontation. But instead I made a dash for a tree a good distance away. I drew my sword from the sheath. I had never run as fast as I did then; my heels were hitting my buttocks. I could hear only my heartbeat and the lioness' growls. For a moment I thought she was pursuing me. I reached the tree and scrambled up it, dropping my sword in the process. Soon I was high up and secure. The tree was swaying and I thought that all the lioness needed to do was look in that direction and she would no doubt know where I was. I could still hear her growling, trying to dislodge the spear from her flesh.

Moments went by and there was silence. Even the birds stopped singing. The baboons were so frightened that they ran for their lives. I climbed another branch higher.

The quiet was broken once again when another calf wailed for help. No Maasai man can hear a cow's cry of agony and do nothing. I was now unarmed, for my spear was with the lion and my sword was down below. So I yelled loudly and clearly for help. By sheer luck an old man happened to be walking by.

When I saw him, I scrambled down the tree, without him seeing me, and picked up my sword. I walked in his direction. We exchanged greetings and he asked me what happened. As I began to explain, he saw my warrior brother Sambeke coming our way. He happened to have been looking after cattle downwind of us and so had heard the loud cries of the lion and the calf. He came running all the way to give a hand. Sambeke had stumbled on a pride of lions devouring the calf I had heard crying while I was up in the tree. They had just killed another calf but had not yet fed on it because Sambeke caught up with them. They scattered in different directions when they saw him coming.

I could tell Sambeke was furious by the way he stared at me: his eyes were spitting fire! He advanced without saying a word to me, his cattle stick raised. It was obvious he wanted to punish me for having let all the mess happen, which suggested that I had not been as vigilant as a good herder should be. He hurried past the old man without a word of greeting or a glance and came for me.

I ran behind the old man and asked him to keep Sambeke away from me. I told the old man that I had speared a lioness and he did not hesitate to beg mercy for me. While dodging Sambeke's stick, I kept saying, "Tell him I speared a lioness! I speared a lioness!" The old man was pleading, "Leave the child alone! Leave the child alone!" My eyes were full of terror and anger at the same time.

As he tried to strike me, Sambeke asked, "What calf was being attacked when you speared the lioness?" I replied, "Rakanja's calf." That slowed Sambeke a bit, and he said, "Let us first try to locate the calf and see."

We found the calf that had been badly mauled by the lioness. There were severe wounds around its mouth and scratches all over its underbelly. From the wounds, you could tell it was a matter of minutes before the calf would die. Now that I had showed Sambeke the wounded calf and proved to him that a lion had attacked it, he calmed down. He started to believe that I probably had speared the lion, but he was not totally convinced. "Do you remember where it was?" he asked. "Around there," I said, pointing, though I wasn't very sure of the exact location. We walked cautiously toward where I had pointed, fully aware of the danger posed by the wounded lioness.

Sambeke, who was very experienced, having killed a lion himself, spotted a wet blade of grass that he picked up and studied. He went ahead of us and asked, "Where do you think you struck the lioness?" "In the kidneys," I replied. I saw Sambeke picking up a leaf with a red spot on it—animal blood. There was not much blood in the area yet because the spear was still stuck in the animal's abdomen. Soon we saw Sambeke returning with my bent spear in his hand, uttering praise: "Such is the Maasai man, such is the Maasai warrior!"

The three of us scrutinized the spear, discovering that it had penetrated the lioness deep enough to cause death. Moreover, stuck to the spear was the hard kidney fat, so easily distinguishable from body fat. Sambeke handed me my spear with the words "Great Maasai warrior!" I was overcome with pride and ecstasy, an immeasurable confidence known perhaps only by decorated Maasai men.

At the kraal that evening, one of the warriors who was also in charge of driving cattle to the watering hole came over to me as I was milking a cow. With his hand extended and a wide smile, he said, "You must have been out of your mind to have speared such an enormous beast. I have never seen one that big!" His words made me feel really good. He added that he had nearly speared the dead beast again, for fear that it was still alive. As he and I continued talking, the rest of my brothers came around and started analyzing how I had approached the lioness, comparing their experiences to mine and complimenting me for my bravery.

I took the calves to the watering hole the next day as usual. Now that we knew the area was teeming with lions, we were more vigilant and ready to defend the herd. I found the carcass of my lioness and cut off the tail and claws. Being still a youth, I was now allowed to celebrate my achievement. I wished that I had been a warrior, for then I could have celebrated in four kraals. I nonetheless proceeded to stick the tail of the lioness on my spear and celebrate alone. I then hid the tail in a tree. Every other day when I drove the herd to the watering hole I would pass that tree, take out the tail, and celebrate some more. I did this until the tail dried out.

News spread quickly that Saitoti's son had killed a lion. Youths of my generation composed songs of praise in honor of me. My father complained jokingly that I did not deserve praise because he had lost two calves while I was killing only one lion, but I responded, "I had only one spear." When the pride of lions in the area realized that we were on the alert for them during the daytime, they tried their luck at night and were no longer as secretive as before. At night we knew where they were, because they roared a lot to mark their territories.

One late evening we heard them rumbling in the lowlands and felt safe because they were far away. As it grew darker, clouds formed and lightning flashed, followed by deafening thunder. We rushed to drive the calves into their pens and build big fires, not only for warmth but also for security—lions are less likely to attack when a fire is burning. Certainly rain could put out the fire, but a large fire is extinguished more slowly than a small one. It started to rain after we had eaten. A light sprinkle was followed by a downpour as we covered ourselves with hides and went to sleep. The raindrops sounded like drumbeats as they pounded our hides. Their monotony lulled us to sleep. Tired as we were from herding, we slept soundly. One warrior was awakened by a stampeding herd; he shouted at all of us to wake up, for there must be danger. As soon as I awoke, I could tell he was right by the way the cattle were anxiously sniffing the air. They were frightened and excited.

The night was pitch-black. The darkness was almost tangible. Sambeke, the senior warrior, afraid that all the cattle were ready to stampede, ordered us to go outside the fence and chase the lions away, for if the cattle were to jump the fence they would fall prey to every predator around and the losses would be in the hundreds.

I had to climb over the fence into the pitch-blackness. Out there were lions at the ready, and I could easily have stumbled into their jaws. I searched for a flaming branch to use as a flare to light my way; I managed to find only burning wood. I could not use the wood as a torch, but could use it as a weapon. Besides, this beacon would make me visible to lions, I thought. I had forgotten that most cats can see as well or better in the night than in the daytime. Reluctantly I felt my way over the fence, and when my feet were firmly on the ground, I started to walk around the kraal fence, using my spear as a feeler and managing to avoid thorns. Sambeke was also over the fence and was making his way around it. We walked slowly because of the darkness. I was about forty paces or so around the fence when there was a huge crash through the thorn enclosure, accompanied by a roar. Flying clumps of bushes hit me. Shaken, I shouted and cried at the same time.

For a while I was not sure whether I myself had been attacked. When Sambeke and I met up again, he asked me if I was all right and I said, "I do not know."

I thought the pride had succeeded in avenging the death of the lioness I had speared. We went around the fence yelling as loudly as we could to keep the night prowlers away. The lion that had burst through the fence had nearly collided with me. He had already broken into the kraal and we happened upon him just moments before he was able to attack any of our animals. As we went around the kraal, we heard lions roaring out a call to group themselves. They must have separated to circle the herd in case they succeeded in making them stampede. Usually one lion would go in the direction of the wind, trying to agitate the herd with its smell, and the others would wait at the base of the kraal, ready to capture any cattle that broke through the fence.

We remained awake and alert all night until dawn. We had managed to protect our sacred herd.

In February 1967, two months after I had killed the lioness, my father summoned all of us together. In the presence of all his children he said, "We are going to initiate Tepilit into manhood. He has proven before all of us that he can now save children and cattle."

Elizabeth of Toro

(excerpt)

Elizabeth Nyabongo

Born in 1936 into one of Uganda's royal families, Elizabeth Nyabongo was educated at Cambridge University, became Uganda's first female lawyer, and pursued a career as a model and actress. In 1974, she joined the government of General Idi Amin, who had taken power three years before. In a chapter of her autobiography called "The Clouds Gather," she describes some of her first intimations that the country's leader was far more ruthless than she had imagined.

As minister of foreign affairs, I had come as close to the seat of power as it was possible for anyone to come. It was a singular honor for the monarchy—the highest position a member of the Uganda royal families had ever held at the Uganda level, apart from the kings. Since the monarchy had been abolished by Obote, there had been a deliberate policy to discredit it, in spite of Amin's initial overtures, but my appointment was a clear recognition of the fact that there is ability and merit in the royals. It was also a landmark, as I was the first woman to hold that glamorous and prestigious position.

But a foreign minister attracts a lot of envy as well as attention. On the very day I was appointed, certain friends and members of my family, with inside knowledge of the Ministry of Foreign Affairs, issued warnings to me about the network of intrigue within the ministry. As early as the sixties, apparently, a report by a Foreign Ministry official had falsely alleged that the ministry was dominated by princes and people from the tribes in the kingdom areas. My sister Gertrude advised me to get a kettle of my own and have my secretary make my tea and coffee. I was therefore fully alert to the internal struggles I was somehow to cope with, as I turned up at my new office in the Parliament building itself.

Lt. Col. Ondonga was waiting to hand over the keys to me. When I offered him my sympathies, he said, "Don't worry, Elizabeth, you had nothing to do with it." I kept on his personal assistant, Emmanuel Gasana, and his private secretary, Elizabeth Bamuturaki. I noticed that the photos of Ondonga had already been removed from the walls, and gave strict instructions that no photos of me should be put up. Meanwhile, congratulatory messages poured in, directed sometimes to Amin and sometimes to me, nearly all of them affirming that the president had made a clever move in appointing me. One person who did not send me a message of congratulations was our ambassador to Ethiopia, Matiya Lubega, who explained later, "You were so much at the center of attention that I feared for you."

However, no amount of excitement and speculation about my appointment as foreign minister could disguise the fact that President Amin was beginning to lose his grip on the regime. The numerous defections by high-ranking personalities in the government rendered him a psychological blow, not least the defections of his own brother-in-law and former foreign minister, Wanume Kibedi. The ministers of finance and of education, and the ambassador to France fled.

Amin was infuriated and made jittery by these defections. It was obvious to me that unless something was said or done to appease him, he would become uncontrollable in his rage. Surprisingly, he accepted my advice as to the best policy to adopt toward such desertion. I told him that perhaps if he ignored what had happened it would die a natural death. He would not impress anyone by hitting out at Kibedi or at the international press, and I begged him not to embark on a witch-hunt against the defectors' relatives, as they were not to blame.

As well as the defectors, Amin had the Lugbaras and the Alur in the Army and elsewhere to worry about. Externally, pressure was also mounting against the president. The Human Rights Commission report on Uganda was about to come out, and he feared being isolated in international forums. He desperately needed the right foreign minister, and it had become more and more difficult to find one. The vital personal qualities of a foreign minister are international experience, equanimity in the face of pressure, and a certain breadth of vision. Amin's policies, however, constituted a perfect recipe for a disastrous foreign policy. As his foreign minister, I was soon reduced to steering him and the country out of crisis after crisis, each one engineered by Amin himself. Certainly, I could never be sure what the president was going to do next, but I was determined to brave it out and to do the best I could for Uganda and my people, taking advantage of the reservoir of goodwill extended to me by the international community, and by the country itself.

My first public function was to address the new Foreign Service officials at the Institute of Public Administration. In my speech, which was printed on the front page of the leading newspaper the following morning, I advised them to adopt as their guiding principle the political maxim: "In politics there are no permanent friends or permanent enemies. The only thing that is permanent is interest." Whereas it had been standard practice to use such occasions for the expression of simple pleasantries, of no serious consequence, it became my practice to use them to introduce political and philosophical ideas.

Shortly after this engagement, I was asked to represent Amin at the independence anniversary celebrations of Czechoslovakia. I was still feeling my way in my new job, but in Czechoslovakia I nearly put my foot in it. The invasion of Czechoslovakia had taken place while I was modeling in London, and I had followed the course of the revolution religiously; the revolution left a permanent mark on me. In my speech at the anniversary celebrations, I went on and on about the heroism of the Czech people, carefully omitting to mention the invasion, or the revolution, or Dubcek (at least by name)—but I referred to President Svoboda as towering like a rock of strength for the Czech people.

The Soviet ambassador had meanwhile been gradually inching toward me, but the Czech ambassador, his wife and other embassy officials, had formed a sort of line of defense around me. No one before in Ugandan-Czech relations had dared to blunder about in the above manner, thereby risking incurring Soviet displeasure, and the Czechs were never to forget my tribute. The reception was televised and Amin ordered it to be screened three times. He told me he was glad I had praised Czechoslovakia, as we had received a lot of arms and military hardware from them.

The Soviet ambassador complained to Colonel Jack Bunyenyezi about Amin having appointed a pro-British minister of foreign affairs, and Bunyenyezi in my presence reported the complaint to the president. However, I made it up with the Soviet ambassador, and accepted an invitation to a dinner he gave in my honor at the Soviet Embassy in Kampala, at which I toasted the special relationship between Uganda and the Soviet Union.

Within weeks of my taking office, a railway crisis broke out between Uganda and Kenya. Kenya had confiscated our railway wagons, demanding that we pay a long-standing debt we owed them, and all transportation between landlocked Uganda and the port of Mombasa was frozen. Amin sent me to see Jomo Kenyatta. I had for years nursed a secret anger about allegations by the international press of nepotism and corruption where Kenyatta was concerned, which was threatening to undermine the legend that had grown up around him. He was a man whom I had much admired, and it hurt me to think that he might be capable of destroying my belief. "You do not belong to Kenya, you belong to Africa, to all of us," I told him, in audience. "How long does it take to create a legend? . . . It takes generations, a lifetime, and when that legend is destroyed, what exactly do you intend to leave your children, and Africa? Money?" "No, not money," he replied. I spoke to him frankly about the accusations that were upsetting me, and asked him to put an end to them if they were true, and to do something to help Uganda. He called in his permanent secretary and said, "Karithi, I am granting all her requests. I want Uganda's wagons freed immediately so that trade can resume." His minister of state, M. Koinange, had been present throughout the meeting, and when we left Kenyatta, he shook his head in disbelief. "It was a very effective mission," he said to me.

I had to see my Kenyan counterpart, Njoroge Mungai, before I left. As he was seeing me off, Ngithi, the editor of the *Daily Nation*, Kenya's largest newspaper, turned up and said to me, "Your predecessor has just been murdered." I was stunned. "Are you absolutely sure?" I asked him. "Absolutely," he assured me. "Someone in Kampala has just given me the news over the phone."

In a state of shock, I returned to Uganda. No one believed Amin when he said that he had had no part in Lt. Col. Ondonga's murder. He explained to a gathering including ambassadors, ministers, Army officers, and civil servants that Ondonga was related to his wife, Kay—which was true—and that since he, Amin, was related to his own wife, that meant he was related to Ondonga, and therefore he had not killed him, as the newspapers were alleging. He told us that Ondonga's body had been found floating near the dam at Jinja, and that he was making arrangements for it to be taken to West Nile for burial.

However, the truth was blatantly otherwise. Lt. Col. Ondonga and a fellow Lugbara officer, Lt. Col. Ombiya, had been removed from their posts in the Army and made ambassadors at the time Amin had been indulging in a purge of senior Lugbara officers. Ondonga became Uganda's ambassador to the Soviet Union until he was appointed minister of foreign affairs. After his hostile dismissal as foreign minister, he had been warned to leave Kampala and return to his native village in West Nile, where Amin was unlikely to risk a direct confrontation with the Lugbara tribe.

Unfortunately, Ondonga hung around in the capital, where he was being guarded by security men loyal to him in the minister of foreign affairs' residence, not far from Amin's own residence. On the day of his murder, Ondonga went just after midday to collect his little girl from kindergarten. As he was arriving at the school, a car with four assassins from Amin's murder squad inside turned up. They hauled Ondonga screaming from his car and, in front of the assembled children, pushed him into the other car and drove off. A teacher rang Mrs. Kay Amin, who drove to the school herself and took Ondonga's weeping daughter back home with her.

That same day, in the evening, Lt. Col. Toko, the former Air Force commander and then a director in the East African community, called me from Nairobi where he was living and working. He was also a Lugbara, and he was also related to Ondonga and to Kay Amin. He said to me, "I am phoning to assure you that we know you've had nothing to do with all this, and you should not be made to feel bad by anyone."

Nevertheless, I couldn't move into Ondonga's former residence, knowing that I would always be haunted by what had happened, and I remained in the roving ambassador's house.

Meanwhile, the machinations in my ministry continued. Apart from the minister of foreign affairs, Amin had appointed a minister of state for foreign affairs, who was responsible for matters arising over the OAU. His office was situated in the presidential office, and he was a member of the Cabinet, but it was clear that he came under my own ministry. Since Amin did not possess the clarity of mind to operate a strict demarcation of duties, the situation was open to misinterpretation and delay. To say to an African foreign minister that she will not be responsible for OAU matters is like telling a British foreign secretary that his jurisdiction does not extend to Wales and Scotland. When Kibedi was foreign minister, there was no such minister of state for foreign affairs, so the same confusion had not arisen. Ondonga had dealt with it militarily—once, Amin, trying to play the divide and rule game again, had included Ondonga and the minister of state for foreign affairs on the same delegation to an OAU conference at Addis Ababa. Ondonga was in charge of the delegation, and when they reached Addis Ababa and arguments arose as to who was to do what, he merely ordered the minister to stay in his room for the duration of the conference; however, I was no soldier and soon became a victim of the confusion.

Matters in my ministry were not attended to because files were with the minister of state for foreign affairs. One day, an important cable arrived at the communication room in my ministry; I never saw it and no action was taken. Amin phoned and angrily demanded to know the name of the person who worked in the communication room. I gave him the name and he hung up. The purpose of his call was to establish whether I knew the identity of every employee in the ministry; if I had failed to give him the name, he could have accused me of inefficiency and negligence.

The muddle reached its peak at the OAU conference for ministers of foreign affairs which was held in Kampala in March 1974, preceding the OAU meeting of heads of state to be held in June in Mogadishu. Since the OAU was the minister of state for foreign affairs' responsibility, he was going to chair the meeting. It was most embarrassing for me, especially as many more ministers than usual were turning up at the conference because they thought I would be chairing. Fortunately, there was to be a Law of the Sea conference at the same time, in Nairobi, and as I had chaired the conference of the landlocked states earlier in the year, in March, in Kampala, I was eager to pursue this. The president gave me permission to go.

During the night before my departure, there was the sound of heavy gunfire in Kampala, very close to my house near the command post. This was the night of Charles Arube's failed coup. I remember my mother and an aunt by marriage, Mrs. Rwakatale, running panic-stricken into my room. Things quieted down, and in the morning, I sent my driver to check if the roads were clear, and also rang the airport to see if it was closed. I knew that I ought to call the president to ascertain that it was still all right for me to leave for Nairobi. I managed to get through and offered my sympathy for Arube's attempted coup. Amin was keen to restore normality as fast as possible because of the OAU conference, so he agreed that I should proceed to Nairobi.

The question of access to the sea was a matter of life and death for landlocked Uganda—even Amin appreciated this. The Law of the Sea conference was a follow-up to the earlier meeting in Kampala, which had issued the Kampala Declaration, but the landlocked states were in the minority and did not have the benefit of having either of the two super powers on their side. The issues the conference had to deal with included the jurisdiction of the coastal states, territorial waters, the continental shelf, the high seas, and the right of access of landlocked states. We maintained that the wealth of the sea was not a monopoly of the coastal states but belonged to humanity. Our broad strategy was that unless the coastal states agreed to an equitable sharing of the sea's wealth and to reasonable access for the landlocked states as part of a new economic order in the world, there was not going to be a Nairobi Declaration. You could say we succeeded, for there was no Nairobi Declaration.

When I returned to Uganda, I found that Amin was still reacting to the coup, and wanted me to implement certain misconceived moves which were intended to close all possible loopholes through which threats to him might come. One of these involved his decision to post two Nubian security men as diplomats to each of our embassies abroad. The president rang me and told me curtly that he wanted these men, twenty-six in all, to report to the embassies at once. Two days later, he came on the line again, wanting to know why the men had not yet left. I told him that if I were to dispatch them without their having received their inoculations, they would be held in quarantine at the airports. Furthermore, after vaccination they were supposed to wait for a certain period before they could leave the country. "This is a military government. You must send off those men in two days' time," Amin barked. I had to go to Kampala City Council personally and beg the health visitors to back-date the men's certificates. They obliged me, and I was able to dispatch the men and report to Amin accordingly.

These men had direct access to Amin and he relied on them to keep informed of any sabotage activities by Ugandans or others abroad. The exercise was destined to fail even before it took off. Most of the men were uneducated and became easy prey to manipulators, who in certain cases used them as instruments to maneuver good officers out of their positions.

In another phone call, Amin informed me that he was with immediate effect moving the passport section from my ministry to the Ministry of Internal Affairs, and that I was to inform all the embassies at once. It had not occurred to Amin that Ugandans who were determined to defect would do so whether they had passports or not. I did as I was bid, but Ugandans continued to defect, and there was quite a racket in illicit passports.

Of no less seriousness was Amin's move to divorce his four wives. These were Kay from West Nile, Mama Malyamu from Busoga in the east of Uganda, Nora from the Langi tribe, and Medina from the Buganda tribe. One Saturday morning, according to my usual routine, I was in my office studying the political reports from our ambassadors. When Amin rang, I was absorbed in the ambassador to Peking's report. Apparently the president had been expecting me at a meeting that morning with an envoy from the president of another African state, and was surprised at my absence. He had just asked the chief of protocol if I had been informed of the meeting, and been told that I had. "Why didn't you come to the meeting? I can have you replaced, you know," Amin said. "That's a matter for Your Excellency to decide," I replied. "However, as you know, the OAU does not come under my jurisdiction."

"I have divorced all my wives," Amin said, suddenly. There was a long silence.

"I am telling you as my foreign minister," Amin added.

"But why, what have they done?" I asked. "Such a move will be terribly damaging for your image, both here and abroad."

"It's too late now, I've already divorced them," he told me. "If I don't want them, no one can force them on me, and no one can force me to live with them."

"Whereas the country might understand your divorcing Mama Malyamu because of your quarrel with Kibedi, or Kay because of your problems with the Lugbara, or Nora because she is related to Obote, you can pin nothing on Medina. Why don't you keep her?" I implored Amin.

The president listened, but he hung up without giving me any indication of what he was going to do. It was clear that his fears for himself were growing; he no longer felt safe, even with his own wives. In the end, he decided to keep Medina; the others were not so lucky.

One Monday afternoon I had driven to Nakassero Presidential Lodge, where I had an appointment to see Amin. After a long wait along with other Cabinet colleagues, it came to my turn. I was about to go in when Henry Kyemba, now the minister of health, entered, looking very grim. He asked me if I'd mind letting him go in before me, as he had something extremely urgent to discuss with the president. He was still with Amin when I was called in to be briefed on my forthcoming mission. I left, leaving Henry with the president, but without the slightest idea what had occurred.

The following day was Tuesday, Cabinet day. By 10:00 A.M. we were all in our seats, with Shekanabo, the minister of public affairs, in the chair—which was always the case except on rare occasions when the president took the chair. My place was between that of Information and Finance. It was Cabinet ministers' practice to refer to each other by the names of their ministries. I was always referred to as "Foreign," and the minister of animal resources and husbandry was referred to as "Animal"—we were forever being teased because of the connotations attached to these two words.

As usual, the ministers were chatting to each other before the meeting was called to order—it was often through these chitchats that we shared important information and alerted one another to possible dangers, which we couldn't normally do over our tapped phones or at friendly gatherings, however small, without inviting suspicion. I remember, after one Cabinet meeting, suggesting to a colleague I'd just been talking to that we continue our discussion a little longer. "Not over my dead body!" he shuddered. "Amin always rings through after Cabinet meetings to check which ministers have stayed behind to talk amongst themselves. If we hang around here talking, you can be sure someone will tell him you and I have been plotting something or other."

"Information," a Nubian called Juma Oris, and "Finance," Simyeyo Kiyingi, had become great friends of mine. Juma Oris suddenly leaned toward me and whispered, "Kay has been killed."

"Kay who?" I asked.

"Kay Amin," he answered.

I ran out of the Cabinet room to Joy Mawalo, the president's secretary, and asked her if I could speak to Amin. She connected me, and I asked him if it was true that Mrs. Kay Amin had been murdered. He replied in the affirmative.

"Could I come in and see you?" I said.

"Why do you want to see me?" he demanded.

"In connection with Mrs. Amin," I told him.

"You can come and see me," he said.

I went into his office and sat down.

"I don't believe that Kay has been murdered," I said. She had been my favorite among Amin's wives. She was gentle and charming, the first Lugbara to be educated at Gayaza High School and the first Lugbara to go to university.

"I've already told you, why do you ask me again?" Amin snapped. "Kay is dead."

"The country is going to hold you responsible," I said quietly. "If your hands are clean, go on television and radio tonight and explain how she came to die."

Amin picked up his phone and told his secretary to summon the minister of information. Oris came in, looking grave.

"The minister says the country will blame me for Kay's death unless I go on TV and radio immediately to explain her death," Amin said. "What do *you* think?"

Juma Oris, still standing, looked on the verge of tears. In a voice loaded with emotion, he said, "The minister is right."

We were interrupted by a knock at the door, and a Nubian called Ismali Sebi, the president's principal private secretary, walked in with three of Kay and Amin's young children.

"Go back to the Cabinet room. I'll come and address you all this afternoon," Amin said to Oris and myself.

We did as we were told, and the meeting proceeded. The afternoon session, however, was destined to be the most memorable Cabinet session I ever attended. Amin turned up accompanied by Odria, the commissioner of police, himself a Lugbara like Kay, and the head of the CID, who happened to be my brother-in-law, Mukasa. The chairman hurriedly vacated his seat for Amin, and two extra seats were brought for Odria and Mukasa.

"I know everyone will blame me," Amin told the electrified Cabinet, "but I don't mind."

With a gesture, he bade Odria and Mukasa to address us on the results of their investigations into Kay's murder. Among the exhibits the police produced as having been found at the scene of the murder was Kay's dress, which I had seen her wearing on several occasions. We were told that, according to Kay's father, who had been staying with her, Kay had been complaining of headaches and generally not feeling well on the day she died. On Sunday afternoon, Dr. Mbalwa Mukasa had come to collect her in his car and they had driven off somewhere. That had been the last Kay's father had seen of his daughter. On the following day, her body was found in the trunk of Dr. Mukasa's car outside his clinic, her legs and arms mutilated. On the same day, Mukasa tried to take the lives of his wife and six children by administering fatal overdoses of drugs, before committing suicide himself. The wife and children were discovered by a neighbor and rushed to the nearest hospital, where they were revived. We were told that they were still in a critical condition, and had not therefore been interviewed by the police.

Throughout the police briefing, I kept glancing at Amin, looking for clues. He was wearing a bright red short-sleeved shirt which highlighted his blackness, and, for the first time, I noticed how large his arms and hands were. Were these the arms and hands of a murderer? I asked myself, frightened. Could he murder the mother of his children? The thought was beyond my comprehension. But I remembered something the Italian ambassador's wife had told me, about how Kay had called her and asked to see her, and how the ambassador's wife had invited her to tea, and how depressed Kay had seemed to be. Her hostess thought it was because Kay was still in love with Amin, even though he had divorced her. But I, and others, am inclined to think she was carrying Amin's child and was depressed at the thought of having an abortion. Dr. Mukasa was notorious for the many abortions he had performed in Kampala. The questions still remained: Had Dr. Mukasa and Kay been followed that Sunday afternoon after he'd picked her up? If he *had* attempted to perform an abortion on her, had he been caught in the act? Or had Mukasa been her lover? Did the doctor really commit suicide, or had he been forced to take his own life by someone else? Many people believe that only Amin could have arranged such a murder.

One report in connection with Kay's death was particularly disturbing. While we were in the Cabinet meeting that Tuesday, Amin had taken his and Kay's children to the mortuary in Mulago Hospital, where he had pointed to Kay's corpse and said, "Your mother was a bad woman." There is not a shred of evidence to suggest that Kay had ever been unfaithful to Amin; if she had, she would have been dead a long time ago. Was he therefore referring to an abortion, or something else? One thing was clear: Kay's death was an ominous sign for the women of Uganda. Up to this time,

Amin's murderous system had claimed few women as victims; I personally know of only one girl, called Pink Kabahenda, whom he accused of having been a spy of Obote. The combination of the soldier and the Muslim made Amin not quite despise women, but made him feel they presented little or no threat—which made Kay's murder even more mysterious. I felt we were entering the murky waters of psychopathy. Was the president a sadist? Whatever he was, this latest incident boded no good for the rest of us.

Nisa: The Life and Words of a !Kung Woman

(excerpt)

Nisa, as told to Marjorie Shostak

Nisa, a member of the !Kung San ethnic group of the Kalahari Desert, was about fifty years old when she met Marjorie Shostak, who began a twenty-month research visit to Botswana in 1969. As Shostak later wrote, "Nisa is a member of one of the last remaining traditional gatherer-hunter societies, a group calling themselves the Zhun/twasi, 'the real people,' who currently live in isolated areas of Botswana, Angola, and Namibia." (The exclamation point in the name of her people stands for a particular type of tongue click in the !Kung language.) Much of her story concerns sexuality and the raising of children, but Nisa also describes how she and her family supported themselves in the traditional culture of the !Kung.

[Translated from the !Kung by Marjorie Shostak.]

We lived in the bush and my father set traps and killed steenbok and duiker and gemsbok and we lived, eating the animals and foods of the bush. We collected food, ground it in a mortar, and ate it. We also ate sweet nin berries and tsin beans. When I was growing up, there were no cows or goats and I didn't know who the Hereros were. I had never seen other peoples and didn't know anything other than life in the bush. That's where we lived and where we grew up.

Whenever my father killed an animal and I saw him coming home with meat draped over a stick, balanced on one shoulder—that's what made me happy. I'd cry out, "Mommy! Daddy's coming and he's bringing meat!" My heart would be happy when I greeted him, "Ho, ho, Daddy! We're going to eat meat!"

Or honey. Sometimes he'd go out and come home with honey. I'd be sitting around with my mother and then see something coming from way out in the bush. I'd look hard. Then, "Oooh, Daddy found a beehive! Oh, I'm going to eat honey! Daddy's come back with honey for us to eat!" And I'd thank him and call him wonderful names.

Sometimes my mother would be the one to see the honey. The two of us would be walking around gathering food and she'd find a beehive deep inside a termite mound or in a tree. I remember one time when she found it. I jumped and ran all around and was so excited I couldn't stop moving. We went to the village to get some containers, then went back again to the termite mound. I watched as she took the honey out. Then, we went home.

Long ago, when we were living in the bush, our fathers brought us plenty of food! And, animals full of fat—that was especially prized. Whenever my father brought back meat, I'd greet him, "Ho, ho, Daddy's coming home with meat!" And felt thankful for everything and there was nothing that made my heart unhappy.

Except if it was someone else in the village who killed something and came back carrying it. Then I'd look and think, "Uhn, uhn . . . that one, the people in the hut aren't giving-people. If they have something, they never give it to us. Even when they do, they don't give enough so all of us can eat. They are stingy people." My heart would not be happy at all, because that would mean we would have to ask. So, the next morning we would sit around their hut. If they gave us a large portion, my heart would be happy and I would think, "Yes, these people, their hearts are close to ours. They gave mother and father some of what they had." Then everyone would eat.

But, there is always one hut in the village where the people kill you when it comes to food. I remember when we were living with a group of Zhun/twasi and they were eating meat from an animal they had killed. My father asked for some, but they refused. I sat there, thinking, "I'll just sit here and wait. When Daddy kills an animal, then I'll eat meat." Because my father was a good hunter.

Whenever I saw others coming back to the village with meat, I'd ask, "Daddy, how come you didn't go out hunting and kill something so we would have meat? Those people over there are the only ones who will be eating today." My father would say, "Eh, but my arrows didn't have any fresh poison on them. If they did, then, just as these others went out hunting, I would also have gone hunting and killed something for you and your mother to eat." Then I'd say, "Mm, those others are the only ones who ever hunt."

When we were living in the bush, some people gave and others stinged. But there were always enough people around who shared, who didn't fight. And even if one person did stinge, the other person would just get up and yell about it, whether it was meat or anything else, "What's doing this to you, making you not give us meat?"

When I was growing up, receiving food made my heart happy. There really wasn't anything, other than stingy people, that made me unhappy. I didn't like people who wouldn't give a little of what they had. Then my heart would feel bad and I'd think, "This one, I don't like." Or sometimes I'd say, "As I am, you're a bad person and I'll never give you anything." But other times, I'd just cry. Sometimes I'd cry all night and into the morning. Once, I cried because someone had trapped a very small bird and I didn't get any of it. I wanted it and just sat there, crying and crying. Finally, people told me, "It's just a tiny bird, stop crying over it."

It's the same today. Here I am, long since an adult, yet even now, if a person doesn't give something to me, I won't give anything to that person. If I'm sitting eating, and someone like that comes by, I say, "Uhn, uhn. I'm not going to give any of this to you. When you have food, the things you do with it make me unhappy. If you even once in a while gave me something nice, I would surely give some of this to you." Because people like that are very bad. When they see food in front of them, they just eat it.

I used to watch my father when he left the village early in the morning, his quiver on his shoulder. He'd usually be gone all day. If he shot something, when he came back, he'd say, "Eh, I went out to the bush this morning and first I saw an animal, a giraffe. But I didn't track it well. Then I saw an eland and struck it with my arrow. Let's wait until tomorrow before we go find it." The next day we'd fill our ostrich eggshell containers with water and everyone would go to where the animal had died.

One time, my father went hunting with some other men and they took dogs with them. First they saw a baby wildebeest and killed it. Then, they went after the mother wildebeest, and killed that too. They also killed a warthog.

As they were coming back, I saw them and shouted out, "Ho, ho, Daddy's bringing home meat! Daddy's coming home with meat!" My mother said, "You're talking nonsense. Your father hasn't even come home yet." Then she turned to where I was looking and said, "Eh-hey, daughter! Your father certainly has killed something. He is coming with meat."

I remember another time when my father's younger brother traveled from far away to come and live with us. The day before he arrived he killed an eland. He left it in the bush and continued on to our village. When he arrived, only mother and I were there. He greeted us and asked where his brother was. Mother said, "Eh, he went to look at some tracks he had seen near a porcupine hole. He'll be back when the sun sets." We sat together the rest of the day. When the sun was low in the sky, my father came back. My uncle said, "Yesterday, as I was coming here, there was an eland—perhaps it was just a small one—but I spent a long time tracking it and finally killed it in the thicket beyond the dry water pan. Why don't we get the meat and bring it back to the village?" We packed some things, left others hanging in the trees, and went to where the eland had died. It was a huge animal with plenty of fat. We lived there while they skinned the animal and cut the meat into strips to dry. A few days later we started home, the men carrying the meat on sticks and the women carrying it in their karosses.

At first my mother carried me on her shoulder. After a long way, she set me down and I started to cry. She was angry, "You're a big girl. You know how to walk." It was true that I was fairly big by then, but I still wanted to be carried. My older brother said, "Stop yelling at her, she's already crying," and he picked me up and carried me. After a long time walking, he also put me down. Eventually, we arrived back at the village.

We lived, eating meat; lived and lived. Then, it was finished.

My older brother, Dau, was much older than I was. Even when I was born, he already had his own hut and no longer lived with us. Later, he married. But when I was still little, he would go hunting and come home with meat. And just as my father knew how to track and kill animals, my older brother also learned. The memories I have about him aren't unhappy ones—they are the times when my heart felt wonderful.

I used to follow him around wherever he went; I just *loved* him! Sometimes, when he wanted to go hunting, he'd say, "Why don't you just sit in the village? Why are you always following me?" I'd stay home and when he came back with meat, I'd greet him, "Ho, ho . . . my big brother's home!"

Sometimes he took me with him, and although I was already fairly big, he'd put me up on his shoulders and carry me. That's part of the reason I followed him around all the time! When he'd see an animal, he'd put me down, track it, and shoot it. If he struck it, we'd return to the village and he would always let me be the first to tell, "My big brother killed a gemsbok!" The next morning, people would go out with him to track it. Sometimes, I was afraid I'd be thirsty and there wouldn't be enough water, so I'd just stay behind.

Sometimes, when I stayed in the village, he'd tell me to set the bird traps. He only told me, never my little brother, because Kumsa always ate the bait, tiny chon or gow bulbs. He loved those little bulbs and just took them away from the birds.

Once, mother went to set some traps not far from the village. After she came back, Kumsa followed her tracks and ate most of the bulbs. When mother went back late in the afternoon, she found a guinea fowl in one of the traps, but the others were empty of both bird and bait.

Another time, Kumsa got his finger caught in one of the traps (as he often did!) and started to cry. I went to him with my older brother. Dau hit him and said, "If you steal the food from the guinea fowl, it won't get caught! Now, stop eating the bulbs! Have you no sense, taking food out of the traps?"

I never did that. I just held the bulbs in my hand and went to the traps. I'd put the bulb in and leave it there for the birds. I'd check the traps later in the day. If a bird was caught, I'd bring it home and my older brother would take the feathers off.

I also set some of my father's traps. I, all by myself. I'd go alone and set them. But my little brother would stay behind, because he really liked those bulbs!

I used to *love* stewed mongongo fruit. If someone was eating some and didn't give any to me, I'd cry and cry until I got some. But once, I had all the fruit soup and mongongo nut meats I wanted, and I had nothing to cry over.

My older brother often went to the mongongo groves and brought back sacks full of nuts. One time, when he came back, he told my mother, "Here are the nuts. Cook them so you and Nisa can eat. But don't cook so many that you give them away. I'm tired, so listen to what I have to say— I don't want these nuts given away, because I'm giving them all to Nisa. Others will help her cook them so she can drink the fruit soup whenever she wants it. Now, I'm just going to rest until this moon dies. Only then will I go out and collect more nuts." I had all those mongongo nuts to myself and I drank lots of fruit soup and ate lots of cracked nuts.

I also remember the time I got burned. My mother had just come back from digging klaru bulbs, and had put them into a pot to cook into soft porridge. I kept asking, "Mommy, give me some. Why don't you give some to me? Mommy, give me some klaru." Finally, to quiet me, she took some she thought was cool enough from the top of the pot and put it in my hand, but it was still too hot. I dropped it and it landed on my leg. Before I could push it off, it burned me, leaving a large wound. I cried and cried and even after it got dark, I kept on crying. My father said, "Chuko, I've told you again and again, you shouldn't do things that cause Nisa to cry and be full of tears. Why don't you understand? Are you without ears? You keep doing things that make her cry. You, the mother of these little children, can't you understand things?"

People say that salt heals burns, so after they washed it out thoroughly, they crushed some salt into very small pieces and put it on. I wasn't afraid and just let them put it on. Then, I cried and watched as the salt made little bubbles on the wound, "Oh, this salt is terrible . . . eeeee . . . eeeee . . .!" The salt almost killed me. Really, it felt as though it was killing my leg. I almost died from the pain.

The burn lasted a long time and made walking difficult. I couldn't get up easily. When I had to go to the bush I would crawl on my hands. My father blamed my mother, "If you ever do something like that to Nisa again, I, an adult, and her father, will do the same thing to you! I'll take you and throw you into the fire. How could you have almost killed a child? Now, she can't even walk! I'd like to throw you into the fire right now. I won't, people say I shouldn't. But if you ever burn her like that again, I will!" My mother said, "You're right. If you were to throw me into the fire, there wouldn't be any wrong done because I was responsible for your child's getting burned. But she really has no sense. There's nothing worth anything in her head yet. She has no sense at all, not even about asking for food to be given to her."

We lived and lived and after a while the burn healed.

I remember another time, when I was the first one to notice a dead wildebeest, one recently killed by lions, lying in the bush. Mother and I had gone gathering and were walking along, she in one direction and I a short distance away. That's when I saw the wildebeest. I went closer to look but got scared and ran away. I called, "Mommy! Mommy! Come look at this! Look at that big black thing lying there." As she came toward me, I pointed, "There by that tree!" She looked, "Eh! My daughter! My little Nisa! My little girl! My daughter has found a wildebeest!" Then she said, "Go back to the village and tell your father to come." She stayed with the animal while I ran back, but we had gone deep into the mongongo groves and soon I got tired. I stopped to rest. Then I got up and started to run again, following along our tracks, ran and then rested and then ran until I finally got back to the village.

It was hot and everyone was resting in the shade. My older brother was the first to see me. "What's the matter? Dad, look. Nisa's coming back alone. Do you think something bit mother?" I ran over to them, "No, Mommy hasn't been bitten . . . but I, I found a wildebeest lying dead in the bush! We had just left the place where the ground dips down and where the trees are thick and when we came to the opening beside the groves, that's where I saw it. I told Mommy to come look. She stayed there while I ran back here." My father and my older brother and everyone in the village followed me. When we arrived, they skinned the animal, cut the meat into strips and carried it on branches back to the village.

After we came home with the meat, my parents started to give presents of it to everyone. But I didn't want any of it given away. I cried, "*I* was the one who saw it!" Whenever I saw them give some away, I followed the person to his hut and took it back, saying, "Did you see the wildebeest? Mommy and I were together and *I* was the one who saw it!" I took the meat away and hung it again on the branch beside mother's hut. People said, "Oh! This child! Isn't she going to share what she has? Is she a child who sees something and doesn't give any of it to others?" But I said, "Did you see it? I myself saw it with my very own eyes, and this wildebeest is *mine*. I'm going to hang it up by my hut so I can eat it *all*."

Later, I went to play. While I was away, mother took the meat and shared it with everyone. When I came back, I asked where all the meat had gone because I couldn't see it anywhere.

Mother and I often went to the bush together. The two of us would walk until we arrived at a place where she collected food. She'd set me down in the shade of a tree and dig roots or gather nuts nearby.

One time I left the tree and played in the shade of another tree. Hidden in the grass and among the leaves, I saw a tiny steenbok, one that had just been born. It was lying there, its little eye staring out at me. I thought, "What should I do?" I shouted, "Mommy!" I just stood there and it just lay there, looking at me. Suddenly I knew what to do—I lunged at it and tried to grab it. But it jumped up and ran away, and I started to chase it. It was running and I was running and it was crying as it ran. Finally, I got close enough to put my foot in its way and it fell down. I grabbed its legs and started carrying it back. It was crying, "Ehn . . . ehn . . . ehn . . ."

Its mother had been close by, and when she heard it call, she came running. As soon as I saw her, I started to run again, still carrying the baby steenbok. I wouldn't give it back to its mother! As I ran I called out, "Mommy! Come! Help me with this steenbok! Mommy! The steenbok's mother is coming for me! Run! Come! Take this steenbok from me." But then the mother steenbok was no longer following so I took the baby, held its feet together, and banged it hard against the sand until I had killed it. Then it no longer was crying; it was dead. I was very happy. My mother came running and I gave it to her to carry.

The two of us spent the rest of the day walking in the bush. While my mother gathered, I sat in the shade of a tree, waiting, and played with the dead steenbok. I picked it up; I tried to make it sit up; I tried to open its eyes; I looked at them. When mother had dug enough sha roots, she came back. We left and returned home.

My father had been out hunting that day and had shot a large steenbok with his arrows. He had skinned it and brought it back hanging on a branch. "Ho, ho, Daddy killed a steenbok!" Then I said, "Mommy! Daddy! I'm not going to share my steenbok. Now *don't* give it to anyone this time. After you cook it, just my little brother and I will eat it, just the two of us."

I remember another time we were traveling. While still on our way, my father and older brother tracked a baby antbear, the animal with almost no hair, with skin like human skin and hands like human hands. After they killed it and we ate it, I started to feel sick and threw up. That's when a serious illness entered my body, and I became very sick. My father did a curing trance for me, laying on his hands, and worked with me until I started to feel better. I was still too young to understand that he was curing me, because I still had no sense about those things. All I knew was the feeling of being sick. All I thought was, "Am I going to die from this sickness?" My father worked on me, curing me with his medicinal powers. I started to feel better and soon I was sitting up; then, I was sitting around with other people. Once I was completely better, I started playing again and stopped having thoughts about death.

An older child understands things and knows when someone is curing her. She thinks, "This person is trying to cure me. Perhaps he will make me better because right now, this sickness hurts very badly. Maybe he'll cure me and take the pain out of my body. Then, I'll be better again." I liked when my father cured us, liked when he did something good and helpful. I'd think about how he was making all of us better. If I was sick, I'd feel my body start becoming healthy again; if someone else was sick, I'd sit and sing for my father as he tranced and cured him. An older child understands and thinks about things like that. But a younger one doesn't have those thoughts.

I remember another time when I got sick after eating meat, the time my older brother killed a wildebeest with his poisoned arrows. I was so happy when I saw him coming back, carrying huge pieces of meat, "Ho, ho, my big brother's brought home meat!" I kept thanking him and praising him. And, fat! It was very fat! I was given a big piece and ate it all, especially the fatty parts. I ate and ate and ate, so much, that soon I was in pain. My stomach started to hurt and then I had diarrhea. My insides were too full from all that fat, and my diarrhea was full of fat as well.

Soon I got better, and we just continued to live.

Another time, I broke some ostrich eggshell water containers and my father hit me. I used to put them in my kaross and go to the water well to fill them. But once one fell down and broke, broke into lots of little pieces.

When I came back, my father had a branch and said he was going to beat me to death. So . . . phfft! I ran away!

But, it happened again. I had taken some ostrich eggshell water containers to the well, and while I was filling one with water, another one fell and . . . *bamm!* I said, "Today I won't run. Even if my father kills me, this time I won't run."

My younger brother Kumsa ran off immediately, to tell, "Daddy! Nisa killed another ostrich eggshell!" My father was waiting for me when I returned. He said, "Tell me, what caused that eggshell to break? Aren't you a big girl already? Still, you broke it?" He hit me and I started to cry. Soon he stopped, "All right . . . it isn't that important, after all."

But after that, whenever someone said, "Nisa, take the ostrich eggshell containers and fill them with water," I'd refuse. I knew if I broke another one, they'd hit me again. "Those eggshell containers don't help me at all. I'll just let them sit over there. Otherwise, you'll kill me." Whenever I was thirsty, I took a small can and went to the well to drink. I'd fill the little can with water, cover it with leaves and carry it back. But I wouldn't touch their ostrich eggshell containers. My mother was the only one who brought back water from the well.

A long time passed without my touching those eggshell containers. And we just lived on.

A Woman Alone

(excerpt)

Bessie Head

Bessie Head was born in 1937 to a wealthy white woman in Pietermaritzburg, South Africa. Her father was an African servant. Head was born in secret and raised by foster parents until she was thirteen, when she was placed in an Anglican orphanage in Durban. A teacher, then a journalist for the South African magazine Drum, *she moved to the Bechuanaland Protectorate (now Botswana) in 1964, where she wrote short stories and novels set in the village of Serowe, her new home. These included* When Rain Clouds Gather, Maru, *and* A Question of Power. *The two short essays below, the first written in 1965 and the second in 1984, two years before her death, convey her deep attachment to the place. She died of hepatitis at the age of forty-eight.*

For Serowe: A Village in Africa

Summertime in Serowe is an intensely beautiful experience. It rains unpredictably, fiercely, violently in November, December, January. Before the first rains fall it gets so hot that you cannot breathe. Then one day the sky just empties itself in a terrible downpour. The earth and sky heaves alive and there is magic everywhere. The sky takes on a majestic individuality and becomes a huge backdrop for the play of the rain. Not ordinary rain but very peculiar rain.

All through December and January the rain sways this way and that on the horizon. The wind rushes through it and you get swept about by a cold fresh rain-wind. Sometimes all the horizon rain sweeps across the village in glistening streams. Then the grass roofs of the mud huts shine like polished gold. The barren earth, grazed to a shred by the goats, becomes clothed by a thin fine carpet of green. Under the trees there is a sudden, lush wild growth of long green grass. Everything is alive in this short dazzling summer. Forgotten are the long months of bleaching scorching sun and intense blue skies. The sky is now shaded with large brooding clouds.

It takes such a long while for the insects to come out of hibernation. But in December the earth teems with them. There are swarms of flies, swarms of mosquitoes and swarms of moths—sometimes as big as little birds. Crickets and frogs are all over in the pools and around the village; there is a heavy rich smell of breathing earth everywhere.

Somehow, by chance, I fled to this little village and stopped awhile. I have lived all my life in shattered little bits. Somehow, here, the shattered little bits began to come together. There is a sense of wovenness; of wholeness in life here. There were things I loved that began to grow in me like patches of cloth . . .

There isn't anything in this village that a historian might care to write about. Dr. Livingstone passed this way, they might say. Historians do not write about people and how strange and beautiful they are—just living. There is so much necessity living they do and in this village there is so much mud living. Women's hands build and smooth mud huts and porches. Then the fierce November, December thunderstorms sweep away all the beautiful patterns. After some time these same patient hands, hard and rough, will build up these mud necessities again.

There are just people of Africa here and endless circles of mud huts. They do not seem to be in a particular confusion about anything. The politicians are very agitated because the whole of Southern Africa is a melting pot, they say. But the women just go on having babies and the families sit around the fire at night chatting in quiet tones. Everybody survives on little and there may be the tomorrow of nothing. It has been like this for ages and ages—this flat, depressed continuity of life; this strength of holding on and living with the barest necessities.

They say this and that about aid. They seem to know nothing of the desperate longing to bring out our own creativeness. In Southern Africa this desperation is fierce because we feel that opportunities to venture out on discoveries of our own are going to be forcibly denied us for a long time. We are all really startled alive by the liberation of Africa, but we have been living in exclusive compartments for so long that we are all afraid of each other.

Southern Africa isn't like the rest of Africa and is never going to be. Here we are going to have to make an extreme effort to find a deep faith to help us to live together. In spite of what the politicians say people are not going to be destroyed. Not now. There is all this fierce hatred and it is real. There are the huge armies prepared for war against unarmed people and we are all overwhelmed with fear and agony, not knowing where it will end.

Some of us cannot battle with this conflict any more. I cannot. But wherever I go I shall leave a chunk of myself here because I cannot think of myself as a woman of Southern Africa—not as a black woman but as an ordinary and wryly humble woman. There was this immense conflict, pressure, uncertainty and insecurity that I have lived with for so long. I have solved nothing. I am like everyone else—perplexed, bewildered and desperate.

A Search for Historical Continuity and Roots

In March 1964, barely a day's journey separated me from one way of life and another. Until that day in March I had been a South African citizen. A very peripheral involvement in politics resulted in a refusal of a passport and I left South Africa on an exit permit. Great events were taking place then. Most of Africa was gaining independence and I was a part of the stirring of the times. It was consciously in my mind that African independence had to be defined in the broadest possible terms. I was twenty-seven years old and had lived those years like most black South Africans, an urban slum dweller who survived precariously, without a sense of roots, without a sense of history. A short train journey and a day later I awoke to a completely new world, Botswana (then the British Bechuanaland Protectorate), and a way of life unknown and unfamiliar to me. South Africa, with its sense of ravages and horror, has lost that image of an Africa, ancient and existing since time immemorial, but in Botswana the presence of the timeless and immemorial is everywhere—in people, in animals, in everyday life and in custom and tradition.

I hope two disparate worlds could be considered to have combined harmoniously in me. I have never been able in my writing to represent South African society but the situation of black people in South Africa, their anguish and their struggles, made its deep impress on me. From an earlier background, I know of a deep commitment to people, an involvement in questions of poverty and exploitation and a commitment to illuminating the future for younger generations. I needed an eternal and continuous world against which to work out these preoccupations. One of my preoccupations was a search as an African for a sense of historical continuity, a sense of roots, but I remember how tentative and sketchy were my first efforts, not finding roots as such but rather putting on layer after layer of patchy clothing. This patchy clothing formed the background to most of my work.

It was my habit to walk slowly through the village and observe the flow of everyday life—newly-cut thatch glowing like a golden hay-stack on a round mud hut, children racing around, absorbed in their eternal games or a woman busy pounding corn for the evening meal. I would pause a while near a yard where a tall, slender woman pounded corn in a stamping block with a long wooden pestle, her bare feet partly buried in a growth of summer grass. It was a scene that had been a part of village life since time immemorial but to me it was as fresh and new as creation itself. The woman's form would sway to and fro with the rhythm of her work, her face closed and withdrawn in concentration. The warm slanting rays of the late afternoon sunlight seemed to transfix that timeless moment in my memory. I would turn and look at the distant horizon. Beyond the last hut, beyond the perimeter of Serowe, the land lay in an eternal, peaceful sleep, the distant horizon hazy and shrouded in the mists of the earth. I would reflect that the dwelling places of all the tribes had been, for ages and ages, just such small, self-contained worlds, busy with the everyday round of living.

Such peaceful rural scenes would be hastily snatched to form the backdrop to tortuous novels. Perceptive fans sensed the disparity, the disparity between the peaceful simplicity of village life and a personality more complex than village life could ever be. They would say: "I like the bits about Botswana life but I found your second/third novel difficult to read . . ."

But it still goes back to a question of roots rather than the small, stolen patchy scenes which would seem implicit in my early work. Later, much later, I became acquainted with the history of Botswana and it was like becoming acquainted with a way of life that was applicable to all the tribes of Africa. The high clamour and violence of South African history dominates all the southern lands so that they are written of in the history books as mere appendages of South African history. Botswana is no mere extension of South African history and the great arid wasteland the history books would have us believe. It was a British Protectorate and as such has a distinct and individual history of its own, a history whereby a colonial power was sensitive to human grandeur, even if it turned up in a black skin, and it was a country that provided one such leader at a crucial moment, Khama the Great, who made known the people's preferences as regards their independence and the ownership of the land. We have a situation where the people never lost the land to a foreign invader and in the rural areas the ancient African land tenure system of communal ownership of the land still operates. It is on this peaceful basis of security of tenure that one begins to assemble the history of the land.

One has so many options and choices of study that are sure, steady and sane and simply another addition to mankind's history. One can concentrate on the impact of Christianity on the tribes, the power and influence of the missionaries and the London Missionary Society and changing patterns of culture and learning. Thus, the refrain of recorded history begins very much the way it began in Europe: "When the Romans first took learning to Europe, the tribes there were just like the tribes of Africa, not knowing anything about learning and progress . . ."

We can look back at the old men, who until the missionaries introduced a new form of learning, were the only libraries the people had and the repositories of all tribal learning and knowledge. We can look back at the earlier religions of the tribes and the persuasive voice of Christianity in modifying and transforming custom and tradition. We can look back on a history that is not sick with the need to exploit and abuse people.

I have found the tensions and balances of the rural parts of Botswana, of a fine order. Enough of the ancient way of African life has survived to enable the younger generations to maintain their balance with comfort and ease, while almost daily with independence, new innovations, new concepts of government and critical, complex situations invade the life of the country. It is in such a world that one puts down some roots in the African soil and one finds a sense of peace about the future.

LESOTHO

Singing Away the Hunger
(excerpt)

Mpho 'M'atsepo Nthunya

Born in rural Lesotho in 1930, Mpho Nthunya spent several years in a brawling South African township near Benoni, married and returned to Lesotho, gained and lost a fortune in livestock, and eventually made a meager living as a housekeeper at the University of Lesotho. Nthunya's story is a tale of extraordinary hardship and suffering—much of it caused or worsened by the cruelty and neglect of family members.

The Land of the Wild Sage

In midsummer, right after Christmas, Alexis took me home to the Maluti Mountains of Lesotho. We packed all our clothes and left the dust, noise, Boer police, and constant fighting of Benoni Location, where Alexis and I had been forced to live as husband and wife since Easter. And we went to Marakabei, my new home.

I didn't know anything about Marakabei and those Maluti Mountains. I saw little hills, we called them mountains, when I was a small child living in Lesotho, near Roma. But always the hills were at a distance. I did not know the size of them. Alexis said the Maluti were very different from the hills of Roma; he said I could not imagine them, and it was true. I was wanting to see my new home and family, and these mountains Alexis told me about, but I was not happy on the way, because I was tired. I tried not to grumble.

We took the trains to Maseru; from Maseru a bus to Roma; and from Roma we had to walk by foot to Makhaleng, which is half the way from Roma to Marakabei. I was four months pregnant with the child who was going to die, and I carried a brown suitcase with clothes for me and Alexis, and Alexis carried a gray bag with more clothes. My feet were tired, tired. We found some people in Makhaleng who let us sleep at their house. They were friends of Alexis, and they gave us food and let us sleep on the floor on sheepskins.

The next day we woke up and began to walk again. We walked the whole day by foot, uphill most of the time, around steep cliffs and winding paths. I began to see what mountains are, but still I did not see mountains like those in Marakabei. When it was late afternoon, the postman passed us on horseback, with an extra horse carrying some mail. Alexis asked the man, "Please, can you put this lady on the one horse? We are going to Marakabei, but she is tired now. It's the first time for her to walk like this, such a great distance." So the postman put me on the horse carrying the mail. This was also my first time to ride a horse, but because I was tired, I didn't even care enough to be afraid I would fall off. Then we go. Alexis is walking by foot, but the postman and I go on ahead of him. Soon the postman has to go a different way, so he leaves me in a small village and says to the ladies, "Please take care of this person. Her husband is coming. She will stay here and the man will come and collect her."

The ladies gave me some *papa* and some *mafi* (sour milk) to eat with it. I was glad to have something to eat. But it was now sunset, and no Alexis. Just as the sun was down, Alexis came running, running very fast and found me. He says, "Marakabei is still a distance away."

We walk on in the dark, stumbling sometimes over the stones, carrying our suitcase and our bag. I keep on asking him, "When are we going to arrive in this place?"

And he tells me he doesn't know when. He laughs, "I told you this place is very far." We were winding in and out between the hills, along a footpath, but I couldn't see what was around me in the dark. I couldn't see the mountains and the cliffsides, so I didn't even know how to be afraid. I smelled the sharp strong leaves of the wild sage that grows all over the Maluti. It was a new smell to me, a clean, wild smell, and I liked it.

Finally we find the house, a large rondavel and many people, Alexis's family. His mother and father are there, and his sisters and brothers, and many children, all wanting to see the new wife of Alexis. We sit down. They give me *papa* and *mafi*, the same thing I ate with the ladies in the village on the way, and I say, "No. I won't eat it."

They say, "What are we going to do now? It is too late to cook sheep." But their father tells them to bring the sheep.

I say, "Thank you," and sit down.

They bring the sheep, show it to me, and kill it quickly. They take the liver and two ribs and put them on the fire and give to me to eat. I eat them with the *papa*. They say, "Oh, maybe she wants tea. They drink much tea in Gauteng, where this Mosotho girl has been living a long time." But there is no tea in that house.

They offer me the drink they make from sorghum, a sour porridge we call *motoho*. I say, "No, I don't eat sour porridge, because it hurts my tonsils."

They go up and down to other people's houses, looking for tea. I didn't know they had no tea there, or I could put some in my suitcase to bring with me. At first I thought they could go to the store to buy some, but they have no stores there. Only mountains. At last they find some tea, and I drink it. Alexis drinks *joala*. And we go to sleep.

The next day I woke up tired, so tired from walking all that way by foot. We slept in the rondavel on sheepskins, and I got up, looked out the door and saw the mountains. I sucked in my breath. "Ah!" I was shocked to see them so near to my face, so big and close, larger than anything I have ever seen. Then I smiled inside myself, thinking, "So this is the Maluti."

The land was quiet, peaceful, and very pleasing to my eyes. I liked the colours, the shapes of the mountain-tops, the way the shadows from the clouds fall and move across the mountains so everything is always changing. Everywhere I could smell wild sage. I like the wild sage and clean mountain wind, the colours of the wildflowers: bright blue, deep yellow, or maybe red and orange like flames of the fire. I like the sounds, the birds and the crickets, the waterfall near the house, the music of sheep-bells and cow-bells, the silence. Most of all I like the silence. The people there are quiet. No fighting, no yelling, and there are no buses, no engines. You can see a few trucks or buses if you go to Marakabei village, which is far away, but it is so still, in the mountains there. Later in my time in the Maluti, sometimes an airplane would pass overhead, and I would wave to it and say, "Fine, go on. You can have those towns you fly to. Say hello to my mother when you pass over her. I am happy to stay here."

I saw that even though the mountains were strange to me, I was going to be at home in them. It was going to be a good life for me. I took a bucket to go to fetch some water, but the path was steep and I didn't know it. I was looking over the edge of the path, afraid I would fall. The people at the stream laughed at me.

I said, "What are you laughing at?"

They were laughing because I couldn't put the bucket on my head, because I was afraid to fall with it on the steep path. So they laughed. They said, "*Hei!* Alexis has wasted his cows on this woman. Is she a woman or a *lekhooa* (white person)?" They thought I was not going to stay in the Maluti, but they were wrong.

I laughed back at them in my heart. They didn't know how tired I was of the town. After only one morning, I knew I wanted to stay there in the mountains. The town had too many people, too much noise all the time, no peace. *Tsotsis,* gangsters were everywhere stealing things, fighting; other people always fighting. There was no peace totally. Basotho were fighting with Maxhosa; men were fighting with wives and girlfriends; men were drinking *joala* and fighting with anybody they see. Every day we saw some people dying in the streets, and when they were fighting, they didn't care whether you were fighting or not; when they found you on the way they could just kill you. I saw that the mountains were a better place, and I knew that I wanted to stay. But I had to learn many things.

When I came back from fetching the water, carrying the bucket in my hands like a white person, people were gathered to the house to come and see me. My mother-in-law chose a name for me and sent a friend of hers to tell me. "Your new name is 'M'atsepo, which means Mother of Trust. We trust you, and so we give you this name." I just looked at her, thinking about it. I didn't say anything. She said, "You are supposed to say, 'Thank you' if you like the name."

And I thanked her.

I was four months pregnant now at this time, but nobody could tell. I knew, and Alexis knew, but he didn't tell his mother when we arrived. After New Year, Alexis went back to Gauteng for work. I stayed there, living with his mother, who was called 'M'anthunya. She loved me very much, and I loved her. We were staying together, going to the fields together. In the fields we fetched maize for meal, or sorghum, which makes bread. We pulled off stalks and put the heads—we call them mealies—in sacks or big basins which we carried home on our heads.

There were two girls, one boy, Ntate Nthunya, 'M'anthunya, and me. Ntate was not working, just sitting, looking out over the mountains, thinking many things. If it's time to harvest, you must go to the fields, everyone except Ntate. 'M'anthunya would grind maize for meal, but I did not know how, because I came from Gauteng. I was a city girl. When they gave me the mealies, I said, "I don't know what to do with these."

They say, "How is this possible? You have not been trained? Your father does not drink *motoho*? Oh, this child! They like to be married, but they don't know anything. This child is useless."

I didn't care. I was laughing, and they were laughing too while they were grumbling. I was just like a fool. They were right, I didn't know how to do anything. So 'M'anthunya started to teach me. She gave me *mabele* (sorghum) and told me to grind it; she said it is softer than maize, it's a good way for me to learn grinding.

I laughed, and I said I couldn't do it.

His family says to Alexis, "Where did you get this *lekhooa*, this white girl?"

He says, "At Roma; from Roma to Benoni. She never used a grinding stone in her life. There was no grinding stone in her mother's house in Benoni."

His mother asks, "So why do you take this girl who knows nothing?"

"You will teach her. I did not marry her to come and fight with the stones here. I married her because I love her. She can come here and see what this life is like, and she can learn. Give her time. Give me the things to be ground and I will take them to the mill until she learns grinding."

First 'M'anthunya taught me to make *joala*, because all the men like to drink it, and if I am a wife I must know this. She showed me the way while she did it. She said, "You cook the water, and when it's boiling, you take the maize, put it in another pot, and take the boiling water and pour it in and stir it. Use a lot of water, and stir it long. Then you wait. When it's not hot, but just a little warm, you take a sour *motoho*, you put it in, just a little bit, so the whole mixture will come to be sour. Next day you cook this *lekoele*. After cooking it, you cool it. When it is cold, bring it together with *mela*, which is like meal. You heat it again. When it is good and sour, it's called *joala* and you put it through a sieve and it's done."

Me, I don't like it. I never make it now. My mother, my father, and my brother don't like it, and I didn't like it too. Many Basotho like to drink it too much, and it causes many problems. Sometimes when I was pregnant I would take just one glass when I was thirsty, but only one glass. They say it is good for pregnant women. But from there, no more.

So. I'm four months pregnant in December. The baby should come in May. I was busy learning many things from 'M'anthunya, and I didn't think much about the baby coming. I didn't know that the baby was going to come in April, a month early and too small to live.

When the summer came to an end and my time was closer for the baby, I began to be sick. I was not knowing what happened in my body. I was very tired and hot. Don't want to eat. Just drink. Basotho say a pregnant woman must not drink so much water; but I drink and drink. Can't get enough. Alexis came at the end of March to take me to see the doctor in Roma. We went on horses, but the trip was very difficult for me, and when we got to Dr. Maema, he said I must go to hospital in Maseru. We thought he meant I should go home and get my things, and come back again to hospital to have the baby, and I knew that before I go to hospital for the baby, I must go first to my parents' home. We didn't understand that Dr. Maema meant I should go now, now, at that very moment, to the hospital. We go back up to the mountains again.

In Lesotho when you are seven months pregnant with your first-born child, you go to your parents' house to do certain Sesotho things, to prepare properly. Your mother-in-law must say when it is time for you to go. My parents moved to Roma at the same time Alexis and I went to Marakabei—in December. We were living in Gauteng all those years because of my father's work, but he was tired, so they were going home to Lesotho when I went to the Maluti.

I was looking forward to seeing my parents again and preparing for the baby. But the way it happened, I did not see them until after the baby died, because my mother-in-law didn't know that I was pregnant, so she didn't send them to me at the right time. I was not counting the time. I thought Alexis told 'M'anthunya, and so I thought it was not my business to ask her when I was supposed to go back to my mother's house, so I said nothing.

When we return from seeing the doctor, we tell 'M'anthunya that I must go to hospital now, and she is surprised. She asks Alexis, "How many months is your wife, when you say the doctor needs her to go to hospital?"

He says "Eight."

She says, "Oh, why didn't you tell me in December when you arrived here that your wife is pregnant? She was supposed to go to her home at seven months and do the proper things."

"What things?" we ask, because we don't know about these things. I know I am supposed to go, but I don't know for what.

"She must put on a little skirt which is only for pregnant women to wear, and a small shirt made of flannelette material with little cap-sleeves, called a *selapa*. Then she puts a red clay on her face, removes her shoes and her head-covering, and waits until the child comes. There are some other things that help her to get ready. Then, when the child comes she takes the *selapa* off her shoulders and wraps the child in it. But now it is too late, so what are we going to do?"

Alexis says, "I don't know, 'M'e. I didn't know you wouldn't ask 'M'atsepo. I thought you would notice she is pregnant."

She says, "I didn't see she was pregnant because she has no stomach. She is so small. Now we have missed something which should be done at seven months. This is not good."

I was sick, and I came to be sicker. I could not travel to go back to the hospital, which was in Maseru. There was a bus from Roma to Maseru, but the only way to get to Roma was by horse, and I couldn't stay on a horse. It was too painful. And in just five days from the time we got home, the child came.

'M'anthunya helped me to bring the baby out, with another lady. But when the baby came, she was tired, and they told me she was not going to live. She passed away after only one day. It was 1950, April. It was my first-born, a girl. And I was such a fool, I was not even sad. I never held my child, because she was sick from the time she was born, and I too was very sick. My stomach hurt, and it was hot. The baby was small, so I was not too sore where she came out, but I was very tired and weak. The thirst went away, and I was hungry, but when I ate I would vomit.

When the baby died, she was taken to *thotobolo,* the rubbish heap. Only women could touch this dead baby that I never touched myself.

All this time Alexis was in town drinking *joala.* He knew I was sick, and after the baby came they told him the baby passed away. He was sad. It was only me, the fool, who was not sad. After about ten days I began to feel better, and I felt I must get up and work.

They cut my hair and put a white scarf on my head, we call it a *tubu.* I have to wear this white *tubu* for a whole month. After that month I have to go to my mother's house and leave the *tubu* and my old clothes there. My mother has to buy me new clothes. I stay with my mother only one week. Then I go back to the mountains. I would like to stay longer with my mother, but I was not supposed to, because I was not visiting. I was just come because it is the practice in Lesotho. I had to go right back to the mountains. But I take only one month in the mountains and I come back to Roma, to be with my mother and to make my church marriage.

Never Follow the Wolf
(excerpt)

Helao Shityuwete

Born in 1934 in southern Angola, Helao Shityuwete grew up to devote himself to the liberation of Namibia, the territory to the south that was formerly known as German South-West Africa. Following World War I, the German territory was given in trust to South Africa, which was expected to help advance it toward independence. Instead, apartheid South Africa plundered its fish, diamonds, and other resources. Educated in mission schools, Shityuwete became a migrant laborer in Namibia, then traveled to Tanzania to join SWAPO, the South West Africa People's Organization, which was fighting for the liberation of Namibia. In the chapter below, Shityuwete describes his perilous crossing back into Namibia. He was later captured, tortured, and sentenced to imprisonment in South Africa, where he served time with Nelson Mandela and others on Robben Island.

We waited for almost an hour before the canoeist appeared. Lying low on the river bank in anticipation of being discovered and perhaps killed was a harrowing experience. We could not relish the beauty of the Okavango River which, because of the incessant rain, was surrounded by lush greenery. We could not see beyond our personal safety and the anxiety of what awaited us on the other side.

We braced ourselves for what was to be our last river crossing. The dugout was so small that it was only able to take two passengers at a time and we would have to make five trips.

The river was about three-quarters of a mile wide where we crossed it and there were no reeds to provide us with cover. If the enemy had been waiting for us on the Namibian side, or appeared on a river patrol, we would have been sitting ducks! We were able to cover our comrades on the first crossing from behind, but we did not know what awaited them on the other bank so we were much relieved when they landed on the other side without incident. After they reconnoitred the bush nearby and found no threat, they set up defences and gave an all-clear sign for the other groups to proceed.

Castro and I were the last to cross. He nearly caused the dugout to overturn due to his clumsiness. The canoeist told us to sit down on the floor of the dugout to help stabilise the craft. Castro, however, chose to squat and clung to the sides, which made us rock from side to side. He panicked and nearly fell overboard. The boat went completely out of control. I felt anger mounting in me after I tried to calm Castro down to no avail. I was ready for a swim, if things went any further wrong. But the pilot remained calm and, being an expert, he did not struggle but let the canoe drift downriver. At the same time he manoeuvred the craft, now powered by the current, towards the Namibian shore. We were about one and a half miles downriver from the crossing and in thick reeds before the pilot regained control and at last landed us on the Namibian shore.

I heaved a huge sigh of relief when I found myself on firm ground. This was the land I loved so dearly and had left two years ago. This was the country I had deserted because it could not offer a bright future for me or my descendants. I returned to you, my Namibia, fully prepared to liberate you from the abhorrent system of apartheid perpetuated by the racist regime in Pretoria. I was prepared to pay the supreme price for your freedom and independence. These were the thoughts that ran in my mind as I struggled up the bank and tried to find my way through the thick bush that grew along the river.

We made it to the others, and because it was not yet dark enough for us to proceed, we made final preparations and wished one another luck. We divided ourselves into four groups—two groups of three each, and two of two each. I was again, as on the river crossing, landed with Castro, and when darkness fell, we were the first to set out. Thirty minutes were to be allowed to pass before the next group followed. All groups were to report to Eliaser Tuhadeleni at Endola, about 300 miles to the west. To get there, we had to head for Rundu, the nearest town, where we had a SWAPO contact.

Here we go, I thought to myself as I heaved my rucksack onto my back. It was 23 March 1966, a date I was to remember as the day when, as a returning guerrilla, I was prepared to play the game according to its rule of kill or get killed. Similar liberation wars had been fought and were now being fought in other parts of the world. Our struggle resembled many national liberation struggles such as that of the Algerians against the French colonialists, or the Angolans and Mozambicans against the Portuguese. It also bore resemblance to historic revolutionary wars fought before ours, to the French Revolution, the American war of independence, the October Revolution in the Soviet Union and the Chinese revolution.

Our struggle was in essence a national liberation struggle against a colonial power, South Africa. A war of deprived, exploited, down-trodden and oppressed and expropriated people. We were fighting to regain what had been taken away from us—our country and our freedom.

I did not regret, not for even one second, having undergone military training. It was essential in our liberation struggle. The time had come and it was now imperative that my training should be put to the test. Here, on this soil, I was prepared to shed my own blood for the freedom of every Namibian, and to shed the blood of the enemy. I felt strong and full of courage now that I was no longer on foreign soil but in my own country. I was ready to meet the challenge. The rain, to our surprise, had stopped when we crossed the river.

We arrived in Rundu at about 0200h and because we could not find our way through the town, we decided to rest and have a little snooze. It was too dark to see farther than our noses, and we did not realise until dawn, when the first light appeared on the horizon, that we were only yards away from the Rundu police station. Though we were aware of car headlights going in and out of the yard, we did not bother to investigate and assumed that it was a garage or something commercial.

We moved away from the police station at first light and located the house of our contact in Rundu. He was not at home but his wife, Helena, invited us in. She asked who we were and why we wanted to see her husband. Because we did not know her or her attitude towards SWAPO, we tried to hide our identities from her and fed her with false information. We left our bags with her and went to the shops. There was an acute shortage of transport from Rundu to the west, so we decided to buy bicycles to be self-sufficient in transport.

We met Shakala and Shilongo on our way to the shops. Shilongo told us that he and two others had managed to get into the compound used by SWANLA [South West Africa Native Labour Association] for recruiting contract workers looking for jobs both in Namibia itself and South Africa. The mission of Shilongo's group was to take up employment in the south with the aim of organising the southerners in political as well as military activities. Shakala told us that he and his two colleagues had met a SWANLA lorry driver who had agreed to give them a lift to Nkurenkure. From there they would march on to Oshikango and then to Endola where we were all going to report to Tuhadeleni.

Rundu was teeming with security police. The Ondangwa as well as Oshikango Native Commissioners were there. Uniformed police in four-wheel drive vans were patrolling everywhere in the dusty town. Police in civilian clothes and in unmarked cars were in evidence everywhere. It was clear that they knew we were in the area, but did not know who we were or what we looked like. We, however, had some idea of what kind of people they thought we were. SWAPO's trademark was known to be beards and most SWAPO members were thought to be in their mid-twenties. To beat these widely held beliefs we had all agreed to be clean-shaven. Dressed in tatters, I walked with a slight stoop like an old man. I had cut myself a walking stick in Angola and wore omukonda (a dagger) to complete the picture of an old man. The deception was perfect and nobody suspected us.

We bought everything we wanted except bicycles, which were sold out but were expected in a couple of days, we were told. I nearly committed an unforgivable mistake in the SWANLA shop. One area of the shop was reserved for whites only and blacks had to point to what they wanted from a distance. Blacks could not hand money directly to the white saleswoman. They first had to give it to the black salesman, who would then pass it over to the white saleswoman after he had "cleaned" it. People entering the shop were sprayed with fly repellent pesticide.

The whole practice infuriated me and, coming from abroad where I had not seen such disgusting behaviour, I just snapped. Speaking in fluent Afrikaans, I refused to leave the reserved "whites only" area. With my elbows on the counter (which was even worse) I did my shopping there and only moved out after I had finished. Watching the white saleswoman out of the corner of my eye, I saw her pulling on the black assistant's sleeves and asking: "Wie is hy? Miskien een van die SWAPO mense. (Who is he? Maybe one of the SWAPO people.)" It was then I realised my big mistake. I had allowed my anger to overcome me and could have given us away. I withdrew from the shop before any further damage was done.

Outside the shop, I found Shakala surrounded by a group of security policemen asking him who he was. He had forgotten to change into tatters. Speaking in fluent Oshikwangari (the language spoken in the area) he beat off all their penetrating questions. Like an inquisitive old man, I stood outside their circle, leaned heavily on my walking stick and listened. When he emerged from the circle, Shakala ordered us to make tracks. He later met us at the house of our contact.

There, the cat was well and truly let out of the bag. Shakala and the lady of the house had been at school together. He desperately tried to deny that she knew him or that he had been abroad in Tanzania. In the end, he admitted that he was Shakala and confessed that we were coming from abroad. Helena told us that she already knew who we were and did not believe anything we had told her earlier. She was aware of everything because the Boers had been announcing on radio broadcasts that they expected a force of about ten guerrillas to enter Namibia. She pointed out many cars belonging to the police and Native Commissioners and their assistants.

She said it was too dangerous for us to hang around the house because of our contact's position within the SWAPO leadership in the area. Besides, police now visited the house regularly because their first-born daughter had left for abroad a couple of weeks earlier. Helena was going to do her washing at the river. It would be better if we went with her, she suggested.

Spotter planes and helicopters were scouring the area around Rundu and flying low over the river. One chopper came to have a closer look at us: we stood gazing up at it like innocent "curious" blacks. Satisfied, it banked away to follow the river's course. Helena told us that police sur-veillance had increased since the night before and that we should avoid hailing a lift because they were checking on everyone going west. They were also checking every car leaving Rundu for either Oshikango or Ondangwa. We briefed her on our mission and the reason we wanted to see her husband, adding that we would be grateful if she could convey our messages to him.

We thanked Helena for her hospitality and at about 1300h on 24 March Castro and I headed for Mupini, about 10 miles west of Rundu. We were heading for the house of Stephanus Haundyange, Shakala's uncle, who lived there. Shakala in the meantime went back to his travel companions.

We arrived safely at Haundyange's. By now our disguise had changed: we were no longer mine workers returning from South African mines. Castro was now an ex-patient of the Uutokota Hospital east of Rundu. I was his cousin who had gone to collect him and we were returning back home to Oukwanyama. We did not tell the old man Haundyange who we were, only that we wanted a place to spend the night.

The following morning we set off down the road which followed the course of the Okavango River. We tried to hail a lift from a SWANLA lorry carrying contract workers back to their homes. Here it was safe to get a lift westward, but there was no room on the lorry. At about 1400h, a horse-man came by: we slipped into the bush to hide. He stopped to talk to herdsmen who were herding their cattle nearby. From our hiding place I could see that he was agitated and I heard him asking the herdsmen whether they had seen three Ovakwanyama criminals on the road there. Immediately I heard the questions, I knew that it was a reference to some of our colleagues. Their group had had a skirmish with the police, I heard the horseman saying.

We decided to change course and we travelled for the rest of the day in thick brush two miles away from the road and the river.

Helicopters and spotter planes were now scouring the woodland along the river and it was difficult for us to approach the river to drink—it being the only source of water. Because the fields were ripe with corn and water-melons, however, we helped ourselves to everything we could get. When it was dark and safe enough for us not to be seen by anybody using the road, we ventured closer to the road. We were then able to survey the movements of police vehicles.

We had just got onto the road when suddenly we saw the powerful headlights of a police vehicle approaching around a bend. We dived into a hedge nearby and then crawled through a corn field away from the road. Fortunately, they didn't see us and passed us lying low in the corn field. When it was safe enough, we left the field and went back to the road. We walked for the whole night and only rested for three hours towards morning. Castro was dead tired and was snoring before he hit the ground.

Mafeking Diary

(excerpt)

Sol T. Plaatje

Sol T. Plaatje (1876–1932) was a founding member and the first general secretary of the South African Native National Congress, which later became the African National Congress. Fluent in seven or more languages, he served as a court interpreter in the town of Mafeking. He kept a diary during the 217-day siege when the town was defended by Colonel R.S.S. Baden-Powell (later to be the founder of the Boy Scouts) against more than 8,000 Boer troops. Plaatje's diary, marked by a lively sense of humor, illuminates the lives of Africans during a siege that was glorified as a triumph of British colonial resolve.

"For the townspeople of Mafeking," wrote the editors of the 1973 edition of Mafeking Diary, *"events took a serious turn for the worse during the month of January. . . . The food predicament was symptomatic: many essential commodities were now being requisitioned. . . . Equally threatening, albeit from a different point of view, was the shortage of ammunition." Ratcheting up the pressure on the people of Mafeking, "the Boer commander saw to it that bombardment from outside was intensified." The Boers' heaviest weapon was a 94-pounder Creusot siege gun, for which "Sanna" was one of several nicknames on the British side.*

January 1900

Monday, 1st

The first day of the first week of the first month in 1900. Not at all a lovely morning. The distant pop of the Mauser distinctly shows that there is no holiday for poor beleaguered us. I tried to go to town but "Au Sanna," going strong, caused me to come back and take shelter. I wonder why some people call her "Grietje," as "Griet" for a thing of her potency would be nearer the mark. She was exceptionally "kwaai" [bad, nasty] all day today. Goodness knows what provoked her.

After I went to town and David and Ebie were breaking-fast the thing smashed within 50 yards from the house. [David Phooko, a constable for the Inspector of Native Reserves, was a friend and distant relative of Plaatje. Ebie was Plaatje's six-year-old cousin Solomon Ebenezer Schiemann, who was visiting Plaatje when the siege began.] David cleared helter-skelter with the coffee which had become insipid. Ebie considered his bread too precious and remained chewing as if nothing had happened. In the afternoon things were very warm. I have developed a nasty fear for "Sanna." She has, since Dingaan's Day, devoted her time to our little gun across the river, and we have now become unused to her. I wonder why she is so hot today.

In the afternoon David stood watching a train of merry girls, amidst whom were Meko's sisters-in-law in the best of millineries, celebrating the new year with several jolly games. All of a sudden "Sanna" came round and spoiled the whole thing. Mr. Briscoe's garden is an intolerably near spot for 94 pounds of mortar to burst while a train of giggling girls are enjoying the first day in the first year of the twentieth century near Bokone—particularly when they were under the impression that it was directed to town. It sent nearly all the merry maidens in different directions. Some lay flat on the ground—it was for dear life—and "Sanna" fairly put them in memory that their lives were dearer and more expensive than their new year's dresses.

One shell burst near Weil's this morning. The employers had a narrow escape and two mules which happened to be about were killed on the spot. One burst near the commissariat yard. A fragment came in contact with one of the labourers and eviscerated him which, in short, means killed him on the spot. A few broken walls completed the total for today. "Sanna" was very hot today, and so was a beastly new 7-pounder to the east of the town which at one time caused me to leave the Market Square post-haste—it was for dear life.

Tuesday, 2nd

The 7-pounder that fired from the east yesterday had been moved round to Jackal Tree during the night. It sent a number of shells into the stadt early this morning, one of which smashed inside the hut of Mma-Mokoloi and emptied its contents on her head. None of the others were injured. The baby at her breast was not even shaken. A shell from "Sanna" hit the east of the stadt, where Ellitson [the local butcher] has put up his slaughter-pole since the siege, and amputated an employee in a most piteous manner—both legs and both arms. He died after this.

Wednesday, 3rd

It was not the 7-pounders which killed Rra-Mokoloi's wife, but a 12-pounder. Opinions differ on the point and some call it 9-pounder; however, its shells are said to be far more dangerous than any yet used by the enemy on Mafeking. It is posted somewhere west of the stadt.

They have turned their attention away from the Rooi-neks [rednecks, i.e., English] and have decided to knock spots out of the "verdomde Kaffers" this morning. They are shelling the stadt from east and west. There is a miscellaneous collection of Natives from Johannesburg who thought that the war would last a month or less. They came here as they thought Mafeking was safe enough to spend the month, after which they would return to the revolutionized Rand. They are a miscellaneous collection and include Pondos, Shangaans, Barotse, Zambezian and South Central African breeds. They are [a] harmless lot of people—some of them live under the two trees on the space between the B.S.A. Police camp and the stadt. They do a little night's toil when they require a little cash to buy grain which they "nona" [fatten] with horseflesh. They are quiet and are waiting for the end of this trouble, and I am sure they would not do any harm to anybody.

This morning I was trying to go to town. I was just near the two trees when the bells rang. There was a horrible smash all round me and I could see the branches of one of the trees flying in the air in a cloud of dust. From under the tree all the men in the shade were raised from four to seven foot high. After the smash I thought that thunder seldom strikes twice the same place, and I pressed my nerves to see how my fellow creatures had been jumped upon by this meanest part of the scum of the German race. But the good lord's potency is marvellously demonstrative when he wishes to frustrate the termination of a wicked man. His good angels had preceded the shell, shifted the men apart, and made a way for it. It burst amongst them in a most indescribable awfulness, but not one of them was hurt. There was a furrow where it ploughed the ground among their bedding. The camel-thorn tree suffered fearfully, but not one of the men got a single scratch. However, I was filled with fear and I turned back to take shelter. I had hardly reached the Meko's when there was another terrific smash. It burst five yards from them; this time the fragment flew over their heads but injured nobody.

Things were a bit quiet about dinner time. The 12-pounder was meanwhile circuiting back to the east. It took up its position, apparently to resume operations in the afternoon, but they had hardly time to digest their lunch of black coffee and ox meat when Baden-Powell's chappies showed them that they had something nasty for Boer flesh in store in

Mafeking. Three 7-pounders, posted within range of the big gun last night, and a little Nordenfeld started to boom one by one. Their shells raised clouds of dust as they demolished the earth-works which form the Boers' entrenchments. The little Nordenfeld is a very great friend of "Sanna's"—we'll call it "three-pounder." It and "Sanna" always had duels resulting in very little success for either side, just like a fight between two bulls of the same age. Three pounds against ninety-four—can anything be funnier? Now just imagine the former being reinforced by three times seven and you have an idea of the duels that ensued. People who in the morning were frightened out of their wits had an opportunity of turning out and watching the artillery duel. The state artillery with proper soldiers directly under their nose had no time to think of shelling a town full of unarmed people, and we walked about as freely as if we were in Cape Town, for they warmed up the Boers until about dusk.

While she was in the west this morning, the 12-pounder managed to kill a volunteer in the White fort. Whilst they were beckoning the stretchers with a Red Cross flag the gun sent three shells into the women's laager. A fragment of the first killed a child of Mrs. Erasmus, prosecutrix in the *Regina versus Emily Bezuidenhout* theft of £90, and wounded a little boy so fearfully that he is not expected to live.

Ma-Mokoloi died today in hospital. This has been an unfortunate day for both man and beast. Two horses were wounded in town, three cows and a goat killed near the stadt, and Mr. Bell's cow received a Mauser bullet in her neck. Poor dame! This is the second Mauser on the neck since the siege.

Another shell burst in the south; we wonder how long this is going to last. Instead of getting brighter, the prospect in front of us is darkening itself. I am inclined to believe that the Boers have fully justified their bragging, for we are citizens of a town of subjects of the richest and the strongest empire on earth and the burghers of a small state have successfully besieged us for three months—and we are not even able to tell how far off our relief is. It is certain that it cannot be too near. As the last despatches told us that the Boers were at Stromberg, Cape Colony and as far down as Estcourt in Natal, this is a capital stroke and fully justified their bragging. It is a shame on the part of the Imperial Government to "kgotla semane" [poke at the wasps] before they have tested their abilities to face it. Now they let us square the account while they lounge on couches in London City, reading their newspapers and smoke their half-crown (2/6) cigars. It is a difficult thing to maintain a bright face when so many are ruining young cheer. In the month of October the British had been victorious against the Boers—so victorious that we were under the impression that the Natal chaps will line the border from the 1st of November. Instead of that being the case, the Boers have since beleaguered Ladysmith and gone traversing the British territory to as far down as Estcourt. Their progress had, according to the last despatches, not yet been checked.

Thursday, 4th

A very quiet day. I was a broken reed all yesterday, and a man from Maritzani arrived just in time to pull me together. All of the Boers in the district have rebelled with the sole exception of Mr. Vos. The latter, a very kind old Dutchman, was our field-cornet at Maritzani. He had been arrested three times and taken to the laager, and on each occasion swore that he will never take arms against the English, even if they wish to shoot him. They have allowed him to go on each occasion. When my informant left Maritzani, however, he had received his final notice: that if he adheres to his views, all of his stock would be taken and his children sent away to Mafeking. He told me a lot more—that the troops had fought at the Vaal river. They have previously been travelling to and fro between Kimberley and the Vaal. Since the fight the Boers are not able to tell where they are. Letters have been received at Maritzani from the laager—that there is no use in fighting the English. They always wish to clear away, but are still there—only in obedience to orders; and various other interesting items.

What makes me to believe everything he says is that he heard of the Game Tree fiasco on Saturday last week. They told him that there was a fight in Mafeking in which the Boers lost 27 men and, it is believed, the English lost many more.

Friday, 5th

It was raining softly all night, and the result is a fair and lovely morning.

The presiding officer at the trial of the girl Bezuidenhout, his honour Major H.J. Goold-Adams, being indisposed, she was remanded *sine die*.

Poor Ngidi came in for a very rough time. He was before the court yesterday on a charge of being asleep while on sentry duty the previous night, and was sentenced to be dismissed. He appeared again this morning on a charge of failing to hand over a bag of kaffircorn. The sentence of the court: seven days H.L. and the confiscation of the kaffircorn. Hard luck on poor little Alfred. The following is the cause of his trouble: during the month of November the authorities, deeming it expedient in view of the approaching hard times, forbade the sale of grain of any sort by the storekeeper. All grain belonging to storekeepers was commandeered, and the government had it retailed cheaply—on economic lines—to the public.

For this purpose they have established a grain store in the stadt, one at the location, and Lippman's in town. Early in December orders were issued to private owners as well that they were to state the amount of grain in their possession, as this drain got a grip of us; and it became imperative that all grain should be collected from private people, and everybody be allowed to buy so little as not to have the slightest chance of wasting anything. It is only by dint of a favour that I was allowed to buy a steen brood ["brick" or loaf of bread] per diem. Therefore it is criminal to have in your possession any quantity of grain beyond what the regulations permit you to purchase from one of these stores run on economical lines.

Rice, barley, oatmeal, and sugar have also been included and their sale is restricted unless one has an order which regulates the quantity he can purchase in a certain shop to last him a certain period. A common person would be enriched by this arrangement, as cash cannot procure whatever one requires—he being allowed to purchase so much worth and the balance all remaining in his till. But our case is different: the regulation diet is cheap enough as the purchase price is also regulated, but it is too small to keep a decent man alive. One can only increase his diet by various unrestricted luxuries, the prices of which rule higher than the clouds.

From an official's viewpoint, this restriction is a wise policy, as it prevents the decrease of our supplies from passing faster than the days of the siege. To the merchant it is a boon, in as much as it enables him to demand whatever he desires for his unrestricted dainties. It is a curse, however, in that the money is circulated at the expense of the private individual's pocket.

From a Serolong [the language of the Barolong people] point of view this whole jumble is more annoying than comforting. For this they may be excused, as the arrangement is in the hands of young officers who know as little about Natives and their mode of living as they know about the man on the moon and *his* mode of living.

It came to their notice that some Barolongali were selling kaffir beer the other day. They look upon it as wasting, or if the scale of this luxury was to continue, they were going to make a case against the party and would have, had the Civil Commissioner not been what he is—a white Native.

They do not know that kaffir beer to the common Morolong is "meat vegetables and tea" rolled into one, and they can subsist entirely on it for a long time. If ever you wish to see the sense of the word economy, observe the kaffir beer by the amount of water poured into the corn to what is yielded. If prohibited, I wonder what is to become of the bachelor, who is a fighting man and soldier and can therefore not brew it for himself, as it is not sold in any of the three [grain stores].

The collection of grain is now going on in the stadt unlike at the location. There it is carried away by the chiefs. The officers are under the impression that when the chiefs reach a hut they take away the last crumb they find in possession of the owner, who would henceforth survive on what they purchase economically from the store. The store has been shut for the last five days, because when the regulation was struck down to 6*d* a time, Barolongali told the storeman he could go to H. This was last Sunday. The store has since been shut. I believe the storeman has gone to Hopetown in obedience to the Black Petticoat Ordinance [apparently Plaatje's term for a protest by Barolong women]. I presume the truth is that the officers are either under the impression the Barolongs are able to purchase from a closer store, or that they can live a week without—for otherwise I cannot comprehend. This causes me to believe that they liken Barolongs to the man in the moon, who is at his place every time there is a full moon. The full moon is always at night, when the store is closed, and the man in the moon could not possibly come down for any grain; and it is their belief that Barolong can do the same: for while this "every-morsel-economical-collection" is in progress, the store shows no sign of reopening—God help these poor beleaguered people.

Ebie has a very bad chest. He has had it for the last few days and he shows no sign of improving. His people "ncoma" [praise or extol] his coughing as that which was never heard in the hut before. Most of the children are down with fever. Further, Molema's cattle and many others have the rinderpest. Mafeking [daughter of Molema] has "setlhabi" [a pain in the chest]—she can hardly breathe. Sickness has formerly not troubled us very much during the siege; sickness was so rare that I have never heard anyone complain of toothache.

With Selabi all the afternoon. He told me of the welfare of my family. If he is not the boldest "cheat" in Bechuanaland, I owe him an apology.

Since the middle of the last month we have been tasting to see if the Civil Commissioner's grapes are ripe; so far we have only been able to discover that they are sweet, but we cannot yet tell if they are ripe or green. There is, however, no likelihood of this being found out until there are no more grapes to taste!

This morning I went round for another taste. I tried to pick only as much as necessary for tasting, when the whole bunch came down on my hand—rather a heavy weight. It weighed about three pounds, but I was not the fool to replace it, although it was far too much more than I required. In the afternoon I saw the "baas" filling his little basket and I went round for another "discovery," viz., what they taste like. Just when I came in, I heard "Do you know who steals my grapes, Patrick?" [Patrick

Sidzumo was the court messenger and a corporal in the "Fingo contingent," a group of African allies of the British.]

I carried on bravely. "No, Sir, I don't."

"Do you know, Plaatje?"

"I am Plaatje."

"Do you know who always steals my grapes?"

"No."

"To steal is no answer . . . By Jove! It is you who always steals my grapes. Can't you fellows do without stealing?"

I thought that the next question might be too unpleasant and I tried to modify the flowing tide before it grew worse, so I began:

"I have only been eating ('eating' mind you and not 'stealing') those in front of the stable, Sir."

"I don't see why you should steal them even if they were at the back of the stable, for your father didn't steal any grapes."

I successfully stemmed the tide when I interpolated:

"Well, my father didn't work for the Magistrate."

He turned around and went on with his business. He was still smiling when he eventually gave me the sweetest bunch in the garden!

Let My People Go

(excerpt)

Albert Luthuli

Albert Luthuli (1898–1967) was the son of a Seventh-Day Adventist missionary. Born in Rhodesia, he moved with his mother to Groutville in South Africa's Natal province after his father's death. His uncle Martin was the chief of the Christian Zulus in the local Mission Reserve. After working as a teacher and principal, Luthuli was persuaded in 1936 to become the new chief. He joined the African National Congress and rose to its leadership in 1952, four years after the Nationalist Party took control of the government and instituted the rigid system of racial segregation known as apartheid.

Following Luthuli's election as head of the ANC, the government removed him from his position as chief and placed banning orders on him for four years, restricting his movement. When the banning orders expired, he attended an ANC conference and was arrested and charged with treason a few months later, along with Nelson Mandela and many other ANC leaders. In 1957, charges against him were dropped and he was released.

Luthuli continued to protest against apartheid despite renewed bans and prosecution. In 1960 he became the first African to be awarded the Nobel Peace Prize, and in 1962 he published his memoir Let My People Go.

The Call of My Village

My decision to leave Adams College, thereby bringing to an end my teaching career, was preceded by a period of indecision. For various reasons, Groutville's domestic affairs were not going very well, and the people desired a change of chief. A body of tribal elders approached me with the request that they be allowed to ask the tribe to consider my replacing the ruling chief. The resident missionary added his voice to theirs. For two years they kept up the pressure, and for two years I answered with excuses.

The truth was that I did not want to become chief. It will be remembered that I had spent some time in my uncle Martin's household while he was at the head of Groutville affairs. I enjoyed my time there well enough, but I saw nothing in his life to attract me to chieftainship—the very reverse.

315

For one thing, my comparative youth inhibited me. I did not feel that I had acquired sufficient experience to rule. For another, my own observation had shown me how difficult it is for a chief to make a living. As things go with us, my income as a teacher was relatively high—just sufficient to make it possible for me to support my wife and the family which was beginning to appear (we had three children at this time) a little above the bread-line. I knew full well that if I became chief the struggle to subsist would become harder, though not desperate. My wife and I talked the matter over during my holidays in Groutville, and each time we decided that it would be best to go on as we were, in the interests of our children.

Added to this, I was at heart a teacher. I had been attracted to the profession right back in the days when I was so deeply impressed by the integrity and ability of many of my teachers at Edendale and Adams. Since that time the calling had had seventeen years to grow on me. I found fulfilment in teaching, and I cannot say that I had much appetite for the taxing days and the endless stream of petty administrative affairs which beset a chief who does his job properly. Alone, and in company with my wife, I turned the matter over. Each time I reached the same conclusion—I would continue at Adams.

I changed my mind quite suddenly. I think that perhaps all the emphasis which Adams had placed on service to the community bore fruit. I recognised now that the call of my people was insistent, and the reasons I gave for declining the request of the tribal elders seemed to me to be excuses for not going to their aid. I was at Adams when I decided to accept, and I wrote to my wife about this decision. I cannot account for the fact that, quite independently, she too had changed her mind about where our duty lay.

There were four candidates when it came to election. I was elected by democratic voting, the Native Commissioner (who conducted the election) informed the head of his Department, and the Government confirmed my appointment as from the beginning of 1936. I left Adams with reluctance, but there was one compensation besides the belief that I was doing my duty—after eight years of holiday and week-end encounters, I could at last live with my wife and family.

It is not easy to describe briefly the function of a chief, since he has a number of activities which are not normally the combined lot of one person in European affairs. To add to the difficulty, a chief does not stand for the same things in white minds as in African. In African eyes a chief possesses certain authority by virtue of his position, while in European eyes all that he has is conferred on him by beneficent whites—he is a sort of appointed boss-boy.

When I became Chief of the Umvoti Mission Reserve, I at once found myself, among other things, a petty administrator, presiding over the day-to-day affairs of about five thousand people living on about ten thousand acres. I did not relish this part of my work much, but what I did enjoy was court work. Within defined limits a chief acts as a magistrate with jurisdiction in civil affairs. At the pleasure of the Governor-General he may have criminal jurisdiction added to this. In common with the other chiefs in the Lower Tugela area I was given criminal jurisdiction. (It was later taken away from all of us and then restored to me alone, I do not know why.)

It was my fortune to be well versed in the fundamentals of what is called Native Law and Custom, so I was able to take up my court work with no great difficulty. But my main pleasure in this activity came from the rewarding attempt to reconcile people who were at variance, and from the debate involved. I love the impact of mind upon mind, and I love thrashing things out in the attempt to get at the truth. The procedures of the court give these things orderliness, and getting at the truth is worthwhile for its own sake. The dying arts of exposition hold great attraction for me.

Tribal courts do not closely follow the pattern with which Europeans are acquainted. Plaintiff and defendant normally represent themselves, and any tribal elder present may question both them and the witnesses. In days before the advent of the white man it was customary for the witnesses to remain in court throughout the trial, but latterly there is a tendency to take European precautions and exclude the witnesses.

I did not like the practice whereby (in my time) court fees and fines, up to a maximum of five pounds or two head of cattle, went into the pocket of the chief, making him an interested party. The Nationalists have made a small improvement here. All tribal moneys go now into the Tribal Treasury.

Besides doing this kind of work, I found myself called upon to be a sort of liaison officer between the Native Commissioner and the tribe, and this brought me a good deal in contact with the Commissioner. On the whole, I got on pretty well with these men. I do not recall quarreling with one, or being taken to task. Some knew very little about their function in a Mission Reserve, others knew more. With the former it fell to my lot to brief them tactfully on many occasions. They either learned as they went along, or else they simply delegated a part of their work to me. For instance, the allocation of land is not the duty of a chief in a Mission Reserve; nevertheless, I found myself allocating land in Groutville right up to the end of my tenure.

Since a chief is answerable for the good order of his territory, I had also to be a kind of chief of police—not, I hasten to add, regular South African Police. I was eager to have the regular police in Groutville as little as possible, and for this reason I saw to it that my own men dealt with all minor breaches effectively and promptly. In my early days as chief I set myself to curb the illicit brewing of beer, and especially of the more deadly concoctions—not because I am a reformer in these matters, but because it reduced the pretext for police raids. Eventually I managed to get one of the Native Commissioners to recognise and permit brewing within defined limits, and I myself encouraged the healthy brewing of *utshwala,* corn beer. Illicit brewing, the result of poverty, continued, but it did lessen.

In all my routine work I was assisted by tribal elders. These men were entirely unpaid. They did their work without any compulsion as a public duty, recognising far better than our rulers that privilege—even if it is merely prestige—carried with it obligation. They worked selflessly, without reward of any kind.

At Adams College I had had no particular cause to look far beyond the walls of the institution. I was, of course, aware of the South African scene, but Adams was in some ways a protected world, and the South Africa outside did not reach in in those days. Our awareness was partly theoretical. Moreover, we were busy.

All that came to an end when I became Chief of Groutville. Now I saw, almost as though for the first time, the naked poverty of my people, the daily hurt to human beings. Evidences of an inadequate tribal structure breaking up under the pressures of modern conditions were all around me.

In Groutville, as all over the country, a major part of the problem is land—thirteen per cent of the land for seventy per cent of the people, and almost always inferior land. The quality of the land at Groutville is comparatively good. But allotments shrink while you watch them, and there is nowhere for the surplus population to go. The average official Groutville allocation is now four to five acres per family. Against this, rural white South Africa owns an average of 375 acres per person.* You can see, by looking at these figures, the hollowness of the white argument, both here and in the Federation,† that the coming of the whites brought us a material prosperity for which we ought to be grateful.

Groutville has a subsistence economy, based mainly on the culture of sugar-cane, started, it is said, by the Rev. Aldin Grout. Cane has the merit

---

* Per person, rural Africans occupy an average of six acres each throughout the Union.

† The Central African Federation was created in 1953 as a federal realm of the British Crown, intended to join the Commonwealth as a dominion. It included Northern Rhodesia, Southern Rhodesia, and Nyasaland—later Zambia, Zimbabwe, and Malawi, respectively. The Federation was disbanded in 1963. [Ed.]

of being a cash crop, and this to some extent lessens the great evils of migrant labour. In a good season an acre will yield thirty tons gross, and this may fetch up to £60. From this the cost of transport and labour must be deducted at an average of 10/- per ton. An acre may thus earn £45 in a season; so that a five-acre allotment will earn £225. But it must be borne in mind that cane is not an annual crop. It takes eighteen months to two years to mature, so that the average annual income of a Groutville farming family may be between £110 and £170. This is up to £150 per year below the bread line, according to the size of the family.

Of course, even on allotments two or three times the size of this, we could not lead a materially prosperous existence. The trek to the cities is inevitable if a man wants his children to have meat as well as porridge—and, as for books, they are high up on the list of seldom attainable luxuries. So the family is broken up, and the worker becomes an uneasy dweller in two unrelated worlds.

It is true, of course, that to some extent we farm uneconomically, and I have often wished that we had the aptitude which Indians have for coaxing, almost conjuring, vegetable crops out of every square inch of the soil. But I doubt whether our faulty tillage is fairly compared with that of Europeans. One day during my chieftainship I was given a lift in his car by a neighbouring white farmer.

"You fellows," his conversation began, "you're just playing around with the soil. If we had this land we'd produce far better crops of cane than you do."

"Our handicap," I said, "is that we lack two things which you've got—fertiliser and machines. I think if we had these our crops would be better. They cost money."

"But doesn't the sugar mill down below help you—the one that buys and crushes our cane?"

"No, it doesn't help us at all."

"Oh! Well, then, why don't you ask Dube* for money?"

"I wonder," I asked, "if you're aware that Dr. Dube finances his school partly from his own pocket?"

My benefactor looked startled. He also seemed to sober down considerably.

"We," he said eventually, "can get short-term loans from the Land Bank."

---

* Dr. Dube, Principal of the Ohlange Institute, was at this time prominent in the African National Congress. At the same time he edited a Zulu newspaper.

"That's the difference. We can't. Your land is their security. Ours isn't."

The Native Affairs Department had a scheme whereby it undertook to supply agricultural officers and African field demonstrators to demonstrate more efficient methods and to produce bumper crops. I set myself when I was chief to co-operate with this scheme. The Government demonstrator decided to persuade Groutville to plant cotton, and I set aside a piece of my own land for him to produce his model crop on.

I ploughed. He planted. My wife tended the crop. The Government demonstrator visited the experiment casually. At the time of reaping he was nowhere to be found. We reaped it in ignorance of the correct methods to employ. He reported the operation to his superiors. That was that. But think of the outcome if I had persuaded some of my people to let their land be fooled around with! And this was a representative experience in my dealings with field demonstrators. I found them slack, uncooperative and indifferent—partly, I think, because they were left largely to their own devices.

I did in fact take the rap from my people over other failures of this scheme. In theory I do not criticise it. In practice it is operated by white authorities who supervise at a distance and have no knowledge of what goes on in the field. I have no reason to think that it has improved since I was chief. It is not properly supervised or participated in. It is another favour bestowed on natives by well-dressed visitors, and African field demonstrators are identified with the white supervisors rather than with the toiling peasant. It fails, on the whole, and its failure is pointed to by whites as yet another piece of evidence that Africans are unteachable.

But even if this scheme worked to the full, even if every square inch of the land were exploited efficiently, even if we could afford equipment and fertilisers, we still have only a fraction of the land which we need. The miracle of making the "Bantu heartlands" blossom as the rose cannot be performed. The whites find that, to live in their accustomed state, they need 375 acres per person. They allow us six. In Groutville, where the land is above average, we get about this for a family.

The whites can find no answer to this problem of land. They have the land. We are denied it. They cannot make the reserves support the excessive human and animal population, but at the same time, as the recent decision of the United Party shows, Africans cannot even be permitted to buy land, for no white electorate will consent to this except perhaps on so petty a scale that it achieves nothing. It is an impasse. It will have to be solved, even though no white Government dare try to solve it. They dare do no more than tinker with the existing situation, and pretend that a little model farming will supply the answer.

Shortly after I became chief I was one of ten Zulu chiefs who were taken on an official conducted tour of the Transkei where experiments in economical farming were being made. There the Government had done something about erosion—but only in places where there were no people. They had in effect created parks. It did not seem like a solution. They were also encouraging experiments in co-operative dairy farming on eight-acre plots under a quit-rent system. The experiment was useful but it did not answer the question: "What happens to eight acres when my children inherit them?"

The benefits of stock limitation were pointed out to us. It is obvious, of course, that any given area can carry only so many head of cattle. White policy all along has been to limit the stock. But they are not likely to persuade us of the desirability of this when we are familiar with the spectacle of white farmers with thousands of head of cattle on spacious ranches.

There is another solution: give us more room.

The tour was pleasant, but it showed us no real way to ease our lot, and even the African councillors whom we met seemed carefully schooled in what to say.

It fell to me and one colleague to describe this tour on our return for the benefit of a meeting of other chiefs. I remained silent on the subject of stock limitation. To my surprise my colleague praised it. He was set upon as though by a swarm of bees, and only when the subject was shelved could order be restored. Cattle-culling is an unreal solution to the problem in South Africa. The problem is: thirteen per cent of the land for seventy per cent of the people. The white version of the problem is: how can we continue to confine them to thirteen per cent of the land, as we are determined to do? Cattle-culling is not the result of facing the real problem, it is the outcome of this white determination to make no concession whatever. That is why, in the present South African setting, I reject it.

It is scarcely surprising, if these things are borne in mind, that when I became chief I was confronted as never before by the destitution of the housewife, the smashing of families because of economic pressures, and the inability of the old way of life to meet the contemporary onslaught. The destruction of our families is not the least of the crimes which white avarice has perpetrated against us. It continues, it increases, in spite of pleading voices raised against it. The results in promiscuity, neglect, and marital trouble, are read by the whites as just another sign of African incapacity. They ignore our pain.

Before I was chief I was in a sense a migrant labourer myself; but when I became a villager the plight of my people hit me hard—and Groutville is by no means the poorest of African communities. Others are condemned to land that will support almost nothing, so that a far higher proportion of workers must spend their lives away from home, in cities where African unemployment is rife and increasing. The Government reaction to this problem of growing unemployment is typical: send the unemployed back to the already overcrowded sub-economic reserves, which they left because of poverty. This sort of decision, to transfer the problem of unemployment from city to country, strikes them as a solution—remove the offence from before white eyes, and it ceases to exist.

It may seem odd, in the face of all this, that when, during my chieftainship, a manufacturing company offered to set up a paper factory in Groutville, the village turned down the application. The idea was put before me by the Native Commissioner, who did not indicate his Department's attitude one way or the other. I submitted it to a tribal gathering—in practice all male adults. (I took the quite revolutionary step of admitting women to these tribal councils. Although the change was accepted by the people without a murmur, ingrained custom tended to keep the women on the outskirts of discussion. But they did come, and though they hung back they did seriously follow proceedings.)

The people turned down the application by a very large majority. In the first place, Groutville had no surplus land for a factory. In the second place, the reserve remained our escape from city life with (among poorly-paid Africans) its demoralising effects, and the people had no wish that Groutville should be transformed into a factory compound. I think, too, that the people recognised with a sound instinct that the motive of the company was to exploit a cheap labour market rather than to enrich Groutville. Such schemes do not, in fact, bring in their wake any appreciable improvement in the African lot. I agreed, therefore, with the decision of my people, perhaps because I am of a conservative cast of mind. I was interested to observe that the Native Affairs Department appeared to approve of our rejection of this scheme.

We were to arrive at another tribal decision which went against Government policy in urban areas. They were then, as now, encouraging the establishment of beer halls by whites in these areas, partly perhaps to counteract the harmful effects of illicit concoctions, and partly to raise money for their schemes which the white parliament and municipalities are reluctant to vote. The Groutville missionary of the time drew my attention to the attempt being made in the neighbouring township of Stanger to open a beer hall. Emphasising the fact that I was acting in a personal capacity, I drew up and submitted a memorandum opposing this. Stanger's application was turned down, but the matter did not end there. One or two local whites remarked to me sourly: "Stanger isn't Groutville."

I do not think that the disappointment which they showed had anything to do with the frustrating of a charitable impulse.

In the course of time Stanger renewed its application. The Native Commissioner called me and said that my personal expression of views was not enough to justify continued opposition to this application. The Department wanted the views of the whole Groutville community. I did not know what the outcome would be. But when the tribe met it opposed the intention of Stanger as strongly as I, albeit for reasons not identical with mine. I recall clearly what one man said, and he summed up the general opinion: "I shall be tempted to waste my money in Stanger, and rob my children of money from which they would benefit. My wife can make beer here."

Although Stanger eventually got Government permission to establish a beer hall, the town did not, after all, carry out its original intention. This is not a matter for regret. There have been no disturbances similar to those which have occurred throughout Natal recently over this very issue. The beer hall has become for us—and especially for the women—a symbol of legal robbery by whites. This is not a new thing, but as the scale and intensity and range of beer hall disturbances latterly (most notably at Cato Manor) show, it has assumed greater proportions than before.

The point is simple. Africans are denied all licit access to alcohol, except in municipal halls. The municipalities use beer halls to raise money in order to meet the cost of public services among Africans—whites will not make their money available for this. The beer halls are therefore profit-making enterprises, and the result is that they produce beer at a cost far beyond the cost of home production. The women know that they can make beer more cheaply at home, they know that when their menfolk drink regularly at beer halls, their families are further impoverished, and they know that beer hall profits are spent on achieving the white man's notion of what is "good for natives." Since this is done at the cost of putting their families even further below the bread line, it is not acceptable.

I do not call in doubt the desirability of public services, such as clinics. But can the existence of such things be justified if they can only exist on impoverishing the poor, and thus reducing the general health of the population they serve? It is obviously a vicious circle. The more clinics we are forced to afford, the less can we afford to feed our children, and the more do they suffer from malnutrition. And of course entire beer hall profits are not spent on clinics. They are spent on whatever seems good to the white man for us.

The most shocking feature highlighted by the beer hall issue is this: why are the social services not there *anyway*? This is said to be a civilised country, and its Government tells us that it is civilised. Yet the social services which are there for the richer section of the community are not there for the poor, except at the cost of the poor being made poorer—though it must be added that this does not apply to the white poor. There are not many of them, but the social services are there for them as for their richer fellows.

One of the results of the beer hall system is, as may be expected, illicit brewing, not only of beer but of more potent concoctions. This in turn brings police raids at all hours, followed by fines or imprisonment, and it provides a lucrative sideline for some whites who buy liquor and resell it at high prices to Africans. Is it really inexplicable that our women boycott beer halls, are antagonistic towards municipal Native Affairs Departments, and have sometimes done damage to municipal buildings (including clinics) put there "for their benefit"? We do not want a few services, ostensibly provided by beneficent whites—at our cost. We want a share in South Africa, nothing less.

Many whites, some missionaries among them, are very stern on the subject of illicit brewing. Up to a point I agree with them about the abstract moral principles. I am an abstainer myself, but I must be realistic and meet the problem in a practical way. I am aware of the evils of "home brewing," particularly of those deadly concoctions which seriously undermine African health. But the illicit sale of concoctions is often the only way which African women have of feeding their children.

There is not enough food on our side of the fence—one African child in three dies from malnutrition in its first year. But across the fence there is enough and to spare.

Nevertheless, there is one ray of light in this squalid picture. This is the effort of various voluntary white groups, and some churches, to provide Africans with such social amenities as they are able to finance and run. But these absolve neither the Government nor the urban authorities from responsibility. And the Nationalist Governments have made our plight worse: not only are their grants to municipalities for such purposes niggardly, but they have greatly reduced grants to indigent, disabled and aged Africans.

What a mockery to call this state Christian!

117 Days

(excerpt)

Ruth First

The daughter of Latvian Jewish immigrants, Ruth First was born in Johannesburg in 1925 and studied at the University of the Witwatersrand, where fellow students included Nelson Mandela and Eduardo Mondlane. As a social researcher and journalist, she was active in the South African Community Party, which her parents helped found, and the African National Congress. In 1949 she married Joe Slovo, who became the head of Umkhonto we Sizwe, the armed wing of the ANC.

First was one of the 157 defendants in the Treason Trial of 1956–1961. Following the Sharpeville massacre of 1960, she was placed under banning orders, and in 1963 she was the first white woman to be detained under the apartheid government's 90-day detention law. Her memoir 117 Days *describes that experience. In 1964 she left the country for England, and in 1978 she moved to Mozambique, where she was the director of the research training program at Eduardo Mondlane University. In 1982 she was killed by a letter bomb addressed to her.*

The Cell

For the first fifty-six days of my detention in solitary I changed from a mainly vertical to a mainly horizontal creature. A black iron bedstead became my world. It was too cold to sit, so I lay extended on the bed, trying to measure the hours, the days and the weeks, yet pretending to myself that I was not. The mattress was lumpy; the grey prison blankets were heavy as tarpaulins and smelt of mouldy potatoes. I learned to ignore the smell and to wriggle round the bumps in the mattress. Seen from the door the cell had been catacomb-like, claustrophobic. Concrete-cold. Without the naked electric bulb burning, a single yellow eye, in the centre of the ceiling, the cell would have been totally black; the bulb illuminated the grey dirt on the walls which were painted black two-thirds of the way up. The remaining third of the cell wall had been white once; the dust was a dirty film over the original surface. The window, high in the wall above the head of the bedstead, triple thick—barred, barred again and meshed—with sticky black soot on top of all three protective layers, was a closing, not an opening. Three paces from the door and I was already at the bed.

Left in that cell long enough, I feared to become one of those colourless insects that slither under a world of flat, grey stones, away from the sky and the sunlight, the grass and people. On the iron bedstead it was like being closed inside a matchbox. A tight fit, lying on my bed, I felt I should keep my arms straight at my sides in cramped, stretched-straight orderliness. Yet the bed was my privacy, my retreat, and could be my secret life. On the bed I felt in control of the cell. I did not need to survey it; I could ignore it, and concentrate on making myself comfortable. I would sleep, as long as I liked, without fear of interruption. I would think, without diversion. I would wait to see what happened, from the comfort of my bed.

Yet, not an hour after I was lodged in the cell, I found myself forced to do what storybook prisoners do: pace the length and breadth of the cell. Or tried, for there was not room enough to pace. The bed took up almost the entire length of the cell, and in the space remaining between it and the wall was a small protruding shelf. I could not walk round the cell, I could not even cross it. To measure its eight feet by six, I had to walk the length alongside the bed and the shelf, and then, holding my shoe in my hand, crawl under the bed to measure out the breadth. It seemed important to be accurate. Someone might ask me one day—when?—the size of my cell. The measuring done, I retreated to the bed. There were four main positions to take up: back, stomach, either side, and then variations, with legs stretched out or curled up. In a long night a shift in position had to be as adventurous as a walk. When my knees were curled up they lay level with a pin-scratched scrawl on the wall: "I am here for murdering my baby. I'm 14 years." The wardresses told me they remembered that girl. They were vague about the authors of the other wall scribbles. "Magda Loves Vincent for Ever" appeared several times in devotedly persistent proclamation. Others conveyed the same sentiment but with lewd words and too-graphic illustrations, and in between the obscenities on the wall crawled the hearts and cupid's arrows. The women prisoners of the Sharpeville Emergency had left their mark in the "Mayibuye i'Afrika" [Let Africa Come Back] slogan still faintly visible. It was better not to look at the concrete walls, but even when I closed my eyes and sank deeper into the warmth of the bed, there were other reminders of the cell. The doors throughout the police station were heavy steel. They clanged as they were dragged to, and the reverberation hammered through my neck and shoulders, so that in my neck fibres I felt the echo down the passage, up the stairs, round the rest of the double-storey police station. The doors had no inside handles and these clanging doors without handles became, more than the barred window, more than the concrete cell walls, the humiliating reminder of incarceration, like the straitjacket must be in his lucid moments to the violent inmate of an asylum.

Six hours before my first view of the cell, I had come out of the main reading-room of the University library. The project that week was how to choose atlases in stocking a library, and in my hand was a sheaf of newly scribbled notes:

> Pre-1961 atlases almost as obsolete for practical usage as a 1920 road map—evaluate frequency and thoroughness of revision, examine speciality maps, e.g. distribution of resources and population—look for detail plus legibility—check consistency of scale in maps of different areas—indexes—explanations of technical and cartographic terms, etc., etc.

The librarianship course was an attempt to train for a new profession. My newest set of bans prohibited me from writing, from compiling any material for publication, from entering newspaper premises. Fifteen years of journalism had come to an end. I had worked for five publications and each had, in turn, been banned or driven out of existence by the Nationalist Government. There was no paper left in South Africa that would employ me, or could, without itself being an accomplice in the contravention of ministerial orders. So I had turned from interviewing ejected farm squatters, probing labour conditions and wages on gold mines, reporting strikes and political campaigns, to learning reference methods, cataloguing and classification of books, and I was finding the shelves poor substitutes for the people and the pace that had made up our newspaper life.

The two stiff men walked up.

"We are from the police."

"Yes, I know."

"Come with us, please. Colonel Klindt wants to see you."

"Am I under arrest?"

"Yes."

"What law?"

"Ninety Days," they said.

Somehow, in the library as I packed up the reference books on my table, I managed to slip out of my handbag and under a pile of lecture notes the note delivered to me from D. that morning. It had suggested a new meeting-place where we could talk. The place was "clean" and unknown, D. had written. He would be there for a few days.

The two detectives ranged themselves on either side of me and we walked out of the University grounds. An Indian student looked at the escort and shouted: "Is it all right?" I shook my head vigorously and he made a dash in the direction of a public telephone booth: there might be time to catch the late afternoon edition of the newspaper, and Ninety-Day detentions were "news."

The raid on our house lasted some hours. It was worse than the others, of previous years. Some had been mere formalities, incidents in the general police drive against "agitators"; at the end of the 1956 raid, frightening and widespread as it was, there had been the prospect of a trial, albeit for treason. I tried to put firmly out of my mind the faces of the children as I was driven away. Shawn had fled into the garden so that I would not see her cry. Squashed on the front seat beside two burly detectives, with three others of rugby build on the back seat, I determined to show nothing of my apprehension at the prospect of solitary confinement, and yet I lashed myself for my carelessness. Under a pile of the *New Statesman* had been a single, forgotten copy of *Fighting Talk*, overlooked in the last clean-up in our house of banned publications. Possession of *Fighting Talk*, which I had edited for nine years, was punishable by imprisonment for a minimum of one year. Immediately, indefinite confinement for interrogation was what I had to grapple with. I was going into isolation to face a police probe, knowing that even if I held out and they could pin no charge on me, I had convicted myself by carelessness in not clearing my house of illegal literature: this thought became a dragging leaden guilt from then on.

The five police roughs joked in Afrikaans on the ride that led to Marshall Square Police Station. Only once did they direct themselves to me: "We know lots," one said. "We know everything. You have only yourself to blame for this. We know. . . ."

It was about six in the afternoon when we reached the police station. The largest of my escorts carried my suitcase into the "Europeans Only" entrance. As he reached the charge office doorway he looked upwards. "Bye-bye, blue sky," he said, and chuckled at his joke.

"Ninety days," this Security Branch man told the policemen behind the counter.

"*Skud haar*" [Give her a good shake-up] the policeman in charge told the wardress.

When we came back from her office to the charge office, all three looked scornfully at my suitcase. "You can't take this, or that, or this," and the clothing was piled on the counter in a prohibited heap. A set of sheets was allowed in, a small pillow, a towel, a pair of pyjamas, and a dressing-gown. "Not the belt!" the policeman barked at the dressing-gown, and the belt was hauled out from the loops. "No plastic bags." He pounced on the cotton-wool and sprawled it on the counter like the innards of some hygienic giant caterpillar. No pencil. No necklace. No nail scissors. No book. *The Charterhouse of Parma* joined bottles of contraband brandy and dagga in the police storeroom.

I had been in the women's cells of Marshall Square once before, at the start of the 1956 Treason Trial, but the geography of the station was still bewildering. The corridors and courtyards we passed through were deserted. The murky passage led into a murkier cell. The cell door banged shut, and two more after it. There was only the bed to move towards.

What did they know? Had someone talked? Would their questions give me any clue? How could I parry the interrogation sessions to find out what *I* wanted to know, without giving them the impression that I resolutely determined to tell them nothing? If I was truculent and delivered a flat refusal to talk to them at the very first session, they would try no questions at all, and I would glean nothing of the nature of their inquiry. I had to find a way not to answer questions, but without saying explicitly to my interrogators, "I won't tell you anything."

Calm but sleepless, I lay for hours on the bed, moving my spine and my legs round the bumps on the mattress, and trying to plan for my first interrogation session. Would I be able to tell from the first questions whether they knew I had been at Rivonia?* Had I been taken in on general suspicion of having been too long in the Congress movement, on freedom newspapers, mixing with Mandela and Sisulu, Kathrada and Govan Mbeki, who had been arrested at Rivonia, not to know something? Was it that the Security Branch was beside itself with rage that Joe had left the country—by coincidence one month before the fateful raid on Rivonia? Was I expected to throw light on why Joe had gone, on where he had gone? Had I been tailed to an illegal meeting? Had the police tumbled on documents typed on my typewriter, in a place where other revealing material had been found?

Or was I being held by the Security Branch not for interrogation at all, but because police investigations had led to me and I was being held in preparation for prosecution and to prevent me from getting away before

---

* One month before my arrest, in July 1963, Security Police arrested Nelson Mandela and other political leaders in a raid on a house in the Johannesburg suburb of Rivonia. That house was used at the underground headquarters of the freedom struggle headed by the African National Congress. In what subsequently became known as the Rivonia Trial, Mandela and his associates were sentenced to terms of life imprisonment for directing sabotage and planning the armed overthrow of the South African Government.

the police were ready to swoop with a charge? At the first interrogation session, I decided, I would insist on saying nothing until I knew whether a charge was to be preferred against me. If I were asked whether I was willing to answer questions, I would say that I could not possibly know until I was given a warning about any impending prosecution. The Ninety-Day Law could be all things to all police. It could be used to extort confessions from a prisoner, and even if the confession could not—at the state of the law then—be used in court, it would be reassurance to the Security Branch that its suspicions were confirmed, and a signal to proceed with a charge. My knowledge of the law was hazy, culled from years as a lawyer's wife only, and from my own experience of the police as a political organizer and journalist. Persons under arrest were entitled to the help of a lawyer in facing police questioning. If they would permit me no legal aid, I would tell them, whenever they came, that I would have to do the best I could helping myself. So I could not possibly answer any questions till I knew if the police were in the process of collecting evidence against me. Nor, for that matter, I decided to tell them, would I say that I would not answer questions. After all, how did I know that, until I knew what the questions were. If they would tell me the questions I would be in a better position to know what I would do. This cat-and-mouse game could go on for a limited period, I knew, but it was worth playing until I found out how the interrogation sessions were conducted, and whether there was any possibility that I might learn something of the state of police information. If they tired of the game, or saw through it—and this should not be difficult—I had lost nothing. Time was on their side anyway. If they showed their hand and revealed by intention or accident what they knew about my activities, I would have told them nothing, and I would be doubly warned to admit nothing. If fairly soon I was to be taken to court I would consider then, with the help of a lawyer, I hoped, the weight of the evidence against me. There was just a chance they might let slip some information, and even a chance—though it seemed remote the first night in the cell—that I might be able to pass it on to the Outside, to warn those still free.

As I dropped off to sleep the remembrance of that neatly folded but illegal copy of *Fighting Talk* rose again. If the best happened I would be released because there was no evidence against me . . . and I would have withstood the pressure to answer questions . . . but I would be brought to court and taken into prison for having one copy of a magazine behind the bottom shelf of a bookcase. How untidy! It would not make impressive reading in a news report.

I slept only to wake again. My ears knocked with the noise of a police station in operation. The cell was abandoned in isolation, yet suspended in a cacophony of noise. I lay in the midst of clamour but could see nothing. Accelerators raced, exhaust pipes roared, car doors banged, there were clipped shouted commands of authority. And the silence only of prisoners in intimidated subservience. It was Friday night, police-raid night. Pick-up vans and *kwela-kwelas*,* policemen in uniform, detectives in plain clothes were combing locations and hostels, backyards and shebeens to clean the city of "crime," and the doors of Marshall Square stood wide open to receive the haul of the dragnet.

Suddenly the noise came from the other side of the bed. Doors leading to other doors were opened, then one only feet away from mine, and I had for a neighbour, across the corridor, an unseen, disembodied creature who swore like a crow with delirium tremens.

"Water, water. *Ek wil water kry*. For the love of God, give me water."

A violent retching, more shrieks for water, water. I caught the alcoholic parch and longed for water.

Twice again I was jerked awake by the rattle of doors to find the wardress standing in my doorway. She was on inspection, doing a routine count of the prisoners. "Don't you ever sleep?" she asked.

Suddenly the door rattled open and a new wardress stared in. A tin dish appeared, on it a hard-boiled egg, two doorsteps of bread, and coffee in a jam-tin mug. Minutes later the crow was retreating down the passage. The wardress led me out of my cell, past a second solitary one, into the large dormitory cell which was divided by a half-wall from a cold water basin and a lavatory without a seat. I washed in cold-water and half a bucket of hot, put on my pyjamas and dressing-gown, was led out again into my little cell, and climbed back into bed. My first day in the police station had begun.

I felt ill-equipped, tearful. I had no clothes. No daily dose of gland tablets (for a thyroid deficiency). My confiscated red suitcase, carefully packed from the accumulated experience of so many of us who had been arrested before, was the only thing, apart from me, that belonged at home, and in the suitcase were the comforts that could help me dismiss police station uniformity and squalor. I sat cross-legged on the bed, huddled against the cold, hang-dog sorry for myself.

---

* The African name for pick-up vans. *Kwela* means "jump," and this is the instruction that police shout at arrested Africans.

The door clanged open and a lopsided gnome-like man said he was the Station Commandant. "Any complaints?" he asked. This was the formula of the daily inspection rounds. I took the invitation. I objected to being locked up without charge, without trial, in solitary. The Commandant made it clear by his wooden silence that I was talking to the wrong man. The catalogue of complaints was for the record, I had decided. I would allow no prison or police official to get the impression that I accepted my detention. But the end of the recital that first morning tailed off on a plaintive note . . . "and I've got none of my things . . . I want my suitcase, my clothes, my medicine. . . ."

"Where's her suitcase?" the Commandant demanded of the wardress, who passed the query on to the cell warder.

"Bring it. All of it. Every single thing."

The cell warder went off at the double. Red suitcase appeared in the doorway, tied up with pink tape. The Station Commandant started to finger through it, then recoiled when he touched the underwear.

"She can have the lot!" he said.

The wardress, peering over his sloped left shoulder at the cosmetics, said shrilly: "She can't have bottles. . . . The bottles . . . we can't have bottles in the cells."

The Commandant rounded on her. One person would make the decisions, he told her. He had decided.

The cell warder retrieved the pink tape and the suitcase stayed behind in the cell. Nestling in it were an eyebrow tweezer, a hand mirror, a needle and cotton, my wrist-watch, all prohibited articles. And glass bottles, whose presence made the wardresses more nervous than any other imagined contravention of the regulations, for it was a strict rule that nothing of glass should be allowed in the cells. I was later to find out why.

Throughout my stay in Marshall Square my suitcase was the difference between me and the casual prisoners. I lived in the cells; they were in transit. I had equipment, reserves. Their lipsticks were taken from them, and their combs, to be restored only when they were fetched to appear before a magistrate in court. The casuals were booked in from the police van in the clothes they had worn when arrested, and if they wanted a clean blouse they had to plead with the wardress to get the cell warder to telephone a relative. I could go to my suitcase. I had supplies. I was a long-termer in the cells.

And Night Fell

(excerpt)

Molefe Pheto

Molefe Pheto studied music in London and became a founding member and the first chairperson of MDALI, the Music, Drama, Arts and Literature Institute. Pheto spoke out against racial segregation in the arts, and he directed three annual Black Arts Festivals in Soweto before he was arrested by South African security police in March 1975. He was held for 281 days, all but ten of which he spent in solitary confinement. The charge, although he did not know this for some time, was that he had helped a mixed-race activist flee the country into Botswana.

The Christmas Party

We arrived at Jan Vorster Square and drove into a maze of a garage in the basement of the building that comprises this massive police headquarters. I sensed immediately that, once there, there was no hope. Miracles, yes, perhaps. The garage was ill-lit and contained a battery of police cars, some of which I had on several occasions seen in the townships. There was an ominous regimentation that immediately descended on everyone.

I was led to a lift which took the four of us to the ninth floor. There the lift stopped and the door opened, showing us a gorilla-like White man in a glass cubicle. He took a scanning look at us as we piled out. To our right, past the cubicle encasing that hideousness, a steel door miraculously slid and slotted itself into a wall. As soon as we went in, the steel door shot out of its wall-slot back into place. There were no door handles, no buttons, nothing. Just a plain pale pink slab of steel and we were sealed in.

I found myself in a corridor containing what seemed like hundreds of offices, facing each other down the stretch of the passageway. It was still early and the place was devoid of human beings. At that time, apart from the monstrous animal we had just passed, whose job presumably was to control electronically the steel door after assessing arrivals, a few Black,

Coloured and Indian Security Policemen were already there, idling, apparently waiting for the Whites under whom they operated. Without these Whites, they were without initiative. Then there were us—Ben Letlaka, myself and the two robots.

The three men led me into a room which I imagined to be Colonel Visser's interrogation chamber. I could feel that in normal office hours, this place must hold people like flies, each one pretending business at this or that. I could feel their numbers even in their absence. And because there were so few then, it felt eerie.

It was not long before the arrival of the important man himself. I did not know him, but as soon as he came in his flourish told me that it must be the "Kernel" in person. He oozed confidence and self-assertion, looking fresh and well groomed. He gave my presence there no importance at all, as if to rub in the fact that I should get it straight, from the beginning, that he had been victorious in having me hauled in.

Soon after his triumphant entry, a whole flotilla of policemen sailed into his room. They rushed into the room where I had been ushered as if they were escaping from someone with a whip who was lashing their backs and behinds.

There were lieutenants, colonels, captains, warrant officers, sergeants, non-commissioned men and new recruits. There were Blacks, Coloureds, Whites and Indians. Some of them were very young and some very old, a whole contingent of them, as though an important instruction were to be given. I could see their heads, particularly the short ones trying to get a better glimpse of this important detainee, as I thought. Others got so close to me I almost thought they were semi-blind. A lot of them shook their heads, making clicking sounds at the same time, as if to say that I had had it. Whether this show had been decided as a campaign to make me nervous, and therefore easier to deal with later, I could never tell; or whether the whole spectacle had been stage-managed, I still could not say. What I did feel was that word had gone round that I had been brought in, as if other detainees before me, involved with me, had loaded the whole whatever-it-was on me.

All the police in this room were babbling away, in Afrikaans, at the same time. I ceased trying to follow their excitement which was obviously aroused by me. Many of these peeping Toms were later to be directly involved in my interrogation. Many I never saw again at close quarters except sometimes in passing, as the process unfolded. At one time there were over a dozen policemen screaming for a better viewing point. They made me feel that I was so "important" that they each had to take an individual look at this finally unearthed subversive.

I felt very frightened. Whatever it was, it must be very serious. Colonel Visser, looking fresh and clean, a blond with blue eyes, seemed absolutely satisfied with his work, as if he had himself effected the arrest after a bloody battle in which he had overpowered me.

Ben Letlaka and his two deaf and dumb mutes shared the glory, doing their best to shield their stinking breaths from their White superiors and trying terribly hard to look as fresh and alert as Visser. Other non-White police seemed to share in this success. I got the impression that they all worked as one. One for all and all for one (for you, South Africa), as one of the lines from the South African Afrikaner anthem, "Die Stem" (the branch or agreement), runs.

Their behaviour was like that of ghetto children I had seen at Christmas parties. The only difference was that the spectacle unfolding before my eyes was being enacted by adults. The other difference was that these were the Security Police!—and I was the cause of their "Christmas party." I even had the impression that they were reacting in this manner as if I had been on the run from them for some time and so it was reason enough for a celebration.

The theory that South African policemen, Black and White, were stupid was never better illustrated than it was on this day. In their private confines, they may perhaps exhibit some modicum of intelligence. But I had seen them in public and at law courts, so ludicrously exposed that I found it hard to believe that it was true. I had seen them fumbling and lying and fabricating, half the time not even remembering their own concocted lies to effect a conviction. Many other times I had seen them in the streets not even knowing why they were arresting people. All they could tell one, at best, was, "You will answer in front," meaning in court.

While all this was happening, together with ever so many goings in and out of Visser's room, I was straining my mind for at least one reason for my detention, besides MDALI activities—the most obvious. I could not think of anything else then. But of course, it could be one of many things, or absolutely none, remembering that this was South Africa. No real reason was needed to haul any Black person into prison. But given the existing conditions, it could be one of a multiplicity of things. . . . A conversation, perhaps, with friends, on the political events in the country. I could remember several such conversations I had had with all sorts of people. Ordinarily, there should be nothing the matter with that, even in South Africa. But with so many ill-paid informers all over the place, anything gets blown up out of all proportion. A conversation like that could be interpreted as plotting the violent overthrow of the state. But none of my imprisoners was letting the cat out of the bag and, in agony, I could not find any reason or probability. At the same time, I was doing the best for myself. Reassuring myself that I should relax and not get ruffled by these antics, I told myself to think out my answers carefully as soon as the interrogation started, and I was certain it would begin soon.

I stole glances at every one of them, to make sure I would recognize them if we should meet in the revolution I wished would happen tomorrow. I felt that perhaps I could then avail myself of the chance to repay them in kind. I felt a particularly burning hatred for the Blacks there, more than any other racial group, for having allowed themselves to be used to humiliate their own kind. Next in line were the Coloureds, their next in rank in the South African human hierarchy and, of course, their "cousins," the Coloured population being a result of the early Boers (White Afrikaners) having bedded the indigenous women, some or most of them against their will. Last, the Indians or Asian stock, the super opportunists. I was infuriated and my head was reeling, aching with anger, choking my impotent throat. The Whites I detested for their hateful superiority and contempt of the Blacks, which they had displayed for three hundred years and more for no reason other than that of colour. All this time, I was made to stand like a prize bull in a market, a black one at that.

"Sit," Colonel Visser barked at me, picking a moment when the din had temporarily quietened. He said the word in Afrikaans, which uses the same spelling as in English but pronounced differently, like "set."

This also happened to be the signal for various others to leave, which they promptly did. I suppose business was about to begin and they all knew the sign.

Colonel Visser and I must have been silent adversaries for some time. Only I did not know it. But he must have had me under observation. This was his moment. He had won the first battle. He had me in custody, in his hands and at his mercy. Many of them had left, except those I considered to have some rank. So the room still had some air of the Christmas party. Visser was himself fussing and burrowing into some papers, files and several documents on his desk, one of which was a thick file with my name on its brown cover.

Shit! I'm in hell, I thought, when I saw the thickness of the file.

He opened his mouth, lit his pipe and started. "Phineas Gaboronoe Phetoe," reading from the mountainous file before him.

"Molefe Pheto! I offer that name as it is my right name." I ventured to put the record straight from the beginning.

"Yourr alibis and aliases! We know about them too."

I did not know what he meant by "them" as I had offered him only one name.

All my life, I had been registered through the various South African department offices as Phineas Gaboronoe Phetoe. Besides Gaborone (correctly spelt), Molefe is my ancestral name. I have been trying and fighting all the time to correct the misspellings and to eradicate the inhumanity of being nameless to no avail. But after he alleged that my correct names were aliases, I decided not to crack my head with what I considered an imbecile. Besides, Visser had already become aggressive.

"Don't lekturre us. You arre herre forr interrrogation. Don't underrmining our intelligence, and you mus be rready to ko-operrate."

The Afrikaners, almost all of them, speak English with strong accents on the letter "c," which sounds like "k," and have long rolled "r" sounds. The "t" also sounds flat. Their English grammar is utterly amusing—come what may, they never seem to master it. These factors made them longstanding jokes in the ghettos of Alexandra Township, Soweto and other places. No day passes without some Black man telling a funny story about an experience involving the Afrikaner and this aspect. In most cases the Afrikaner is aware of this inability and is very sensitive about it. It is worse with the rural Afrikaners, all of whom take exception to educated Black people.

Personally, I am not bothered whether the Afrikaner speaks English well or not. I see it as their planned resistance, as they have not forgotten their historical enmity with the English. But at another level, if anything demonstrates that the Black man has better learning ability, then this is a case in point. With all the facilities and opportunities their government provides for them, the Afrikaners are still incapable. It could also be a reason for their denying us opportunities, for fear of being outdone. Visser was no different, and neither were the rest of the police I was later to come into contact with.

I steadied myself for the worst. Visser kept on looking into the file which seemed to contain everything about me. My life history. He tilted it away from me in such a manner that, much as I tried, I could not glimpse a thing.

Then he rattled out all my past travels abroad. "You have been overrseas," referring to the time when I was a music student at the Guildhall School of Music and Drama, in London. "To London, came back to South Africa, then left again back to England, Frrance, London, Ghana," and here he stressed Ghana.

"You are correct."

He glowered, as happy as a monkey. "You see! Therre is nothing we don't know about you. Now yourr job is to tell us everrything. Not forr us to tell you. Now. What ken you ko-operrate us with?"

I told him that I thought he was to ask me the questions.

"Oo! I ken see you refuse to ko-operrate."

He took a deep breath and looked at me through the smoke he had just emitted from his pipe. I believed he was also sizing me up. The others remained fierce-looking, standing like steel statues beside me. All the non-Whites had left. Visser looked at his remaining White colleagues, as if he had to get their acquiescence to continue. Apparently, all the White policemen who had remained behind in the room knew something about what I was supposed to have been involved with.

"Do you know Krris Weimer?"

I tried hard to remember. Nothing happened. I tried harder just in case, to save myself. Still nothing clicked. But I knew that I had never heard the name before. I wasn't sure whether this Kris or Chris Weimer was White or Coloured, since the names of Coloured people and Afrikaners in South Africa are similar both in spelling and pronunciation. It certainly was not an indigenous name. If anything, I had anticipated being asked about people with Black names. This was getting too much.

"No!" I shook my head.

"No?" He imitated me, making it look funny, calculated to solicit laughter from his audience. "I see!" Visser said slowly, his pipe back in his mouth, held back in place by a strong bite.

They all looked at each other. Five White men, three of whom were extremely hefty like the hideousness I had encountered when I came out of the lift with my escorts. Visser and another were not as big, on the elderly side, particularly the other who was sinewy and worn-out.

"Errik Molobi? Do you know that one?" pronouncing the second name so badly I could not recognize it.

I had heard the name before. In Black communities, several clans share the same name. In fact, a cousin of mine by marriage was a Molobi. But his "European" name was not Eric.

"No. I do not know Eric Molobi. I have never heard the name before," I told him, or rather, them. To all intents and purposes, they were all taking part in the interrogation by proxy. They were following everything that was going on and I expected any one of them to throw in his bit at any time, even a punch, if I annoyed them enough.

The five White men again exchanged glances. I had the feeling that they thought I was resisting. But they showed no emotion nor indication of what they thought. I noticed confidence in them as though to say, "You all start that way, but sooner or later you begin to talk."

"Do you know Johnny Rramrrock?"

"No."

"Kenny Klarrke?"

"No."

The questions and names were coming much faster. The fact that Visser was not even repeating them took me off guard for a while. I started thinking that perhaps they believed me and were not really bothered. Well, at last, we were getting somewhere, progress.

"Pat McGluwa?"

"No. I don't."

"A certain Zabane, Aprril?"

"No."

One of them, whom I christened "Mother Hen" because he behaved like a hen over her chicks, with his huge size and busy hands, talkative, walking in and out, raging, menacing me, thrusting his fat fleshy face into mine, annoying me because it had sweat bubbles like wet pimples, said, "He's shitting us, and we'll shit him too."

Then he turned to me and said in perfect SeSotho, one of my native languages, "Hey, we are not here to play. We are working here," his voice loud, as if I had challenged them or was not aware that they were at work.

While I was wondering where he had learnt the language so well, his boast—because that is what it was—alerted me that whatever happened, I should not use any of the vernaculars; the possibility was that a lot of them there could speak one of them. Sometimes I would answer that I did not know what they were asking me, so as to clear my mind when they pursued the question. I had realized that if I didn't give a positive answer, the question came back a number of times.

I did that in the case of Sefton Vutela.

"And Sefton Vutela? Do you know him?"

"No!" I lied.

"You don't know Vutela?" Visser was getting angry. He seemed sure that I must know Vutela. He was right. I knew Vutela very well.

I was aware that Visser was absolutely certain that I knew Vutela, by the way he insisted, showing, I suppose in an off-guarded moment, surprise that I said I didn't. In the meantime, I tried to remember very quickly any awkward moment that might make it difficult for me if I finally agreed that I knew Vutela.

Vutela was a political personality of high courage when I first met him. He had been harassed by the Security Police for a long time in Johannesburg. At the time he was living in Botswana in exile. He had fled South Africa after he had been banned, in the early sixties. He took off while awaiting trial for continuing to engage in the activities of a banned organization, so the charge read. When he was let out on bail, he headed for the border.

I first met Vutela at the Witwatersrand University Library, where we were both employed as "library shelvers," when in actual fact the work we were doing was that of library assistants. We fought many battles together. First, against the library authorities for what we considered unjust treatment of us, and against the university administration's bureaucracy. In all these problems, Vutela stood principled and would never desert, whatever the odds. Indeed, I knew Vutela.

"Oh, yes. I know Vutela . . . if you mean the one in Botswana!" I had already clearly decided what to say without compromising myself politically, or in any other way. That his exile situation had nothing to do with me. That there was nothing wrong in knowing a man who lived in exile. That politically, I was not involved with him.

However, in South Africa, in interrogation, things do not work out that way. If you know someone in exile, you automatically are involved with him. I told Visser and company that Vutela and I met and became friends when we worked together as library assistants at the Witwatersrand University Library. That I was aware of his political involvement in the country then, and of his status in Botswana. In Botswana, I told them, we had met on the basis of the past and on no other.

"You want us to believe that!" Visser said, enunciating all the words, implying that I was taking them for fools. Of course they did not believe me and it would have been naïve of me to think that they did.

It was the next question that brought out sweat all over me. Over my hands, body and forehead. And it was the first question Mother Hen had asked, apart from the threats he had made to me.

"Who took Clarence Hamilton away?" He looked me straight in the eye. Mother Hen must have decided that shock treatment was better. Whether I was going to be sincere in my denial or not, it was a chance he considered worth taking. His eyes stuck into me to record my reaction. He had asked the question slowly, clearly, but not too slowly. Just the right pace to produce the effect he desired. I went to pieces inside, but remained stoic. I dared not show that I was shaken.

I knew Clarence Hamilton very well. He had recently joined the Mihloti Black Theatre group, whose performances I directed. Prior to that, he was a drama student at the African Music and Drama Association in Johannesburg, a Black arts learning centre, where I was musical and cultural programme director.

At about the same time that I first met him, Clarence Hamilton had been one of a group of youths who had organized a boycott of lessons at the Coloured school he attended near Johannesburg. He was alleged to have distributed pamphlets encouraging his fellow students not to attend classes as sign of protest against the celebration of Republic Day in South Africa, implying that Coloured people had nothing to be jubilant about as they had no stake in the country, the same as the Black people. The Security Police in Johannesburg reacted sharply to this; coming from Coloured youths, the protest showed the very solidarity that the régime would need to nip in the bud. There were disturbances at his school, culminating in the detention of Clarence Hamilton. He was later charged, tried, found guilty, but was allowed out on bail to await sentence. Clarence did not honour his bail. He ended up in Botswana, the neighbouring independent state, an exile.

"Who took Clarence Hamilton away?" Mother Hen repeated the question.

"I don't know." I had made a quick decision.

So far, my system of delaying tactics was working. But I was sure it was not successful. Somewhere, there was bound to be a slip.

At that moment, one of the older policemen in the room interrupted the proceedings, speaking in Afrikaans: "Where are his things?"

I did not know what things he was talking about. Another replied that they had nothing from me. He was told that I had been collected by Bantu Constable Ben. Yet another added that they had better go and search the house, "*voor die goed verdwyn*" (before the things disappear). The policeman who first asked where my things were continued, still in Afrikaans, "You know how they are," meaning of course we Black people. That given the slightest chance, nothing they could use against me would still be in the house. Books, pamphlets and material like that. We were supposed to be notorious for our stealthy manners; we could not be trusted. He was right. The people of the ghetto would have covered for me as soon as they knew I had been unjustly detained, for that was what it was. No one had the right to detain any Black man against laws the Black man had no hand in making. The ghetto would do anything to frustrate the police. I too would do the same for a fellow Black. It was then that I understood what the "things" were: whatever the search might have produced. So, at that time, there was nothing they could show or refer to in incriminating me.

While the discussion was going on about the "things," I had some respite from Mother Hen's piercing questions. But not for long. He was back as soon as he had had a break. "You say you don't know who took your friend away?"

"No. I don't. . . ." I did not finish the answer I was going to give.

Thud! Mother Hen hit me hard directly on the forehead, dead centre between my eyes, with the three middle fingers of his right fist folded as in karate, the middle knuckle making the first painful contact before the other knuckles. The pain, the force, and the surprise element—like his questions—brought a flood of immediate tears to my eyes.

"We have methods to conscientizing people into remembering. We are working here. We don't sleep," repeating his stock-in-trade remark about them not "sleeping there." Mother Hen was fond of and boastful about what he considered to be the Black Consciousness terminology. He would rattle off the words in as pompous a manner as he could find: "Solidarity, pig, motherfucker, the man, conscientize and afro!"

I could not find any reason for this exhibitionism. If Mother Hen was trying to impress me, I could not see what he would gain by it. Incidentally, he seemed to be the most educated of the lot there. His English was better than that of most Afrikaners I have had the chance to listen to.

Just when I thought the music had begun again, they all suddenly went into another room, summoning a Black policeman, one of the many loitering there, to guard me. But they were soon back.

"*Kom!*" (Come!)

These men seemed to conduct themselves in a disorderly manner which at times relieved me from tight corners, while at other times had me with my back against the wall.

Anyway, the order had been given. "*Kom!*"

The Christmas party ended as suddenly as it had begun. Some of the police had come to Visser's room out of curiosity. Some had remained in the room because they seemed to help each other all the time, like actors cuing each other. Some were to remain with me for a long time, day after day, for weeks and months.

Their sudden withdrawal from Visser's room to another must have been to hold a small conference that decided to go and search my house. As they said earlier, I had been brought in by Bantu Constable Ben, who had not searched the house, or was not allowed to do so without White supervision, or was considered not educated enough to know what to look for, or was not even trusted.

"*Kom!*"

Their demeanour made it clear to me that they knew in a little while I would talk. They showed no immediate hurry to squeeze the information from me. They had all the time in the world, and they told me so; out of experience, they expected me and all detainees to offer resistance, as a matter of course, before the methods to break us were resorted to. They were not in a hurry at all.

"*Kom!*"

I Write What I Like

(excerpt)

Steve Biko

Steve Biko was born in 1946 in King William's Town in the Eastern Cape. As a medical student at the University of Natal, he was involved with the National Union of South African Students (NUSAS) and went on to found the South African Students' Organisation (SASO). At a time when the African National Congress and Pan-Africanist Congress were banned by the government, SASO filled the political vacuum by evolving into the Black Consciousness Movement. In 1972 Biko was expelled from the university, and the following year he was banned by the authorities. Despite this, he played a key role in organizing the protests that culminated in the Soweto Uprising of 1976.

The first passage below is extracted from Biko's testimony in a case against SASO and the Black Peoples Convention that extended from 1975 into 1976. David Soggot was the assistant counsel for the defense. The second passage is from an interview Biko gave a few months before he was detained and beaten to death. Biko died on September 12, 1977.

What Is Black Consciousness?

Soggot: Now, I think that brings us to the 1971 second GSC [General Students' Council]?

Biko: Yes.

Soggot: Now, I do not propose to take you through the whole of that in any way, I merely want to refer you to certain aspects of the Resolution passed at that GSC. If you look at paragraph 1: "SASO is a black student organization"—have you got that?

Biko: Yes.

Soggot: Would you just read that please, paragraph 1?

Biko: "SASO is a black student organization working for the liberation of the black man first from psychological oppression by themselves through inferiority complex and secondly from the physical one accruing out of living in a white racist society."

343

Soggot: Now, the concept of Black Consciousness, does that link up in any way with what you have just read?

Biko: Yes, it does.

Soggot: Would you explain briefly to His Lordship that link-up?

Biko: I think basically Black Consciousness refers itself to the black man and to his situation, and I think the black man is subjected to two forces in this country. He is first of all oppressed by an external world through institutionalised machinery, through laws that restrict him from doing certain things, through heavy work conditions, through poor pay, through very difficult living conditions, through poor education, these are all external to him, and secondly, and this we regard as the most important, the black man in himself has developed a certain state of alienation, he rejects himself, precisely because he attaches the meaning white to all that is good, in other words he associates good and he equates good with white. This arises out of his living and it arises out of his development from childhood.

When you go to school for instance, your school is not the same as the white school, and *ipso facto* the conclusion you reach is that the education you get there cannot be the same as what the white kids get at school. The black kids normally have got shabby uniforms if any, or no uniform at school, the white kids always have uniforms. You find for instance even the organisation of sport (these are things you notice as a kid) at white schools to be absolutely so thorough and indicative of good training, good upbringing. You could get in a school 15 rugby teams. We could get from our school three rugby teams. Each of these 15 white teams has got uniforms for each particular kid who plays. We have got to share the uniforms amongst our three teams. Now this is part of the roots of self-negation which our kids get even as they grow up. The homes are different, the streets are different, the lighting is different, so you tend to begin to feel that there is something incomplete in your humanity, and that completeness goes with whiteness. This is carried through to adulthood when the black man has got to live and work.

Soggot: How do you see it carried through to adulthood, can you give us examples there?

Biko: From adulthood?

Soggot: Yes.

Biko: I would remember specifically one example that touched me, talking to an Indian worker in Durban who was driving a van for a dry-cleaner firm. He was describing to me his average day, how he lives, and the way he put it to me was that: I no more work in order to live, I live in order to work. And when he went on to elaborate I could see the truth of the statement. He describes how he has to wake up at 4 o'clock, half past four to walk a long distance to be in time for a bus to town. He works there for a whole day, so many calls are thrown his way by his boss, at the end of the day he has to travel the same route, arrive at home half past 8 or 9 o'clock, too tired to do anything but to sleep in order to be in time for work again the next day.

Soggot: To what extent would you say that this example is typical or atypical of a black worker living in an urban area?

Biko: With I think some variance in terms of the times and so on and the work situation, this is a pretty typical example, precisely because townships are placed long distances away from the working areas where black people work, and the transport conditions are appalling, trains are overcrowded all the time, taxis that they use are overcrowded, the whole travelling situation is dangerous, and by the time a guy gets to work he has really been through a mill; he gets to work, there is no peace either at work, his boss sits on him to eke out of him even the last effort in order to boost up production. This is the common experience of the black man. When he gets back from work through the same process of travelling conditions, he can only take out his anger on his family which is the last defence that he has.

Soggot: Are there any other factors which you would name in order to suggest that—to explain why there is this sense of inferiority, as perceived by you people?

Biko: I would speak—I think I have spoken a bit on education, but I think I must elaborate a little bit on that. As a black student again, you are exposed to competition with white students in fields in which you are completely inadequate. We come from a background which is essentially peasant and worker, we do not have any form of daily contact with a highly technological society, we are foreigners in that field. When you have got to write an essay as a black child under for instance JMB [Joint Matriculation Board, the governing body for secondary education] the topics that are given there tally very well with white experience, but you as a black student writing the same essay have got to grapple with something that is foreign to you—not only foreign but superior in a sense; because of the ability of the white culture to solve so many problems in the sphere of medicine, various spheres, you tend to look at it as a superior culture than yours, you tend to despise the worker culture, and this inculcates in the black man a sense of self-hatred which I think is an important determining factor in his dealings with himself and his life.

And of course to accommodate the existing problems, the black man develops a two-faced attitude; I can quote a typical example; I had a man working in one of our projects in the Eastern Cape on electricity, he was installing electricity, a white man with a black assistant. He had to be above the ceiling and the black man was under the ceiling and they were working together pushing up wires and sending the rods in which the wires are and so on, and all the time there was insult, insult, insult from the white man: push this you fool—that sort of talk, and of course this touched me; I know the white man very well; he speaks very well to me, so at tea time we invite them to tea; I ask him: why do you speak like this to this man? and he says to me in front of the guy: this is the only language he understands, he is a lazy bugger. And the black man smiled. I asked him if it was true and he says: no, I am used to him. Then I was sick. I thought for a moment I do not understand black society. After some two hours I came back to this guy, I said to him: do you really mean it? The man changed, he became very bitter, he was telling me how he wants to leave any moment, but what can he do? He does not have any skills, he has got no assurance of another job, his job is to him some form of security, he has got no reserves, if he does not work today he cannot live tomorrow, he has got to work, he has got to take it. And if he has got to take he dare not show any form of what is called cheek to his boss. Now this I think epitomises the two-faced attitude of the black man to this whole question of existence in this country.

Soggot: The use of the word "black" in literature and as part of western culture, has that figured at all?

Biko: Sorry?

Soggot: The use of the word "black," what does black signify and how is it used in language?

Judge Boshoff: Is it a comprehensive term?

Biko: If I understand you correctly, the reference I think of common literature to the term black is normally in association also with negative aspects, in other words you speak of the black market, you speak of the black sheep of the family, you speak of—you know, anything which is supposed to be bad is also considered to be black.

Soggot: We have got that, now in that context . . . *[Court intervenes]*

Judge Boshoff: Now the word black there, it has nothing to do with the black man. Isn't that just idiom over the years because darkness usually, the night was a mystery for the primitive man? I mean I include the whites when I talk about primitive man, and when he talks about dark forces, he refers to forces that he cannot explain, and he refers to magic, black magic; isn't that the reason for this?

Biko: This is certainly the reason, but I think there has been created through history and through common reference—all the attitudes which are associated with exactly that kind of association—also go in regard to the black man, and the black man sees this as being said of magic, of the black market, precisely because like him it is an inferior thing, it is an unwanted thing, it is a rejected thing by society. And of course typically (and again in the face of this logic) whiteness goes with angels, goes with, you know, God, beauty, you know. I think this tends to help in creating this kind of feeling of self-censure within the black man.

Soggot: When you have phrases such as "black is beautiful," now would that sort of phrase fit in with the Black Consciousness approach?

Biko: Yes, it does.

Soggot: What is the idea of such a slogan?

Biko: I think that slogan has been meant to serve and I think is serving a very important aspect of our attempt to get at humanity. You are challenging the very deep roots of the black man's belief about himself. When you say "black is beautiful" what in fact you are saying to him is: man, you are okay as you are, begin to look upon yourself as a human being; now in African life especially it also has certain connotations; it is the connotations on the way women prepare themselves for viewing by society, in other words the way they dream, the way they make up and so on, which tends to be a negation of their true state and in a sense a running away from their colour; they use lightening creams, they use straightening devices for their hair and so on. They sort of believe I think that their natural state which is a black state is not synonymous with beauty and beauty can only by approximated by them if the skin is made as light as possible and the lips are made as red as possible, and their nails are made as pink as possible and so on. So in a sense the term "black is beautiful" challenges exactly that belief which makes someone negate himself.

Judge Boshoff: Mr. Biko, why do you people then pick on the word black? I mean black is really an innocent reference which has been arrived at over the years the same as white; snow is regarded as white, and snow is regarded as the purest form of water and so it symbolises purity, so white there has got nothing to do with the white man?

Biko: Right.

Judge Boshoff: But now why do you refer to you people as blacks? Why not brown people? I mean you people are more brown than black.

Biko: In the same way as I think white people are more pink and yellow and pale than white.

Judge Boshoff: Quite . . . but now why do you not use the word brown then?

Biko: No, I think really, historically, we have been defined as black people, and when we reject the term non-white and take upon ourselves the right to call ourselves what we think we are, we have got available in front of us a whole number of alternatives, starting from natives to Africans to kaffirs to bantu to non-whites and so on, and we choose this one precisely because we feel it is most accommodating.

On Death

You are either alive and proud or you are dead, and when you are dead, you can't care anyway. And your method of death can itself be a politicizing thing. So you die in the riots. For a hell of a lot of them, in fact, there's really nothing to lose—almost literally, given the kind of situations that they come from. So if you can overcome the personal fear of death, which is a highly irrational thing, you know, then you're on the way.

And in interrogation the same sort of thing applies. I was talking to this policeman, and I told him, "If you want us to make any progress, the best thing is for us to talk. Don't try any form of rough stuff, because it just won't work." And this is absolutely true also. For I just couldn't see what they could do to me which would make me all of a sudden soften to them. If they talk to me, well I'm bound to be affected by them as human beings. But the moment they adopt rough stuff, they are imprinting in my mind that they are police. And I only understand one form of dealing with police, and that's to be as unhelpful as possible. So I button up. And I told them this: "It's up to you." We had a boxing match the first day I was arrested. Some guy tried to clout me with a club. I went into him like a bull. I think he was under instructions to take it so far and no further, and using open hands so that he doesn't leave any marks on the face. And of course he said exactly what you were saying just now: "I will kill you." He meant to intimidate. And my answer was: "How long is it going to take you?" Now of course they were observing my reaction. And they could see that I was completely unbothered. If they beat me up, it's to my advantage. I can use it. They just killed somebody in jail—a friend of mine—about ten days before I was arrested. Now it would have been bloody useful evidence for them to assault me. At least it would indicate what kind of possibilities were there, leading to this guy's death. So, I wanted them to go ahead and do what they could do, so that I could use it. I wasn't really afraid that their violence might lead me to make revelations I didn't want to make, because I had nothing to reveal on this particular issue. I was operating from a very good position, and they were in a very weak position. My attitude is, I'm not going to allow them to carry out their program faithfully. If they want to beat me five times, they can only do so on condition that I allow them to beat me five times. If I react sharply, equally and oppositely, to the first clap, they are not going to be able to systematically count the next four claps, you see. It's a fight. So if they had meant to give me so much of a beating, and not more, my idea is to make them go beyond what they wanted to give me and to give back as much as I can give so that it becomes an uncontrollable thing. You see the one problem this guy had with me: he couldn't really fight with me because it meant he must hit back, like a man. But he was given instructions, you see, on how to hit, and now these instructions were no longer applying because it was a fight. So he had to withdraw and get more instructions. So I said to them, "Listen, if you guys want to do this your way, you have got to handcuff me and bind my feet together, so that I can't respond. If you allow me to respond, I'm certainly going to respond. And I'm afraid you may have to kill me in the process even if it's not your intention."

Zambia Shall Be Free

(excerpt)

Kenneth Kaunda

Kenneth Kaunda was born in 1924, the youngest of eight children of a Church of Scotland minister. He became a teacher and headmaster before involving himself in nationalist politics. In 1955 he was jailed for two months with his colleague Harry Nkumbula, the president of the Northern Rhodesian African National Congress. Kaunda eventually broke from the ANC and formed his own Zambian African National Congress in October 1958. The new party was banned the following March, and Kaunda and others were detained, an experience described below. In 1964 Kaunda became the first president of an independent Zambia, a position he held until 1991. Since his retirement, he has served as a roving ambassador for Zambia and has been active in the fight against AIDS.

Arrest and Detention

The day had been unusually hot for March and the out-of-season drought made the little ones who lay uncomfortably sprawled on their communal mats rather tired. In a two-roomed house, number 257, New Chilenje township, ten of us lived. There were two nieces and a nephew besides my wife and our five sons. Our nephew and our firstborn shared our small kitchen. There they lay, looking more like pieces of firewood than human beings. The youngest two shared our tiny bedroom with us and the rest occupied the other room. It was everything—bedroom, living-room, dining-room—and before we secured a New Chilenje two-roomed house number 280, this room was also used as the Zambia office. In fact, it was here that the resolution to form the Zambia African National Congress was passed. The congestion and the discomfort I knew to be hard on my wife who was expecting our sixth child, but she did not complain. This suffering has, however, now been a source of great laughter between the Kapwepwes and ourselves for, in their own moments, Mama Salome Kapwepwe and my wife very seriously

351

questioned the wisdom of their husbands starting a new political party. Had we not suffered enough when serving in the African National Congress and was it not time we went back to a normal life, the life we had known in pre-Congress activities? However, this was carefully hidden from us.

On 10 March, one of our informants came to report that all senior police officers from all Provinces had been meeting at their territorial Headquarters and he knew we were going to be arrested, either on that day or the following. We, therefore, began to prepare ourselves by combing our offices and homes clean in so far as our valued papers and books were concerned. We placed these with people we could trust and those we knew the police could not suspect and invade. By this time we had already sent out to Tanganyika Mr. Lewis Changufu. We did not have sufficient funds but Mr. Ben Kapufi, then a business man in Broken Hill, offered to assist us. The original idea was that both Mr. Munukayumbwa Sipalo and Mr. Reuben Chitandika Kamanga, National Secretary and Deputy National Treasurer respectively, would leave the Protectorate, but lack of funds prevented this.

On 10 March nothing unusual happened. On the 11th, it was clear that we were being shadowed in a very unusual way and we knew the reason for it. Late that evening about five of us got together. It is now difficult to say why we met. Perhaps our souls and bodies needed coming together. However, we were together for some good hours until someone joked it would be better that one should be arrested in the presence of his own family, and that sent us all to our respective homes. All of us had heavy hearts even though each tried hard not to display it. By the time I got home all but my wife were fast asleep. I could not find our lock so I used a pair of scissors in place of a lock.

I must have been asleep for an hour when I opened my eyes and noticed that a motor vehicle was approaching our home and had floodlit our bedroom. My watch read 1 A.M. I began to dress and told my wife to do likewise. Before we could go through there was a loud knock at our cattle-kraal-type door. In a very firm voice I said, "Just a moment, please." This was followed up by a big push and the pair of scissors gave way and, in the twinkling of an eye, there was a policeman in uniform right in our bedroom.

He immediately ordered me to put my signature to a piece of paper which he would neither show nor read to me. Normally, I would have refused to sign something that I knew nothing about, but this time I looked at my wife and then my two boys with their startled faces and without the slightest resistance I signed a document not knowing what it was. Up to now, I cannot explain my action. It was not as though I was taken by surprise. I knew they were coming and my mind was steady in so far as I can remember . . . so it could not be a surprise. However, he ordered that I should pack up one suitcase while his two colleagues filled their Land-Rover with my books and papers. The younger of our two nieces sat up just as I was getting out and shouted, "Za-za-za." And just as suddenly as she had started up she fell back and slept. The whole small Land-Rover was full of my books and papers; so much so that I perched on my own otherwise valuable property with my left hand handcuffed to an African plain-clothes man and my right to that of a white assistant inspector in uniform. My wife, who had followed us outside, was told by the policeman, who obviously was leading the operation, to report at the D.C.'s office for ration money. With this, my long journey to some unknown destination started. I was rushed to the Woodlands police station. I discovered later that the man in charge did not trust the signature I had given him and so I had to thumb-print his document. From this police station, he rushed at a terrific speed past Government House, the Secretariat, the High Court and on to King George Avenue which joined Cairo Road. Six miles from Lusaka on the Great North Road towards Broken Hill, we swerved into a very large gravel pit where some contractor had dug out ballast for the road. I thought the whole police force was centred there for the night. There must have been some forty police vehicles around. The man in charge of our unwelcome expedition reported to his superiors about his big catch and I was immediately conscious of scores of hungry and fixed glances. My suitcase was thrown to the ground and someone opened it and began to make a thorough search of all my clothes and then threw them down carelessly. After this I was pushed into a near-by Black Maria where I found two of my colleagues, Simon Kapwepwe and old John Mumbi. A few minutes later we were joined by Chipowe who was Lusaka Chairman.

The fact that we did not know where we were going made us very uncomfortable. We tried to speak to the two police officers who were in charge at this time but they would not talk, so we decided to be unruly and started singing. They did not like it, so they threatened to separate us if we continued. We thought that would be terrible in the circumstances so we stopped, but this gave me an opportunity to talk and rather unconcernedly I said, "I am very glad that I am going to see my mother at last." One of the two men fell into our trap. Laughing very loudly and obviously enjoying himself he said, "You have a hope. You are going right in the opposite direction." Well this wasn't much but at least we knew we were not going home. Incidentally, all of us five were ex-Chinsali.

It must have been between 3 and 4 A.M. when all officers and their men left except for a car, a Land-Rover and our Black Maria. At 4 o'clock we started moving. We went round and round Lusaka for about an hour and then we shot straight for the airport where we found a full force of security men. I was called out first and two hefty police officers escorted me to a waiting 44-seater plane, the engines of which were already running and ready for immediate take-off. My hands were twisted as they took me to the aeroplane. At a quarter past five we took off for our unknown destination. Our next port was Ndola. As we descended, we could see a big police truck surrounded by Land-Rovers and we knew we were stopping to pick up some more "trouble-makers." Sure enough we were joined by Hyden Dingiswayo Banda, Nephas Tembo, J. K. Mulenga, R. Kapangala, Joseph L. Mulenga and Ralph Kombe from Broken Hill. I remember as we were airborne again we were offered some corned beef and biscuits. Someone told the captain (a police officer) that I did not take meat but there was nothing the poor man could do. After some time, I went along to the lavatory. An African constable followed me. I protested vigorously to the captain for this intrusion into my privacy, but our good captain could only regret and told us those were his orders so I decided to withdraw. After some two hours we landed at Balovale landing ground. I spent some few hours there and was then sent on the last lap of my long journey to my unknown destination. At 6 P.M., I was handed over to the D.C., Kabompo. There Frank Chitambala joined me and thirty minutes later, we arrived at our new "home."

In *Black Government?*, which I wrote with the Rev. Colin Morris, I said, "We are engaged in a struggle against any form of imperialism and colonialism not because it has as its agents white men but because it has many more wrong sides than good ones." Here is an illustration of what I mean. After our first breakfast at Kabompo, we decided to take a stroll. To our surprise villagers ran away from us as we approached them. Men stood near trees ready to climb up should we approach them. Mothers dashed to their houses with babies in their arms. When this was repeated about three times, we thought it right to find out what was happening and, on investigation, we found out that those in authority had spread a very wicked story about us. Villagers had been told that these Zambia men were cannibals. They especially liked children since these provided tender meat. Anyone who would go to this extent of telling lies in order to maintain his position I think calls for mental treatment, but this is imperialism at work. In *Black Government?* I also said, "It is an arrangement that will corrupt the best of men regardless of their colour, creed or religion." I can't imagine these same people who do such things in Africa doing these things in Britain, but out here they are defending a wrong system. However, very soon we settled down and our people around soon came in good numbers to listen to the good tidings of Freedom. In fact, we became so effective that only a month after we had been there we received individual orders banning us from addressing any meeting at all.

Our movements were restricted to a limited area so we tried to while away our time in as useful a way as we could in the circumstances. We began our mornings with baths and breakfast after which Frank and Musonda, who joined us after two weeks, would go out to look for provisions; then they would join me at our open-air office. Some very strange things happened there. One very hot morning, I was wearing a very simple form of sandal and had no shirt on, only a vest. I had been reading very hard but at this time I stopped suddenly. My thoughts began wandering. I wondered why man could not come closer to nature and be a friend with all that we fear today. I thought to myself if only we could be like little children we might play around with deadly snakes like the puff adder. At this juncture, I looked down and saw the head of a very big snake just passing the small toe of my left foot. I cannot explain my behaviour here but I looked on calmly. My uninvited, unwelcome and deadly poisonous visitor was a black mamba about five feet long. (After Mr. John Gaunt called me a black mamba, I often wondered why this particular member of "my family" did not stop to greet me. It could be my ignorance of the Mamba language!) Some good five minutes must have elapsed when all of a sudden I jumped up and dashed away into my bedroom. The swift snake must have been a mile away by then.

After lunch, we would take a rest and we would go back to our open-air office again until 5 P.M. I would then take my long evening walk while Frank and Musonda would prepare our evening meals. It was during these walks that another of these strange things happened. Before this time, I used to admire much that is in nature but never before had I come so close to nature and never before had I actually fallen in love with nature. This is what I mean. Before this, I had defended quite sincerely, controlled "Chitememe System" and "Soil Conservation" as well as game reserves. I had done this because of my personal experience at home. Around Lubwa we had plenty of game, trees and grass. But as our gun population grew, game became less and less. Today hunters have to go to Chiefs Chibale and Lundu in the Luangwa Valley to hunt game. Trees disappeared until some method of control was resorted to. We had to work hard to save our soil at the Mission Station from erosion by making contour ridges. This was my experience before Kabompo days, but quite a new attachment to nature grasped me here. I would walk for about a mile and then come to rest at a very high place overlooking one of the most beautiful scenes in the country at that time of the year. Here the silent waters of the Kabompo River gather in one great sheet of water. On both sides of the river are huge trees, deep green in the rainy season. They seem to be jealous of one another and appear to be pointing fingers of strange accusation at each other as the wind blows them backwards and forwards. Just as this one great sheet of water makes a sharp bend at the grassy feet of this princely high ground of Kabompo Boma, the silent waters burst into noisy protest as they clash with the enduring rocks.

Here I would sit in silent meditation removed from this world. Here I seemed to be getting nearer and nearer to understanding the language of nature. I studied the various shapes of trees and this gave me great pleasure. As the quiet breeze blew from the River Kabompo the trees and the grass around seemed to dance to a strange tune which made me feel that I was in the midst of music which would never come the way of my ears. However, there I sat, while minutes ran into hours. During these periods lions, leopards, hyenas, snakes and all animals seemed to accept one name, creatures of God the Almighty, and seemed to agree that they should not hurt each other. At time, Frank Chitambala would get worried about my long absence and would come looking for me. After this experience, I decided to get myself a camera, hoping to photograph trees from various angles that pleased me and to build up an album of such shapes. At this time more than ever before I began to wrestle with the idea that trees and all growing things must have a language of their own but that God's creation that passes all men's understanding has kept this a secret, and that some day this secret will be revealed to man in the same way as so many have already been revealed. I have bought my camera since coming out of jail but the factor of time is against my Kabompo detention days' ambition. I still hope to fulfil this some time.

Our influence around Kabompo was not confined to schoolboys and villagers only. I had a habit of using a rough sort of staff as a walking stick. Within a month almost every Boma messenger was walking around with one. So did a good number of schoolboys, much to the annoyance of the officials, who started giving lectures on how not to behave. Life was not all rosy at Kabompo. I almost lost my life at one time. I had a serious attack of dysentery followed by a sharp attack of malaria and then I suffered from a series of colds and coughing attacks. In so far as my health was concerned I did much better when I was re-arrested and sentenced to prison. There are other sad memories of Kabompo. One day I went to see the District Commissioner about the insufficiency of our allowances. I arrived at the offices at 8:30 A.M. At 9:30 A.M. the Hon. William Nkanza, member of the Legislative Council for North West arrived. He waited for forty-five minutes but the D.C. could not see him. We were just told to wait. Mr. Nkanza went back but I still continued to wait. At 12 noon I went past the messenger posted near the D.C.'s door to stop anyone from going in. My patience was completely exhausted. I knocked at the door very angrily and entered without his asking me in. He shouted at me to get out but I refused and instead demanded to be told why he had kept me waiting for three and a half hours. He replied that he was drafting something for me to sign. I shouted back saying surely it would have been good manners to let me know and then I would not have wasted my time. How would he have liked it if someone else had treated him as he had treated me?

At this juncture, he lost his temper and called me names. Silently I went straight for him. He left his chair and we went round and round his table as he called for his head messenger. The head messenger came in and stood between us as we looked at each other like fighting cocks. Our newly found peace-maker was an old man for whom I had great respect and, when he pleaded with me not to do anything, I looked at my friend and saying, "I respect the head messenger more than I do you," I left. An hour later, the D.C. came to my open-air office to make us sign certain documents. They were the orders—already referred to above—banning all three of us from addressing any meetings for three months.

With the People

(excerpt)

Maurice Nyagumbo

*Maurice Nyagumbo (1924–1989) is not one of the best known of the ac-
tivists who brought independence to Zimbabwe. But while the memoirs of
many politicians are preoccupied with meetings, speeches, and unsettled
scores, Nyagumbo's has a revealing directness and honesty. After independence, Nyagumbo became a cabinet minister in the government of Robert
Mugabe. He was embroiled in a scandal over the misallocation of cars and
committed suicide when prosecution seemed imminent. Some said that any
enthusiasm Mugabe may have had for rooting out corruption in his government ended with the death of his friend.*

Primary School

As my parents had taken up the peasants' life at Munyena, they now
needed someone to watch out for the baboons, which came to destroy the
crops on the land. My father thought that I could do the job. It was a terrifying experience because, for me, a baboon was a terrible monster even
to look at. Each time my parents and I went to the land, I was supposed
to stay on a high place so that I could see in all directions.

However, my father soon realised that the problem could not be
solved in that way. Each time he left me on a high place, I went to hide
myself behind some bush in order to be away from the baboons which I
was certain would eat me. One afternoon, as I was hiding, a baboon on its
way to the land came in my direction, and I started to scream as I rushed
towards my parents. My father came running since he thought perhaps I
had been bitten by a snake. However, the baboon was startled by my
screaming and ran away too. My father could not convince me that I
would not be devoured.

In order to keep me in the high place where I could see the baboons
coming, my father got some fibre ropes and tied my feet to a stump. But

this caused another problem as I used to cry the whole day. Nevertheless, this problem was less evil as it chased away the baboons. One day my father had just finished tying me to the stump and I had just started crying when my granny Tswari, the first wife of Nyagumbo, arrived. She immediately ordered him to untie me and while he was busy doing so she started hitting him with her walking-stick. As soon as my father had finished untying me, he took flight. My grandmother took me away to her own land to stay with her, so my father's problem remained unsolved.

In 1931, Tswari died and this left me without a home. I was forced to go back to my parents, though this time things were much better as I now had two little brothers to play with. The three of us used to go to the land very early in the morning. No baboons came near the crops because we made a lot of noise throughout the day. We never had a break in our job of looking after the crops, since there was always some crop on the land at every season of the year. After the harvest in June, my parents planted rice in the swampy places. With my two young brothers, Douglas and Ezekiel, I looked after the growing rice crop which attracted cattle and goats during the dry season. This crop was harvested in November, when maize, rupoko, corn, pumpkins and many other crops were planted.

In 1933, a school was established at Mutenure village, about two miles away from our village. It was later known as Mukuwapasi School. We had one teacher, an old man called Mr. Samuel Munyave. Although he appeared to have only passed Standard One, he was the most brilliant teacher we ever had. As soon as the school opened, it was flooded with pupils of various age-groups. There was a group which included married men and women; another, of big boys and girls, numbered about two hundred and was the largest group; a third group consisted of pupils aged between fifteen and twenty years old. All these groups were kept separate. The last group was ours, aged from eight to fourteen.

We would arrive at school at seven o'clock in the morning and were then divided into our class-groups. As soon as we had sat in our classes, everyone, big or small, was required to keep silent. Anyone who misbehaved was severely dealt with. Each class was given a particular subject and everyone was expected to do the best she or he could do. In most cases, children in our age-group were asked to write certain letters on the ground. We could not afford to be playing but had to do what we had been asked to do.

I did not do very well at this school because my cousin Harrison and I used to play truant. During the winter season, the two of us would get up very early and go to a mountain where we made a fire to warm ourselves. As soon as we saw others coming from school, we joined them and went back home. The two of us remained in Sub. B until 1935. In 1936, our parents decided to send us to St. Faith's Mission as boarders. We were supposed to leave for the mission on 27 January 1936. Unfortunately, I fell ill with bronchitis and was taken to Rusape Hospital. I did not recover until April of the same year, and Harrison went to St. Faith's alone.

When I had recovered, I left the hospital and went home to join the others at Mukuwapasi School. I now had more incentive to learn as it had become obvious that I had to go to a boarding school the following year. In November I went to St. Faith's Mission to register for the next year. Sister Esther, the principal, accepted me and told me to bring three pounds for school fees on 27 January 1937. I was very happy after this interview as I was going to join my cousin after a separation of a year.

On 27 January 1937, Harrison and I left for St. Faith's arriving at about five o'clock that afternoon. About thirty minutes after our arrival, we were summoned to the principal's office and, after a roll-call, were asked to pay in our school fees. Then we went to what was called the children's dormitory. There were no beds and we slept on mats made of reeds. By this time, nearly all the boarders had arrived. The newcomers were asked to fall into line by twos, and we formed a very long line since there were so many of us. All the "oldcomers" were carrying long sticks.

From here, we were told to march to the stream called Jordan, and as we marched along we were told to sing a song which went as follows:

Tiri, manyukama,
Tiri, manyukama,
Ti-ne tswi-na
Ti-ne tswi-na
Hati-gona, kugeza,
Hati-gona, kuzidza.

In English, the words mean:

We are the newcomers,
We are the newcomers,
We are dirty,
We are dirty,
We do not know how to wash ourselves,
We have not acquired education.

At the stream, we were told to undress and to jump into the water. After swimming for about five minutes, we were told to come out and dress, then to march to the school dining-room. When we had had our supper, we marched to our dormitories. Our hall prefect in the children's dormitory was Davis Dzuda. We prepared our beds and the newcomers were told to go to sleep. At nine o'clock, all lights went out. Then the old-comers started to hit us. I immediately hid myself in between the suitcases at the centre of the floor and I stayed there until the next morning.

These activities of beatings, marchings, singing and many other treat-ments being meted out by the oldcomers went on for the whole month. One Sunday evening, as we were having supper, Vincent Chipunza came with a bone full of fat and asked me to keep it for him. I wrapped the bone in a newspaper and put the parcel in my suitcase. About two weeks later Vincent came for his bone and I quickly collected it and gave it back. From that day onwards, all my troubles of being a newcomer came to an end, for Vincent became my friend and protector. The day ending the beating, singing, and marching was marked by a football match between the old-comers and the newcomers. The newcomers had to be careful not to score as that tended to prolong the suffering period. Even if the newcomers were all good players they had to let the oldcomers score as many goals as they needed.

I entered Standard One at St. Faith's Mission. My class teacher was Mr. Elijah Chitsike who later became a priest. During the first three-month term, I completely failed to comprehend any of the subjects, which included Arithmetic, English, Reading, Nature Study and Shona. The results of my first term examination were very discouraging and Mr. Chit-sike recommended to the principal that I be sent back to Sub. B in the sec-ond term. But as they could no longer allow any boarder to attend Sub. B, Sister Esther, the principal, decided that I should be given another chance. We went home for three weeks' vacation and during this time I busied myself just as if I was at school. I had little time for play and whenever I found myself with a problem in any subject, I went to Harrison who was now doing Standard Two.

When we went back to school, Mr. Chitsike was surprised with my progress. Throughout that second term, I worked very hard in all the sub-jects, and each time I needed any help I went either to Harrison or to Vin-cent who was in Standard Three. In August we wrote our second term examination and I came fifth in a class of forty-five pupils. Again, during that holiday, I kept myself busy with my books. Among those who were above me in the last examinations was a girl, and that disappointed me very much. I did not want a repetition of that in the final examination.

In September we went back to school. Apart from class work, Stan-dard One had gardening classes during the afternoons from Mondays to Fridays. I used to have excellent marks in gardening as my two beds of tomatoes, rape and carrots were always the best in the whole garden. We wrote our final examinations towards the end of November and the results were announced on 14 December. I was number three in our class but again the same girl was number one. We had a closing concert that evening and left for our homes the next morning.

I was due to enter Standard Two the following year, and as I wanted to work so that I could avoid being beaten by a girl, I borrowed Harrison's Standard Two books. I again spared no time that holiday but kept myself busy studying. When we went back to school in January 1938 our teacher in Standard Two was Mr. Langton Walter, a Coloured from Bulawayo who was a very good teacher, especially in the subject of Hygiene.

The mail-bag at St. Faith's Mission was collected on Saturday mornings by schoolboys. This year, I was among those four given the task of collecting the post. Going to Rusape every Saturday morning became a privilege for me and Freddy Shayamunda as we could always collect food parcels on our way back: my grandmother was still staying at Nyahada village, which was on our way, and Freddy's father worked as a salesman at an Indian shop in Rusape. Each time we arrived at the post office, we stood by the window where we handed in and received the mail-bag. We were strictly prohibited from entering the post office through the door. This was used only by Europeans, although there was no written notice of that regulation.

One Saturday morning, it started raining heavily as we were about three miles from Rusape. When we arrived at the post office, the window was closed but the door was open. As there was no veranda where we could shelter, we stood by the window in the soaking rain. After a while, Stephen Shumba, the oldest boy among us, decided to walk in through the door in order to hand in the mail-bag. Within a few seconds, Stephen was flung outside by a fat white man who followed and kicked him. The three of us ran to Savania Store where we stood watching helplessly while our colleague was being kicked by this huge man. Later, Stephen got up and ran to the Native Commissioner's office where his uncle worked. When the uncle saw his nephew screaming and being pursued by the white man, he avoided Stephen, who immediately ran into the Native Commissioner's office. The huge white man followed him and within a few seconds Stephen was being beaten by two white men on the veranda of the office. After a while, Stephen managed to extricate himself and ran towards us. By this time, his face was swollen up, and we walked back to the mission without the mail-bag. As we were passing the place where Freddy's father worked, an Indian woman noticed Freddy's swollen face and offered to wash and bandage the wounds. From there, we walked fast to the mission which we reached at about five o'clock.

We went to Sister Esther and reported the matter. As Father Arthur Knight, the priest in charge at the mission, was not available, Sister Esther decided to wait until Monday. Stephen was ordered to bed. Early on Monday, Sister Esther and the four of us drove down to Rusape in a mission truck. When we arrived, the Sister and Stephen went into the post office while the three of us waited outside. Within a few moments, Stephen was thrown out by the same huge white man who told Sister Esther to "stay outside with the kaffir." As she came out, Sister was sobbing, which was her normal way of expressing disapproval of anything, even if a child misbehaved in class.

She took Stephen by the hand and walked to the Native Commissioner's office, but as she was about to enter, the Native Commissioner shouted that she should wait outside with the native. Sister Esther stood on the veranda with Stephen. After some time, the Native Commissioner came out and asked her what she wanted to do with the native. She replied that she only wanted to know why the boy had been beaten.

The Native Commissioner said, "You must teach the native boy how to behave. Do not waste too much time in teaching him how to speak English." Immediately he had finished saying these words, he walked into his office and banged the door.

Sister Esther sobbed as we went back to the truck, and drove back to the mission. On arrival, Stephen who had obtained further injuries on his face that morning, received treatment at the dispensary and was sent to bed. The Sister decided to wait for the priest in charge of the mission. On Wednesday afternoon, when he returned from his trip, Sister Esther told him all that had happened at the post office and at the Native Commissioner's office. On Friday afternoon, the four of us boys were summoned to Father Knight's house. Here we were told never to cause trouble again in the future and that if we did, we would be expelled from the mission. Although we tried to argue that we had not intended to cause any trouble, we were unable to convince Father Knight. We were all shocked by his reaction.

However, we continued to go to the post office. Stephen joined us after three weeks when he had recovered. One Saturday morning, as we waited outside the post office for our mail-bag, a European boy riding on a bicycle bumped into Weston Madziwa and fell to the ground. Weston helped the white boy to stand up, but a big white man who came running from the opposite side pushed Weston aside and took the white boy, who was now crying. The same white man returned and accused Weston of having assaulted the white boy. Before Weston could reply, the white man started hitting him. As we protested, several other Europeans came and started hitting us with their fists. When police arrived, the four of us were taken to the charge office where we were caned with four strokes each. I felt very bitter against white people after this incident. We had not done anything to that white boy. There was absolutely nothing wrong with us and we did not deserve that punishment.

After our thrashing, we were taken back to the post office by the police and we collected our mail-bag. We walked back to the mission with great difficulty as our buttocks were bleeding from cuts. Our faces, too, were swollen from our beating by the white men at the post office. We also realised that Father Knight had threatened us with expulsion if we caused more trouble. Now that trouble had occurred, we decided not to tell anyone, including Sister Esther. Instead of arriving at about half past four as usual, we arrived at six o'clock. Sister Esther was waiting in her office. After giving her the mail-bag we walked away, but she noticed that Freddy had difficulty walking and she called us back to explain. However, before Freddy was able to, Sister noticed that every one of us had a swollen face and she demanded to know what had happened. Stephen Shumba related everything to her and also told her about the threat we had received from Father Knight. Sister Esther sobbed for quite some time before she told us to go to the dispensary where we were bandaged. We were then told to go to bed.

Although we were unable to go to Sunday service the next morning, we managed to attend our classes on Monday. On Friday morning, the four of us were summoned to the principal's office where we found Bishop Paget, Father Knight and Sister Esther. We were told to get into the mission truck, and we all drove to Rusape police charge office. On arrival, the bishop asked one of the policemen why the schoolboys had been caned. The policeman replied that we had caused a lot of trouble and had assaulted a young European boy the previous Saturday morning. They asked to see the young European boy the police claimed had been assaulted and were told that the boy and his parents were not in town that day. At this stage we were told to leave the office while the bishop, Father Knight and Sister Esther remained with the police.

Some time later, they emerged and we drove back to the mission. From that day onwards, big boys replaced us on the Saturday mail collection. These two incidents at the post office really changed my attitude towards education and also towards the white man. I actually thought that the white men had bullied us at the post office only because we were young boys, and decided that when I grew up I was going to retaliate if any white man bullied me. Of course, at the time I had no knowledge of the facts of the situation in the country.

The results of our final examination that year were announced on 14 December and I was number one in the class. At last I had achieved what I had always dreamed about. I received many books and pencils for my achievement. The next morning, we all went to our homes. There were about ten boys from Makoni village and about fifteen from Rugoyi village and also five from our village, and we all used to walk together on our way home. We used to pass through the farm of a white man by the name of van der Merwe. We had just passed his house when we heard the sound of a fast moving car behind us. As we jumped out of the road, the car suddenly stopped, and we realised that the white man was up to some trouble so we ran away in different directions. The white man chased after three big boys, while our group disappeared in the tall grass and went home.

After they had run a short distance, the big boys, who were carrying heavy luggage, decided to stop. When the white man caught up, he hit one of them with a sjambok. The three big boys got hold of the white man and gave him a thorough beating. When we arrived home that evening, we did not tell our parents about it. The next day, police came and arrested us all. Our parents accompanied us to Rusape police station where we found all the other boys. We were made to stand in line while the white farmer and the police looked at every one of us. The three big boys were soon picked out and we were caned with five strokes each. We were then told that the road which we had been using to walk to school was now closed to the public. This meant that we would have to travel a distance of fifty miles to St. Faith's Mission instead of only eight miles in our case, or three miles in the case of those who came from Makoni village.

My father did not see any point in my continuing to attend St. Faith's which had now become further than St. Augustine's Mission, so the next morning he went to St. Augustine's to ask for a school place for me. He returned the same evening with the news that he had obtained one. On 26 January 1939, I was among three boys and five girls who walked through Mount Jenya, Zongoro, Muchena and Tsambe on our way to school, where we arrived at about half past five in the afternoon. Within a few minutes of our arrival, we were all summoned to the principal's office to pay in our school fees.

Here, too, newcomers suffered harsh treatment although we were not beaten as at St. Faith's Mission. Instead we were made to sing songs which praised the education institutions in the country. Both the accommodation and the food were much better than at St. Faith's. The only thing I did not like here was that we were required to speak English for six days of the week, from Monday morning to Saturday evening. The system with which debates were held was also very bad for me. Every Friday evening, a debate on a different topic was held and a panel of speakers was arranged. These speakers were selected from the junior to the senior classes and, once you were selected, it became compulsory.

I caused laughter on the first occasion I was included on the panel. There were four of us, including a girl from a senior class, and I was supposed to be the second speaker that evening. The topic was: "Which is the best method to keep a man's wealth, in money or in livestock?" When my turn came, I moved myself to the third speaker's place but the chairman noticed and demanded that I get back in position. I was then forced to stand up to speak. As I stood, I found myself completely dumb and unable to utter a word. When other boys and girls started to whistle and mock me, I sat down. But the chairman ordered me to stand. By this time, everybody was laughing and I took the opportunity to say a few words which could not be heard by anyone because there was too much noise. As soon as people stopped making a noise, I sat down. When the chairman asked me to stand up again, I protested and told him that I had already spoken.

This helped me greatly, and from that day onwards I worked very hard to improve my spoken English. After about six months, I was able to debate intelligently and logically on any topic. I did not go home during the June and September holidays but remained at school working for money I needed to buy clothes. In September I was busy watering flowers at the nuns' quarters at the mission when Sister Pauline came to tell me that a war had been declared between Britain and Germany. She told me that all the people should pray to God that the British win the war, because if Germany won the war the whole world would suffer under Nazi domination.

I believed what Sister Pauline said. Although I had seen cruelty among some English people at Rusape post office, I had also seen that among the missionaries were some very good English people who treated Africans as human beings. From that day, a bell was rung at twelve o'clock every day and everyone at the mission was required to attend a special church service.

Among my friends at St. Augustine's Mission was Lucian Ndlovu from Bulawayo. The two of us used to speak about going to Johannesburg to seek employment, because Lucian's father was working there. We believed that workers in South Africa were better paid than in Rhodesia. But my friend Lucian was ahead of me, in Standard Five. I still had a desire to speak better English. We wrote our final examinations towards the end of November and the results were announced on 13 December. I was number two and I was terribly disappointed because a girl came first.

We went home the next day, this time travelling by train, and arrived at Rusape at noon. After we alighted from the train we walked in a long file along the Inyanga road. At home, I met Solomon Mutasa who had just come from Bulawayo where he had been working. He had succeeded in getting a school place at St. Faith's Mission where he intended to study the English language for one year. He told me that after that he intended to go to Johannesburg. I told him of the plans Lucian and I had made and we agreed that we should all leave for Johannesburg after the school examinations in December 1940.

In February 1940, a debate was held at the school on the topic: "Should the Africans in this country assist Britain in its war against Germany?" This topic was very controversial. Among the speakers was Samuel Madekurozwa who spoke last and was one of the two who were against assisting Britain. Although his partner, Joshua Nyamunda, had also spoken very strongly against assisting Britain, Madekurozwa went further to explain "notorious British colonial history," especially that of this country. He told the audience that the Africans of the country had no obligation to help Britain, whose nationals had butchered and tortured the inhabitants of the country during 1896–7. Madekurozwa pointed out that Africans of the country had become parasites because they had been declared homeless by the British colonists here.

Immediately after the debate that evening, Samuel Madekurozwa was expelled from school. His expulsion served as an eye-opener to me as I still had some illusions about missionaries. I now realised that they were birds of the same feather as other settlers. Since my arrival at St. Augustine's Mission, we had been made to understand that all debaters on any topic were to discuss the subject independently without fear of antagonising the school authorities. But this expulsion was to disprove the theory of "independence."

I went home during the June holidays as I wished to finalise my arrangement with Solomon. I had been assured by Lucian Ndlovu of our plan to leave for Johannesburg in December of that year. Here at home, Solomon and I agreed that the matter should remain a secret between the two of us. After the holidays, I joined a group of boys and girls who boarded the train at Rusape and travelled a rowdy journey to school. We sang and danced on the train till we arrived at Umtali that afternoon. The school truck made four trips from the railway station to the mission. Lucian had three pounds for pocket money that term, a great deal of money for a schoolboy at that time, but before we left for the mission that afternoon Lucian and I had already spent ten shillings on sweets.

Throughout that year, I found it hard to concentrate on my studies as I was thinking of going to South Africa. During the September holidays, I decided to remain at the mission to work for some money which would help me on my way. I was to receive twenty-five shillings and I intended to keep it for the journey. We wrote our final examinations towards the end of November, and on 14 December, we travelled by train to Rusape. I told Lucian to expect Solomon and me in two days' time.

When I arrived home, I went straight to see Solomon who had just come back from St. Faith's Mission. He said that he would not be ready in two days as he had to wait for his brother who was coming home for the Christmas holidays and was going to give him the necessary money for the journey. I said that I could not wait because of the arrangements I had made with Lucian. We eventually agreed that Lucian and I would wait in Bulawayo for Solomon. I then went to my parents and told my father that I was required to leave for Bulawayo the next morning as the "Pathfinders" were camping at the Matopos hills. My father gave me the five pounds which I asked for.

The next day I woke up very early, packed my clothes in my suitcase and left for Rusape. I boarded the train at about eleven in the morning and arrived at Bulawayo at seven the following morning. I searched all over the platform for Lucian but was unable to find him. I knew that his parents were living in Makokoba Location but I had not taken the trouble to find out the address. I then went into the waiting-room and sat on a bench. After a while, I went to the ticket office and asked for a ticket to Kimberley. A European lady in the office asked whether I had a pass and I gave her my school pass, but she told me to go and get a travel pass from the Native Commissioner's office. The name "Native Commissioner" terrified me. I did not want a repetition of what I had experienced at Rusape. I walked back to the waiting-room, but when I got there my suitcase was not where I had left it on the bench.

I immediately reported the missing suitcase to an African constable who was on the platform. The only clothes I now had were those I was wearing, a school blazer, grey trousers, a pair of black shoes and a cap. The constable looked around and searched everyone on the platform for my suitcase, then asked me to accompany him to the charge office to make a statement. After I had given the statement, he offered to take me to the Native Commissioner's office, where a messenger took me to the Native Commissioner. I told him that I was coming from school and that my father had sent me to see my brother who was seriously ill in Kimberley Hospital. I produced the school pass and the Native Commissioner gave me a travel pass. I was very happy and walked quickly to the station. I showed the lady the travel pass and paid twenty-five shillings for a ticket to Kimberley.

The Kimberley train had already gone, but the one to Johannesburg was leaving at three that afternoon. I bought some meat pies and two bottles of cold drink and boarded that train. I travelled the whole night and arrived at Lobatsi at about nine the next morning. Here I found some African women selling food. Since I was now feeling hungry, I decided to buy some biltong and some sour milk. Although I did not understand what the woman was talking about, I just bought the stuff and started eating. But a Tswana man sitting next to me, who must have observed that I did not understand the Tswana language, asked me whether I ate horse meat. I said no, and started spitting out the bits of meat I still had in my mouth, but it was too late. I had already done a lot of eating and we had left Lobatsi. I also discovered that the milk I had bought was goat's milk.

We arrived at Mafeking at midday, and I alighted from the train as it was going on to Johannesburg. I went and sat on a bench in the waiting-room. After about two hours, two African men came and asked me where I was coming from and where I was going. When I told them, they asked me to accompany them to what they called the charge office. I followed them, and just as we were almost outside the town we entered what appeared to be an empty building. Suddenly the two men grabbed me, took four pounds from my trousers pocket then ran away. I left the building crying for my money and wanted to go and report the matter to the police. I met a European policeman on the way and told him of my plight. He insisted that I speak in Afrikaans and when he saw that I could not understand the language he walked away. I saw that the police were not prepared to help me. I was very much afraid to go back to the waiting-room. I now had only thirty-five shillings in my blazer pocket.

I decided to walk along the railway line towards Kimberley so that I could avoid the robbers and get the train at the next siding. This was about three in the afternoon. I had travelled about five miles from Mafeking when I came across what I thought was a siding. Within the few minutes I stood there, the train passed at a terrific speed. Realising that the place was not a siding as I had thought, I started walking again. It was about five o'clock. After I had gone just a short distance, I saw a trolley approaching. The white men in it stopped and asked me something in Afrikaans which I could not understand. Since I did not answer their enquiries, the white men jumped from the trolley and, as they came towards me, I ran to the western side of the railway line.

I did not stop running until it had become dark. There was no moonlight and, though it was not raining, the sky was full of black clouds. I was a bit confused and did not know exactly where I was. But I knew that I was on the western side of the railway line. After a while, I began walking in an eastern direction. It was difficult to go fast because there was a lot of tall grass and thorny bushes. I continued to walk until I reached the railway line. It was now very late in the night and I started to walk south along the line. I saw lights ahead and believed it was a town, so I travelled faster as I wanted to get there quickly. A while later, I looked behind me and saw something I thought was a donkey or a mule with a lot of fur on its mane. It was possible to see its outline by the starlight. Each time I stopped to make a proper observation of the animal, it also stopped and looked at me. Whenever I continued to walk, it did the same. I then reached the place where I had seen lights, but to my surprise there was only a massive building, adjacent to which were several huts enclosed by a high fence of barbed wire. There was no sign of movement but there was the sound of a mine-stamping machine. Following a small path which led to the railway line, I saw a platform with a structure which I took to be a waiting-room. I went in and closed the door with an iron hoop from inside. There was a bench in the room where I lay down.

I had slept for only a few minutes when the door was flung open. After a time, I heard a movement outside the room but I did not attempt to close the door again as I did not want to make any noise. I could not sleep again as I was very much afraid. I believed that the door had been banged open by the robbers who had taken my money at Mafeking and that they had followed me. I remained in the same position till morning. I could hear people's voices but I did not want to reveal myself, for I was still thinking of the robbers. The talking continued, then someone came to the waiting-room and saw me. He started to speak to me in Tswana but soon discovered that I did not understand what he was talking about. He then asked in English where I was coming from. I told him, and the man was very surprised that I had survived the lions which he said were prowling around the waiting-room during the early hours of that morning.

As this man continued to speak to me, he saw that I was shivering and he came to help me stand up. When I started to walk out, I realised that my trousers were wet with urine and I asked the man to wait a minute. He told me not to worry as he fully appreciated my predicament. He then told me to stand in the sun. All the people on the platform, both men and women, came and stood around. They seemed very surprised to see me. Soon the train arrived and we boarded it. The man who had helped me bought some coffee and buns which we all ate. He said that everybody who had seen me in the waiting-room that morning believed that I was the luckiest man in the world.

We travelled together to Vryburg, where my good friend left me. I went on to Kimberley, arriving at about eight in the evening. I alighted from the train and went to sleep in the waiting-room.

Nkomo

(excerpt)

Joshua Nkomo

*Joshua Nkomo (1917–1999) was the founder of the Zimbabwe African
People's Union (ZAPU), which led the early stages of the struggle for an
independent Zimbabwe. One of eight children, he became a carpenter,
schoolteacher, social worker, trade union organizer, and leader of Rhodesia's
Railway Workers Union. From 1964 to 1974 he was held at the remote
Gonakudzingwa Restriction Camp along with other opponents of Ian
Smith's white minority regime, including Maurice Nyagumbo, Ndabaningi
Sithole, Edgar Tekere, and Robert Mugabe. In 1963 Sithole and Mugabe had
split from ZAPU, forming two factions of what was called the Zimbabwe
African National Union (ZANU).*

*As the leaders of two separate armed forces, Nkomo and Mugabe over-
threw the Smith regime. Parliamentary elections held in 1980 split largely on
ethnic lines, and Mugabe took power as the first prime minister of Zimbabwe.
Nkomo was appointed minister without portfolio. He was later accused of
leading a coup against Mugabe and he fled the country, as recounted below.
North Korean–trained troops massacred villagers in Nkomo's stronghold of
Matabeleland, and after Nkomo's return to Zimbabwe he allowed ZAPU to
be absorbed in ZANU, a move he later said was motivated by a wish to avoid
further bloodshed. After his death in 1999, Nkomo was declared a national
hero and buried at Heroes Acre outside Harare.*

Leaving Zimbabwe

Just before dawn on 8 March 1983, I crossed the dry river-bed into
Botswana, driven into exile from Zimbabwe by the armed killers of Prime
Minister Robert Mugabe. Over the decades of our struggle for freedom I
had grown used to the hostility, even the hatred, of governments representing the tiny white minority of my fellow-citizens. But nothing in my
life had prepared me for persecution at the hands of a government led by
black Africans. This book will, I trust, make clear what had gone wrong
and why. But first I must explain how I got away and lived to tell the tale.

Over a year had passed since I was dismissed, on trumped-up charges, from the government of Zimbabwe. All that time Robert Mugabe and his party colleagues had sought, without success, to link me and my party, Zapu, to the armed bandits operating in the western province of Matabeleland. Instead of trying to prevent the unrest that was inevitable after fifteen years of armed struggle, the government seemed intent on creating rebellion and suggesting that I was at the head of it. In the rural areas thousands of people—many of them my supporters, many innocent even of that offence against the ruling party—had been massacred by the Fifth Brigade, the force specially trained by North Korean advisers to operate independently of the official army and police.

Whole villages had been burnt to the ground, cattle slaughtered, women raped. Soldiers who had fought gallantly under my command for our country's freedom were arrested and tortured. Some were tried, acquitted by the courts—and then redetained without trial under the arbitrary laws inherited from the colonial period. My family and my friends were threatened, my passport was impounded, my speeches calling for unity and justice were methodically suppressed as the press and broadcast media were brought under total state control. But still the ruling party could not provoke me to disloyalty towards the nation I had struggled to liberate.

Prime Minister Mugabe had publicly called for violent action against my person. He said, quite falsely, that I was trying to overthrow his government. Speaking of my party, he said: "Zapu and its leader, Dr. Joshua Nkomo, are like a cobra in a house. The only way to deal effectively with a snake is to strike and destroy its head." On Saturday 5 March 1983, his men at last moved against me in person. Despite instructions from the police that I should report to them every time I left my house in Bulawayo, I was taking various precautions: that Friday night I had spent with relatives in the eastern suburbs (the former European area of the town, my own home being in the more crowded western district that was formerly reserved for Africans).

On Saturday morning came the news that the old African townships were cordoned off by the army and the police, while the men of the notorious Fifth Brigade were conducting searches within the cordon. Early in the afternoon we heard that my own house had been searched, that the Fifth Brigade commander had checked that it was indeed my home, and had left.

I was furious at this invasion of my home, and I resolved to go there and check it out. My hosts urged me not to go but, seeing that I was determined, my wife insisted on coming with me. I told my security man to drive off across the deserted town. As we approached the cordon of soldiers and police he flatly refused to go on, saying that if by any chance he survived what was bound to happen, he would get the blame for exposing me to danger. My wife agreed with him, and for almost two hours we drove aimlessly around the deserted city, discussing what to do. In the end caution prevailed, and we drove back to the former European suburb where we had spent the night.

About 8 P.M. there was a telephone call. There had been shooting at my home, and sporadic fire was continuing in the neighbourhood. My driver and two other members of my household were known to be dead: there might be more casualties, but nobody was certain. The Fifth Brigaders were still asking the neighbours where I was, but those who knew were not saying. Never before had I wished that I were dead, but I wished it then. I wished I had died when Ian Smith's raiders had attacked my house in Lusaka and missed me by an hour. Then I would have died at the hands of the enemies of my people. But now the attempt on my life was being made on the orders of the African government of Zimbabwe, by people claiming to act on behalf of the nation that I had worked for decades to create. It was the bitterest moment of my life.

Later it became clear what had happened. The Fifth Brigade men had entered my house, searched it and found me absent. They had then questioned my people about where I was, and on getting no reply had shot three of them out of hand. They had then rampaged through the house, smashing up the kitchen and aimlessly breaking the furniture. Apparently for their amusement they had also damaged three of my cars, putting rifle-butts through the windscreens and ripping the upholstery.

This was sheer, unprovoked murder and hooliganism, directed at me but striking at people whose only offence was to have served me loyally. Robert Mugabe had decided to have me out of the way, and he evidently did not care what method was used. But I hold the legitimate government of Zimbabwe innocent of this atrocity. Mugabe was acting not as prime minister, but as leader of his party, Zanu. I had once asked him directly: "What is the supreme organ in Zimbabwe?" He had answered: "The supreme body in Zimbabwe is the central committee of Zanu (PF), my party." I told him that could not be so: that the supreme organ of the country could only be its elected parliament, speaking for all the people. As the prime minister chosen by parliament, Robert was the top man of the country. But as leader of his party he was just a politician like me, with the same rights but no more. As leader of Zanu he acted outside the law: but the law and the constitution of Zimbabwe remain in force, and I hold the ruling party, not the lawful government, responsible for the attempt on my life.

It was my wife maFuyana who determined what I was to do. "It appears to me," she said, "that your friends have gone out of their minds. Now that they have come straight out to kill you, you have got to leave. If you survive abroad you can return, and help the country out of its present problems. If you stay you will die, and there will be no repairing the damage that will do Zimbabwe." I pleaded with her that we should stay together, since if I left her alone they might well kill her and the children too. But she insisted that nobody should leave their country in time of trouble unless it was absolutely necessary. It was her duty, and the children's, to stay and see things through. But equally it was my duty to go, since only if I survived would there be a hope of peace and reconciliation. She was weeping: when I argued that I too should stay she accused me of being selfish. And so I gave in to her argument. Once more I was heading into exile.

To leave Zimbabwe was the toughest decision I ever had to take. I knew my enemies would say I had run away, and I expected they would invent stupid stories about my flight. That clown Herbert Oshewokunze, the minister of home affairs, told the newspapers I had "escaped" disguised as an old woman. Who ever saw an old woman of my height and my weight, with a clipped moustache and one of the best-known faces in all Africa? And if the police had information about this large old lady, why did they not arrest her? Anyway I did not escape, I decided to leave and I left. For a year I had lived the life of a hunted animal. I could hide no longer. On the Monday I had been summoned to report to the police: if I reported, the killers would follow me from there, and if I did not report I would be declared a fugitive suspect, with every soldier and policeman in the country licensed to shoot me out of hand. Those were the arguments for leaving. I resisted them until my wife's words sank in. Then I said, "Right, I'll do it." I did it, and surprised even myself.

Once the decision was taken, we sent our people out to reconnoitre the roads, first to the south-west and then southwards, towards the Botswana border fence which is, at its nearest, about a hundred kilometres from Bulawayo. All that Sunday the men kept coming back to report that it was impossible to pass. Every few kilometres there were road-blocks and men with guns, soldiers or police or men from the security service and the Fifth Brigade.

As commander-in-chief of the Zipra army during the war against the previous regime, I had acquired some knowledge of military tactics and—more important—of the military mind. I knew that every minor road would be blocked. But something told me that they would never expect me to do the simple thing and drive right down the main highway towards the border. That is just what we did. At half-past midnight we set off down the road to Plumtree, beyond which the main road and railway pass on to the Botswana frontier-post. The timing was chosen to pass through Plumtree at about 2:30 or 3 A.M., when soldiers in any army are inclined to take a nap. That was the chance we took, and it worked. I must add that the only people to know of the plan were my wife and the young men who accompanied me. I deliberately left my son and daughter, and her husband, out of it. It was best they did not know, in case of repercussions later.

The leader of our group was Makhathini Guduza, a member of the central committee of Zapu. He drove off first in the truck, a half-ton pick-up with a canopy, together with one man. They were unarmed. I rode behind in the station wagon with Jackson Moyo and three other young men: we had two AK rifles and three pistols ready for use. Guduza's vehicle kept about two hundred metres ahead of ours, so that we could clearly see each other's lights. We had arranged a simple set of signals. If he saw something suspicious on the road, he was to stop and keep on all his lights including the brake light. If he then switched everything off, it meant that all was clear, and we were to pull up to him for a discussion. But if he left all his lights on the four passengers in my care were to get out and move clear of the road with our weapons, and our driver was to move cautiously ahead.

If it came to fighting, the plan was that one of the boys would stick by me, and the others were to fan out right and left before opening fire, to give the other side the impression that there were a lot of us. Then I as commander was to shout, "Close up!", and on that word of command we would retreat, join up, and try to work our way forward around the obstacle in the direction of the border. We were perfectly ready to shoot if it came to that: I did not like it, but there it was.

So we drove out through the former white suburbs to join up with the main road. In Bellevue, just before we picked up the highway, we passed a single car. Between there and Plumtree, a distance of just under ninety kilometres, we met no others. Ten kilometres short of Plumtree we stopped: Guduza went ahead to scout, and I and my three boys took up defensive positions on the roadside. In Plumtree, we knew, there was a government force of about two thousand men. Guduza came back and reported that they seemed to be there all right, but asleep: there were no police on the road, and the townships were dead quiet. I said, "Let's go," we sandbagged the pick-up, and I got in the back with three guards and the guns. That was how we drove right into Plumtree, turning left at the township as we entered it, and so on southwards on the Mpandeni road. Now it was only ten kilometres to the border. We knew this was the riskiest part, but our headlights showed nothing but the rabbits jumping around.

Next we had to find the place where we knew the border fence was unguarded, and this was where we made our first mistake. We turned down the wrong track, and found ourselves at a dead end by a little country school. I took the risk of waking up the teachers, who directed us back towards the highway—and there once again we took a wrong turning, which we realised when the lights of Plumtree once again came up in front of us. As we turned back the sky was starting to brighten in the east, and we knew there was very little time. But at last we identified the corner, drove down the dusty track and came to the village we were looking for. A countrywoman, up early fetching water, pointed to the line of trees and the river-bed just beyond them that marked the border. We drove down and turned left at another track, stopped at the bank of the dry Ramakwabane river, and walked across to the two border fences on the Botswana side. I am no lightweight, but the boys pushed and I climbed the fence, and at last we were over in no-man's-land, and up again to the Botswana fence. It was exactly twenty past six in the bright morning when I climbed down the wire onto the safety of Botswana soil.

From then on it was all welcomes. The chief of the nearest village had been my pupil for a while back in 1939, when he lived on the Zimbabwe side of the border. He greeted me and sent for the local headmaster, who organised transport to take me to Francistown, where the police took over. By 9 P.M. that night we were safe in Gaborone, the capital, and lodged on the orders of the president of Botswana in a small house. For the past two days I had barely rested. Now the tension was over, and I fell into the unconsciousness of deep sleep.

An African Heritage

My parents were born when my country was still free. The government was in the hands of the people, directed by custom and tradition. My father, Nyongolo, was born about 1880, my mother five years later. They were children when Cecil Rhodes and his column of raiders raised their flag on the hill of Harare: around that hill spread the city of Salisbury, now called Harare once again.

They were teenagers when the occupation was completed in 1897, after the superior weapons of the settlers, assisted by British troops, had subdued the combined resistance of the Shona- and the Ndebele-speaking peoples. At the end of that war the commander of the invading soldiers sent out his men to shoot and kill at least two thousand natives, at random, "to instill fear of the white man by the native." The settlers then established a "loot committee" to share out the cattle and other livestock, and to parcel out our land into estates.

I was myself seven years old when the British government handed over effective power to the settlers of what was then Southern Rhodesia, who chose self-government in preference to becoming a fifth province of South Africa. From that time on the nation was dominated by a tiny section of its population: the struggle against minority rule was to be the problem of my life. But the benefit of this new form of government was that it defined, once for all, our national borders. In the old, pre-colonial days the territories of each of the peoples in the land were defined only by custom: their vagueness led to raids and counter-raids in search of cattle, food or women. Now there was no reason why all of us should not unite and develop an unquestioned sense of national identity.

I was born on 7 June 1917, the third of eight children. Alice was born in 1910, then Paul (who sadly died in 1939), then myself, Joshua. After me came Mackenzie, who left us and may now be living somewhere in South Africa; then twin girls (but only Othilia survived infancy); then Stephen; then Edward, the last-born, in 1927.

My parents were Christians, workers for the London Missionary Society at the settlement of Tshimale, in Matabeleland. They were among the first of our people to be married in church, and my father's elder brother, Mapokwana, questioned the wisdom of such marriages, saying that the limit of a single wife restricts the growth of the clan. Just after Alice was born, the missionaries sent my father to be trained as a teacher at their Tiger Kloof School in South Africa.

My mother told me again and again how she and my father worried about me as a baby. For almost the whole of my second and third months of life I caused them sleepless nights with my screaming. My parents consulted a traditional doctor, who gave me some of his medicine. The results gave my parents a new cause for concern. I became unnaturally quiet, unable even to cry like a normal baby. They thought I might even have lost the power to speak, but the doctor assured them that there was nothing to worry about, I would talk when the time came.

This made me a late talker and a shy child. I could not keep up with the other children, and kept running back to my mother. I adored her; I was a mother's boy. My weakness made me backward in our games, and at the sport of stick-fighting. I was slow to follow the other boys in herding, first the calves and then the full-grown cattle. Even when I went to school and found myself coming first in all my classes, from Standard 1 to Standard 6, I felt the other boys were better than me.

In later life that lack of confidence has been both my strength and my weakness. Because I felt the others were ahead of me, I always struggled to keep ahead of their standards. But because I had so much trust in my mother I have believed I could rely on other people as I did on her. In all my dealings with people I have acted trustingly, and have found out too late when I have been betrayed. My comfort has been to trust in and be trusted by the masses.

After three years of study in South Africa, my father Nyongolo returned to find that the mission station at Tshimale was being run down. The white people had chosen it for their own area, and the missionaries had decided to move their school to a nearby community, named after its chief, Bango. It was a lovely place, in the high rainfall area of the Matopos foothills, south of the city of Bulawayo. The rivers Semukwe and Tshatshane flowed nearby from the Matopos, bringing year-round water for the people and the livestock. In this delightful place I was born, and so were Paul, Mackenzie and my sister Othilia. As children we swam in the pools and raced in little canoes. We snared small game, birds and rabbits and squirrels, and even the little beavers. There were steep slopes of water-polished granite, where we would slide on makeshift sledges made of *iSikhukhukhu,* a shrub with slippery branches. In due course the white people claimed it too for their own, and once more we had to move on.

Bango's village was like many others in Africa, a cluster of homes, spaced out 500 metres or more apart. Each home was made up of several round huts. My father, having only one wife, had five huts for the whole family. Chief Bango himself, with five wives and many more dependants, had twenty-five or thirty huts, simple structures of upright poles plastered with the clay that we call *udaka,* and conical roofs of grass thatch. The focus of the home was the kitchen hut, with its central hearth and three stones to support the cooking pot. There were no windows and no chimney, so the smoke had to find its way out through the gap between wall and roof, where ears of grain were stuck so that the smoke could cure them against weevils.

The community at Bango lived by subsistence farming. Each man tilled as much land as he could handle, and kept as many animals as he could get. Father, although a teacher, was entitled to farm like any other member of the community, and his travels to South Africa had brought him into contact with better methods of farming. Luposwa, one of Chief Bango's brothers, had similar experience of better ways of farming, and together they produced much more than most local subsistence farmers. Together they began trading in their surplus grain.

Soon my father and Luposwa Bango became the proud owners of one of the little two-wheeled donkey carts that we called Scotch carts: later they bought a much larger trolley-wagon, with four wheels. Gradually their improved farming methods spread to the other farmers of the community, and the partners began to buy grain in bulk and sell it to the white miners and traders nearby. With their extra earnings they bought more cattle, sheep, goats and donkeys.

Father's income came from his farm and his trade. But he continued to teach as well, and he and his partner Luposwa Bango became preachers together in the mission church. The missionaries did more than spread the gospel. They actively promoted the building and maintenance of local primary schools, teaching arithmetic, English and Sindebele as well as religion. The mission provided books, slates and chalk, and paid the teachers—although the pay was as low as ten shillings a month.

The school building was erected by the whole community, and served also as a church. The benches were simply logs with their tops flattened, set up on sticks for legs—or sometimes they were low walls, fifteen inches high and six inches wide, that the children sat on. The blackboard was black clay plastered directly onto the wall and polished with a smooth stone.

By no means all parents wanted their children to go to school, especially if they were girls. Sometimes the missionaries made gifts to the family to entice the children to school. In most local communities only about a quarter of the people went to church, most of them being women; only a small proportion even of them formally became Christians. Most people stuck to their traditional religion, which the white people mistakenly described as ancestor worship; in fact the African people of what is now Zimbabwe worship almighty God who is a spirit, and with whom they communicate through their ancestors.

With my brothers and sisters I started my education before I was old enough to go to school. Father gave lessons to us and a few neighbours' children, teaching us reading and writing. I did not like it at the time, since it interfered with my games, but I felt the advantage when the school years began and I had a start on the other children. Before my school-days I had learned a lot, too, from my mother's readings from the Bible, and they had a great impact on me, coming from someone I loved so much. It was not until later in life that I saw how the Israelites' occupation of Palestine resembled that of our country by the white settlers, and began to become disenchanted with the story that told how that occupation was sanctioned by God.

Our upbringing was strictly Christian. There were Bible-readings, hymns and prayers every night before bed. We were taught not to eat any food prepared for our neighbours' traditional worship, and strictly instructed not to touch liquor or tobacco—injunctions that I have respected all my life. My wife has brought up our children in the same standards—I would wish to have done so myself, but I have been so many years absent from my family, in exile or in prison. As I have grown older I have remained a religious man, but not so much specifically a Christian. That there is a God I devoutly believe—but a God of all mankind, not just of a selected people.

Going to school with the other children of the community was a relief, sitting in the classroom with a number of others. It was freedom not to be right under my father's eye and subject to his rages, when he would throw chalk and even the slates at us if we could not remember the previous day's lesson. There was safety in numbers, with a teacher who did not know me so well.

When I went to school my mother wanted me to look smart, and bought me some short trousers. This was an embarrassment, since all the other boys wore the *amabhetshu*, a little loin-cloth of skins suspended round the waist by a thong. (Girls wore a small cotton skirt, and in those early days neither boys nor girls wore a top, until later vests and blouses began to be the rule.) So each day I left home in my shorts, but with my little *amabhetshu* in my satchel, and on the way to school I would hide behind a bush, pull off my shorts and slip on my leather garment. Then on the way home I would do the same the other way round, making sure that none of my school-mates knew what I was up to.

Once the effort to please my school-friends earned me a big beating. In our house there was always a big 14-pound bag of sugar for the tea and coffee my parents drank as teetotalers, and I was used to taking spoonfuls of it to make delicious cups of sweet water. It seemed to me a good idea to share this delicacy with my friends, and to have a supply of sweet water for everyone. So I stole a half bag of sugar, took it to a pool of clear water, tipped it in and stirred. My friends and I were very disappointed to find that the pond tasted no sweeter and was full of mud as well: and when Mother found what I had done I got a thorough thrashing.

As I grew older my circle of friends widened, including children who did not go to school as well as those who did. In the long evenings and under the moonlight we played games, and gradually my early backwardness fell away and I gained confidence. For the boys there were special gatherings in an area set aside outside the fence of a home, where the older boys told us boys' stories, and sometimes men would tell us of bygone wars, how to hunt, how to use our sticks for defence or attack, how to share the special parts of the animal set aside for men after it has been slaughtered. We would pass the roast pieces around the group of boys, each one taking a bite in turn, in a ritual of brotherhood.

The girls, for their part, would gather inside the yard of a home to hear from a grandmother what girls needed to know—how to prepare different foods, how women of old used to manage family matters even better than women of the day. Sometimes too there were gatherings of boys and girls together, always in the girls' meeting place, where we would hear old stories—*insimu*—with moral lessons for the young. These tales influenced me as much as the Bible: they are the oral history of our people, passing our knowledge down from generation to generation.

It was the duty of the boys to herd the cattle, sheep and goats, and we were proud of our special rights at milking time. It was the boys who decided whether the milk from a cow that had newly calved should be drunk by us in our male enclosure or sent to mother for the use of the whole family. As the greatest of treats, we would milk a cow directly into our mouths—I loved the foam of it, and the gentle warmth of the fresh milk.

Our animals were individual beings to us, not just possessions. I could recognise the footmarks of our own cattle, and distinguish the lowing of our own oxen and the bleating of our own sheep—though how that was possible I do not know any more. We loved our beasts so much that it was hard to part with them for slaughter or for sale. Father got our agreement to the sale of our favourites only by a trick: he would point to a group of cows or of oxen and ask if we agreed to the sale of one from that group. When we returned from school we would find that the missing one was our favourite after all, and the house was almost in mourning.

Between the ages of eight and fourteen I became much attracted to the traditional religion of our people. With my friends I would steal away from home in secret to the ceremonies of our non-Christian neighbours, joining in the dancing and the singing, and even partaking, despite my parents' strict orders, of the food that had been specially prepared for the ceremony. To me their worship was more lively and attractive, and seemed more serious, than that I had seen in the Christian church. It went on without a break, sometimes for two or three days and nights, maybe even more.

In Bango's community both the Ndebele and the Kalanga languages were spoken interchangeably within the community. The Christian word for God was translated as *uMlimu* in the Ndebele and *Mwali* in the Kalanga language. This God, it seemed to me, was the same whatever language was being used, and the same too in the Christian and the traditional faiths: I could not understand why there had to be such a clear line of demarcation between them—but I was too young at the time to question what my elders told me.

It was later that I made the connection between religion and nationalism. I learned that the missionary Robert Moffat had been the interpreter when the so-called agreements were made by which Cecil Rhodes claimed to have been granted rights by the last king of our country, Lobengula. I learned too that Moffat had previously said of Lobengula and his regime: "This savage kingdom must be destroyed if Christianity is to take root in this area." Lobengula and his councillors asserted that they had never agreed to the concessions that Rhodes, through Moffat as interpreter, claimed to have been granted. But the only man who could say what had really transpired was Robert Moffat, and his Christian conscience.

As the spirit of Zimbabwean nationalism came to the fore again in the early 1950s, I examined for myself the power of the traditional faith of my people, and visited the shrine where Mwali resides in the Matopos hills. Well before dawn, at about 3 A.M., William Sivako and Grey Mabhalani Bango, the nephew of the chief of my father's village, accompanied me to the place called Dula. We were led by a frail old man along an ancient track: some twenty others were with us, each bringing his own problem.

The place was an overhanging slab of granite. The old man, our guide and leader, told us to squat down a few metres from the rock-face: he squatted in front of us, between us and the rock. He commanded us into a soft rhythm of clapping. Suddenly a voice like that of an ancient man began to call us by our names: "You, son of Nyongolo, and you, son of Sivako, and you, son of Luposwa Bango—what do you want me to do for you? How do you expect me to accomplish it? When I told King Lobengula what not to do, he did it. I told King Lobengula not to fight against his cousins who were coming into the land, his cousins without knees.* But Lobengula ignored my instructions, and he fought against his cousins, I know," the voice went on, "he was compelled by some of his chiefs who wanted to destroy him, he listened to them and not to me."

I replied, as leader of the group, "*Babamkhulu,* grandfather, we have come to ask you to give back this land to your children, the people of this land, including the cousins against whom Lobengula fought."

"Yes, my children," said the voice, "I will give you back your land. It will be after thirty years, and after war. That is because Lobengula failed to

---

* "The people without knees" was a term applied to early white visitors whose legs were mysteriously concealed by their trousers.

heed my word. My children of Bechuanaland will get back their land before you, because Sikhume Khama listened to my word and did not fight his cousins."

About sunrise we heard the wind blowing strongly but we did not feel it. The voice said: "Goodbye, my children."

I cannot explain this event, but it happened and the prophecy came true. The other people accompanying us witnessed it: their own problems were not attended to, and they left amazed. We, for our part, left disappointed because the answer to our prayer was gloomy. For thirty years I kept the secret that the voice had foretold a long and costly struggle.

At this place in the Matopos hills all our rulers, from the Monomotapas four centuries ago to Lobengula, the last of our kings, have paid homage, and so have the ordinary people. During the years of colonialism the people continued to go there, respectful of their own religion. In 1974, when I was released after more than ten years in prison, I was told that the voice of the shrine had issued a message. It had said farewell, and ceased speaking to the people, but their complaints and pleas would still be heard. Perhaps as people become more "civilised," God takes a step back.

Towards the end of our dry season, in August, September and October every year, the people attend upon the shrine to pray for rain, health and peace. I once spent a week in attendance at this festival, and I was left in no doubt of the faith and sincerity of the African religion. Men and women dedicate themselves for a period to the shrine, sleeping in the open, rolling in the ashes, singing and dancing all the time. The Christian religion seeks life after death for the individual, while our African religion seeks rain, health and peace in the world for all mankind.

"A Letter to My Mother"
Chenjerai Hove

Chenjerai Hove, born in 1956, is a novelist, poet, essayist, and journalist. He was educated at Marist Brothers Secondary School in Dete, inside the boundaries of Zimbabwe's Hwange National Park, and at the University of South Africa and University of Zimbabwe. His first novel, Bones, *published in 1988, won the Zimbabwe Literary Award and the Noma Award for Publishing in Africa. He was the first president of the Zimbabwe Writers Union and a founding board member of the Zimbabwe Human Rights Association.*

Dear Mother,

It is a long time since I talked to you, now that your ageing ears can hardly hear the faint voice on this side of the telephone. But then, I sometimes wonder at the futility of writing this letter to you since you can't even read. Your eyes too are giving up, and you did not go to the mission school to learn the tricks of the written word. My late Angolan friend, Antonio Jacinto once wrote a poem about a lover who wanted to write his woman a letter, but then the man tragically realised that even he too cannot write, and his woman could not read:

> . . . but you can't read
> and I—oh the hopelessness—I can't write.

Remember the day I arrived in my new town, one of my many stops on this journey that is life. The rains at the airport in Stavanger brought me memories of you working in the fields, not shielding yourself from the warm raindrops. I remembered you then, way back in February, 2005. For I knew you would have composed an instant poem to celebrate first raindrops, those songs about the fish eagle up in the sky, the harbinger of rain, giving life to people, animals and plants.

Here they still have not stopped cursing the rain. I always remind them that one who curses the rain is a witch who wishes that life should not be brought to this earth. But no, they still curse at their gentle, thunderless rain. They prefer the sun instead. Or the white snow which paints the street white as if cotton wool has embraced the whole earth. My fear of snow still persists, especially when it hardens and becomes slippery ice.

For me, a step on ice is a potential disaster. Ice is more slippery than the muddy clay soils of your maize fields. Norwegians hardly fall on ice. They float on it like Arabs walking on sand, never sinking, never falling. They even run races on the ice and win competitions! Can you imagine?

Oh, Norwegians, the things they do!

They built the city of Stavanger on the edge of the sea, as if to block it from coming further inland. Sometimes I dream that the houses hanging by the cliffs will one day fall into the sea.

By the way, I forget that you have never seen the sea. I remember you telling me stories about the place where all rivers poured their waters, in our language, gungwa (the water to quench all thirsts). It is just that, and Norwegians are people of the sea. They play in it, swim in it, dive in it, ride fast boats in it and fish there. They travel over the sea to many places. All their towns and villages are by the sea: it brings them everything they want, friends and enemies, food from faraway places, and petrol which they discovered under the depths of the sea. The sea is full of so many creatures which you find on their plate for almost every meal. According to Norwegians, if you don't eat fish, like me, you are supposed to be miserable.

Yes, there is petrol under the water. I know you may not understand how petrol can be found under the water, but Norwegians found it many years ago. It is the source of their wealth just as the soil, cattle and people are our own wealth.

Petrol has made them rich, and they seem to forget that many years ago, they were poor, and so became wanderers to other lands in search of life and fortune, just like us.

Still, they have not given up their first question when I meet them. "Where do you come from?" they ask, as if they learnt that question the first thing they were born. I have come to accept it as their greeting. I laugh at them when they refuse to accept that I have now become some kind of one of them. But then I think we are also like them. We called ourselves "vanhu" (the people) and all strangers had other names. I have come to know that every people is like that; everyone else is something else, and we are the only genuine "vanhu" (the people) and human dignity is "hunhu," a good person, always measured on how the stranger fits into our ways of life.

"The weather is cold, and Norwegians are cold," one African I met said to me when I arrived. It might be true. I have also discovered that

Norwegians are like a diesel engine, they take time to warm up to you. As they warm up to a stranger and become friends, they are prepared to die for you. Their warming up is slow but sure, like a good diesel engine!

> winter comes with skis
> summer brings some smiles,
> if it does not rain.

Normally, Norwegians are deep in silence. Forget about the noise you hear in the streets of Harare, or in the village in Gotami's country down there in Chireya. Here they are silent, and it is the silence which explodes into your ears as soon as you arrive in their lands. No, they are not afraid of strangers. They are too shy to venture into the life space of anyone, including their own people. It takes time for them to remove that veil of silence which sometimes shields them so much from the possibility of laughter and the good humour which enkindles the human spirit in times of sorrow and despair.

Norwegians have their own traditional dish: boiled potatoes, vegetables and lamb. I have tried it and not thought much of it. They tell me it comes from the old days when they were still poor. I prefer my own Zimbabwean sadza (thick maize flour porridge) with goat or beef stew, and rice with chicken on Sundays and Christmas. You should have seen how many hours I spent searching for maize flour in the shops. When I found it, the evening meal was the best I had ever had for months. It surprises me when I see Norwegians eat small pieces of chicken and a few green vegetables and call it a meal.

For a dinner with a Norwegian, I make sure I have some money in my own pocket, just in case. It is not like home where people invite you for dinner in the restaurant and all you have to bring is a sharp appetite. Here, when the bill comes, you have to know what you ate and drank so you split the bill. At first it shocked me. With time I got used to it. I now know that sometimes when they take the family for a meal, wife and husband look into their individual pockets to pay. It is probably a healthy arrangement since no one drinks from their uncle's purse in these lands. Everyone is their own uncle!

Women and men, that is an interesting topic. The women of Norway are strong. They rule the house and ensure that everyone cleans the house, takes the dog for a walk, and takes the children to and from school. Everyone cooks and everyone washes the dishes. So different from home where the man is the father of the house, some kind of king. Not here. The women are tough: they can even expel the man from the house if he neglects his duties. The women of these lands do not tolerate mischievous men like the women of home.

I know you come from the old generation where you were taught to think that a woman without a man is nothing. Here most women don't even want to marry their men. They just live together, like what we call "kuchaya mapoto" (living together sharing the pots). I talked to many young Norwegians about marriage and they always look at me as if I am crazy. "I don't want trouble," one Norwegian friend says to me.

You will not believe it: but this country is expensive. The price of a pint of beer is the same as the price of a whole goat back home. A loaf of bread costs the same as three live chickens. Can you imagine!

But Norwegians manage well. I walk down the street and the only thin people I see are usually always foreigners. Everyone can afford three good meals a day if they want, plus a place to sleep. If their government was like our government in Zimbabwe which sometimes enjoys destroying people's houses, Norwegians would all have died a long time ago in the cold. What we call "cold" is really "warm" for Norwegians.

You see mother, I am writing you so you can understand my new life and the people I share it with.

I was not too surprised to find that Norwegians enjoy the company of dogs and cats. They keep them as friends, not for hunting or killing the rats. No. And they keep them inside the house. I am told some even share their beds with the dog or the cat. What a scandal it would be back home.

But they are better than the French. You remember I was in France before I came here? The French love their dogs and cats. They are prepared to die for them. I once joked with a woman who always walked around with a tiny little dog. She sometimes carried it in her basket, with the head popping out as if it were in a circus. I joked that where I come from we eat dogs, but added that I would not worry about her little dog because it was too small to make two small bowls of dog soup. The woman broke down crying. She threatened to report me to the police: that I wanted to eat her dog. It took me time and energy to calm her down and convince her that it was only a joke.

Norwegians and the French spend so much money on dog food and care. Not like home where dogs wait for left-overs of everything. I understand the Germans are even worse. When I once said to a German friend "I don't want to be treated like a dog," he laughed and said he would prefer to be treated like a German dog. "Dogs have a better life here than people," he said. We laughed it off, but I think it is true. A missing dog is big news in the papers.

But in my city, there is a woman who has a house full of cats. Her life is dedicated to caring for abandoned cats. People think she is mad, but she does not mind. At least she is assured of never seeing a rat in her house!

Norway has such a beautiful array of mountains, hills, valleys and rivers intricately woven together into one. I wonder where anyone who intends to farm could have done it. Small farms miserably scatter through the valleys, with a few sheep dotted on the landscape, or maybe a cow or two. What they call a farm in these parts is really the size of a large garden in our country. No wonder why they buy most of their food from other parts of the world. Just the other day I ate Namibian impala meat in a restaurant. It was delicious, but I missed the bones that should have come with it. In these parts, they do not like the joy of struggling to tear off meat from bones during a meal.

The only wild animal that Norwegians can hunt is one called a reindeer. I have seen one a year ago when I travelled north. It is like some big wild goat up there in the mountains. Reindeer steak tastes like buffalo which, as you know, I never liked in my youth when the hunters used to kill them for us in the 1960s.

No, I should not spend so much time writing about animals. It makes me homesick, thinking about all those elegant giraffes, elephants and lions roaming our countrysides.

You will wonder if they also have elections here. Yes, of course. The other day I was walking in the street in the gentle rain. Four young men and two women stopped me to give me flowers. A red rose. They were campaigning for their political party by giving voters flowers, they told me. I almost fainted in shock. I told them that in my country they would be wielding sticks, stones and pangas to threaten me with death if I did not vote for their party. Remember the ruling party militias who stopped you and threatened to beat you up if you did not have a party card? Here they would probably have bought you a drink and given you a rose. It is a different world.

Only recently, I was flying to the capital, Oslo. The captain announced to us: "Welcome to Your Majesty and to all you ladies and gentlemen." I looked around and did not see any majesty around. Since I was the only African on the plane, I thought they had mistaken me as some kind of royal because of our Mazvihwa royalty. But then, Majesty is for a woman. I asked a stewardess whether this was a joke of some kind.

"No," she smiled. "The Queen of Norway is sitting right there in front," she pointed.

Then I was puzzled. No special security. No special seat for the Queen. Economy class like everyone else. It reminded me of another trip where I sat next to a young woman. When we introduced each other, it turned out she was the minister of defence. In another city, I was the Guest of Honour to open a literature festival, and the minister of culture was to speak after me.

The minister had also arrived late because of a technical problem on her plane. When I suggested that she should have grabbed the nearest plane and "re-routed it" to her destination, she looked sternly at me and said: "You want my government to fall, hey? The people will force us to resign tomorrow morning."

In all this, I thought of home: how no one would ever sit next to President Mugabe in economy class, how I would probably never be allowed to sit next to the minister of defence, how security police would have sealed off the whole airport if the President was arriving or leaving, and how there would have been hired dancing women with dresses "decorated" with the face of the president.

Mother, in this country, I think power has not yet gone to their heads. Maybe it was in their heads long ago and the people managed to push it out and place it on the proper shelf of humbleness and service to the people.

Maybe your attacks of malaria will already be haunting you. There is no malaria in this country. The little mosquitoes they have are as harmless as pieces of flying paper. No one bothers much about them. But this is not to say there are no diseases here. They have different kinds of illnesses, some to do with the mind, others to do with eating too much wrong food, and maybe others to do with a life controlled too much by watches and clocks. You should see how they walk in the street. They rush to everywhere as if in a permanent state of emergency. Slowing down might help reduce some of their tensions.

I sometimes think they do not use the medicine called laughter enough. They have forgotten that laughter drives out sorrow from the human heart and mind. I wish they could read the poem called "Laugh" by Tanzanian poet Shaban Roberts:

Laugh to heal your wounds, laugh to
send away your troubles,
Laugh to allow the body to grow in
health and vigour.

Mother, you might wonder if there are other strangers like me in my town. Yes, I meet them. Most of them are escapees from one misfortune or other. They tell me bitter memories of their original homes, home bitter home, they remind me. Like me, they miss home, but they loathe the possibility of returning to the jaws of poverty and political repression.

It is Christmas time now. I hope this time they will go to church. Most of the time the churches are empty but over the years religion has become part of the way they think and organise life. For Christmas, they buy and buy and buy and buy as if possessed by the spirit of shopping. It is Christmas without the poor baby Jesus Christ, born in a dirty cattle pen.

As winter has swallowed everybody and taken away their bright smiles, I see their faces yearning for summer already. Norwegians love to celebrate summer. It is the return of the sun which vanishes soon after the afternoon meal in winter. Summer is time for festivals in this country. There is a festival for everything: literature festival, oil festival, humour festival, dance festival, wine festival (although they do not make wine), jazz festival, rock festival, food festival, everything comes with a festival. That is the way it was many years before the coming of the missionaries who taught us that festivals to celebrate the rain were pagan.

So, mother, you can see how complex life is here, with its ups and downs. As I yearn for the voices of home, I begin to think there are more downs here than ups. The voices of home, the music of our birds and the beauty of our setting sun, they weave patterns in my dreams as I live this never-ending desire to be home one day.

I hope the thunderous rains have come by now. Maybe the maize you planted is already the height of a small child. Every sun which rises give me fresh memories of you, and every early sunset reminds me that I am in other lands. Maybe one day we will sit together, switch off the street lights and gaze at the beauty of that lovely African moon which displays the image of a rabbit with large ears. Maybe I will be older, but I will not have given up the idea of being young.

Now I know that there are so many streams to the river of knowledge, and one of them is to live in other lands.

Your Son,
Chenjerai

Permissions

Index
of Authors and Titles

Abani, Chris, 133
Aboulela, Leila, 85
Abouzeid, Leila, 65
Adichie, Chimamanda Ngozi, 141
"African 'Authenticity' and the Biafran Experience," 141
Ahmed, Leila, 21
An Algerian Childhood, 5
And Night Fell, 333

Biko, Steve, 343
Blouin, Andrée, 175
A Border Passage, 21

Childhood in Madagascar, 221
"A Cold But Fertile Ground," 85

A Daughter of Isis, 31
Dawes, Kwame, 115
Detained: A Writer's Prison Diary, 205
The Devil That Danced on the Water, 163
Dib, Mohammed, 5
Dibango, Manu, 99
Dongala, Emmanuel, 185
Dumoux, Christian, 221

Elizabeth of Toro, 265
"Encounters," 5
"Ethics and Narrative: The Human and Other," 133

"The Family House," 239
Farah, Nuruddin, 239
A Far Cry from Plymouth Rock, 115
First, Ruth, 325
Forna, Aminatta, 163
The Fraternal Bond, 59

Ghana: The Autobiography of Kwame Nkrumah, 107

Hatzfeld, Jean, 193
Head, Bessie, 287
"Hollywood, Pirated Videos, and Child Soldiers," 185
Hove, Chenjerai, 387

Ibn Battuta, 43
I Write What I Like, 343

Jelloun, Tahar Ben, 59

Kaunda, Kenneth, 351
Khadra, Yasmina, 11

Lalami, Laila, 71
Let My People Go, 315
"A Letter to My Mother," 387
Look & Move On, 51
Lumumba, Patrice, 169
Lumumba Speaks, 169
Luthuli, Albert, 315

Machete Season, 193
Mafeking Diary, 307
Mahjoub, Jamal, 77
Mancham, James R., 229
Matar, Hisham, 37
*Memoirs of an Arabian Princess
    from Zanzibar,* 247
Mrabet, Mohammed, 51
Murangira, Jean-Baptiste, 193
My Country, Africa, 175
"My Father's English Friend," 125

Ndibe, Okey, 125
Never Follow the Wolf, 301
"New World Alphabet," 201
Ngũgĩ wa Thiong'o, 205
*Nisa: The Life and Words of a
    !Kung Woman,* 277
Nkomo, 373
Nkomo, Joshua, 373
Nkrumah, Kwame, 107
Nthunya, Mpho 'M'atsepo, 293
Nwaubani, Adaobi Tricia, 151
Nyabongo, Elizabeth, 265
Nyagumbo, Maurice, 359

*One Day I Will Write About This
    Place,* 215

117 Days, 325
Ousmane Sembène: Interviews, 155

Paradise Raped, 229
Pheto, Molefe, 333
Plaatje, Sol T., 307

"The Rabbit Club," 37
"Reform, in the Name of the
    Father," 151
Return to Childhood, 65
Ruete, Emily, 247

Saadawi, Nawal El, 31
Saitoti, Tepilit Ole, 255
"Salamanca," 77
Sankara, Thomas, 91
Sembène, Ousmane, 155
Shityuwete, Helao, 301
Shostak, Marjorie, 277
Singing Away the Hunger, 293
"So to Speak," 71

Thomas Sankara Speaks, 91
Three Kilos of Coffee, 99
The Travels of Ibn Battuta, 43

Wainaina, Binyavanga, 215
With the People, 359
A Woman Alone, 287
The Worlds of a Maasai Warrior,
    255
Woubshet, Dagmawi, 201
The Writer, 11

Zambia Shall Be Free, 351

About the Book

African Lives, a pioneering anthology of memoirs and autobiographical writings, lets the people of Africa speak for themselves—telling stories of struggle and achievement that have the authenticity of lived experience.

The anthology presents selections from the work of many of Africa's finest writers and most significant personalities from across the continent and spanning several centuries. Enhancing the material, Geoff Wisner's introduction and biographical notes provide important context for the selections and also highlight the challenges that African memoirs pose to the preconceptions of Western readers. The result is a book that is both an absorbing read and a valuable resource for courses on Africa.

Geoff Wisner is author of *A Basket of Leaves: 99 Books That Capture the Spirit of Africa.*